15⁻

READINGS IN EVALUATION RESEARCH

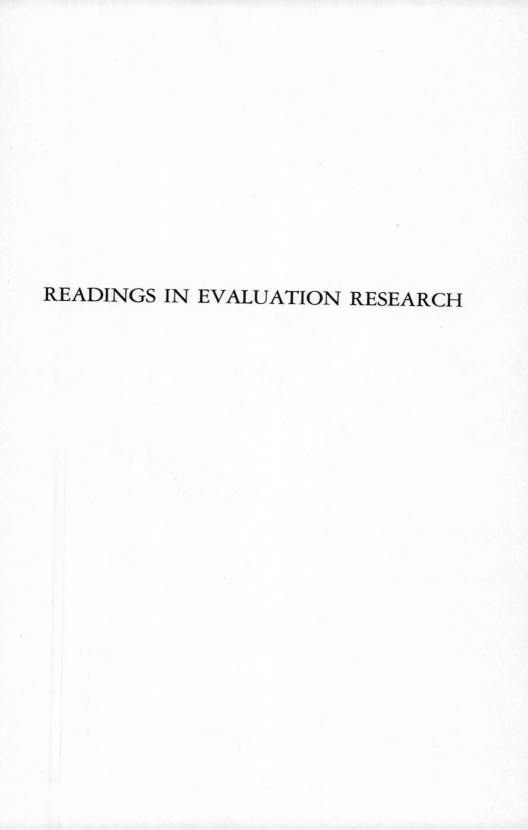

Readings
in
Evaluation
Research

SECOND EDITION

EDITED BY

Francis G. Caro

Russell Sage Foundation

New York

300.723
C22r

Russell Sage Foundation
230 Park Avenue, New York, N.Y. 10017

Library of Congress Catalog Number: 76–12706
Standard Book Number: 87154–201–3

CONTENTS

v

FOREWORD

The evaluation research field has seen remarkable growth in the brief six years since the publication of the first edition of Francis Caro's *Readings in Evaluation Research*. Growth has occurred within the field itself, in the amount of governmental and private sector funding for evaluation studies, in the number of investigators who identify themselves as evaluation researchers, and in the attention paid to evaluation research in graduate academic programs. The growth is evident in other ways as well: in efforts to improve the methodology of evaluation research, in attempts to solve the practical and political problems that often plague the implementation of studies, and in the emergence of professional associations for persons within the field. Most importantly, evaluation research is now an established part of the complex processes that engage planners and policy makers responsible for determining which service programs should be implemented, expanded, and terminated. Not only do program staff in governmental agencies and in private service organizations look to the results of evaluation research studies in reaching decisions on the allocation of scarce resources and on choosing from available social action strategies, persons at the highest policy levels—in federal cabinet offices in the Office of Management and Budget, and in the General Accounting Office and in their state and local counterparts—also attest to the utility of evaluation research.

In revising *Readings in Evaluation Research,* Dr. Caro has selected a number of new articles that highlight recent methodological developments in the field, report on current substantive studies in various service areas, and discuss current controversies and issues of both a methodological and political character. At the same time, he has retained useful pieces from the first edition, so that the reader will have a sense of the historical developments in evaluation research.

The first edition of Dr. Caro's anthology filled a gap in the available literature, particularly since research investigators and resource practitioners often had limited familiarity with the broad spectrum of work in evaluation research, and their scholarly reading usually was (and is) confined to materials in their own discipline or profession. The book also was used widely as a text or as supplementary readings in graduate courses and occasionally undergraduate courses in social science departments and professional schools.

With the growth of the evaluation research field, a number of other successful collections of readings, as well as several texts, have appeared. However, *Readings in Evaluation Research* has more than currency to commend it. Rather, it is Dr. Caro's diligent effort to provide a broad overview of the book that especially recommends this volume. This overview of evaluation research and the introductions provided for the various sections are highly useful commentaries on the present state of evaluation research. I expect that the book will continue to receive wide use in evaluation research courses and as a resource book for investigators, planners, and policy makers.

Indeed, the very fact that the second edition must compete with a number of high quality texts and edited volumes on evaluation research is gratifying to Russell Sage Foundation. For more than a decade, the Foundation has been intensely involved in stimulating the growth and development of the field of evaluation research and in increasing the utility of evaluation studies for planning and policymaking purposes. While, of course, it is impossible to attribute any particular development in the field to the Foundation's efforts, we do believe that Francis Caro's volume as well as the other monographs published by the Foundation and the informal consulting activities of the Foundation staff have contributed to the vitality of the contemporary evaluation research endeavor.

HOWARD E. FREEMAN

Los Angeles, California
January 1977

PREFACE

Interest in evaluation research has been greatly stimulated by a concern for domestic social reform. A desire for improved social conditions has been combined with a demand for more productive and efficient intervention programs. Searching questions have been raised about the adequacy of organized programs in such institutional sectors as health, justice, education, employment, housing, transportation, and welfare. In an atmosphere charged with demands for rapid and significant change, a great many innovative action programs have been introduced. Some reformers have urged that the quest for more effective institutions be orderly and cumulative. They have argued that careful program evaluation is needed as a basis for continued planning and have recommended that the methods of social research be utilized in the evaluation of reform programs. Conspicuous failure of some programs to fulfill public expectations and concern for the soaring costs of services have added greatly to interest in careful program evaluation.

The present volume brings together material about evaluation research drawn from a variety of sources. Professional writing about the topic has been scattered because evaluation research is an application of methods of social research that falls between traditional disciplinary interests and a number of applied social science fields. Included in the book are both general statements about evaluation research and specific case materials. The general articles address such issues as the nature of the evaluation task, the role of evaluation research in programs of directed change, the organizational context in which evaluation research is conducted, and the methodological strategies appropriate for evaluation research. The case materials include treatment of problems in the establishment of the evaluation research role and reports of findings of completed evaluation research studies.

The readings are intended for students and professionals concerned with directed social change. Although the book is most clearly pertinent for those who actually conduct evaluation research, it has important implications for social planners and administrators who are potential consumers of the product. (The crucial quality of researcher-policy maker collaboration is emphasized in several articles.) Particularly in the selection of case materials, an effort was made to suggest the wide range of problems to which evaluation research might fruitfully be addressed.

An advantage of a set of readings over a conventional text is that it can more readily convey differences in the ways in which issues are conceived and addressed. Yet, collections of articles often disappoint those who seek an integrated view of a field. The editor has attempted to accommodate the latter interest in the introductory chapter, which is a broad review of writings about evaluation research, not limited to the selections included in the book. The overview chapter is an updated and expanded version of a paper by the editor entitled "Approaches to Evaluative Research: A Review," which appeared originally in *Human Organization* (28, 1969, pp. 87–99). The general readings are divided into three groups: basic issues, the organizational context, and methodological issues. Inevitably, the articles did not lend themselves to easy categorization. Some are pertinent to more than one section. In order to protect the integrity of the individual articles, a decision was made to print each in its entirety. The placement of some articles in various sections in the volume, therefore, is somewhat arbitrary.

A bias built into the volume is its consistent sympathy for programs of directed change and the contribution of evaluation research to those programs. It is assumed that social researchers can resolve the ethical questions that may be raised about their professional participation in programs of directed social change, particularly when no more can be expected than gradual and moderate change.

The second edition differs from the first largely in that in the second there is greater emphasis on examples of completed evaluation research projects. Since the publication of the first edition, there has been substantial activity in the evaluation field. As a result, case material which is particularly useful for instructional purpose is now more readily available than it was several years ago.

I would like to express my appreciation to my wife, Carol B. Caro, who assisted me with the editing of the second edition. Howard Freeman provided impetus and valuable suggestions for the second edition as he did for the first. Funding from Russell Sage Foundation encouraged me to take on the new edition. Finally, Edith Oxley deserves to be acknowledged for helping with typing and preparation of the manuscript.

FRANCIS G. CARO

New York City
January 1977

READINGS IN EVALUATION RESEARCH

EVALUATION RESEARCH: AN OVERVIEW

Evaluation in recent years has come to be recognized as a distinct and important dimension of social programming. Not only has there been a growth in public concern about social problems, but there has been an increasing recognition of a need for sophistication in the design and administration of social programs. The time when goodwill, dedication, and hard work were thought to be sufficient in ameliorating social problems is behind us. Failure of highly publicized, attractive programs to fulfill their promise has helped to create demand for careful program review. Recognition that public and private expenditures for social programs are substantial at a time when resource limitations are becoming increasingly evident adds to the demand for productivity and efficiency in social programs. All of these factors contribute to the growing attention being given to social program evaluation.

BASIC ISSUES

This book is concerned with evaluation research or evaluative research (the terms are used interchangeably), an approach to evaluation that makes use of methods of social research. For evaluation generally or evaluative research specifically to be useful it is important that its scope, methods, and limitations be well understood. The matter of definition is a good starting point.

Evaluation Defined

Program evaluation has two essential dimensions, one concerned with judgment and the other with information. Programs are conducted to achieve a goal, end, or outcome that is valued. Program evaluation produces judgments regarding the degree to which desired outcomes have been achieved or can be achieved. It leads to conclusions regarding the worth of organized efforts. Information is of critical importance in the evaluation process. Performance as known through verifiable procedures is related or contrasted to goals. The method through which information is obtained is often a central point in evaluation. Both Suchman (1969) and Scriven (1967) include both the empirical and judgmental domains in their definitions. Suchman defines evaluation as "the determination . . . of the results . . . attained by some activity . . .

3

designed to accomplish some valued goal or objective." Scriven simply defines evaluation as a "methodological activity which combines performance data with a goal scale."

Approaches to Methods of Evaluation

Evaluation in a broad sense is a part of everyday life. Without the guidance of any formal procedures, all of us continually make evaluative judgments about the full range of purposeful human activity. In social programming, crucial decisions both at levels of policy and individual treatment are often based on informal evaluation. Recognition of the variability and fallibility of informal evaluations, however, has stimulated interest in the formulation of standardized procedures which, if faithfully executed, would yield sound evaluative judgments. Formal evaluation has become a widespread and diversified activity. Several rather distinct approaches to formal evaluation methodology have emerged and are used somewhat independently.

Accreditation is perhaps the oldest and most firmly established approach to formal evaluation concerned with social programs. Particularly in education and health, accrediting agencies often examine and make public judgments regarding program quality. In some cases licensing is contingent on a favorable judgment by an accrediting agency. Accreditation methodology characteristically involves comparisons of program inputs with standards established by professionals. In educational accreditation, for example, physical characteristics of classrooms, ratio of library books to students, and the level of education of faculty members are important dimensions. Information is usually obtained through site visits. Importantly, accreditation is more concerned with potential than actual achievement. (For a more complete discussion of accreditation methodology, see Glass, 1971.)

Program analysis represents a second evaluation tradition that is distinguished by its emphasis on program activities. Project records concerned with client characteristics and client-practitioner exchanges provide the information base for this approach to evaluation. The extent to which clients are attracted to and retained by programs and the characteristics of clients are typical concerns. Actual performance is often compared to an externally derived standard of performance. Similar programs are often compared on their performance characteristics. Program analysis differs from the accreditation approach in that it deals with actual operations rather than program potential. Program analysis is limited by the scope of program records. Because program records rarely go beyond information about treatments, program analysis usually cannot include consideration of long-term treatment effects.

Evaluation research may be considered a third tradition that is distinguished by its central concern for outcomes of treatment. It attempts to determine whether changes sought through an intervention actually come about. Further, evaluation research is concerned with the question of whether observed changes can reasonably be attributed to the intervention. Evaluation research, therefore, makes use not only of scientific method but procedures designed to test for causal connections. It is the evaluation research approach with which this volume is primarily concerned.

Cost analysis is still another distinct approach to evaluation. At its most basic level, cost analysis seeks to account for program expenditures. The amount spent overall and in various categories is related to an external standard. The possibility of illegal diversion of funds is a primary concern. Cost data are also used for policy purposes. Data on program resource cost, cost per unit of service, and cost associated with achievement of desired outcomes are of great value to decision makers. In human services programs, however, sound attribution of costs to various program components is often surprisingly complex. More importantly, attempts to conduct cost analyses for policy purposes are frustrated often by weakness of data on program operations and effectiveness.

Program Development

Evaluation may be viewed as a phase in systematic program development. Ideally, action programming is preceded by a planning process that includes: (1) identification of problems; (2) specification of objectives; (3) analysis of the causes of problems and the shortcomings of existing programs; and (4) an examination of possible action alternatives. Evaluation follows program implementation and provides a basis for further planning and program refinement. (Although evaluation follows implementation, it is, of course, desirable that evaluation activities begin prior to implementation.) The planning-action-evaluation cycle may be repeated indefinitely until objectives are realized or until problems and objectives are redefined. Results of evaluation may be used to modify programs while they are in progress. When evaluation is viewed as part of a process of planned change, the use of evaluation findings in decision making becomes a key concern.

Evaluation research may be concerned with stable and well-established programs or with new programs for which viable administrative patterns are being sought. Scriven (1967, p. 43) introduces the terms "formative" and "summative" to distinguish between these two concerns. Formative evaluation is designed to improve a program while it is still fluid; summative evaluation is designed to appraise a product after it is well established.

Evaluation Research in Historical Perspective

Anticipation of formal social experimentation and evaluation research can be traced back to the writings of early social scientists. Application of the scientific method in the development of social legislation was predicted by Lester Ward in 1906.

> When people become so intelligent that they know how to choose as their representatives, persons of decided ability, who know something of human nature, who recognize that there are social forces, and that their duty is to devise ways and means for scientifically controlling those forces on exactly the same principles that an experimenter or an inventor controls the forces of physical nature, then we may look for scientific legislation. (p. 338)

More explicitly, F. Stuart Chapin called for sociological experimentation in an article published in 1917. Chapin cited the utopian communities of the nineteenth century as examples of experiments but characterized them as trial-and-error rather than scientific experiments. Chapin expected that knowledge of social conditions eventually would be sufficient to permit precise sociological experiments.

An actual evaluation research study was reported by J. M. Rice, an educator, in 1897. Rice used a standardized spelling test to relate the length of time spent on drill to spelling achievement. By comparing schools that varied in their emphasis on drill, he generated data that he used to argue that heavy emphasis on drill did not lead to improved achievement.

Between 1920 and 1940, attempts were made to use empirical research methods to determine the effects of programs of directed social change in a variety of settings. Experiments concerned with productivity and morale among industrial workers were begun in the 1920's by Elton Mayo (1933) and extended by Fritz Roethlisberger and William Dickson (1939). The application of experimental method to the study of medical effects of public health programs was well enough established in the 1920's to be celebrated in Sinclair Lewis's *Arrowsmith* (1925). Best known of the early sociologically oriented evaluative research contributions to public health is Stuart Dodd's study of the effects of a health education program on hygienic practices in rural Syria (1934). Dodd administered standardized measures of adequacy of public health practices in experimental and presumably isolated control villages both before and after the introduction of educational clinics.

Chapin and his associates at the University of Minnesota, stimulated by the social reform concerns of the Depression, conducted evaluative research on such topics as the effects of work relief compared to direct relief, the effects of public housing on project residents, and the effects of treatment programs on juvenile delinquents (Chapin, 1947).

In spite of Rice's early work and the heavy emphasis on testing and student evaluation which began in the early part of the century, educators were relatively late in developing concern with program evaluation. Writing in 1935, Ralph Tyler urged that progressive schools be seen as experiments in education and formally evaluated as such.

An important and relatively early social psychological contribution which may be considered evaluative is Theodore Newcomb's study of students at Bennington College (1943). Newcomb attempted to determine the effects of participation in an experimental college program on the personalities and attitudes of students.

An important social research contribution to social policy issues was made during World War II by a group of sociologists headed by Samuel Stouffer in the Research Branch of the Information and Education Division of the U.S. Army. Extensive evaluative research was conducted in that setting on the effects of films and other forms of mass communication (Hovland, Lumsdaine, and Sheffield, 1949).

After World War II, a number of impressive evaluative research studies were contributed by social psychologists concerned with social issues. Much of the stimulus for that work came from the interest in experimental research in field settings generated by Kurt Lewin and his associates in the late 1930's (Lewin, 1948). The experimental work of Lippitt and White on the effects of autocratic and democratic leadership styles on the performance of groups of children is well known (Lippitt, 1940). In the postwar period, Lewin and his colleagues turned their attention to issues such as the effects of programs designed to change attitudes toward minorities, effects of programs designed to apply group dynamics principles in industry, and the effects of community organization activities on the morale of residents of a housing project (Festinger and Kelley, 1951). Another frequently cited psychological contribution to the evaluation research literature during this period is Riecken's (1952) evaluation of a volunteer work camp. Other major evaluative research reported in book form during this period include Powers and Witmer's (1951) study of a delinquency prevention project; Hymen, Wright, and Hopkins' (1962) work on a summer camp experience for college students; Wilner and associates' (1962) work on the implications of public housing for health and social psychological adjustment; Weeks' (1958) research on the effects of an innovative program for the treatment of delinquents; and Meyer, Borgatta, and Jones' (1965) experimental research on the effects of social work intervention.

The rediscovery of poverty and related domestic problems in the early 1960's led to a renewed interest in evaluative research. Social scientists who participated in the development of early antipoverty programs urged that these efforts be viewed as experiments and that evaluative research be emphasized. The "Grey Area" Projects sponsored by the Ford Foundation and the delinquency prevention projects of the President's Council on Juvenile Delinquency, which were forerunners of the Office of Economic Opportunity Programs, included extensive evaluative research components staffed by social scientists (Marris and Rein, 1967, pp. 191–207). Although the early emphasis on formal planning and evaluative research did not survive in the Office of Economic Opportunity's Community Action programs, federal administrators in a variety of agencies concerned with domestic social programs have sponsored research on the effects of their programs. Program evaluation in education was given an important stimulus by an evaluation requirement written into the Elementary and Secondary Education Act of 1965. Evaluation research has a particularly important contribution to make in the demonstration program approach which has been widely employed in recent years by federal agencies.

That evaluation research should be an integral part of innovative social programming is now well established in federally sponsored projects. A number of private organizations that specialize in evaluation research have emerged in recent years and compete for federal evaluation contracts. (For analysis of the status of H.E.W. sponsored evaluations, see Bernstein and Freeman, 1975). Large-scale formal social experimentation has been attempted under federal sponsorship. Rivlin (1971) has played a particularly important role in stimulating interest in using formal experiments to address major social policy issues. Major experiments concerned with income maintenance and housing allowances have been carried out.

Factors Affecting Investment in Evaluation Research

Interest in evaluation research is likely to be greatest among groups predisposed toward gradual and moderate change. Where change is thought to be undesirable or impossible, little interest in evaluation is to be expected. Groups demanding rapid and radical social change are also unlikely consumers of evaluative research both because their inclinations tend to be ideological rather than empirical, and because evaluative researchers are generally not able to fill their information needs rapidly enough.

Emphasis on evaluative research is most appropriate where it is expected that program effects will not be directly and immediately evident (Coleman, 1969). Large-scale social programs tend to be characterized by not only subtle and diffuse outcomes, but also substantial social distance between policy makers and recipients of services. When they are close to clients, policy makers may be reasonably confident of their own informal evaluations of programs. As their distance from the client population increases, however, policy makers may recognize the need for more formal evaluation procedures (Trow, 1967).

In principle, evaluation activities may generate judgments regarding effectiveness on such varied dimensions as programming approaches (remedial reading or income-maintenance programs); administrative units (schools, departments, or agencies); individual practitioners (physicians or teachers); or recipients of services (patients, clients, or students) (Cronbach, 1963). In practice, for reasons to be discussed, evaluators who are primarily concerned with program effectiveness usually deliberately avoid making judgmental statements regarding particular administrative units, practitioners, or recipients of services.

Another way to look at evaluation is as a programming input, which may be subject to evaluation just like other inputs. In cost-benefit terms, the cost of evaluation should be related to the benefits that evaluative data and judgments contribute to programming efficiency or effectiveness. A heavy investment in formal evaluation is most likely to be justified when a program is expensive, when its impact is potentially great but uncertain, and when there is a great potential for diffusion of programming concepts. Glass (1971) further contends that decisions to conduct evaluative research should reflect estimates of the cost of evaluation, the extent to which program effectiveness is uncertain, and the cost of implementing alternate programs.

Organizational Arrangements

Theoretically, evaluative research may be undertaken without any formal sponsorship, it may be based upon a wide range of value perspectives, and its findings may be reported to a variety of audiences. In practice, however, because of problems of cost and access to information, formal evaluation is usually a sponsored activity. External funding agencies (such as private foundations or the federal government) and top administrators of action organizations are the most common sponsors. Whether they are an internal unit of an organization or outside consultants, evaluative researchers are usually linked directly to persons high in the administrative structure of the action organization. Therefore, those who actually carry out the programs to be evaluated are subordinate to those to whom evaluators report. Sponsorship often affects the issues addressed by evaluation and the manner in which results are reported. Consequently, evaluators may not fully serve the interests of the general public, practitioners, and recipients of services.

Evaluation Research and Basic Research

From the point of view of a behavioral science, evaluation research represents an application of the scientific method that is quite different from basic research. Some insist on a sharp distinction between research and evaluation, whereas others classify evaluation as a form of research. Wrightstone (1969) suggests that "research is more concerned with the basic theory and design of a program over an appropriate period of time, with flexible deadlines, and with sophisticated treatment of data that have been carefully obtained." Evaluation, on the other hand, "may be concerned with basic theory and design, but its primary function . . . is to appraise comprehensively a practical . . . activity to meet a deadline. . . ." Suchman (1969) argues that the distinction between basic research and evaluative research is one of purpose rather than method. Evaluative research applies the scientific method to problems that have administrative consequences, whereas basic research is concerned with problems of theoretical significance. Cherns (1969) distinguishes between pure basic research, which arises out of perceived needs of an academic discipline, and action (evaluative) research, which is concerned with an ongoing problem in an organizational framework and involves the introduction and observation of planned change. He also points to differences between the types of research in diffusion and generality. Basic research has a great potential for generality, but a limited potential for immediate utilization. By contrast, evaluative research has limited potential for generality, but great potential for immediate utilization.

Evaluative research represents only one form of applied research, since research may contribute to social policy without assessing the effect of specific interventions. Research on the causes of problem behavior, the incidence and concentration of patterns of social problems, and on public knowledge of and attitudes toward existing services may all have important policy implications without being specifically evaluative.

For social scientists interested in contributing to programs of directed change, evaluative research is only one possible role. Alternately, social scientists may contribute to training programs and engage in consulting activities. Brooks (1965), for example, suggests that social scientists may provide ideas for experimentation and encourage the greatest possible rationality in the planning process. They may aid in the identification of objectives and action alternatives and prediction of consequences of possible courses of action. (See also Bennis, 1965; and Likert and Lippitt, 1953.)

At the same time that evaluative research provides social scientists with an opportunity to contribute rather immediately to programs of directed social change, it involves the researcher in a number of ethical issues. If evaluation involves an experimental design, the researcher must address the issues that generally apply in experimentation with human subjects. On the one hand, risks to which experimental subjects may be exposed must be weighed; on the other hand, good reason may have to be found to withhold a promising treatment from members of a control group. (Frequently, the burden of the argument for a control condition falls on the evaluator.) When evaluation research involves data collection through interviewing or observation, the researcher must concern himself with issues of privacy and confidentiality as he would in any field research. (For more thorough discussions of ethical issues in evaluative research and social experimentation, see Riecken and Boruch, 1974; and Rivlin and Timpane, 1975.)

THE ORGANIZATIONAL CONTEXT

Problems in Establishing and Maintaining the Evaluation Research Role

Although there is often a strong rationale for a central role for formal behavioral evaluation, effective participation of evaluative researchers in social programming is much less common. Looking at evaluation from an organizational and occupational perspective, some practical problems in establishing and maintaining the evaluation role become apparent.

Traditionally decision makers have not given evaluative research a major role in policy formation and change in social programming (Rossi, 1969). Policy has been formed without considering what kinds of evaluative data would be needed to sustain the worth of a program. Objective evidence of the effects of programs has not been demanded as a basis for modifying programs. Satisfied with informal evaluation, administrators often include evaluative research only when it is specifically required by a funding agent.

Administrators may regard evaluative research as expensive and of little practical value; but in addition, they may have important covert reasons for resisting formal evaluation. The very presence of an evaluation component invites administrators to consider the possibility that their policies do not lead to the effective realization of announced objectives. Because administrative claims for programs are usually optimistic, evaluative research results are almost inevitably disappointing (Rossi, 1966). Campbell (1969) observes that ambiguity in results helps to protect administrators where there is a possibility of failure. Freely available facts would reduce the privacy and security of some administrators, making them vulnerable to inquiries about their effectiveness. In addition, administrators may resent evaluators who raise questions about basic organizational premises or suggest evaluative criteria that may be embarrassing to the organization.

Horowitz (1969) identifies several other reasons why administrators of an action organization may consider applied social scientists who belong to an internal research unit as troublesome. Social scientists often demand preferential treatment, creating resentment among other employees. Social scientists often want direct access to top decision makers, thereby threatening by-passed bureaucrats. Furthermore, the extracurricular involvements of social scientists, such as writing, teaching, and lecturing are often resented.

At the same time, administrators interested in evaluative research have often found it difficult to recruit and hold qualified behavioral scientists. Like other scientists, behavioral scientists often prefer to be oriented toward the general scientific community rather than the needs and goals of the organization that employs them (McKelvey, 1969). Scientists typically wish to do research that will contribute to a scientific body of knowledge. Administrators, on the other hand, typically expect that scientists on their payroll will do research that contributes directly to the goals of their organization. Social scientists who like to be able to publicize their work also resent the norm of secrecy, which prevails in some organizations (Horowitz, 1969). In contrast to administrators who want social scientists to work within the framework of established policy, social scientists may want to challenge an agency's ideological premises (Horowitz, 1969). In addition, some social scientists have been concerned that agreement to undertake the evaluation of a program may be interpreted as implicit commitment to the philosophy or goals of the program. Evaluative researchers, then, may give a program a legitimacy they believe it does not deserve (Ferman,

1969). Also, social scientists have been deterred from engaging in evaluative research by the low prestige accorded to applied research in academic settings, exasperation with the methodological and administrative problems of conducting research in an action setting, and disagreements regarding the use of research results.

Problems in Administration of Evaluation Research

Successful administration of evaluation research depends on cooperation from agency administrators and practitioners charged with implementing action programs. Even though they often advocate extensive collaboration and communication with administrators, evaluative researchers typically insist that they hold ultimate responsibility for research design and execution. Administrative interference with what social scientists consider to be critical issues in the design and execution of research is seriously resented (see, for example, Smith *et al.,* 1960).

Whether or not researchers are agency employees, they are readily drawn into staff-management conflicts. A number of observers have noted that acceptance of evaluative research is often accompanied by suspicion of research at lower levels. (See, for example, Rodman and Kolodny, 1964; Lippitt, Watson, and Westley, 1958; Argyris, 1958; Whyte and Hamilton, 1964; and Likert and Lippitt, 1953.) Because evaluation is linked to top administration and involves examination of the activities of staff subordinates, evaluators are sometimes suspected of being management spies. Staff practitioners anxious to avoid criticism of their work are likely to attempt to conceal real or imagined shortcomings. Such steps may add greatly to the evaluator's difficulties in obtaining valid data.

Research neutrality is also likely to pose a problem with practitioners who consider a strong value commitment to their programs important. Scriven (1967), for example, reports the complaint of some practitioners that the skepticism of evaluative researchers may dampen the creativity of a productive group. Argyris (1958) argues that research neutrality leads to subject alienation which, in turn, produces anxieties in the researcher that result in invalid observations.

Purely mechanical demands of data collection may also create a burden. Practitioners typically, and perhaps correctly, consider themselves overburdened with record keeping. Characteristically, even when record keeping is emphasized, records are not sufficiently accurate or complete to satisfy research criteria.

Conflict between research and service goals may interfere with the collection of data called for by research designs. When a research design calls for action inconsistent with immediate service goals, practitioners may disregard research needs in favor of providing services. Compounding the problem, practitioners may "neglect" to inform evaluators when clients have been shifted from one treatment condition to another because of service considerations.

Different conceptions of efficient use of time may lead to mutual annoyance. A professional evaluator, for example, is not accustomed to turning in daily time sheets. His failure to do so can be interpreted as a sign of indolence by an administrator concerned with time and cost factors. Bynder (1966), reflecting on his research work in a social work unit of a general hospital, observes that "thinking is not a tangible use of time, and, therefore, could not be accepted in an agency which measured work in terms of clients interviewed, physicians contacted, meetings attended, and pages written." An insecure social scientist may respond by engaging in "busy work," which satisfies the immediate demands but which may be detrimental to long-term evaluation objectives.

Status ambiguities may further strain relationships. If an evaluator has more formal education but less clinical experience than his administrator and practitioner counterparts, conflicts may result. The social scientists may display an academic disregard for practical problems. Administrators and practitioners, in turn, may be defensive about their educational inferiority and highly sensitive to what they interpret as the snobbism of evaluative researchers. Sometimes threatened practitioners have claimed that evaluators are incompetent because they do not understand the practical problems of an action agency. Evaluative researchers, perceiving themselves as exposed and defenseless members of a minority group in an action organization, have sometimes reacted at this point by looking for ways of returning to an academic setting.

The publication of the results of evaluative research may create two basic problems. (See, for example, Rodman and Kolodny, 1964.) Agencies often impose controls on the publication of "sensitive" data because a negative report may threaten not only the agency's public image but also its access to funds. Even if it is agreed that project results should be reported, there may be disagreements about publication credits. The evaluative researcher who contributed the research design, data analysis, and writing may regard the report as a scientific publication for which he is solely responsible. The administrator, emphasizing the content of the project, may believe he deserves major recognition for conceiving and implementing the program.

A final important issue is the availability of funds for evaluative research. Action organizations nearly always operate within tight budgets. Administrators typically attempt to use funds to provide as much service as possible. The cost of the elaborate data collection and analysis that evaluative researchers consider essential, however, may represent a substantial proportion of the total project budget. Given the often intangible and uncertain contribution of evaluative research, requests for evaluation funds may be among the first to suffer when the budget is curtailed.

Problems in the Use of Results of Evaluation

Since the ultimate purpose of evaluation is to contribute to the effectiveness of action programs, implementation of research results is a critical phase in the process. Yet numerous writers have warned that even the most carefully designed and executed evaluative research does not automatically lead to meaningful action. (For some examples of cases in which findings of evaluative research were ignored or rejected by program administrators, see Rossi, 1966; and Hall, 1966.) Disregard for results of evaluation appears to stem from a variety of sources.

Some of the nonuse of evaluation results is attributable to limitations of the research itself. In discussing demonstration projects, Rein and Miller (1967) note that evaluative research often cannot produce results early enough to be a major factor in short-term policy decisions. J. Mann (1969) similarly reflects on the dilemmas of rigor, timing, and utility of evaluation: "The better the study, the longer it takes, and consequently the less usefulness it may have. Conversely, the sloppier the procedure, the more likely it is to provide information on questions of interest even though this data will be of doubtful validity." Weiss (1966) further indicates that the influence potential of evaluation may be limited because results are indefinite, show only small changes, and fail to indicate the relative effectiveness of various components or the reasons for a program's success or failure.

Of basic importance in cases where pertinent evaluation results are ignored is the evaluator's lack of authority. Since the evaluator is an advisor, policy makers are under no obligation to accept his recommendations. Nonuse of evaluation findings is sometimes explained by the fact that evaluation was included for the "wrong reasons." Downs (1965) points out that professional advice is sometimes sought to justify decisions already made or to postpone action. Several commentators have suggested that an evaluation component is sometimes supported because it lends an aura of prestige to an action enterprise (Rodman and Kolodny, 1964; Bynder, 1966; Rosenthal and Weiss, 1966; and Schulberg and Baker, 1968). An administrator may support an evaluator in the hope that he may provide other services—for example, the organization of information to justify grant requests (Miller, 1965a; and Luchterhand, 1967). As previously indicated, evaluation is sometimes included in action programs only because it is required by law or the administrative regulations of a funding agent. In these cases evaluation results may be ignored because administrators do not adequately understand or appreciate their relevance. Discrepancies between the findings of evaluative research and informal evaluations, personal convictions and professional ideologies of decision makers, and judgments of the competence of evaluators also contribute to the nonuse of evaluative research findings (Sadofsky, 1966).

Disagreements regarding evaluative criteria sometimes contribute to nonuse of findings. Rossi (1969) observes that administrators sometimes discount evaluation findings by claiming that the "real" goals of the project were not measured. Schulberg and Baker (1968) question the wisdom of the usual practice of building evaluation on the public goals of an organization because administrators may have no intention of achieving those goals. An evaluative researcher, then, may be ineffective because he misread the administrator's real intent. Campbell (1969) and Deutscher (1975) also call attention to the vulnerability of evaluations in which only a portion of the potentially important outcomes are addressed.

Basic Strains between Evaluative Research and Administration

Relations between evaluative researchers and administrators are likely to be strained in the introduction, execution, and utilization of evaluative research. Many of the specific obstacles to effective collaboration identified here can be summarized by consideration of several basic orientations in which administrators and evaluative researchers are likely to differ markedly: service versus research, specificity versus generality, methods, status quo versus change, explanations for failure, and scientific versus administrative experience.

Service versus Research

In contrast to the practitioner who is concerned with the immediate and specific application of knowledge, the evaluative researcher is responsible for the acquisition of knowledge. The service-research strain is most evident in field settings where research and service perspectives call for opposite courses of action. An evaluative research design may call for the assignment of a client to a control group when, from a service perspective, it appears preferable that he receive the experimental treatment. (See, for example, Argyris, 1958; Freeman, 1963; and Perry and Wynne, 1959.) In addition, evaluative researchers, reflecting their academic backgrounds, are likely to have greater appreciation than practitioners for the acquisition of knowledge for its own sake.

Specificity versus Generality

In contrast to administrators who emphasize the solution of immediate problems, researchers are more often interested in long-term problem-solving. Similarly, administrators emphasize the uniqueness of their agency and program, while researchers prefer to generalize in both time and space. What is of theoretical significance to the scientist may be trivial from a practical viewpoint. (See, for example, Shepard, 1956; Warren, 1963; Merton, 1957; Rodman and Kolodny, 1964; and Cherns, 1969.)

Methods

Although administrators and researchers may agree that methods used in program development should be "rational," they often do not mean the same thing by that term. Evaluative research, for example, requires explicit statements of objectives and strategies to which administrators find it difficult or undesirable to commit themselves (Schulberg and Baker, 1968). Administrators may be displeased with evaluative research which, in emphasizing organizational outputs, often tends to neglect administrative activities that are needed to maintain the organization as a viable system (Etzioni, 1960). At another level, the researcher's commitment to scientific decision-making procedures may run counter to the administrator's confidence in intuition. Evaluative researchers have a professional interest in being able to show that the scientific method is superior to conventional wisdom as a basis for decision making (Ferman, 1969).

Status Quo versus Change

Implicit in the evaluation role are attempts to discover inefficiency and to encourage change. Administrators, however, usually prefer to conceal inefficiency for which they may be held responsible and resist disruptive change. A claim to superior knowledge of human affairs predisposes social scientists to dramatize inadequacies in the conventional wisdom upon which programs are often based. Administrators, on the other hand, look for evidence of success of past and current programs to assert their competence. Evaluative researchers are thus predisposed to see a need for change whereas administrators are inclined to defend their efforts and maintain the status quo. (See, for example, Argyris, 1958; and Ferman, 1969.)

Explanations for Failure

Evaluators and administrators are likely to emphasize different explanations for the persistence of social problems. Again, apparently because of a desire to assert their competence, administrators tend to accept the validity of the theoretical premises on which their programs are based. Attributing failure to the inadequate application of their approaches, administrators are likely to call for the expansion of present efforts. Evaluators who are free to question program premises often attribute failure to an inadequate understanding of the basic problem. They are likely to suggest that a radically different programming approach is needed if the problem is to be addressed effectively. In arguing that what is needed is "more of the same," the practitioner may also serve his professional interest in expanding the demand for his services. Evaluative researchers similarly have vested professional interest when they argue that more effective programming requires an expanded emphasis on evaluation.

When both administrators and evaluators acknowledge difficulties in implementing programs, administrators are likely to look for explanations that are idiosyncratic (incompetence or emotional instability) and moral (dishonesty or laziness) in contrast to social scientists, who emphasize amoral and structural factors. Part of the issue is the social scientist's sensitivity to the impact of organizational structure on the particular job-holder. Insiders, on the other hand, tend to explain organizational behavior in terms of the personal characteristics of the individuals involved. Also related is the evaluative researcher's more secularized explanation of human behavior, which leads him to emphasize factors outside the realm of free choice.

Scientific versus Administrative Experience

Because the evaluation researcher typically approaches social action from the perspective of scientific method and an academic discipline, his knowledge of program operations is likely to be highly incomplete. Political constraints, budgetary problems, and limitations of personnel and facilities are among the program dimensions whose importance researchers often underestimate. In the same sense, it is difficult for administrators with limited research background to appreciate the intricacies of research design, measurement, and data analysis.

Client Activism

Much of the innovative social programming in recent years has been directed toward reducing the incidence of poverty. At the same time, the minorities who represent a substantial proportion of the poor have been growing more self-conscious as groups. Stimulated by the civil rights movement and professional community developers, minority activists have taken a significant interest in local community affairs, including the social programs directed at the poor. As clients or spokesmen for clients of antipoverty programs, they have pressed for extensive participation if not full control of these programs at the levels of both policy and implementation. Antipoverty programs consequently have often been surrounded by substantial and continuous conflict over such matters as representation on and authority of boards, employment policies and practices, and the substance and administration of programs. Beyond the direct programming implications of minority activism, the movement has added to the challenges confronting the evaluative researcher.

Even though evaluative researchers may firmly believe that their efforts ultimately contribute to the cause of the poor, minority activists may confront them with a hostility similar to that which they direct at other middle-class professionals. The basic issues that strain evaluator-administrator relations even more thoroughly set evaluation researchers apart from low-income program clients. Preoccupied with the immediate, tangible, dramatic, and personal, the minority activist is likely to be impatient with the evaluator's concern with the future, abstract concepts, orderly procedures, and impersonal forces. In contrast to the activist who often seeks to generate open conflict, the evaluative researcher typically emphasizes cooperative approaches to problem-solving. The evaluator may also find himself in an awkward position in the power struggle between client spokesmen and professional administrators. If his entree to the program is through a funding agency or a professional administrator, the evaluative researcher is likely to be mistrusted immediately by minority activists who see him as a potential spy. Indeed, if evaluative criteria are limited to those acceptable to administrators, and if evaluation findings are subject to administrative review prior to being publicized, client spokesmen have good reason to challenge the evaluator's contribution.

Some of the minority activist's hostility to evaluative research is also attributable to a more general antipathy toward social resarch. Minority spokesmen frequently complain that they have been "surveyed to death." Perhaps for some social research has come to symbolize the powerlessness of the poor. The poverty spokesman resents that social research on poverty has nearly always been initiated by outsiders and addressed to issues defined by outsiders. The poor have been encouraged to cooperate by rhetoric that links research to desired social goals; yet, it is difficult for them to see tangible benefits stemming from social research. In fact, many activists cynically view research as a substitute for needed action. General antagonism toward social research is also linked to the activist's political ambitions. The independent social scientist who does poverty research is a potential competitor for the indigenous leader who would like to control the flow of information from poverty areas. The local spokesman for the poor has reason to be anxious if his claims are challenged by respected social scientists.

Strategies for Establishing and Maintaining the Evaluation Role

A number of experienced evaluators have suggested strategies for dealing with the problems that can be expected in establishing and maintaining the evaluation role.

Inside versus Outside Evaluators

A basic administrative issue concerns the comparative advantages and disadvantages of "inside" and "outside" evaluators. The inside evaluator is a staff member in the organization whose programs are evaluated; the outside evaluator is an outside consultant. The following are some of the arguments that have been presented in favor of outsiders: (1) they tend to be better able to maintain their objectivity; (2) they are more likely to be able to include evaluative criteria that question basic organizational premises; (3) they may be able to mediate more effectively where there is extensive internal conflict; (4) they usually are better protected from problems of marginality and status incongruity; and (5) they are better able to avoid unwelcome nonresearch tasks.

It has been suggested that insiders have the following advantages: (1) they are usually able to develop a more detailed knowledge of the organization and its programs; (2) they are in a better position to do continuing research. Likert and Lippitt, 1953; Weinberger, 1969; Weiss, 1966; McEwen, 1956; and Rodman and Kolodny, 1964, are among those who have addressed themselves to these arguments. Van de Vall (1974) reports on a survey concerned with applied social research in a number of organizational settings which showed that findings of research done by insiders were more often used in decision making than studies conducted by outside researchers. Van de Vall attributes the greater influence of internal researchers to their more effective communication with policy makers.

Luchterhand (1967) points out that outsiders cannot always be counted on to be more objective than insiders. When they are concerned with maintaining good relations with clients, outsiders may slant their interpretations to accommodate their client's interests. Alienated inside evaluators, on the other hand, may be inclined to report on their agency's programs with stark objectivity. Yet, funding agencies, spokesmen for clients, and the general public usually consider the reports of external evaluators more credible. As Lortie (1967) points out, persons and organizations cannot be trusted to act as judges in their own case. Their self-appraisals cannot be accepted without question. When evaluation is conducted for the purpose of accounting to an outside body, use of external evaluators appears preferable. If, on the other hand, evaluation is conducted to assist an organization in its program development efforts, an internal evaluation unit may be able to contribute more effectively.

Establishing Relationships

If the evaluative researcher hopes to contribute to internal program development, he should take early steps to establish effective ties with those who make key decisions regarding programming. Sensitivity to the locus of decision making is, therefore, important. Relations with administrators are always important, but in more decentralized and democratic organizations evaluative researchers may find it appropriate to work more closely with the professional practitioners (such as physicians, social workers, and teachers) who are most concerned with the substance of programs. Some have pointed to the importance of the evaluator's organizational position. (See, for example, Argyris, 1958; Bennis, 1965; Rosenthal and Weiss, 1966; Suchman, 1967a; and Whyte and Hamilton, 1964.) The evaluator's prestige and power are considered to be positively related to the likelihood that his findings will be implemented. If the evaluator is an insider, it is important that he have a prestigious position within the organization. Similarly, if he is an outsider, it is helpful if he has strong professional and organizational credentials. It is also important for an outside evaluator to be linked to someone of high status in the action organization—a relationship that Sussman (1966) calls the "Merlin role." When he makes status claims, the evaluator, however, must also consider the possible resentment of staff subordinates. If they believe he receives more status prerogatives than he deserves, they may not cooperate fully.

As he begins working with agency representatives, it is important for the evaluator to create what Likert and Lippitt (1953), call an "image of potential." The evaluator must, for example, provide administrators and practitioners with assurance of his technical competence, his understanding of the action setting, and his personal integrity and decency (Warren, 1963).

A mutual clarification of expectations at an early stage in the relationship may be useful. Administrators should, for example, be informed of some of the limitations of the contribution of evaluative research. Evaluators might need to explain, for example, that their work cannot resolve fundamental value issues nor can it, by itself, resolve deep-seated conflicts between administrators and their staff or between the agency and its clients. If evaluation is to be used for program development purposes, evaluators should attempt to gauge the extent to which policy makers may be willing to tolerate challenges to their basic premises. An early agreement regarding the manner in which evaluation results will be publicized is also desirable. If the purpose of the evaluation is summative and it is externally sponsored, there should be advance agreement on the extent to which persons and organizational units will be identified in published reports. The evaluative researcher's interest in pursuing professional research interests should also be discussed. For his work to be relevant in the action setting, the evaluative researcher may have to postpone the pursuit of some of his personal intellectual interests. It may be desirable for the evaluative researcher to reach an early and explicit agreement with the funding agency and program administrators on the extent to which he is free to use his time and project data for professional research purposes. In addition, the evaluative researcher should inform himself not only about available action alternatives, but also the timing of decision making. If evaluation findings are to be used, evaluation must be addressed to pertinent action issues and results must be available when needed.

Cooperation in Task Definition

Evaluators may be able to make a greater contribution if they can modify the policy maker's expectations. Sadofsky (1966), for example, suggests that the program operator's fear of failure may be diminished if action projects are accepted as experiments. Failure, then, can be seen as a learning opportunity. Weiss (1966) recommends that instead of judging programs in simple success or failure terms, the administrator should be encouraged to ask questions about the relative effectiveness of alternative programs.

In general, evaluators should work closely with administrators in establishing evaluative criteria first, so that evaluators may become more fully aware of administrative concerns; and second, so that administrators may become more committed to the evaluation process (Freeman and Sherwood, 1965). Collaboration in the identification of criteria or goals may help evaluators base their work on variables more explicit, realistic, and perhaps more comprehensive than the objectives shown in official program documents. Stake (1967), however, strikes a note of caution. He argues that administrators or practitioners should not be expected to work at the high level of abstraction required for the writing of behavioral goals. Rather, evaluators should draft statements of objectives that attempt to reflect and clarify the intent of administrators. Coleman (1969) similarly points out that because administrators are often not fully aware of their decision-making criteria, evaluative researchers may have to discover these criteria for themselves.

As a number of writers have pointed out, evaluative researchers need to consider a wide variety of potential program effects, including those which are unintended and undesired. Scriven (1969), for example, emphasizes the evaluator's responsibility as a professional to focus his efforts on appropriate evaluative criteria. Campbell (1969), concerned with undesired side-effects, recommends that several outcome measures be used, including those recommended by "loyal opponents." Deutscher (1976) suggests that by observing programs in operation and through discussions with practitioners, evaluators may become aware of important evaluation issues that are not apparent in program proposals. Because of limited evaluation budgets and the relatively narrow range of alternatives which the administrator sees as open, however, the evaluator often finds it prudent to narrow the range of his inquiry. Aware of his lack of power, but hopeful of being able to influence policy makers within a limited but significant range of decision alternatives, the evaluator may find it desirable to ignore some potential evaluative criteria.

Cooperation of Program Staff

It is important for the evaluator to take steps to obtain cooperation not only from administrators, but also from subordinate staff members. Staff support is critical if programs are to be carried out as designed and if program records, essential for evaluation purposes, are to be maintained. Staff cooperation, however, cannot be taken for granted. A basic problem here is that the evaluator's relationship with top administrators puts the evaluator in the same organizational position as an inspector or policeman. If he hopes to obtain staff cooperation, the evaluator must insist that program evaluation is quite different from the evaluation of individuals or organizational units. Thus, Likert and Lippitt (1953, p. 611) emphasize that staff members must be assured "that the objective of the research is to discover the relative effectiveness of different methods and principles and that the study is in no way an attempt to perform a policing function. The emphasis must be on discovering what principles work best and why, and not on finding and reporting which individuals are doing their jobs well or poorly. . . ."

Staff subordinates must, then, be given emphatic assurance of confidentiality and anonymity. It is also desirable to be able to obtain a commitment from administrators to share evaluation findings openly with subordinates. If evaluation efforts are to add to the record-keeping duties of practitioners, evaluators may be wise to provide practitioners with added compensation or staff support to assure their cooperation.

Feedback

Because of pressure to produce results quickly, timing may be a critical concern in the organization of evaluation efforts. Time pressures must, of course, be given strong considerations in selection of a methodological strategy. Grobman (1968) further suggests that evaluators use a formal planning procedure such as Program Evaluation and Review Technique (PERT) to assure that evaluation work will be completed within a tight time schedule. In some cases, evaluators may wish to report interim findings either to aid in an immediate decision problem or to keep administrators interested in the evaluation process. Early feedback, however, may be a problem for evaluators if it leads administrators to change programs substantially before enough cases have been observed to satisfy the requirements of an experimental design.

Use of evaluation findings may depend on the manner in which results are reported. Clear, concise, and even dramatic presentations of findings are helpful in attracting attention to evaluation findings. Sadofsky (1966) warns that delivering results to an administrator publicly and without warning may produce a defensive reaction. Written reports may be supplemented with personal meetings with administrators. Mann and Likert (1952) recommend a series of small group meetings from top administrative levels through the ranks of subordinates to facilitate communication of results and to stimulate interest in following through on the action implications. They argue that the pressures generated in small groups increase commitment to implementation of recommended changes. Argyris (1958) proposes another strategy. He suggests first asking administrators and practitioners for their own diagnoses, to reduce the likelihood that they will reject research findings as too obvious.

Strategies for Obtaining Cooperation from Client Spokesmen

Where client cooperation with evaluation may be an issue, support of client spokesmen should be sought at an early stage. Funding agencies or administrators should initially explain the rationale for evaluation and the allocation of funds for this purpose. Participation of client spokesmen in the selection of an evaluator may also be advisable. Since employment opportunity is a central concern among minority activists, it is desirable for evaluators to employ some members of the population served by programs. (Such a commitment may make it necessary for the evaluator to place more emphasis on staff training and supervision than he would otherwise.) Even more than staff subordinates, client spokesmen need persuasive assurance that confidential personal information will be used only for overall evaluation purposes. They also need to be convinced that unlike basic research, evaluative research is designed to have rather immediate action implications. Client spokesmen need assurance that evaluation results will be available to them and that they will have full opportunity to participate in their interpretation. An evaluator may be able to satisfy some of the personalistic concerns of poverty groups by spending enough time with minority spokesmen so that they know and trust him as an individual.

In some situations the level of conflict between client spokesmen and established agencies may be so great that cooperation in program evaluation is not a realistic possibility. In these cases it may be preferable for each group to sponsor its own evaluation enterprise. Funding agencies may find it advisable in these cases to provide organized client spokesmen with the funds needed for their independent evaluation of programs.

METHODOLOGICAL ISSUES

The methodological principles that apply to the evaluation of social programs are the same as those of general behavior science inquiry. However, certain problems of measurement and design arise with some regularity in evaluative research.

Measurement

A basic step in evaluation is the identification of objectives and their measurement. Suchman (1966) suggests that the formulation of objectives has five aspects: (1) the content of the objectives (i.e., that which is to be changed by the program); (2) the target of the program; (3) the time within which the change is to take place; (4) the number of objectives (if they are multiple); and (5) the extent of the expected effect. Freeman (1965), Suchman (1967a), Greenberg (1968), and Weiss (1966) are among those who urge a distinction among immediate, intermediate, and ultimate objectives. Measurements that focus on immediate and intermediate objectives are particularly important when evaluation results are needed before ultimate objectives may be realized. If a program is justified on the basis of ultimate objectives but evaluative research is limited to immediate and intermediate objectives, the plausibility of the hypothesized causal link between intermediate and ultimate objectives must be subjected to very careful analysis. When programs fail to realize ultimate objectives, data on accomplishment of more proximate goals may be useful in explaining the program's limited success. If immediate and intermediate objectives are used as substitutes for ultimate objectives, however, the burden is on the evaluator to argue the validity of the hypothesized links to ultimate objectives. When programs fail to realize ultimate objectives, utilization of a hierarchy of objectives may also be useful in accounting for their limited success.

Input Measurement

Because the realities of program operations are often inconsistent with public project descriptions, measurement of program inputs has also been recommended. Greenberg (1968), for example, terms observation of administrative patterns and analysis of service statistics as "quasi-evaluation." Coleman (1969) further urges a distinction between resources as allocated by organizations and services as actually received by clients. Analysis of these administrative data may be useful for preliminary program screening purposes. To the extent that organizations are unable to deliver services to clients, expectations of program effectiveness, of course, are diminished. As discussed previously, it is also helpful for the evaluator to anticipate and measure possible unintended effects of programs, including the undesirable ones. Scriven (1967) further recommends that evaluators consider secondary effects of programs, which include impact on the individuals and organizations who conduct programs and those who regularly interact with program beneficiaries.

Original and Secondary Data

Identification of variables is, of course, only a first step in the measurement process. Evaluators are often confronted with serious obstacles in seeking the valid, reliable, and sensitive measures they need. Lerman (1968) and Campbell (1969) are among those who point to the shortcomings of the agency records upon which an evaluator often depends. When he uses agency records, the evaluator must consider that these data may reflect the organizational, professional, and individual interests of the record keepers as much as they do the behavior that they are intended to measure.

Because his information requirements are relatively refined and because the quality of agency records is frequently poor, the evaluator must often collect his own data, thus creating additional problems. Data collection may add enormously to the cost of evaluation. Administrators and practitioners may object either because data collection interferes with the time available for programming or because it may jeopardize client or community acceptance of the program. Evaluators, on the other hand, may be concerned that their data collection activities may artificially enhance client awareness of the program, thereby altering its apparent or actual effectiveness. The evaluator may cope with these data collection problems by using unobtrusive measures (Webb *et al.*, 1966) or by disguising the relationship between his data collection and the program (Seashore, 1964). He may also address these problems through his selection of a research design. Campbell (1957) suggested use of the Soloman four-group design or a design requiring only post-test measurements. (See also Suchman, 1967a; and Wuebben, 1968.) Although Hyman, Wright, and Hopkins (1962) review evidence indicating that sensitizing or practice effects of pretesting are often negligible, the evaluator is clearly advised to take steps to guard against this potential source of measurement error.

Freeman (1963) urges that evaluators use behavioral rather than attitudinal measures of program objectives because policy makers are more likely to be impressed with behavioral data. Deutscher (1969) similarly argues in favor of direct behavioral measures because they pose fewer validity problems than do procedures designed to provide estimates of hypothetical behavior.

Beyond the sensitizing effects of measurement, practitioner and client awareness of evaluative criteria and measurement procedures can have important undesired effects on the way in which programs are administered and received. (See, for example, Weiss and Rein, 1969, and Deutscher, 1976.) The danger is that administrative units, practitioners, or clients may artificially redirect their behavior to affect the outcome of evaluation. The problem is particularly acute where incomplete sets of evaluative criteria and imperfect measures are used to judge the performance of participants. Considerable attention has been given to this problem in higher education, for example, where it has been argued that faculty are often excessively concerned with publishing and students are overly preoccupied with grades. By emphasizing their concern with program concepts rather than specific participants, evaluative researchers may be able to deal with this problem effectively.

Timing of measurement is often another serious issue in evaluative research. (See, for example, Freeman and Sherwood, 1965; Hyman and Wright, 1967; and Harris, 1963.) Often it is not clear how soon program effects can be expected, and how stable and durable changes brought about by programs will prove. Ideally, the problem is addressed through continuous or at least repeated measurement of output variables. Many evaluative researchers, however, find that they have only an opportunity for a single post-treatment measurement. The timing of such a measurement may have most important implications for the outcome of evaluative research.

Design

The Problem of Control

To assure that changes in measured behavior can be attributed exclusively to the program at hand, evaluative researchers prefer to be able to employ some form of an experimental design. From an evaluation perspective, it is desirable that clients be assigned randomly to treatment and control groups. Adequate control, however, is difficult to achieve in an action setting. Suchman (1967b) cites two obstacles to the effectiveness of use of control groups: (1) service orientation—administrators, practitioners, and client representatives are reluctant to withhold services from those who might benefit from them; and (2) self-selection—it is difficult both to refuse service to those who seek it and provide service to those who resist it. In discussing the evaluation of community-wide programs, Greenberg (1968) points out the added problem of finding truly equivalent communities. Where control groups are not possible, experimental control may be approximated through some design adjustments. One approach is to match participants with nonparticipants and compare them through the use of analysis of covariance. Campbell and Erlebacher (1970), however, warn that matching may produce regression artifacts that seriously bias the results. The time-series design (Hyman, Wright, and Hopkins, 1962; Campbell and Stanley, 1963; Campbell, 1969; and Gottman, McFall, and Barnett, 1969) is an alternative through which the treatment group is used as its own control through repeated measurements of outcome variables, beginning well before program implementation.

Lerman (1968) argues that evaluators should resist the common assumption of administrators that evaluation be based on those who complete treatments. Rather, evaluation should be based on the population in need of services. He points out that the issue is particularly critical among private agencies that can select their own clients.

In action settings it may be possible to use comparison groups when control groups are unacceptable. Unlike the control group which receives no treatment, the comparison group receives an alternate treatment. Where policy makers are committed to the principle of providing additional services, a comparison-group design may actually provide more useful information than a design using only a strict control.

Social programs usually cannot be expected to produce a dramatic impact. If evaluation is to document subtle but important changes, large samples or highly sensitive designs are necessary (Freeman, 1963). The conservatism that often prevails in academic research regarding rejection of null hypotheses may also be inappropriate in the formulation of decision criteria in evaluative research. Rather, evaluators may wish to be cautious in drawing negative conclusions regarding innovative programs (Miller, 1965b).

Program Practitioner Interaction

A persistent problem in the design of evaluative research is the separation of effects of program content from those of the characteristics of practitioners. Staff enthusiasm and confidence may be critical variables in innovative programs. Design adjustments are particularly difficult where the number of practitioners is small. Greenberg (1968) suggests that program personnel be rotated between treatment and control conditions. Unless very carefully supervised, such staff rotation, however, may encourage an eclecticism in practice that compromises the distinction between the experimental and control conditions. Special train-ing and supervision of practitioners may be introduced to reduce variability in practitioner behavior. Alternately it may be possible to conduct some programs with minimal practitioner-client contact.

Program Recipient Interactions

Program recipients may contribute to the effect of an intervention through their feelings of self-importance as persons selected for special attention (Hawthorne effect) or through their faith in the program (placebo effect). The impact of these effects is likely to be particularly great when the program is new and experimental and when participants are volunteers. Scriven (1967) suggests the use of multiple experimental groups to separate these effects from those of programs. He urges that enthusiasm be held constant while treatments are varied. Trow (1967), however, points out that some administrators may try to capitalize on Hawthorne effects by attempting to build an experimental climate into their normal programming. Sommer (1968) similarly argues that the Hawthorne effect is not an extraneous disruptive influence; rather it is an important and ever-present factor in any field situation. As he puts it, "En-vironmental changes do not act directly upon human organisms. They are interpreted according to the individual's needs, set, and state of awareness" (p. 594). If the effects of social programs are to be fully understood, it seems to be important that the client population's predisposition toward and interpretation of programs be an integral part of comprehensive evaluative research.

New programs often pose special difficulties for evaluators. On the one hand, the evaluative researcher must be prepared to deal with the positive effects of novelty, special attention, and enthusiasm. On the other hand, he must look for some strictly administrative problems in implementation which can account for the failure of an otherwise soundly conceived program (Hyman and Wright, 1967). It is particularly important for administrators of innovative programs to be free to modify their procedures on the basis of their early experiences in implementation (Marris and Rein, 1967). These modifications pose an enor-mous problem for evaluation if research designs call for a lengthy commitment to a highly specific set of procedures. If, as Glass (1971) recommends, evaluators focus on program concepts rather than specific procedures, their experimental designs may be able to accommodate procedural adjustments as long as basic concepts remain intact.

Program outcomes may also be affected by many other variables that cannot

be controlled in a single evaluative study. Among these are the physical characteristics of the program site and the duration and intensity of the program.

Because action programs are often ineffective and because experimental
evaluation is often very expensive, Rossi (1966) recommends a two-phased
approach to evaluation. First correlational designs would be used to identify
promising programs. Then powerful controlled experiments would be conducted to evaluate the relative effectiveness of those programs that passed the
initial screening.

Diffuse and Unstable Programs

Tight experimental designs are most easily implemented in the evaluation of
programs conducted by highly centralized organizations with extensive voluntary or involuntary control over clients. Prisons, hospitals, and residential
schools are typical of such organizations. Where programs involve a number of
autonomous organizations, are conducted by practitioners with considerable
personal and professional autonomy, and are directed at client populations
whose willingness to cooperate is highly uncertain, evaluators often must be
satisfied to use limited methodological tools.

The community-wide antipoverty programs of the 1960's were among those
in which it is most difficult for evaluators to use well-controlled experimental
designs. The relative contributions of various components of these large-scale
programs were difficult to determine because of uncontrolled exposure of clients
to several programs. It was also difficult to determine the extent to which new
programs were supplements to rather than substitutes for earlier programs.
Weiss and Rein (1969) further argue that in the case of these highly diffuse and
unstable programs, it is particularly difficult to select and operationalize evaluative criteria that are broad enough in scope to reflect a program's full range of
consequences—especially those that are unintended.

In these settings the evaluator must look for research strategies that are
realistic and, at the same time, yield a maximum of useful information. Particularly in the case of completely innovative programs where evaluation results are
needed at an early stage, informal research approaches usually associated with
exploratory research may be most appropriate. Observational techniques and
informal interviewing may provide more useful rapid feedback than can formal
experimentation. (See, for example, Weiss and Rein, 1969.) Lazarsfeld, Sewell,
and Wilensky (1967) observe that because the decision process in these programs is continuous, evaluation must take place at many points. They recom-

mend concurrent evaluation, a procedure through which records are kept of all decisions including information on rejected alternatives and expected outcomes. Perhaps as Benedict *et al.* (1967) suggest, what is needed is evaluation that combines rigorous experimental data with a "natural history" account of events and actors before, during, and after program implementation.

CONCLUDING THOUGHTS

Clearly, evaluative research is an activity surrounded by serious obstacles. Satisfied with informal and impressionistic approaches to evaluation, policy makers are often reluctant to make the investment needed to obtain verifiable data on the effects of their programs. Evaluative researchers are typically confronted with problems of measurement and design, which greatly restrict their ability to reach unambiguous conclusions. Abrasive relations with practitioners and clients can add to the evaluator's difficulties in obtaining information. Evaluative research is often addressed to a distressingly narrow range of issues, and results not fully or widely disclosed. At the same time, policy makers often ignore highly pertinent findings of evaluative research. Little wonder that many social scientists regard evaluative research as a dubious enterprise.

Yet, there is a strong argument for emphasizing evaluative research in social programming. This country spends enormous amounts for social service programs (including health and education). At the same time the effectiveness of many of these programs is seriously questioned. Increases in program costs tend to be much more conspicuous than improvements in the quality of services. If it is agreed that social programs should be strengthened and that improvement is most likely to come about through the use of rational methods, it is clear that the evaluation role is vital. Because the results of social programs are often not obvious, the methods of empirical research are needed to obtain precise information on program effectiveness.

Evaluative researchers can take a number of steps on their own to improve their contribution to program development. They can become more skillful in applying their methodological tools to specific evaluation problems. By becoming more knowledgeable about the decision problems of action organizations, evaluators can recommend more appropriate evaluation strategies. Greater personal familiarity with action settings may make evaluators more effective in working with practitioners and clients. The climate for evaluation might be improved if evaluators were to place more emphasis on educating administrators, practitioners, and client representatives regarding the role of evaluation in program development. Evaluators might also develop more effective ways of communicating the action implications of findings. Behavioral scientists who assume administrative roles in programs can also help by showing how programs can be structured to accommodate evaluation requirements.

If, however, evaluative research is to make its full contribution, substantial changes must be made in society's overall approach to social programming. Legislators and other public officials reflecting widespread public concern must raise significantly their demands for the effectiveness and efficiency of programs. In addition, they must learn to focus more on program goals so that they can assume a more experimental attitude toward specific programming strategies. Such fundamental changes in attitude would lead to greatly expanded interest in evaluative research. If there were more serious emphasis on performance standards and the search for more effective program approaches, evaluative researchers more often would be able to obtain the political and administrative support needed to employ powerful experimental designs. Behavioral scientists who hope to contribute to the effectiveness of social programs through evaluative research need to concern themselves, then, not only with immediate methodological and organizational problems but also with the larger issues concerning the social context in which social programs are conducted.

REFERENCES

Argyris, Chris. "Creating Effective Relationships in Organizations," *Human Organization* 17: No. 1, 34–40, 1958. Reprinted in *Human Organization Research* (edited by R. Adams and J. Preiss). Homewood, Illinois: Dorsey, 1960, pp. 109–123.

Barnes, Louis. "Organizational Change and Field Experiment Methods," in *Methods of Organizational Research* (edited by Victor Vroom). Pittsburgh: University of Pittsburgh Press, 1967.

Benedict, Barbara, *et al.* "The Clinical-Experimental Approach to Assessing Organizational Change Efforts," *Journal of Applied Behavioral Science* 3: 347–380, 1967.

Bennis, Warren. "Theory and Method in Applying Behavioral Science to Planned Organizational Change," *Journal of Applied Behavioral Science* 1: 337–360, 1965.

Bernstein, Ilene N., and Howard Freeman. *Academic and Entrepreneurial Research: The Consequences of Diversity in Federal Evaluation Studies.* New York: Russell Sage Foundation, 1975.

Brooks, Michael. "The Community Action Program as a Setting for Applied Research," *Journal of Social Issues* 21: 29–40, 1965.

Bynder, Herbert. "Sociology in a Hospital: A Case Study in Frustration," in *Sociology in Action* (edited by A. Shostak). Homewood, Illinois: Dorsey, 1966, pp. 61–70.

Campbell, Donald T. "Validity of Experiments in Social Settings," *Psychological Bulletin* 54: 297–312, 1957.

Campbell, Donald T. "Administrative Experimentation, Institutional Records, and

Nonreactive Measures," in *Improving Experimental Design and Statistical Analysis* (edited by Julian Stanley). Chicago: Rand McNally, 1967, pp. 257–291.

Campbell, Donald T.   "Reforms as Experiments," *American Psychologist* 24: 409–429, 1969. [Reprinted in this volume, No. 12, pp. 172–204]

Campbell, Donald T., and Albert Erlebacher.   "How Regression Artifacts in Quasi-Experimental Evaluations Can Mistakenly Make Compensatory Education Look Harmful," in *Compensatory Education: A National Debate,* Vol. III of *The Disadvantaged Child.* New York: Brunner-Mazel, 1970.

Campbell, Donald T., and J. C. Stanley.   "Experimental and Quasi-experimental Designs for Research on Teaching," in *Handbook of Research on Teaching* (edited by N. L. Gage). Chicago: Rand McNally, 1963, pp. 171–246. (Reprinted as *Experimental and Quasi-experimental Designs for Research.* Chicago: Rand McNally, 1966.)

Chapin, F. Stuart.   "The Experimental Method and Sociology," *Scientific Monthly* 4: 133–144, 238–247, 1917.

Chapin, F. Stuart.   *Experimental Designs in Sociological Research.* New York: Harper and Brothers, 1947.

Cherns, Albert.   "Social Research and Its Diffusion," *Human Relations* 22: 209–218, 1969.

Coleman, James S.   "Evaluating Educational Programs," *The Urban Review* 3, No. 4: 6–8, 1969.

Cronbach, Lee J.   "Course Improvement Through Evaluation," *Teacher's College Record* 64: 672–683, 1963.

Deutscher, Irwin.   "Looking Backward: Case Studies in the Progress of Methodology in Sociological Research," *American Sociologist* 4: 35–41, 1969.

Deutscher, Irwin.   "Toward Avoiding the Goal Trap in Evaluation Research." Paper prepared for American Sociological Association meetings, Montreal, Canada, August 1974. [Reprinted in this volume, No. 14, pp. 221–238]

Dodd, Stuart.   *A Controlled Experiment on Rural Hygiene in Syria.* Beirut: Publications of the American University of Beirut, Social Science Series, No. 7, 1934.

Downs, Anthony.   "Some Thoughts on Giving People Economic Advice," *American Behavioral Scientist* 9: 30–32, September 1965. [Reprinted in this volume, No. 4, pp. 67–72]

Elmer, Manuel.   Chapter 13 of *Social Research.* "Experimental Research," New York: Prentice-Hall, 1939.

Etzioni, Amitai.   "Two Approaches to Organizational Analysis: A Critique and a Suggestion," *Administrative Science Quarterly* 5: 257–278, 1960.

Fairweather, George.   *Methods of Experimental Social Innovation.* New York: Wiley, 1967.

Ferman, Lewis A.   "Some Perspectives on Evaluating Social Welfare Programs," *The Annals of the American Academy of Political and Social Science* 385: 143–156, September 1969.

Festinger, Leon, and Harold Kelley.   *Changing Attitudes Through Social Contact.* Ann Arbor: University of Michigan Press, 1951.

Freeman, Howard E.   "Strategy of Social Policy Research," *Social Welfare Forum,* 143–156, 1963.

Freeman, Howard E., and Clarence C. Sherwood.   "Research in Large-Scale Intervention Programs," *Journal of Social Issues* 21: 11–28, 1965. [Reprinted in this volume, No. 13, pp. 205–220]

Freeman, Howard E., and Clarence C. Sherwood. *Social Research and Social Policy.* Englewood Cliffs, N.J.: Prentice-Hall, 1970.

French, John. "Experiments in Field Settings," in *Research Methods in the Behavioral Sciences* (edited by L. Festinger and D. Katz). New York: Holt, 1953, pp. 98–135.

Glass, Gene. "The Growth of Evaluation Methodology," *AERA Curriculum Evaluation Monograph Series,* No. 7. Chicago: Rand McNally, 1971.

Glueck, Eleanor. *Evaluative Research in Social Work.* New York: Columbia University Press, 1936.

Gottman, John M., Richard M. McFall, and Jean T. Barnett. "Design and Analysis of Research Using Time Series," *Psychological Bulletin* 72: 299–306, 1969.

Greenberg, B. G. "Evaluation of Social Programs," *Review of the International Statistical Institute* 36: 260–277, 1968. [Reprinted in this volume, No. 10, pp. 137–158]

Grobman, Hulda. *Evaluation Activities of Curriculum Projects: A Starting Point.* Chicago: Rand McNally, 1968.

Hall, Richard. "The Applied Sociologist and Organizational Sociology," in *Sociology in Action* (edited by A. Shostak). Homewood, Illinois: Dorsey, 1966, pp. 33–38.

Harris, C. W. *Problems in Measuring Change.* Madison: University of Wisconsin, 1963.

Hayes, Samuel P. *Measuring the Results of Development Projects.* New York: UNESCO Monographs in the Applied Social Sciences, 1959.

Herzog, Elizabeth. *Some Guidelines for Evaluation Research.* Washington: U.S. Government Printing Office, 1959.

Horowitz, Irving. "The Academy and the Polity: Interaction Between Social Scientists and Federal Administrators," *Journal of Applied Behavioral Science* 5: 309–335, 1969.

Hovland, C., A. Lumsdaine, and F. Sheffield. *Experiments in Mass Communication,* Vol. 3 of *Studies in Social Psychology in World War II.* Princeton, N.J.: Princeton University Press, 1949.

Hyman, Herbert, and Charles R. Wright. "Evaluating Social Action Programs," in *Uses of Sociology* (edited by Paul Lazarsfeld, William Sewell, and Harold Wilensky). New York: Basic Books, 1967, pp. 741–782.

Hyman, Herbert, Charles Wright, and Terence Hopkins. *Applications of Methods of Evaluation.* Berkeley: University of California, 1962.

Lazarsfeld, Paul, William Sewell, and Harold Wilensky. "Introduction," in *The Uses of Sociology.* New York: Basic Books, 1967, pp. i–xxxiii.

Lerman, Paul. "Evaluative Studies of Institutions for Delinquents: Implications for Research and Social Policy," *Social Work* 13, No. 3: 55–64, July 1968. [Reprinted in this volume, No. 11, pp. 159–171]

Lewin, Kurt. *Resolving Social Conflicts.* New York: Harper and Brothers, 1948.

Lewis, Sinclair. *Arrowsmith.* New York: Collier, 1925.

Likert, Rensis, and Ronald Lippitt. "Utilization of Social Science," in *Research Methods in the Behavioral Sciences* (edited by L. Festinger and D. Katz). New York: Holt, 1953, pp. 581–646.

Lippitt, Ronald. *Studies in Experimentally Created Autocratic and Democratic Groups.* University of Iowa Studies: Studies in Child Welfare, 16, No. 3, pp. 45–198, 1940.

Lippitt, Ronald, Jeanne Watson, and Bruce Westley. *The Dynamics of Planned Change.* New York: Harcourt Brace and Co., 1958.

Lortie, Dan C. *The Cracked Cake of Educational Custom and Emerging Issues in Evalua-*

tion. Paper presented to the Symposium on Problems in the Evaluation of Instruction. Los Angeles: UCLA, December 1967.

Luchterhand, Elmer.   "Research and the Dilemmas in Developing Social Programs," in *The Uses of Sociology* (edited by Paul Lazarsfeld, William Sewell, and Harold Wilensky). New York: Basic Books, 1967, pp. 506–521.

McEwen, William J.   "Position Conflict and Professional Orientation in a Research Organization," *Administrative Science Quarterly* 1: 208–224, 1956.

McKelvey, William.   "Expectational Non-complementarity and Style of Interaction Between Professional and Organization," *Administrative Science Quarterly* 14, No. 1: 21–32, March 1969.

Madge, John.   *The Origins of Scientific Sociology.* New York: Free Press, 1962.

Mann, Floyd, and Rensis Likert.   "The Need for Research on the Communication of Research Results," *Human Organization* 11, No. 4: 15–19, 1952. [Reprinted in this volume, No. 9, pp. 125–134]

Mann, John.   "Technical and Social Difficulties in the Conduct of Evaluative Research," *Changing Human Behavior.* New York: Scribners, 1965, pp. 177–190.

Mann, John.   "Evaluating Educational Programs," *The Urban Review* 3, No. 4: 12–13, 1969.

Marris, Peter, and Martin Rein.   *Dilemmas of Social Reform.* New York: Atherton Press, 1967.

Mayo, Elton.   *The Human Problems of an Industrial Civilization.* New York: Macmillan, 1933.

Merton, Robert.   "Role of the Intellectual in Public Bureaucracy," in *Social Theory and Social Structure.* New York: Free Press, 1957, pp. 207–224.

Meyer, Henry, Edgar Borgatta, and Wyatt Jones.   *Girls at Vocational High.* New York: Russell Sage Foundation, 1965.

Miller, S. M.   "Evaluating Action Programs," *Trans-action* 2, No. 3: 38–39, March–April 1965. (a)

Miller, S. M.   "Prospects: The Applied Sociology of the Center-City," in *Applied Sociology* (edited by Alvin Gouldner and S. M. Miller). New York: Free Press, 1965, pp. 441–456. (b)

Newcomb, Theodore.   *Personality and Social Change.* New York: Holt, Rinehart, and Winston, 1943.

Perry, S. E., and Lyman Wynne.   "Role Conflict, Role Redefinition, and Social Changes in a Clinical Research Organization," *Social Forces* 38: 62–65, 1959.

Powers, Edwin, and Helen Witmer.   *An Experiment in the Prevention of Juvenile Delinquency: The Cambridge-Somerville Youth Study.* New York: Columbia University Press, 1951.

Rein, Martin, and S. M. Miller.   "The Demonstration Project as a Strategy of Change," in *Organizing for Community Welfare* (edited by Mayer N. Zald). Chicago: Quadrangle Books, 1967, pp. 160–191.

Rice, J. M.   "The Futility of the Spelling Grind," *Forum* 23, pp. 163–172, 409–419, 1897.

Riecken, Henry W.   *The Volunteer Work Camp: A Psychological Evaluation.* Cambridge, Mass.: Addison-Wesley, 1952.

Riecken, Henry W., and Robert F. Boruch.   *Social Experimentation—A Method for Planning and Evaluating Social Intervention.* New York: Academic Press, 1974.

Rivlin, Alice. *Systematic Thinking for Social Action.* Washington, D.C.: Brookings Institution, 1971.

Rivlin, Alice, and P. Michael Timpane (eds.). *Ethical and Legal Issues of Social Experimentation.* Washington, D.C.: Brookings Institution, 1975.

Rodman, Hyman, and Ralph Kolodny. "Organizational Strains in the Researcher-Practitioner Relationship," *Human Organization* 23: 171–182, 1964. Reprinted in *Applied Sociology* (edited by Alvin Gouldner and S. M. Miller). New York: Free Press, 1965, pp. 93–113. [Reprinted in this volume, No. 5, pp. 73–93]

Roethlisberger, Fritz, and William Dickson. *Management and the Worker.* Cambridge, Mass.: Harvard University Press, 1939.

Rosenthal, Robert. *Experimental Effects in Behavioral Research.* New York: Appleton-Century-Crofts, 1966.

Rosenthal, Robert, and Robert Weiss. "Problems of Organizational Feedback," in *Social Indicators* (edited by Raymond Bauer). Cambridge: MIT Press, 1966, pp. 302–340.

Rossi, Peter H., "Boobytraps and Pitfalls in the Evaluation of Social Action Programs," *Proceedings of the American Statistical Association,* 1966, pp. 127–132. [Reprinted in this volume, No. 15, pp. 239–248]

Rossi, Peter H. "Evaluating Educational Programs," *The Urban Review* 3, No. 4: 17–18, February 1969.

Sadofsky, Stanley. "Utilization of Evaluation Results: Feedback into the Action Program," in *Learning in Action* (edited by June Shmelzer). Washington: U.S. Government Printing Office, 1966, pp. 22–36.

Schulberg, Herbert C., and Frank Baker. "Program Evaluation Models and the Implementation of Research Findings," *American Journal of Public Health* 58, No. 7: 1248–1255, July 1968. [Reprinted in this volume, No. 3, pp. 54–63]

Scriven, Michael. "The Methodology of Evaluation," in *Perspectives of Curriculum Evaluation.* American Educational Research Association Monograph Series on Curriculum Evaluation. Chicago: Rand McNally, 1967, pp. 39–83.

Scriven, Michael. "Evaluating Educational Programs," *The Urban Review* 3, No. 4: 20–22, February 1969.

Seashore, Stanley. "Field Experiments with Formal Organizations," *Human Organization* 23: 164–170, 1964.

Shepard, Herbert A. "Nine Dilemmas in Industrial Research," *Administrative Science Quarterly* 1: 295–309, 1956.

Smith, Joel, Francis Sim, and Robert Bealer. "Client Structure and the Research Process," in *Human Organization Research* (edited by R. Adams and J. Preiss). Homewood, Illinois: Dorsey, 1960, pp. 41–56.

Sommer, Robert. "Hawthorne Dogma," *Psychological Bulletin* 70, No. 6: 592–595, 1968.

Stake, Robert. "The Countenance of Educational Evaluation," *Teachers College Record* 68: 523–540, 1967.

Suchman, Edward. "A Model for Research and Evaluation on Rehabilitation," *Sociology and Rehabilitation* (edited by Marvin Sussman). Washington, D.C.: Vocational Rehabilitation Administration, 1966, pp. 52–70.

Suchman, Edward. *Evaluative Research.* New York: Russell Sage Foundation, 1967. (a)

Suchman, Edward. "Principles and Practices of Evaluative Research," in *An Introduc-*

tion to Social Research (edited by John Doby). New York: Appleton-Century-Crofts, 1967, pp. 327–351. (b)

Suchman, Edward A.   "Evaluating Educational Programs," *The Urban Review* 3, No. 4: 15–17, February 1969. [Reprinted in this volume, No. 2, pp. 48–53]

Sussman, Marvin.   "The Sociologist as a Tool of Social Action," in *Sociology in Action* (edited by A. Shostak). Homewood, Illinois: Dorsey, 1966, pp. 3–12.

Trow, Martin.   "Methodological Problems in the Evaluation of Innovation." Paper presented to the Symposium on Problems in the Evaluation of Instruction. Los Angeles: UCLA, December 1967.

Tyler, Ralph.   "Evaluation: a Challenge to Progressive Education," *Educational Research Bulletin* 14, pp. 9–16, 1935.

Van de Vall, Mark.   "Utilization and Methodology of Applied Social Research: Four Complementary Models," *Journal of Applied Behavioral Science* 11, No. 1: 14–38, 1975.

Walsh, John.   "Anti-Poverty R & D: Chicago Debacle Suggests Pitfalls Facing OEO," *Science* 165: 1243–1245, 1969.

Ward, Lester.   *Applied Sociology.* Boston: Ginn and Co., 1906.

Warren, Roland.   *Social Research Consultation.* New York: Russell Sage Foundation, 1963.

Webb, E. J., D. Campbell, R. Schwartz, and L. Sechrest.   *Unobtrusive Measures: Nonreactive Research in the Social Sciences.* Chicago: Rand McNally, 1966.

Weeks, H. Ashley.   *Youthful Offenders at Highfields.* Ann Arbor: University of Michigan Press, 1958.

Weinberger, Martin.   "Evaluative Educational Programs: Observations by a Market Researcher," *The Urban Review* 3, No. 4: 23–26, February 1969.

Weiss, Carol H.   "Planning an Action Project Evaluation," in *Learning in Action* (edited by June Shmelzer). Washington: U.S. Government Printing Office, 1966, pp. 6–21.

Weiss, Carol H.   "Utilization of Evaluation: Toward Comparative Study." Paper presented to the American Sociological Association, September 1966, Miami Beach. Printed in *The Use of Social Research in Federal Domestic Programs,* Part III, *The Relation of Private Social Scientists to Federal Programs on National Social Problems,* Washington: U.S. Government Printing Office, 1967, pp. 426–432.

Weiss, Robert S., and Martin Rein, "The Evaluation of Broad-Aim Programs: A Cautionary Case and a Moral," *The Annals of the American Academy of Political and Social Science* 385: 133–142, September 1969. [Reprinted in this volume, No. 16, pp. 253–262]

Wholey, Joseph S., John W. Scanlon, Hugh G. Duffy, James Fukumoto, and Leona M. Vogt.   *Federal Evaluation Policy.* Washington, D.C.: The Urban Institute, 1970.

Whyte, William F., and Edith Hamilton.   *Action Research for Management.* Homewood, Illinois: Dorsey, 1964.

Wilner, Daniel, *et al.*   *The Housing Environment and Family Life.* Baltimore: Johns Hopkins Press, 1962.

Wrightstone, J. Wayne.   "Evaluating Educational Programs," *The Urban Review* 3, No. 4: 5–6, February 1969.

Wuebben, Paul.   "Experimental Design, Measurement, and Human Subjects: A Neglected Problem of Control," *Sociometry* 31: 89–101, 1968.

PART I
BASIC ISSUES: PROGRAM DEVELOPMENT
AND SCIENTIFIC INQUIRY

The idea of applying the methods of science to the management of social problems is very appealing. Science implies an order and rationality that contrasts to the conflict and disorder which often plague efforts to deal with community problems. Evaluative research attempts to link directly the realms of scientific inquiry and organized social problem management. The articles in this section address themselves to basic questions about the effort to bring together these disparate spheres of activity.

Perhaps primarily of historical interest is Stephan's plea for experimental social research on the effects of programs of directed change generated in response to the Depression. Although it voices greater optimism and is written with a greater rhetorical flourish than a social scientist might dare to express today, the paper's basic message is similar to more recent statements of the potential contribution of evaluative research. Stephan's article also invites a sobering question. If the contribution of evaluative research was so clearly recognized so long ago, has the approach been as productively developed in the interim as might have been expected?

Suchman offers a clear and concise statement of the purpose and method of evaluative research. He argues that the logic of evaluative research is identical to that of basic or nonevaluative research. Evaluative research differs only in that value is attached to the dependent variable. Suchman goes on to point out that evaluative research provides a scientific basis for testing the principles of program administration.

Schulberg and Baker distinguish between what they call goal attainment and system models of evaluation. The goal attainment model focuses rather narrowly on the overt objectives of a program and the strategies through which those ends are pursued. The system model is broader than the goal attainment model because it also concerns itself with organizational survival interests. Schulberg and Baker argue that when the design and administration of evaluative research reflect system concerns, findings are more likely to be used.

1. Prospects and Possibilities: The New Deal and the New Social Research

A. Stephen Stephan

Mankind in a test-tube is the hope and aim of social science.

Students of human behavior have long envied the chemists and physicists who are releasing the secrets of nature through experimentation and laboratory procedure. The exacting methods of the laboratory have been responsible for the phenomenal advance of the physical sciences. The gap between the accumulated knowledge of the physical sciences and the social sciences is largely explained by the difference in the exact methods of the former and the floundering methods of the latter. Man knows more about the atom than he knows about himself.

The promise of a more exact knowledge of human relations must come from a development of experimental methods that will approximate in precision the techniques of the laboratory scientists. No one, however, can deny the progress in the social sciences. But with all the exacting methods developed, the economists, sociologists, and political scientists, have suffered from a lack of large-scale experimental set-ups to match the every-day resources of their brother scientists in the laboratory.

The current enthusiasm over planning and the planning schemes now being devised by the alphabetical corporations of the Federal government furnish some hopes that this deficiency may be partially remedied. The blueprints of these agencies and the carrying out of their plans may well be looked upon as the creation of experimental laboratories for the social scientists, and for the social workers, educators, and administrators who may profit from their research.

These laboratories set up by the planning agencies of the New Deal permit a more effective use of the experimental method in the research projects of the social scientists. This research in turn would not only be an addition to science but would also be a form of social auditing for the planning authorities in noting and accounting the changes wrought by the programs. The investigator combines here the rôles of scientist and citizen.[1] Hence there is a practical relationship between planning, experimentation, and social auditing for both social scientist and administrator. Excellent examples of the possibilities in this direction lie in the wholesale changes in social behavior brought about by the repeal of prohibition, the program of the Tennessee Valley Authority, and more particularly, the low-cost housing and slum-clearance projects of the Housing Division of the Public Works Administration.

The essence of the experimental

method in social research, as Chapin has pointed out,[2] is the study of social behavior through observations made under controlled conditions. It is an attempt to conduct research by keeping constant as many forces or factors as possible which may influence a given social situation. This procedure permits the elimination of these forces or factors as disturbing elements causing a certain form of social behavior and allows the investigator to concentrate attention and analysis on variable or non-controlled disturbing and causative factors. When a criminologist uses the device of a control group in his investigation he is utilizing a familiar and perhaps most commonly employed experimental technique. He compares a non-delinquent group with a delinquent group and tries to have the non-delinquent group match the delinquent group as nearly as possible in education, nationality, economic status, and other similar factors known by experience to influence a certain form of social behavior. He cannot say that the delinquency is precipitated by membership in a certain nationality group or that it is due to a certain economic status, for these two factors would be constant and present in both the delinquent and non-delinquent groups. He must look for the influence of other factors and for other explanations. This is all similar to the work of an Arrowsmith in testing the effectiveness of a certain serum in curing a particular disease. One group is inoculated and another is not. Both groups are given the same food and live under the same conditions, these are constant factors. The variable factor is the inoculation. If the inoculated group gets well *ergo* mighty medicine says it's no doubt due to the inoculation.

It goes without saying that the enormous planning enterprises and the experimental situations which these plans set up make of Soviet Russia a paradise for the research social scientists. Russia is the most colossal experimental laboratory for the study of human nature ever created by man. At no time in the stream of human history has there been as violent and as wholesale a transformation in the living conditions of so large a segment of humanity, for the U.S.S.R. is one-sixth of the earth's surface and one-twelfth of its population.

The emphasis upon experimental methods in the social sciences is not a vicious attempt on the part of those social scientists interested in this approach to order people around and regiment their behavior. The business of these scientists is to study, not administrate. These students merely hope to use the more exacting techniques of observation and investigation, the value of which is attested by the history of science, in perfecting an important addition to logic and insight for the advancement of human welfare through the power of a more exact knowledge.

Adequate social planning demands a knowledge of the field of operation of the planning programs, be it foreign exchange or slum-clearance. Planning, furthermore, calls for a rigid observation and "control" over the possible factors which may affect a given situation. "Control" is an attempt to observe and measure the forces put into operation and the results produced by these forces. A certain percentage of reduction of the gold content of the dollar may raise prices so much, or the transfer of the slum population of River Bottom to the model community of Sunlight Gardens reduce by a certain percentage the number of delinquents in a given population.

Control in many instances is made more effective by the fact that the planning agency is the source of many of the new influences and forces which are made to operate in setting up and changing certain social situations. Control further means that large-scale experiments are set up for influencing human behavior and that these controlled situations approximate the wished for experiments in the more exact physical sciences. All this calls for some form of social auditing to determine the effect of the forces set in operation by the planning authorities. Planning unaccompanied by research is of little avail since only by research can we find out what changes for better or for worse have been brought about by these plans.

Many of us can see all this in the economic maneuvers of the Federal agencies in such projects as that of managed currency and the programs of the AAA. However, not as many of us can appreciate the fact that there are programs of a more social nature in the repeal of prohibition, the work of the Tennessee Valley Authority, and the projects of the Housing Division of the PWA in terms of the changes in social behavior which these programs may effect.

Repeal calls for a comparison of the drinking habits of the nation during three periods: "before prohibition"; "during prohibition"; "after repeal." This field in particular has been notoriously neglected by the social scientists. So infinitesimal is our knowledge of the social effects of the legal and illegal consumption of liquor that instead of relying on the findings of careful research we have to base our opinions on the colorful utterances of Al Smith and the thunder of Bishop Cannon. This condition exists despite the fact that the country is now a virtual laboratory for every type of experiment from wet to dry spots, from state control to free and open sale of liquor.

In the Tennessee Valley mountaineers are being hurled from primitive conditions to living in an industrial empire made possible by giant power. They are going to be different folk from what they once were. Electricity will give them the shock that will make them jump from the eighteenth to the twentieth century. What changes in the social habits of these people will be brought about by this radical alteration of their environmental conditions?

Public housing programs will mean that people nurtured in the slums and then permitted to live in modern communities of low-cost homes will perhaps behave differently from the way they once acted. America has been woefully negligent in providing adequate housing for its lower-income groups. We are beginners in public housing and have much to learn from the continental and English housing experts who, despite the devastated finances of their countries, have built thousands of apartments and homes.

Vienna, Hamburg, London, and Moscow, are excellent testimonials of their skill and zeal. It is along these lines that we want to emphasize for purposes of detailed illustration, the possibilities of planning, experimentation, and social auditing in the low-cost housing and slum-clearance projects which the Housing Division of the PWA is developing in a dozen or more cities throughout the nation.

Enthusiasm regarding these housing projects has waxed and waned, but enough headway has been made in Atlanta, Louisville, New York, Cleveland, and other cities[3] to warrant the belief that low-cost housing will be a reality in some cities if only for the purpose of demonstrating what can be done. Through this program the housing authorities are planning to alter the living conditions of great bodies of the population in a number of cities.

Do slums make slum people or do slum people make the slums? Will changing the living conditions significantly change the social behavior of the people affected? The public housing projects may furnish the made-to-order test-tubes to help in answering these fascinating and bewildering questions.

The accumulating studies of the sociologists reveal the slums as the sore spots of our modern industrial civilization. In the slum areas of our urban centers are found high rates of delinquency, adult crime, dependency, tax delinquency, sickness, malnutrition, insanity, and similar conditions, together with such characteristic groups as delinquent gangs and institutions of vice. These institutions and conditions epitomize the so-called viciousness of the slum. The implication is that if these people lived under more wholesome conditions there would not be as much delinquency, dependency, sickness, among them. No doubt—but how much less delinquency, dependency, sickness? Compare a slum group with the people living in a suburb. Less delinquency, dependency, and sickness? To be sure. But the people living in the suburbs are not similar to the people living in the slums in terms of certain significant factors. They are usually wealthier, better educated, healthier, than the slum dwellers. The layman would call this an unfair comparison. The best way we can answer this problem, perhaps, is to compare the social indices (rates of delinquency, dependency, adult crime, sickness, and similar factors) characteristic of a given population while living in the slum with the social indices of the same or a similar population after living in the changed environment of a model community. This would mean a "before and after" study. In other words we would have to employ the exacting techniques of an experimental approach. This would permit controlled observation and enable us to know with more precision the difference which may occur in social behavior accompanying a change in social environment brought about by the altering of living conditions. Graphically, it would be like transferring a population mass from Test Tube 1 of Liquid A to Test Tube 2 of Liquid B and finding out what happens.

Certain of the social indices may be

reduced to monetary items in terms of costs to the government (costs of delinquency, adult crime, dependency, police protection, sickness, and similar factors) and a comparison made of the costs to the government preceding and following slum clearance or the transference of a slum population to a model community on more open land. Specifically, such a program may reduce delinquency and adult crime. The cost-per-delinquent and the cost-per-adult-criminal may be computed and the differential in lower costs to the state that may result from the housing program calculated. A computation may be made of the social cost differential in favor of the new communities which may be logically considered a governmental and social saving. Such a body of data may even serve as a basis for recruiting financial support to future housing programs.

The experimental method in a research program of the kind suggested would depend on the plans of the housing authorities and the developments accompanying these plans. Suppose the program for the city of Metropolis is that of slum clearance (we shall call this Plan I), with a significant part of the old population of former residents returning to live in the rebuilt community. Then the investigator would have to compute the social indices in terms of rates of delinquency, dependency, adult crime, sickness, and like factors, of a sample population for whatever number of years he decides is satisfactory for his purpose before slum clearance, and follow the same procedure for the sample group after the population had

taken up residence in the model community and after it had been "exposed" to the living conditions of a more wholesome environment. Hence he would study the social indices in their "before" aspects, and later in their "after" aspects, and then figure out the *differences* in these social indices. These differences the investigator would attribute to the changed living conditions for he would have held a number of significant factors constant. Why? Because the same population was studied throughout the investigation and the principal variable was that of differences in living conditions. But suppose a research bureau decides to make a study of this sort *after* the slum population had moved to the new community. Will it mean that the study could not be inaugurated? Not necessarily, for the investigator would then become a contemporary archeologist and comb the records of the city from the juvenile court to the social agencies for his data. In any event he would have to do something of this sort whether he began his study before or after the slum was cleared.

Now the identical procedure of study may be followed in Plan II, a much better program (as we shall point out later), of transferring a population from the slum to a model community built on more open land, perhaps in the suburbs. The same "before and after" analysis may be made of a sample slum population moved to a less congested area.

The slum clearance program of Plan I as a gesture towards better housing for a congested population is an unsatisfactory procedure in many instances. This springs out of the very nature of the slum in our unplanned and unregulated modern American cities. Slums are typically found where rents are low but where space values tend to rise.[4] They are located on speculative and highly priced properties, for they are on the fringe of the commercial areas and the hope of the landlords is that the central business district will incorporate the slum. All this is based, among other things, on the belief that urban populations will continue to increase, a belief not substantiated by recent population statistics. Stability of population means a curb on speculation and a more realistic basis for land valuation. But where speculative values exist and high cost land is purchased for slum clearance a large slice of the cost of rearing the new structures is eaten up by the land and hence huge apartments are constructed with the possible resultant of a greater congestion than was apparent before the slum was cleared. This would mean rents beyond the reach of the lower income groups. However, through expert handling and accumulation of land, the Housing Division of the PWA is attempting to make possible the valuation of slum property on a realistic utility rather than on a speculative basis. Slum clearance is perhaps not unsatisfactory in the aspects mentioned here for cities under the 250,000 class.

The purchase of more open land for the construction of model homes, as suggested in Plan II, is the best policy. This means that cheaper lands can be utilized and more money spent for basic housing and community planning for parks, playgrounds, streets, and ample sunshine. Community planning is an indispensable part of adequate housing.[5] Furthermore, there is no need in this late day to have thousands of people jammed in close quarters within close proximity to their work. Rapid and cheap transportation enables workers to be within easy distance of the factory, office, and workshop, though they live miles away.

The hitch in Plans I and II comes in the distinct possibility that the new residents in a model community may not all come from a particular slum locality. The new development of Sunlight Gardens in Metropolis may have residents drawn from Slums A, B, C, and perhaps a number of neighborhoods of a not-so-slummish character. We shall call such a possibility Plan III. Does this mean we shall have to abandon the experimental approach? Not necessarily. After things have settled in Sunlight Gardens the investigator would analyze the social indices of its population. Then the investigator would assume the rôle of a social Arrowsmith and try to get a satisfactory control group. His control group would be a slum population which continued to live in the slum. The investigator, we shall say, finds such a population in the slum of the Roundhouse District. But he would have to get a slum control group that as nearly as possible matched the population of Sunlight Gardens on such factors as nationality, religion, education, economic status, and similar conditions. Then he would analyze the social indices of his slum control group and after computing these measuring sticks compare these indices with the social indices of Sunlight Gardens and compute the *differences* in these indices. Now the closer the control group of the Roundhouse District is to the population of Sunlight Gardens the more nearly the investigator would be on safe ground in concluding that the differences in the social indices were due to differences in living conditions. We would hence be in a better position to gauge the benefits of model housing to the people of Sunlight Gardens.

A check on the results obtained above and supplementary qualitative analysis may be secured through a clinical study of the population of Sunlight Gardens. Case studies of the past behavior of the population, or enough of the population to furnish a good sample, as reflected by such indicators as delinquency, dependency, sickness, and like factors, of the Sunlight Gardeners could be made before they took up residence in the new community. Similar case studies on the same items could then be made after the population had lived for some time and had been "exposed" to the environment of the model community. A comparison may then be effected and the differences in the results obtained credited to a large degree to the variations in housing and living conditions.

The change of residence from the slum of River Bottom to Sunlight Gardens may permit an important qualitative analysis of the subtle influence of a variation in living conditions on the personalities of the Sunlight Gardeners. Down on congested Delancey Street little Joe never would play baseball with the gang. He was afraid of cars, an auto had run over him once. In a crowded apartment on the same block old Mr. Flannagan would grumble all the time because a room full of children wouldn't let him read his newspaper in peace. In Sunlight Gardens Joe could play ball on the playground and Mr. Flannagan would stop grumbling, there would be plenty of room in the house and the children would be in the open air. It would be an ideal set-up for a psychiatrist.

Bold are these plans and pious are the hopes that engender them. The "before" and "after" aspects of experiments need auditing. Studies of the character mentioned and particularly of the social effects of public housing need to be prosecuted for certain selected communities by some great public spirited foundation as the Russell Sage or as an adjunct of the housing project itself. A minimum study from the point of view of social policy would be a census of the population after residence in the model community to find out the character of the group attracted to the new environment. The economic experiments of the administration from the NRA to the AAA are being studied by the governmental agencies and the Brookings Institution of Washington. Why not studies of social experiments?

NOTES

1. See Read Bain, "Scientist as Citizen," *Social Forces,* March, 1933, pp. 412–15, for an excellent and timely discussion of how the cloistered objectivity of the scientist makes him oblivious of his rôle as citizen.

2. See F. Stuart Chapin, "The Experimental Approach in the Study of Family Group Patterns," *Social Forces,* December, 1932, pp. 200–07. Also, F. Stuart Chapin, "The Problem of Controls in Experimental Sociology," *The Journal of Educational Sociology,* May, 1931, pp. 541–51.

3. See Harold L. Ickes, "The Federal Housing Program," *New Republic,* December 19, 1934, pp. 155–57.

4. Nels Anderson, "The Slum Endures," *Survey,* March 15, 1927, 799 ff.

5. See Albert Mayer, "New Homes for a New Deal," *New Republic,* February 14, 1934, pp. 7–9. Also Albert Mayer, "Housing: A Call to Action," *Nation,* April 18, 1934, pp. 435–36.

2. Evaluating Educational Programs

Edward A. Suchman

By and large, researchers have been reluctant to undertake evaluation studies. The basis for such resistance lies mainly in the general inadequacy of many of such studies judged by scientific standards. While this poor reputation may be justified from past experience,[1] the shortcomings are not inherent in the conduct of evaluation studies. The purpose of this paper will be to formulate some of the basic issues involved in viewing evaluation as research and to point out some of the ways in which such studies can be improved.

DEFINING EVALUATION

The key conceptual elements in a definition of evaluation from a methodological point of view are (1) a planned program of deliberate intervention, not just any natural or "accidental" event; (2) an objective or goal which is considered desirable or has some positive value, not simply whatever change occurs; and (3) a method for determining the degree to which the planned program achieves the desired objective. Evaluative research asks about the *kind* of change desired, the *means* by which this change is to be brought about, and the signs according to which such change can be recognized.[2]

However, an evaluation study should do more than "pass" or "fail" a program (an administrative goal); it should attempt to find out *why* a program was or was not effective (a research goal). The answer to this question "why" requires an analysis of such factors as (1) the attributes of the program itself that make it more or less successful; (2) the population exposed to the program in terms of which subgroups are reached and which affected; (3) the situational context within which the program takes place, such as auspices, locale, competing programs, and public opinion; (4) the different kinds of effects produced by the program, such as cognitive, attitudinal, or behavioral, long or short term, unitary or multiple, including special attention to any negative side-effects. In this sense evaluation involves more than judging; it also encompasses research on conditions affecting success or failure.

This emphasis upon the analysis of *why* a program is more or less successful underscores the evaluator's responsibility not to take as "given" the administrator's definition of his program. One of the major contributions of an evaluation study lies in an analysis of the program being evaluated in terms of its objectives, the assumptions underlying these objectives, the specific program activities designed to achieve these objectives, the rationale for believing that these activities are capable of attaining the objective, the separation of the "idea"

Reprinted with permission from *The Urban Review,* a publication of the Center for Urban Education, Vol. 3, No. 4, February 1969, pp. 15–17.

of the program from how it is being carried out, and the determination of criteria for observing the extent to which the objectives are being attained. Few of the answers to these questions can be directly obtained from program personnel; they are largely the product of careful observation and analysis on the part of the evaluator himself.[3]

It follows from the above that the design of the evaluation study must provide for testing underlying assumptions, for examining processes by which objectives are attacked, for looking at program content separate from program operation, for providing measures of unanticipated, negative consequences, and, in general, for formulating the evaluation project in such a way that one learns as one evaluates. Obviously there are administrative constraints upon how detailed such an analysis can be, but the goal should be to approach the evaluation as one would any research project—to understand how "theory" and "operation" are linked together in the program being evaluated.

EVALUATIVE VS. NON-EVALUATIVE RESEARCH

Let us examine briefly the underlying logic of the evaluation process. First, we distinguish between evaluation as the general social process of making judgments of worth regardless of the basis for such judgments, and *evaluative research* as referring to the use of the scientific method for collecting data concerning the degree to which some specified activity achieves some desired effect. Our concern in this paper is obviously with the latter.

Science is concerned with the study of process or the interdependence of events or phenomena. In non-evaluative or basic research this process (greatly over-simplified) usually involves the test of some hypothesis concerning the relationship between an independent or "causal" variable and a dependent or "effect" variable: i.e., "the more *a*, the more *b*." Basic research proceeds to test the "validity" of this hypothesis and to elaborate upon the control variables which account for or modify the relationship of *a* to *b*.

The same basic logic applies to evaluative research. The independent variable *a* becomes the goal to be achieved. However, unlike basic or non-evaluative research, value becomes attached to *b* as something desirable, while *a* becomes the object of deliberate, planned intervention. The non-evaluative hypothesis "the more *a*, the more *b*" becomes the evaluative hypothesis, "by changing *a* (through a planned program), the probability of *b* (which I judge to be desirable) increases." Thus evaluative research tests the hypothesis that "Activities *A, B, C*, will achieve objectives *X, Y, Z*."[4]

But just as the non-evaluative hypothesis "the more *a*, the more *b*" requires further testing in terms of some control factor *c* which may destroy or modify the relationship, the evaluative hypothesis concerning the relationship of activity *a* to objective *b* requires critical examination according to control factors which test (1) whether it was really activity *a* that achieved objective *b*, and (2) which elaborate upon how and why the activity was able to achieve the objective.[5] *This is the heart of evaluative research.* First, to ascertain whether program *a* is associated with the occurrence of objective *b*; second, to "prove" that this association is a "true" one—that *a* was demonstrably responsible for *b;* and then third, to elaborate upon the conditions which determine or modify the ability of *a* to achieve *b*.

Using this approach, evaluation becomes research. The significant difference between basic or non-evaluative research and applied or evaluative research is one of purpose and not of method. Both types of studies attempt to utilize research designs for data collection and analysis based upon the logic of the scientific method. The evaluative study applies this model to problems which have administrative consequences, while non-evaluative research is more likely to be concerned with theoretical significance. But the validity of both types of studies rests equally upon the degree to which they satisfy the principles of scientific methodology.

To be sure, the above difference in purpose has important ramifications for determining how a problem is defined and attacked. For example, evaluative research is more likely to emphasize the study of variables which lend themselves to manipulation or change or to be more concerned with the immediate, concrete time and place relevance of one's findings than non-evaluative research which places its emphasis upon explanation rather than manipulation and upon abstraction as opposed to specificity. While undoubtedly evaluative research creates greater personal involvement in outcome than non-evaluative research, this distinction is apt to be exaggerated into questions of honesty or bias not at all inherent in differences between the two approaches.[6] To be sure there are more administrative constraints upon the evaluator both in the choice of his problem and in the interpretation of his findings, but again these are interpersonal problems and should not be confused with methodological problems. The question is one of norms and values, not of principle.[7]

A RESEARCH MODEL FOR EVALUATION

In social research we generally deal with multicausal models in which no event has a single cause and each event has multiple effects. No single factor is a necessary and sufficient cause of any other factor. These logical conditions of a "multiplicity of causes" and an "interdependence of events" applies equally to evaluative research. It means that activity *A* becomes only one of many possible actions or events which may bring about (or deter) the desired effect. Furthermore, both activity *A* and effect *B* will have many other effects or consequences. The significance of this model of "causality" is that evaluations of success must be made in terms of conditional probabilities involving attacks upon causal factors which are only disposing, contributory, or precipitating rather than determining. The effect of any single activity will depend upon other circumstances also being present and will itself reflect a host of antecedent events. Any single activity will, in turn, have a great many effects, many of them unanticipated and some of them even undesirable.

Thus, any "explanation" of the success or failure of program A to achieve effect B must take into account the preconditions under which the program is initiated, the events which intervene between the time the program begins and the time the effects are produced, and the consequences that follow upon the effects. Thus no program is an entity unto itself but must be viewed as part of an ongoing social system.[8]

It is important to point out the relationship of theory to action in terms of the above model. The evaluative hypothesis, "Activities A, B, C, will achieve objectives X, Y, Z," implies some logical reason for believing that the program of activities as the independent or stimulus variable has some causal connection to the desired objectives as the dependent or effect variable. There must be some theoretical basis for linking the program to the objectives. The question "Does it work?" presupposes some rationale as to why one might expect it to work.

In this sense, evaluative research may be viewed as a form of *social experiment*. These social experiments test the validity of the hypothesis that the action program has the power to affect certain "causal" processes related to the development of the desired effect. The ideal evaluation study tests under field experimental conditions the hypothesis that activity A will attain objective B *because* it is able to influence process C which affects the occurrence of the objective.[9]

If a program is unsuccessful, it may be because the program failed to "operationalize" the theory, or because the theory itself was deficient. One may be highly successful in putting a program into operation but, if the theory is incorrect or not adequately translated into action, the desired changes may not be forthcoming: i.e., "the operation was a success, but the patient died." Furthermore, in very few cases do action or service programs directly attack the ultimate objective. Rather they attempt to change the intermediate process which is "causally" related to the ultimate objective. Thus, there are two possible sources of failure (1) the inability of the program to influence the "causal" variable, or (2) the invalidity of the theory linking the "causal" variable to the desired objective. We may diagram these two types of failure as follows:

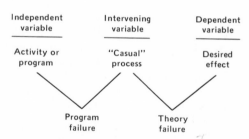

According to this analysis, evaluative research tests the ability of a program to affect the intervening "causal" process. Non-evaluative or basic research, in turn, tests the validity of the intervening "causal" process as a determinant of the desired effect. For example, the evaluation of an obesity clinic may show whether attendance leads to a loss of weight, but whether such a loss of weight decreases the incidence of heart disease is a question for non-evaluative medical research. Similarly, a project Head Start may succeed in increasing the curiosity of culturally deprived pre-schoolers, but whether increased curiosity leads to higher educational aspirations is a matter of theory and non-evaluative research. This is probably the reason why so few evaluations can show any direct effect of a program upon ultimate objectives.[10]

EVALUATIVE RESEARCH AND ADMINISTRATIVE SCIENCE

Evaluation as the study of the effectiveness of planned social change can play an important part in the development of a field of administrative science. With its emphasis upon understanding why a program succeeds or fails, evaluative research is a strategic source of knowledge about principles of program administration. In fact one might argue that evaluative research provides the main scientific basis for testing or validating principles of program administration.

From an administrative point of view, evaluation becomes an ongoing process related to all stages of program planning, development, and operation. Each stage has its own set of objectives and means for attaining these objectives which become subject to separate evaluations. These evaluations feed back information to the program administrator at each stage

and permit him to determine when and how to proceed from one stage to another. We may view these stages as interrelated with the objectives of each preceding stage being means toward formulating the objectives of each succeeding stage. Thus an evaluation of the planning process is judged in terms of its success in program development. The developmental program, in turn, has as its objective the formulation of an operational program. Evaluation at this stage attempts to assess the relative success or failure of various attempts or approaches to the problem being attacked. Thus, this stage provides an excellent opportunity for "experimental" research. Finally, the operational program is evaluated in terms of its ability to achieve the desired objectives as specified in the planning process. As we have discussed previously, such operational program evaluation should stress an analysis of program process as well as end results.

The above approach to program administration has often been characterized by the term "scientific management."[11] The key to its success lies largely in its utilization of the scientific method for making decisions. The central position of evaluation in this process underscores our concern with the development of evaluative research in as methodologically rigorous a manner as possible.

NOTES

1. See, for example, the criticism presented in Ernest M. Gruenberg, editor, "Evaluating the Effectiveness of Mental Health Services," *Milbank Memorial Fund Quarterly,* January 1966, Volume 44, Part 2.
2. Elizabeth Herzog, *Some Guide Lines for Evaluative Research.* Washington, D.C.:

U.S. Department of Health, Education, and Welfare, Social Security Administration, Children's Bureau, 1959, pp. 9–36.

3. Charles R. Wright and Herbert H. Hyman, "The Evaluators," in Phillip E. Hammond, editor, *Sociologists at Work*. New York: Basic Books, 1964, pp. 121–141.

4. Edward A. Suchman, *Evaluative Research: Principles and Practice in Public Service and Social Action Programs*. New York: Russell Sage Foundation, 1967.

5. Detailed treatment of this model is given in Herbert Hyman, *Survey Design and Analysis*. Glencoe, Illinois: The Free Press, 1955; Hans L. Zetterberg, *On Theory and Verification in Sociology*. Totowa, New Jersey: The Bedminister Press, 1963; and Paul F. Lazarsfeld and Morris Rosenberg, editors, *The Language of Social Research*. Glencoe, Illinois: The Free Press, 1955.

6. Abraham Kaplan, *The Conduct of Inquiry*. San Francisco: Chandler Publishing Company, 1964, pp. 381–82.

7. Gideon Sjoberg and Roger Nett, *A Methodology for Social Research*. New York: Harper and Row, 1968, pp. 70–76.

8. Edward A. Suchman, "Principles and Practice of Evaluative Research," in John T. Doby, editor, *An Introduction to Social Research*. New York: Appleton-Century-Crofts, 1967, pp. 327–351.

9. F. Stuart Chapin, *Experimental Designs in Sociological Research*. New York: Harper and Brothers, 1947 (rev. 1955).

10. Edward A. Suchman, "A Model for Research and Evaluation on Rehabilitation," in Marvin Sussman, editor, *Sociology and Rehabilitation*. Washington: Vocational Rehabilitation Administration, 1966, pp. 52–70.

11. Joseph F. McCloskey and Florence N. Trefethen, editors, *Operations Research for Management*. Baltimore: Johns Hopkins Press, 1954.

3. Program Evaluation Models and the Implementation of Research Findings

Herbert C. Schulberg and Frank Baker

A source of great dismay to both the researcher and the clinician is the difficulty encountered in trying to apply the findings of a research project. This consternation is particularly acute in the research specialty of program evaluation, since both the program administrator and program evaluator undertake studies with the fullest and sincerest intention of utilizing the resulting data. The reasons for the gap between research and implementation are varied and considerable attention has been devoted in recent years to analysis of personal and organizational resistances to change. This paper restricts its focus to the issues specifically relevant to program evaluation and program modification and then describes implications of different evaluation research models for the implementation of research findings.

A common approach among those concerned with the utilization of research findings has been the study of the processes through which information flows among scientists. In his review of this broad field, Menzel[1] was able to identify and classify many different types of information-receiving behavior on the part of scientists and to suggest numerous leads for further research. For the past six years the American Psychological Association has been engaged in a wide-ranging study of scientific information exchange and the entire November, 1966, issue of the "American Psychologist" is devoted to a report on this project.

In one of the papers, Menzel[2] discusses five interrelated themes about scientific communication which he considers central to the understanding of this process. Perhaps most relevant to the topic of program evaluation and modification is Menzel's notion that acts of communication constitute a system. He conceives of the flow of scientific information as a set of interaction processes in a social system. As the information-receiving actions of any one individual often involve several of his roles, Menzel urges a systemic view of the problem. The changes and innovations introduced in any one component of the system will have their consequences on the utilization and efficacy of other components.

In considering the processes which intervene between the completion of research and its ultimate application, Halpert[3] identified several barriers to useful communication. The obstacles originate with both the researcher and the clinician. In a perhaps overly stereotyped fashion, we may describe the researcher as suspecting malicious surreptitiousness among those charged

Reprinted with permission from *American Journal of Public Health,* Vol. 58, No. 7, July 1968, pp. 1248–1255.

with the implementation of his findings and inappropriate defensiveness in striving to maintain the status quo. Conversely, the administrator alleges that the researcher's findings have been presented in an unnecessarily frustrating, abstract manner and that the findings have precious little application to the complex reality of his program. If we are to accept Halpert's contention that "a test of the efficacy of communication is its ability to translate research into altered behavior of key individuals,"[4] we then must sadly conclude that much program evaluation has been unsuccessful.

Proceeding from this conclusion, one should then ask a series of questions whose answers may contain guide lines for future developments. The most basic question is whether the research and clinical enterprises are so antithetical in their nature that they inevitably will be in conflict, particularly when the researcher contends that his findings necessitate modifications in clinical practice. Although we are all familiar with practitioners to whom professional autonomy is so sacrosanct that it even prevents the intrusion of research findings, over the years there have been sufficient examples of research and evaluation directly affecting clinical practice to conclude that under appropriate conditions evaluation and practice can be harmonious. Many of the recent program developments in the field of community mental health stem from demonstrations that alternative patterns of care, e.g., day hospitalization, are preferable to ones used previously and that increased flexibility is possible.

It becomes important then to determine what the appropriate conditions are for bringing program evaluation and clinical practice closer together and to develop them in such a way that they have greater applicability. We will consider now the purposes of program evaluation and the alternative approaches for enhancing the implementation of findings.

PURPOSES OF EVALUATION

Even though it is impossible to identify all of the factors associated with the administrator's decision to evaluate an activity, it is essential to identify as many of them as possible. Many aspects of the evaluation procedure itself, and certainly its later utility, hinge upon the administrator's or the organization's motivation in initiating the evaluation. Earlier papers by Greenberg and Mattison[5] and Knutson[6] highlight the complexity of this matter. Knutson thought that the implicit and explicit reasons for program evaluation fall into two categories: (a) reasons that are organization oriented, and (b) reasons that are personally oriented. In both categories values of an unspecified nature exert powerful influences upon decision-making in ways unrecognized by those participating in the process.

The relationship of evaluation purpose to subsequent utilization of findings is indicated in many ways. If the administrator is concerned with achieving status and impressing his peers, he will select for evaluation a program of widespread interest. The evaluation of a relatively obscure service will attract little of the administrator's energy initially and even less if the implementation of findings requires the overcoming of staff resistance.

The purpose of evaluation similarly will affect the depth of investigation to be undertaken and the level of critical analysis to be completed. Knutson suggests that the administrator's orientation will determine the selection of evaluation criteria, since what is valid evidence to one person will not be accepted as such by others. Controversy frequently arises between those subscribing to a "cost analysis" criterion and those advocating a criterion of "human suffering alleviated." In a period of increasing competition for the limited funds in governmental budgets, legislators and economists often reject a program which entails a higher cost per unit of service even when it has been evaluated as successful. The many instances of "successful" demonstration programs which cease operation after the initial funding period demonstrate how the evaluation criteria satisfactory to the professional may leave the legislator unimpressed.

EVALUATION MODELS

In seeking to conceptualize the various approaches to evaluation, two research models stand out: (a) the goal-attainment model, and (b) the system model. The characteristics and limitations of each will be described as they affect the implementation of research findings.

Goal-Attainment Model

There is popular agreement among those concerned with program evaluation that one of the most critical and

also difficult phases in this process is clarification of a program's objectives. This emphasis stems from a conception of evaluation as measurement of the degree of success or failure encountered by the program in reaching predetermined objectives. Related to this conception of evaluation is the assumption that if specific program objectives can be defined, then the appropriate methodology and criteria for assessing the program will be selected correctly. The specification of objectives and goals in the evaluation process is considered by some to be so essential that Freeman and Sherwood[7] suggest that if the evaluation researcher is to act responsibly as an agent of social change, then he should actively participate in developing the program's goals. Having failed to do this, he may find himself in the position of either evaluating incorrect objectives or of never even being told what objectives are to be studied.

Accepting the significance of goal clarification as an integral component in the evaluation process, one can proceed then with well-defined methodologies for determining the degree of success achieved in attaining the goal. This *"goal-attainment* model" of evaluation has been widely described in the literature (e.g., Herzog[8] and Knutson[9]) and it has many of the characteristics of classical research. Freeman and Sherwood maintain that evaluation research seeks to approximate the experimental model as much as possible and, when this cannot be achieved, then quasi-experimental designs should be employed. Knutson distinguishes between evaluation of progress, which is conducted during the course of the program, and evaluation of achievement, which measures change between the base line period and some ultimate point in time when the program is expected to have produced results. The data and criteria selected for evaluating progress toward intermediate goals are different from those used in evaluating achievement of final objectives.

In spite of the methodological rigor evident in the "goal-attainment" model of evaluation, a relative lack of concern is found within this approach for technics of implementing findings. Although evaluation research usually is distinguished from other research by virtue of its closely knit relationship to program planning, only rarely has this interweaving been evident in fact. An exception can be found in James's[10] description of the goal-attainment evaluation process as a circular one. It starts with initial goal-setting, proceeds to determine measures of the goal, collects data and appraises the effect of the goal, and then modifies the initial goal on the basis of the collected data.

Nowhere is any indication found, however, of the manner in which the evaluator can insure closing the circle of the evaluation process in the goal-attainment model. More often than not, the previously linked series of cooperative processes between evaluator and administrator break down at the point of goal modification. What had been a reciprocal relationship of mutual benefit suddenly becomes an antagonistic arrangement marked by the stereotyped interpersonal perceptions described earlier in this paper.

What are the characteristics of the goal-attainment model of evaluation

that render it relatively ineffective at the point of implementing findings? First, we must consider that one of the supposedly major assets of this model may be mythical in nature. The researcher, attempting to avoid the bias of imposing his own objectives as criteria of the organization's effectiveness, turns instead to the administrator for a statement of the goals to be used as criteria. However, in gaining this "objectivity" and utilizing an unbiased evaluation model, the researcher potentially has sacrificed much of the significance of his work. Etzioni[11] forcefully notes that organizational goals, particularly public ones, have an illusory quality in that they may never have been intended to be realized. When this is the case, the program administrator will be troubled very little by the researcher's finding that his previously enumerated organizational goals are not being achieved. Never having meant to attain the goals studied by the researcher, the administrator sees no need to alter his program to accommodate the findings of the researcher. The program evaluation has little impact upon the organization since the researcher had little understanding of the administrator's purpose in participating in the study.

A second limitation in implementing the findings of the goal-attainment model of evaluation is the relatively circumscribed perspective with which this evaluation model views an organization. Since the model assumes that specific goals can be evaluated and modified in isolation from the other goals being sought by the organization, it constitutes an artificial, if not fallacious, approach. A wide body of literature in the field of organizational study (e.g., Rice[12] and Sofer[13]) highlights the interrelated nature of goals and the manner in which modification of any one is constrained by characteristics of the others.

An example of this process of interrelated goals can be found in studies of the ways in which large mental hospitals establish administrative and clinical structures which will permit them to function in an optimal manner. The hospital administrator is faced by the need to deploy limited resources in such a way as to maximally benefit new admissions as well as long-term patients. Achieving the goal of optimal functioning is further complicated by the fact that the mental hospital as an organizational system is faced with many tasks besides its clinical one. The treating and discharging of patients must be considered as just one among several legitimate tasks including training, research, custodial care, and so on, which affect the over-all framework of the institution's administrative and clinical structure.

A recent study by Schulberg, Notman, and Bookin[14] of the treatment program at Boston State Hospital found that although the total number of inpatients not involved in any specific form of therapy had been reduced by 50 per cent between 1963 and 1965, geriatric patients have received little additional treatment in this period. The implication of this finding is clear-cut in the sense that one aspect of the hospital's treatment program is not functioning up to par and modification of this clinical service's structure seems warranted. What are the obstacles, then, to immediate implementation of the findings in this evaluation of goal attainment, i.e., treatment for all patients.

It becomes immediately evident that alteration of the geriatric unit's treatment program must have reverberations in many other facets of the hospital's total operation. Change in the technological component of the system, therefore, cannot be accomplished without equal attention to the implications of change for social aspects of the system. The goal-attainment model of evaluation often has restricted itself to recommendations about either altered forms of technology or administrative structure, without adequately considering the constraints imposed by other competing factors.

Returning to the services of a geriatric unit, the hospital superintendent might accept the findings of the previously cited treatment survey as a matter requiring his immediate attention and decide to increase the level of care on this unit by assigning additional psychiatric residents to it. In doing so, however, the superintendent must, first, overcome the widespread resistance of many residents to working with this aged population; second, operate within the constraint of his training program's guide lines regarding length of time that residents will spend on any one service; and third, consider the imbalance that will be created in other parts of the hospital by transferring additional residents to this unit. Realizing the complexity of these constraints, the superintendent may possibly decide that although the findings of the evaluation were certainly illuminating, they provide him with little guidance on the merits of altering the present situation in the face of the difficulties that change would create.

It is suggested that this brief example of the fate befalling an evaluation of goal attainment is representative of the process through which many studies have passed at the point when administrators considered implementing their findings.

System Model

In view of the implementation limitations inherent in the goal-attainment model of evaluation, what alternative is available to the researcher concerned with the utility of his findings? An approach which warrants more attention than it has received in the program evaluation literature is the system model. It is described by Etzioni[15] who points out that the starting point in this approach to evaluation is not the program's goal, as it is in the goal-attainment model of evaluation. Instead the system model of evaluation is concerned with establishing a working model of a social unit which is capable of achieving a goal. Unlike the study of a single goal, or even a set of goal activities, the system model is that of a multifunctional unit. It recognizes that an organization must fulfill at least four important functions for survival. In addition to the achievement of goals and subgoals, the system model is concerned with: the effective coordination of organizational subunits; the acquisition and maintenance of necessary resources; and the adaptation of the organization to the environment and to its own internal demands. The system model assumes that some of the organization's means must be devoted to such nonobvious functions as custodial activities, including means employed for maintenance of the organization itself. From the viewpoint of the system model, such activities are functional and actually increase organizational effectiveness.

In contrast to the goal-attainment model of evaluation which is concerned with degree of success in reaching a specific objective, the system model establishes the degree to which an organization realizes its goals under a given set of conditions. Etzioni indicates that the key question is: "Under the given conditions, how close does the organizational allocation of resources approach an optimum distribution?"[16] Optimum is the key word and what counts is a balanced distribution of resources among all organizational objectives, not maximal satisfaction of any one goal. From this perspective, just as a lack of resources for any one goal may be dysfunctional so may an excess of resources for the goal be equally dysfunctional. In the latter instance, superfluous attention to one goal leads to depressed concern for the others and problems of coordination and competition will arise.

It should be noted that this model of evaluation is a more demanding and expensive one for the researcher. Instead of simply identifying the goals of the organization and proceeding to study whether they are attained, the system model requires that the analyst determine what he considers a highly effective allocation of means. This often requires considerable knowledge of the way in which an organization functions but it carries with it the advantage of being able to include in the analysis much more of the collected data than is possible in classical research design.

Another system model concept deserving consideration in regard to program evaluation is feedback mechanisms, i.e., the processes through which the effects of organizational actions are reported back to the organization and compared with desired performance. Inadequate utilization of research findings is an indication of blocked feedback and thus represents an organizational problem legitimately subject to scrutiny. The system model, therefore, provides not only a more adequate model for determining the types of data to be collected but it also has utility for determining the factors associated with effective or ineffective integration of the findings.

Turning now to the problem of utilizing the system model in producing change, several studies will be cited as examples of how this approach can be applied. An almost classic instance of the greater ability of the system model than the goal-attainment model to offer the program director sufficient guidance for implementing change can be found in the work of the Cummings[17] relative to mental health education. They started out to study to what extent and in what directions attitudes toward mental illness could be changed through an intensive educational program. After completing the six-month program, the Cummings found virtually no change in the population's general orientation,

either toward the social problem of mental illness or toward the mentally ill themselves. If the goal-attainment model had been pursued, the researchers might simply have concluded that mental health education is ineffective and that the program should be dropped. Instead the Cummings shifted to a system model of evaluation and considered their data within the context of the functions, both manifest and latent, that traditional attitudes toward mental health play for the community as a social system. From this perspective, the researchers were able to formulate several hypotheses explaining the failure of their mental health education effort and to suggest possible concrete avenues for bringing about future change.

Another example of the use of the system model in evaluating program change can be found in studies[18,19] of the changing mental hospital. Baker[20] contends that viewing the hospital as an open system exchanging inputs and outputs with its environment promises to permit improved evaluation and program modification as the organization moves toward provision of comprehensive services. Three categories were identified by Baker for focus and intensive study: (1) the intraorganizational processes of the hospital; (2) the exchanges and transactions between the hospital and its environment; and (3) the processes and structures through which parts of the environment are related to one another. When attempting to implement the findings from one category, it becomes immediately evident that change may potentially affect the others as well. In a community mental health program the linked interdependence of all components in the system is of particular concern since modification of any one element can only occur within the framework of change for the entire system.

The system model suggests a variety of linkages and feedback mechanisms which can be used to bridge the gap between research findings and program modification. Individuals who have contact with the organization's environment as part of their regular work are considered in the system model to occupy "boundary roles." These people are particularly crucial for research implementation since they often are the first to receive information from external sources about the effectiveness of programs.

Boundary roles may occur at all levels of the organization but they usually are found at the top and bottom of the administrative structure. The program administrator at the top of the structure acts as a filter of research results because of his strong commitment and participation in the implementation of new programs. Negative evaluation of the program's effectiveness, however, may reflect adversely on his decision to back the program and in such a situation research findings may not be utilized properly. On the other hand, those occupying boundary roles lower in the organizational hierarchy often cannot make effective use of evaluation results because they do not have the formal authority to influence individuals at levels higher than themselves. A lower-level boundary role incumbent

may pass on only that information which he thinks his superiors want to hear.

Since most health organizations lack a unit or individual specifically concerned with the translation of research into practice, it is suggested that planning divisions be established as one way to fill this void. The planner, being in a relatively objective and highly placed position for analyzing the total organization, can be sensitive to both the data emerging from program evaluation as well as to the unique characteristics of his facility. He, thus, can gauge the flexibility and constraints of his system in accepting the changes suggested by the results of evaluation.

To assist the feedback of research findings to the program administrator, increasing attention is being given to scientific communication. Professional information experts, librarians, abstractors, editors, and others, are employing a variety of hardware-oriented technics for making information more readily available to those who engage in even minimal information-seeking behavior. Examples include computer search programs, abstracting services, review papers, and various types of professional and interdisciplinary conferences. Perhaps these modern technics will partially solve the problem of researchers reporting their findings in forums and language which are foreign to program developers. These devices may be of particular importance when the research conducted in the focal organization is reported elsewhere by the researcher who is without a clear contract to feed back his findings to the organization under study.

A last problem to be considered in the development of feedback mechanisms is the time discrepancy that often occurs between administrators and evaluators. The time dimension of those closest to program implementation is often shorter and more variable than that of the evaluator who focuses upon a more distant horizon. It is suggested that feedback can be enhanced by the design of evaluation procedures which more appropriately fit the schedule decision-making needs of an organization, and which have data available at a time when they can be used for planning.

SUMMARY

In seeking to conceptualize possible approaches to program evaluation,

two research models stand out: (a) the goal-attainment model, and (b) the system model. The characteristics and limitations of each were described as they affect the implementation of research findings. It is contended that the system model, by focusing upon the various factors determining research design and interpretation of the data, offers more promise for programmatic utilization of the evaluation findings. The system model also has utility for determining the factors associated with effective integration of the findings. It is suggested that organizations establish planning divisions because of the problems of blocked feedback to the organization of information on its performance and in order to insure translation of research.

NOTES

1. Menzel, H. Review of Studies in the Flow of Information Among Scientists. Bureau of Applied Social Research, Columbia University (Jan.), 1960. (Mimeo.)

2. ———. Scientific Communication: Five Themes from Social Science Research. Am. Psychologist 21: 999–1004, 1966.

3. Halpert, H. H. Communications As a Basic Tool in Promoting Utilization of Research Findings. Community Mental Health Journal 2: 231–236, 1966.

4. Ibid., p. 231.

5. Greenberg, B. G., and Mattison, B. F. The Whys and Wherefores of Program Evaluation. Canadian J. Pub. Health 46: 293–299, 1955.

6. Knutson, A. L. Evaluation for What? Proceedings of the Regional Institute on Neurologically Handicapping Conditions in Children held at the University of California, Berkeley, June 18–23, 1961.

7. Freeman, H. E., and Sherwood, C. C. Research in Large Scale Intervention Programs. J. Soc. Issues 21: 11–28, 1965.

8. Herzog, Elizabeth. Some Guide Lines for Evaluative Research. Washington, D.C.: Gov. Ptg. Office, 1959.

9. Knutson, A. L., op. cit.

10. James, G. Evaluation in Public Health Practice. A.J.P.H. 52,7: 1145–1154 (July), 1962.

11. Etzioni, A. Two Approaches to Organizational Analysis: A Critique and a Suggestion. Admin. Sc. Quart. 5: 257–278, 1960.

12. Rice, A. K. The Enterprise and Its Environment. London: Tavistock Publications, 1963.

13. Sofer, C. The Organization From Within. London: Tavistock Publications, 1961.

14. Schulberg, H. C.; Notman, R.; and Bookin, E. Treatment Services at a Mental Hospital in Transition. Am. J. Psychiat. 124: 506–513, 1967.

15. Etzioni, A., op. cit.

16. Ibid., p. 262.

17. Cumming, Elaine, and Cumming, John. Closed Ranks: An Experiment in Mental Health Education. Cambridge: Harvard University Press, 1957.

18. Schulberg, H. C.; Caplan, G.; and Greenblatt, M. Evaluating the Changing Mental Hospital: A Suggested Research Strategy. Ment. Hyg. 52: 218–225, 1968.

19. Baker, F. An Open-Systems Approach to the Study of Mental Hospitals in Transition. Paper presented at annual meeting of American Psychological Association, New York (Sept. 2), 1966.

20. Ibid.

PART II
THE ORGANIZATIONAL CONTEXT: ESTABLISHING AND MAINTAINING THE EVALUATION RESEARCH ROLE

The task of evaluation research is to determine the effects of programs conducted in an organizational setting. Often the results are used to help a sponsor decide whether an organization deserves continued support, or to assist the administering organization itself in modifying its programming. Effective working relationships with those who administer programs, therefore, are critical for evaluative researchers.

In devising an evaluative research plan, the social researcher and his client may do well to consider various evaluation alternatives as investment strategies. Downs urges that the cost of research be considered in the light of the economic benefits the research might be expected to yield. (He notes that decision makers tend to underestimate the contribution of research, whereas researchers tend to overestimate its value.) Downs also warns social scientists who assume consultant roles that their advice is often sought less for its substance than as a ploy in organizational politics.

Serious strains in researcher-practitioner relationships are common. Rodman and Kolodny emphasize organizational structure rather than personality variables in accounting for these difficulties. Practitioners, for example, have reason to be concerned that researchers will use their special ties to administrators to report on practitioner errors. The authors recommend that efforts to alleviate these strains focus on the social organization of the action agency.

House analyzes the highly charged political circumstances that surround the evaluation of innovative programs in higher education. Evaluators are advised to be prepared to deal with not only the ideology built into project proposals but also with "saga," that is, the collective understanding of unique accomplishment that surrounds a project. House illustrates how a balanced evaluation narrative can be regarded as negative by project staff because the evaluation challenges the "blemish-free" public image staff have cultivated for the project. The career ambitions of innovators require that the imagery be kept intact. Political enemies are ready to use any negative data as ammunition with which to attack the project.

Concerned with the fact that program performance usually does not improve following evaluation, Horst and associates take issue with explanations that are focused on the evaluation process. Rather, they argue that evaluation deficiencies often can be traced to three problems rooted in the programs themselves: (1) lack of definition of problem, intervention, and outcome; (2) lack of logic linking resources, implementation, and outcome, and (3) lack of management willingness or ability to act on the results of evaluation. The authors recommend that programs be preassessed to determine whether the three conditions for adequate evaluation are present before formal evaluations are attempted.

A study of the organizational context in which evaluative research is conducted is reported by Weiss. Uncertainties regarding the purpose of evaluation, conflicts among researchers, administrators, and practitioners over research decisions, instability in the staffing of evaluation units, and difficulties in meshing program and evaluation timing are documented. Weiss identifies several basic conditions that she believes should be present before evaluation grants are made.

Mann and Likert emphasize the importance of effective communication of research results in organizational settings. They address themselves particularly to the problem of motivating staff members to accept the action implications of research. Their argument is that research results are most likely to be used when staff members have an opportunity through group discussions to participate in the interpretation of data.

4. Some Thoughts on Giving People Economic Advice

Anthony Downs

I. INTRODUCTION

Surprisingly, economists seem to have developed few theories about how to give other people advice effectively. True, there is a vast literature on how to make decisions. There are also extensive writings on which types of advice from economists can be considered purely scientific, and which must also be considered partly ethical. Finally, there are tons of books and articles concerning the substantive issues which advisors are likely to grapple with.

Nevertheless, there is a significant gap in both empirical data and theory concerning the kinds of relationships likely to develop between an advisor and the decision-makers who seek his counsel. Therefore, in this brief article, I will set forth a few thoughts on this subject developed in the course of acting as an economic consultant to a wide variety of clients, ranging from Latin American politicians to New England storekeepers.

II. ADVICE AND THE COST OF MAKING MISTAKES

A practicing economic consultant soon learns that many clients, and even some consultants, do not understand the elementary economics of information. The logical purpose of seeking advice or information before acting is to reduce the likelihood of making an expensive mistake. Therefore, the amount which should be invested in advance research depends upon the potential costliness of making such a mistake.

In this sense, a "mistake" can be failure to make a 200% profit instead of a 100% profit, as well as sustaining a loss. Hence this is just another way of saying that information should be obtained in order to maximize potential gain. Nevertheless, I prefer the "mistake-minimizing" approach because it illuminates two major misunderstandings concerning the economics of information which I often encounter.

The first is under-estimating the value of doing research before acting. This error is most often made by decision-makers themselves. They have a natural incentive to minimize research because they have to pay for it, and good advice is usually expensive. For example, many developers are unwilling to spend even $10,000 analyzing the crucial aspects of a potential investment involving five or ten million dollars. Yet a mistake causing the loss of just two percent of their investment would cost them from $100,000 to $200,000. True, getting advice normally requires cash-on-the-barrelhead; whereas its pay-offs may be way off in the future. Nevertheless, in the complex, highly

Reprinted from *American Behavioral Scientist,* Vol. 9, No. 1, September 1965, pp. 30–32, by permission of the Publisher, Sage Publications, Inc.

competitive, and uncertain environment of most large public or private ventures launched today, it is all too easy to make a tremendously expensive blunder—perhaps a financially fatal one—when relying strictly on "seat-of-the-pants" judgments. Although this truth is being accepted by more and more practical decision-makers, I believe that the vast majority of large-scale private and public decisions still suffer from serious under-investment in advanced research —particularly research into alternative policies. This is related to the myopia of looking at problems too narrowly—which will be discussed later.

An exactly opposite misunderstanding is surprisingly prevalent among consultants themselves. It is most often found among those who are primarily academicians but occasionally venture into the real world to advise "men of action." An exaggerated version of their typical error is proposing—or doing—$100,000 worth of research to solve a $10,000 problem. Moreover, they often fail to come up with a definite answer, since they believe more research is required to produce one! Such over-investment in research stems from ignoring the limited costs of making a wrong decision in certain situations. Thus, a man whose house is worth about $25,000 would be foolish to spend $10,000 to have it appraised. Even if he sold it for less than it was worth through sheer ignorance, he would be very unlikely to make even a $5,000 error. He could certainly protect himself from this large a blunder by investing under $500 in research.

A second cause of over-investment in research is intellectual fascination with *solving the problem* instead of *advising the decision-maker*. The primary purpose of advice is to insure that the decision-maker makes the right choice in a given situation. There are often significant secondary purposes, too, which we will discuss later. In some cases, the right choice for the decision-maker becomes clear relatively quickly. This may occur in the midst of a planned data-acquisition program, even before information which originally appeared "vital" has been gathered or analyzed. Sometimes it is worthwhile to continue such a program just to be sure nothing crucial has been overlooked, or because of the secondary purposes of advice. But in many cases, further research amounts to pure window-dressing. Yet some consultants who are oriented towards arriving at intellectually satisfactory solutions to problems may press on with expensive research because their expositions are incomplete without it. And without an aesthetically complete analysis, they are often unwilling to formulate useful recommendations, since they are *explanation-oriented* rather than *action-oriented*.

III. SOME DIFFICULTIES COMMONLY ENCOUNTERED IN GIVING ADVICE

Having examined two important *general* misunderstandings concerning the usefulness of economic advice, I would now like to discuss a few of the more specific difficulties which advisors frequently run into.

The first is that many people who seek advice do not understand the real nature of their problems. They know that something is wrong, but their attention is normally focussed upon the symptoms rather than the disease. *Hence nearly half of the contribution made by an economic consultant in most cases is helping his clients clearly define their problems.* Once that is accomplished, the solutions are in some cases obvious.

Properly defining the problem is often complicated by the client's belief that he already knows what it is. Most of the time, he is wrong because he conceives of his difficulties too narrowly. A retail firm may say to us, "Find four cities with the following characteristics in which to locate stores." Then it will present us with a set of characteristics which is inappropriate in terms of the firm's true objectives. For example, one firm requested us to locate store sites within 200 miles of Chicago so they would be within half-a-day's travel time from the main office. When we pointed out that jet aircraft placed both coasts and much of the rest of the country within that time span, they radically shifted their horizons. This illustrates that decision-makers tend to think in terms of traditional or habitual categories which are often unduly narrow in relation to their needs.

A common manifestation of this bias is the "one-best-way" approach to problems. Having perceived a problem, the decision-maker quickly devises a basic approach to solving it, and then devotes a great deal of attention to how that approach should be carried out. Only then does he seek professional advice—not on what approach to use, but on the details of its execution.

Hence our first task is often to convince him to let us consider some alternative approaches too. This may be touchy because it requires him to admit that he might have acted too hastily in concentrating on one approach. Yet we are firmly convinced that several alternative approaches to most major problems should be carefully examined—at least on paper—before any one of them is selected for execution or even detailed investigation. For example, people often ask us to study the market for a specific land-use regarding a given site; whereas the best strategy would be to start by examining its potential regarding a number of different uses.

Thus, one set of difficulties in giving advice arises because decision-makers do not call upon the objectives and fresh viewpoint of outside advisors soon enough so that the latter can focus on the whole problem.

Paradoxically, another set of difficulties arises because many decision-makers have an exaggerated idea of the precision with which economic advice can be rendered. They believe that we have standardized, well-tested, and extremely precise methods of making quantitative forecasts about variables which in reality are extraordinarily difficult to measure or forecast. This leads to the following problems:

1. Many people postpone getting economic advice until the very last second before a decision must be made. Their confidence in our methods, or perhaps their last-minute realization that other methods are inadequate, often causes them to seek

our counsel so "late in the game" that only sketchy advice can be given. An extreme but true example is a discount store operator who called me and said, "I have a thirty-day option on this property, and twenty-eight days have expired. What can you do for me?"

2. Decision-makers often place excessive reliance upon specific quantitative estimates in making subsequent plans. We believe that most clients are correct in demanding numerical approximations of key variables instead of vague generalities. However, they tend to forget that these numbers are sometimes rough estimates, rather than precise measurements. For example, many of our clients require that we estimate future store volumes as single numbers rather than ranges because they want to develop gross building volumes, floor plans, and merchandise layouts from those numbers. Also, every real estate appraisal is stated as a single number, although it is often the midpoint of a confidence interval.

IV. THE "SECONDARY" USES OF RESEARCH

In many cases, the client—not the advisor—insists on the compilation of data, analysis, and illustrations which are logically superfluous in terms of the decisions at hand. This reveals a crucial fact which every consultant soon learns: *many people seek professional advice not because they want to know how to make right decisions, but for reasons largely unrelated to the advice itself.* Examples of such "secondary" uses of advice are as follows:

1. Using outside advice to settle an internal dispute among Board members or other high-ranking officials. In many cases, the particular resolution recommended is less important than having a policy on which all concerned can agree *because* it was devised by an "objective" outsider.

2. Using an impressive report to provide justification for decisions already made on grounds largely unrelated to the reasoning presented in the report (although that reasoning is entirely correct). This is more likely among public agencies than private firms.

3. Using a report by a reputable advisor to verify findings previously arrived at by an interested party. An example is making a feasibility study for a shopping center which the developer shows to an insurance company to get long-term financing. In such cases, if the advisor's "stamp of approval" is to retain any widespread acceptance in the long run, he must maintain a strictly impartial objectivity even though his client would like him to be a strong advocate.

4. Using outside advisors as explicit weapons in a struggle for power. Thus:

(*a*) An official may use a report to "prove" that his own operations should be expanded, or his pet policies adopted.

(*b*) An organization may try to obtain a report to "disprove" the wisdom of allowing a rival to expand. Financial institutions often fight potential rivals in this manner.

(*c*) An official may use a report by a well-known advisor primarily to call attention to himself, or to get his superiors to consider a problem they have consistently ignored when he brought it up himself.

(*d*) One official may seek to weaken

the power of another by having the latter's operations subjected to thorough study. Since almost every operation can be improved, such studies *initiated by outsiders,* are normally considered threatening by those being studied.

5. Conducting further research as an excuse for deferring any immediate action regarding some issue which is highly controversial, or as the first step in burying the issue without any action at all.

Two vital observations must be made about such "secondary" uses of advice. First, these logically "secondary" purposes of advice are frequently far more important than the usual primary purpose (i.e., discovering which choice is optimal). This is true because most major decisions in our complex world involve the interaction of many individuals or organizations. Hence even the most dynamic "men of action" usually need to obtain the support and concurrence of others in their decisions. Since they themselves are bound to be judged as advocates, they often have difficulty convincing others of the feasibility of their recommendations without documented analysis and opinions from advisors well-known as *non*-advocates.

Second, merely because the person who hires an advisor wants to use him as a tool in advancing a certain cause does not mean that the advisor himself must become an advocate of that cause. On the contrary, his usefulness to the advocate as a means of obtaining support from others is directly proportional to his reputation for objectivity and impartiality. Naturally, no advisor can long maintain such a reputation unless he is impartial.

Moreover, even though decision-makers may *initially engage* an advisor primarily to substantiate views they already hold, this does not mean that the substance of his advice is irrelevant. In fact, because such clients may not have been thinking as much about substantive questions as about political ones, the advisor can sometimes discover extremely significant factors they have overlooked. Hence he may even shift the focus of their interests from "secondary" issues to the substance of the decisions at hand. As a result, he sometimes finds himself in a crucial position in relation to *both* "secondary" and substantive issues.

On the other hand, an advisor often discovers that he is being used at least in part as a pawn in a quasi-political struggle, either within a single organization, or among different ones. Such "politics" exist in every large organization, since its operations inevitably involve the personal ambitions and goals of its members as well as its formal social functions. Normally, when an advisor first arrives on the scene, he can only dimly grasp the "jockeying for position" going on all around him. The speed and accuracy with which he can sense the subtleties of the situation, and unravel the often complex power relationships involved—all without making an unwittingly tactless blunder—may determine both how long he remains on the scene and how significant a contribution he can make.

Such circumstances usually require extreme tactfulness and sensitivity in human relations, as well as the normal analytical talents associated with giving economic advice. The advisor must simultaneously (a) maintain his standards of professional objectivity and integrity and (b) consciously either assist certain officials in attaining their "secondary" objectives, or assiduously avoid involvement.

The rarity of the combination of traits required in these situations makes top-level economic consultants extremely valuable. The best advisors are always sensitive to *both* the "secondary" and purely technical issues at stake in the situations where their counsel is sought. *They do not approach giving advice as purely intellectual problem-solving, but as assisting specific people to make the decisions that will help them attain their personal and organizational objectives.* This certainly does not imply that advisors must compromise their intellectual integrity in any way. Rather, it implies that they see each situation in its *full context* of social, organizational, and personal implications. It is the challenge of providing such "full-range-response" to the needs of a wide variety of people in a whole spectrum of different situations that makes giving economic advice such an exciting and stimulating profession.

5. Organizational Strains in the Researcher-Practitioner Relationship

Hyman Rodman and Ralph Kolodny

Social science researchers have, to an increasing extent, been moving into clinical settings, such as mental hospitals, general hospitals, child guidance clinics, and social work agencies, and into other professional settings, such as schools and courts. It is well known that problems arise when a social science researcher enters a clinical agency or some other professional setting. What we are interested in exploring is whether there are similarities in the problems faced by researchers and practitioners in these professional agencies, and whether certain of these problems stem from the organizational structure of the professional agency. We shall deal primarily with the relationships between researchers and practitioners in health and welfare agencies, under those conditions where only one or a few researchers are part of a larger agency.[1] We feel, however, that our remarks have implications for research endeavors in any professional agency.

Most of the writings on researcher-practitioner relationships are based upon the personal experiences of their authors in one or several collaborative attempts. While this is also true of our report, we have in addition made a serious attempt to read the writings on researcher-practitioner relationships, and to highlight some of the major themes that emerge in these writings. Moreover, we focus upon some areas of stress and some reactions to these areas of stress that are only barely touched upon in the writings we have seen. Although we have not, by any means, attempted to cover all writings on researcher-practitioner relations, and although we have not automatically referred to every reference we have seen, those references that we included in this paper constitute a fairly substantial bibliography on researcher-practitioner relationships. For an overlapping bibliography on researcher-practitioner relationships, and more generally for references to other forms of interdisciplinary team research, the reader is referred to the excellent bibliography to be found in Luszki's book.[2]

In their less charitable moments researchers complain that practitioners

Revision and expansion of two papers, one presented at the annual meeting of the Society for the Study of Social Problems, in St. Louis, Missouri, August, 1961, and the other at the Michigan Sociological Association meeting in Albion, Michigan, in November, 1961. The paper had its start while the first author was a Russell Sage Foundation post-doctoral resident at the Boston Children's Service Association. It was also aided in part by a grant from the Social Research Foundation to Merrill-Palmer Institute.

Reproduced by permission of the Society for Applied Anthropology from *Human Organization*, Vol. 23, No. 2, 1964, pp. 171–182.

"can't see the forest for the trees" while practitioners, in turn, wonder whether researchers "can see the human beings behind the statistics."[3] This kind of problem, as well as others, frequently plagues the relationship between researchers and practitioners. In attempting to locate the difficulties that arise in the course of this relationship, reference is often made to personality differences or to personality problems. Blenkner talks about

> traits of temperament of a lasting character

that divide researchers and practitioners.[4] In their discussion of anxieties associated with research in clinical settings, Mitchell and Mudd suggest the existence of a

> deeply instilled bias for the "intuitive" on the part of the clinician against the bias for the "logical" of the researcher.[5]

They also suggest that many clinicians, in their first anxiety reactions toward research processes with their clients,

> are reacting to inexperience, the unknown [and that] if their anxiety persists as evidenced in their continued inability to discuss or accept the fact that clients are not harmed by research procedures it can but be labeled as "neurotic anxiety."[6]

It is true, of course, that one cannot understand practitioner-researcher difficulties unless attention is paid to personality variables as they apply to the behavior of individuals or groups of individuals in particular professions. At the same time, it seems to us, an understanding of these difficul-

ties is likely to be incomplete if we do not also take a close look at those factors, other than personality variables, that may influence the actions and feelings of practitioners and researchers toward one another.[7]

In this paper, we will be focusing on one such factor, the formal organization of the clinical agency, and we will attempt to spell out some of the ways in which the strains which may be found between researchers and practitioners are built into the formal organization of the agency. Our purpose in so doing is not to discourage the undertaking of research in a clinical agency but to show the ways in which agency structure of necessity conditions the response of researchers and practitioners to each other, so that the strains which arise between them may be better understood and managed. Since our aim is to illuminate problem areas our attention will be devoted to stresses and difficulties rather than to an examination of the more benign aspects of researcher-practitioner interaction. It should be noted, therefore, in the interest of keeping a balanced view, that despite these stresses, satisfying and productive working relationships have been developed in a good many agencies among administrators, researchers, and practitioners.[8]

THE RESEARCHER AS EVALUATOR

There is general agreement on the need for research activity in clinical agencies. The literature is replete with suggestions and even demands that practice be subjected to systematic investigation. There are many reasons advanced for undertaking research, such as the benefits accruing to staff by way of increased morale and sharpened perceptions of the possible consequences of their techniques. The ultimate purpose of research, however, is to evaluate as thoroughly as possible the effectiveness of practice (although it is recognized that "research cannot produce here and now the 'ultimate' evaluation of efforts to bring about psycho-social changes in individuals").[9] This evaluative orientation is reflected in such statements as the following:

> As more time, energy, manpower and funds have been devoted to mental health, as more scientifically trained professional workers have become involved in the problem and as competition among community programs of all types for manpower and public funds has increased, the need for methods of evaluating mental health activities is obvious. It becomes mandatory that more scientific evidence be furnished if and where this is possible, or otherwise lack of knowledge concerning the results of enormous human effort can lead to wastage, furtherance of untested beliefs and possible counter trends which may obstruct the onward march of hard won progress.[10]

One aspect, then, of the relationship between researcher and practitioner is that the former may be evaluating the work of the latter. At the outset, therefore, practitioners may be threatened by the researcher and ambivalent about the undertaking of research, since the researcher, whether he likes it or not, is in the position of possibly showing up the work of the practitioner. Inherent in the role of the researcher is the conception of a corrective agent who, through his findings, will help practitioners to improve their practice. Researchers in social work write of their

> focus on developing more "knowledgeable" ways of proceeding towards social work goals.[11]

One cannot avoid an implication here that the agency practice upon which they are or will be doing research has been characterized by less knowledgeable ways of proceeding towards social work goals, prior to research. Although the researcher may want to see himself as an enabler in his relationship with the practitioner rather than as an evaluator, the corrective and evaluative aspects of his position as he takes his place in the structure of the agency are sensed and reacted to by the practitioners. As Wilensky and Lebeaux point out, objectivity has a critical tone to it, and

> what the social scientist thinks of as "objective investigation" the practitioner often takes as "hostile attack."[12]

Subsequent resistances on their part cannot be dismissed as merely irrational, for these, in part, are reactions to be expected to the researcher's role in the organization.

The painful aspects of the evaluation process for the practitioner cannot be glossed over.

> A public relations man who usually operates on the basis of shrewd guesswork is likely to feel his "status" is in danger when an outsider threatens to question his guesswork by scientific method.[13]

The practitioner's convictions (and his occasional doubts) that his efforts are helpful often lead to an ambivalent attitude toward research which purports to test whether his efforts really are helpful. This attitude is neatly reflected by Wirth in a review of Albert Rose's book, *Regent Park: A Study In Slum Clearance.* Wirth writes:

> It is good for those of us who are interested in low-cost housing programs to have all of these convictions written down; yet it must be recognized that these conclusions are by no means satisfactorily documented and validated. Much more study remains to be done before we have evidence on hand definitely to assay the costs and benefits of public housing. Most social workers, however, are prepared to take the benefits for granted even without adequate proof in the firm conviction that the benefits will show up in time.[14]

The questioning attitude which the researcher must necessarily assume in carrying out the basic purposes for which he has been employed is likely to be irritating to the practitioner. This is not because the practitioner is naive or blind to inadequacies in practice. Often it is because the probing of the researcher, at least initially, comes as an extra burden to the already overworked practitioner. The researcher's persistent request for evidence rather than impressions may be felt as carping and quibbling by the practitioner with a host of patients or clients to be seen. As Naegele phrased it, researchers kept therapists on their toes by asking, "How do you know?" and therapists kept researchers on their toes by asking, "So what?"[15]

Assaying this situation, Pollak, in his comments on research in social work, has noted that to date researchers and social workers have collaborated under circumstances most likely to cause friction because they meet each other at the point of evaluation, which places the researchers in the position of critical analysts and induces defensiveness in the social workers. Pollak suggests as a remedy for this situation that researchers begin not with evaluative studies in agencies but begin rather by working with the social workers on projects in such a way that the workers are able to perceive the researchers as helpful colleagues, rather than as critics.[16] Such pre-evaluative, collaborative work may have the advantage of teaching researchers more about the complexity of the problems that practitioners deal with. Researchers are then likelier to try to develop research instruments that will better reflect the complexities of practice. This may be a chastening experience for a researcher, but it may also contribute to a reduction of practitioner defensiveness and a heightening of mutual respect.

Even under these conditions, however, certain threatening features of the research process remain, for built into the researcher's function from the very beginning is the role of innovator. The situation is parallel to what would be found within an industrial organization where the research department and the production department may be at odds because the former has a vested interest in searching out ways to alter the production process and in discovering inefficiencies while the latter has a vested interest in resisting changes that would upset the department and possibly reflect upon its inefficiency. In the same vein, in the relationship between researchers and teachers of psychotherapy in mental hospitals, the teachers may look upon research as an effort

> to undermine established authority and to destroy what the teachers are building within the limits of the administrative Procrustes.[17]

It is not only the evaluative aspect of the researcher's job which leads to organizational strains between researcher and practitioner. Actually, the very ways in which the activities of researchers and practitioners are organized and the monetary and prestige values attached to these different sets of activities also have a definite bearing on the strains. A clinical agency is organized to help or treat the clients or patients that it serves; this is its basic function. A number of such agencies, however, are also engaged in a certain amount of research work. A question of some importance, therefore, is the place the research activities find within the agency and the consequences that stem from the differences between research activities and clinical activities.

It is possible to further develop our analogy between the line and staff functions of an industrial organization and the service and research functions of a clinical agency.[18] The workers on the line are engaged directly in the manufacture of a particular product, while the staff members serve in an advisory capacity. In a similar way, the practitioners in an agency are engaged directly with therapeutic goals, while researchers serve in an advisory capacity, or, at any rate, their findings may be looked upon as having advisory potentiality.

Like the staff workers in an industrial organization, the research workers in a clinical agency have an inconsistent status. On some criteria they rank higher than the practitioners, and on other criteria they rank lower. For example, the research workers are often younger than the practitioners and they have had less, if any, clinical training or experience. On these criteria they rank lower. On the other hand, researchers have usually had more formal academic training, they are evaluators of the practitioners and they are closer to the administrator. On these criteria they rank higher. This makes for status inconsistency, and, as some studies have shown, there is a tendency for various forms of dissatisfaction or desire for change to develop in such a situation.[19]

WORK AND TIME ORGANIZATION

An additional factor that transforms the hyphen between researcher and practitioner into a thorn is the extreme difference between the research job and the therapeutic job.[20] The way in which time is organized by the researcher and the practitioner is one difference. The practitioner is engaged in a continuous job with a number of clients or patients who are seen at regular or irregular intervals over a period of time. His time schedule is organized by the sessions with clients or patients which are held in his office, or, occasionally, in his clients' or patients' homes, and his appointment calendar reflects his hour-to-hour "busyness" and shows relatively few empty spaces. The researcher, however, is working on a project; his time is much less organized on an hour-to-hour and day-to-day basis; there are often large blanks in his appointment calendar. Of course, the researcher's time may be as tightly organized as the practitioner's if he is conducting a series of research interviews, but after the interviews are completed, they must not only be recorded, but also examined and analyzed and written up into a final report or article or monograph. It is clear, therefore, that the researcher's activities and his organization of time differ markedly from the practitioner's. That these differences are not always appreciated is illustrated by the following brief phone conversation in which one of the writers was involved:

> SOCIAL WORKER: I wonder when you would have time to get together with me?
> RESEARCHER: Well, I am free on Tuesday afternoon, or anytime Wednesday or Thursday would be O.K.
> SOCIAL WORKER: Boy, that's quite a schedule; you're really living the life of a lotus-eater!

The comments of Ekstein and Wallerstein are interesting in this regard. They note that teachers of psychotherapy in mental hospitals sometimes see researchers in these settings as

> living a parasitical life, free from schedules and responsibilities.[21]

One aspect of the differences in time organization between practitioners and researchers is the fact that the practitioner focuses upon a series of individual cases, while the researcher focuses upon a general problem. This occasionally gives rise to the attitude that the researchers are not interested in the individuals and the practitioners are not interested in the general problems. Practitioners, for example, may complain bitterly about the fact that their own or other agencies accept or reject clients or patients on the basis of whether or not their problem happens to fit the research interest of people at the agency. In addition, they frequently object to changes in their service routine which are called for by a research project and they may, as a final expression of protest, actually undermine such a project.[22]

Researchers, on the other hand, may complain about the fact that practitioners get so bound up with their patients or clients that they object to the use of follow-up studies or control groups. Florence Hollis has written on this point:

> This study would have been strengthened immeasurably had it been possible to follow up the cases, at say a year after closing. There is considerable resistance to such follow-up in the casework field. In the writer's opinion there is very little rational basis for this resistance. There will always be certain individual cases which it is impossible or inadvisable to follow but these would be the exception rather than the rule.[23]

In addition, Martin Wolins, in referring to the use of control groups in social work, has commented that,

> in suggesting control groups I am advocating denial of service, strongly opposed by every social work practitioner to whom I have mentioned it.[24]

Making use of control groups is especially difficult in public agencies.[25]

The problems between researcher and practitioner are compounded by the fact that the practitioner, who is expected to cooperate with the researcher, may have demands placed upon him that require him to change his procedures. One area in which change may be asked of the practitioner is in terms of fuller and more frequent recording. For the researcher, the recording of data is extremely important; he cannot hope to carry out his task unless he can get all of the data he needs. The practitioner, as he actually carries on his job, accords less importance to recording. Even in social work, despite the prominent place recording is given in the literature and despite the belief commonly held by those from related disciplines that social workers over-ritualize their work through voluminous recording and that with regard to recording

> they seem to do too much of the work
> that psychologists and psychiatrists
> seem to do too little of,[26]

recording is in fact not often attended to with anywhere near the diligence agency administrators hope for. This is attested to, for example, by the notices one sees posted from time to time advising workers that vacations cannot be taken until recording is brought up to date, and by the workers who spend many days, prior to leaving an agency permanently, catching up on their recording. The practitioner may feel that the essential points he is concerned with can be remembered, and by saving time from recording, he can devote more time to

doing what he considers his basic job—clinical work. In addition, because of the strong democratic ethic among social workers, certain items like race, religion, and national background may not be recorded, especially on a client's face sheet, and this may lead to difficulties for the researcher.[27] The different nature of research work and clinical work introduces a different attitude toward recording, and it is easy to see that these different attitudes will have consequences for the researcher-practitioner relationship.[28]

CREDIT AND ANONYMITY

Another problem that may arise from the different roles being played by researcher and practitioner concerns the credit that is assigned for the publication of research reports. To the researcher, publication represents the culmination of his work, and he expects to get primary, if not sole, credit for publication. The practitioner who has cooperated with the researcher, however, typically feels that he has contributed a great deal to the research report and expects to get substantial, if not equal, credit for its publication. The researcher who has had to overcome the resistance of the practitioner may tend to minimize the work that the practitioner has done, while the practitioner who has had to sacrifice important time that could have been devoted to what he considers the more essential service job may maximize the work that he has devoted to research.[29] If, in addition, the research report is largely exploratory and descriptive, and makes use of case material that has been supplied by the practitioner, the latter has all the more reason to feel that he should get a considerable amount of credit for the final published report. Thus, one aspect of the problem is that, due to the roles they play, the researcher and the practitioner have differing perceptions of the size of the contribution that the latter has made. This is compounded by the fact that the researcher ordinarily writes up the final report,[30] and decides upon the credit to be given to other participants on the project. He not only sees things differently from the practitioner, but he also has a limited number of possibilities from which to choose in assigning credit. Perhaps the television industry has an easier time handling this problem because the credit to be assigned is part of a contractual obligation, and because there is more scope for indicating greater and lesser stardom. The researcher who is publishing an article is often faced with the choice between co-authorship and footnote mention—and there is a wide gap between the two. In addition, certain journals, due to space limitations, are reluctant to accept articles with more than two or three authors, and may want to edit out footnotes that give thanks to a long list of participants in a research project. This, of course, adds to the strains that are faced in the relationship between researcher and practitioner.

Space limitations do not enter the situation when book publication is involved, and it is, therefore, possible to arrive at a more just distribution of credit under these circumstances. Here, between magnanimous co-authorship and mere footnote mention,

lie the additional possibilities of secondary authorship ("with the assistance of" or "with the collaboration of") and of more or less protracted mention in the Preface or Acknowledgments. The problem is not however simply one of space limitations or the choice of a just distribution of credit, but also one in which the various role-players may have quite a different notion of what is just.

Publication credit is therefore a sensitive issue, and is usually not discussed until the research report has been written, and it may not be discussed even then.[31] This is another area in which the researcher has power, and through which he can broadcast credit (or blame) to a large audience. Because of this, the researcher has another channel through which he can exert pressure upon the practitioner to gain his cooperation; that it may not even occur to the researcher to discuss publication with the practitioner certainly does not lessen this pressure. It may also be significant that social science researchers are often very responsive to the canon of confidentiality that protects the people from whom or through whom they gather their data. So much so, in fact, that they may all too readily grant anonymity to those who would prefer a share of the credit.

THE PATTERNS OF COMMUNICATION

We have indicated so far how the role of the researcher and the nature of the organization in which he carries out his activities can create strains between practitioners and researchers. Another source of strain which must be taken into account can be found in the communication patterns of the researcher.

When research first begins in a clinical agency, it is almost always a creation of the agency's administration. The administration may feel that research work holds out the only hope for new findings and techniques that can cut down on the continually increasing demands for service or that can help to meet these demands more effectively. The publication of research results from a particular agency also provides one of the most effective ways of gaining prestige for the agency. For these reasons research work is usually established because of needs that are expressed by the administration rather than by the practitioners. In addition, according to some writers, it is the administrator who is expected

> to work through the resistance [to research] of inexperienced board members and staff.[32]

This puts the researcher in a clinical agency in a unique position. His work has been created by the administration and it is with the administration that he has his main contacts, at least initially. This special position of the researcher will usually mean that he is not attached to any of the service departments of the agency. It might also involve the creation of a special research group which, by name, often becomes a patrician institute among plebeian departments. In those instances where the researcher is part of a service department—perhaps because he is working both as a practitioner and as a researcher—he may

have certain responsibilities to the head of the service department and also to the administrator of the agency. In such instances the formal organization may lead to a certain amount of strain and the administrator, researcher, and especially the department head, may all wonder, at times, to whom the researcher really belongs.

There is perhaps another factor that binds the researcher and administrator together. This is the "loneliness" that Schmidt sees within the administrative position,[33] and the administrator may therefore welcome a researcher as someone to talk to in a way that he cannot talk to the regular members of his staff.

THE PROBLEM OF MARGINALITY

The special tie that the researcher has with the administrator cannot be too strongly emphasized. The formal organization of his job, at least in the beginning, both isolates him from the rest of the agency and at the same time binds him closely to the administrator. The researcher's activities are different and he is also not usually part of a regular agency department. For these reasons he has a marginal position within the agency.[34] Even his research findings are marginal to the agency in the sense that they are usually published for a much wider audience. As compared to the research department in an industrial organization, the research department in a direct service agency makes fewer suggestions that require changes on the part of the worker in the organization. The complexity of the service task makes it much more difficult for the researcher to suggest changes in clinical practice. It is indeed a reflection of the weakness of the researcher's position that most of the changes he asks for are to enable him to carry out his research task, and are not changes to improve service that are suggested by his theoretical background or his research findings. It is, therefore, not surprising that difficulties develop in those situations where the researcher must work closely with the practitioners in order to carry out his task. The researcher's marginal position both with respect to the structure of the agency itself and the profession in which workers in the agency are engaged deserves close study. His role may be thought of by practitioners as a luxury role which is perhaps useful but certainly not essential to the carrying out of the agency's task and commitment to the public. He is not a part of the line organization of the professional agency. His formal training is in an academic rather than a clinical field which can lead to conflict with the practitioners about the appropriate way of viewing and understanding human behavior. Actually, the orientation of the researcher to personal and social problems may not be greatly different from that of the clinical practitioners, but his structurally marginal position and his inconsistent status[35] may lead him, at times, to feel isolated, without support, and unessential to the agency. In some cases it may make him a useful target for negative feelings displaced from authority figures who are part of the supervisory chain and structure.

The practitioners within an agency share a professional culture which they act out in their daily experiences. This is so regardless of whether they do or do not identify with one specific agency. The lone or the few researchers within a clinical agency are strangers who may be vitally interested in the professional culture of the society in which they reside, but who nevertheless maintain their own distinctive customs and beliefs. They do not commit themselves to the mores of this new society to the same extent that its members do, and their acceptance by the society, therefore, is always conditional and tentative.[36] Like the traditional marginal man the researcher and what he does may be thought of as somewhat mysterious. As a social worker laughingly remarked to one of the writers,

> Nobody knows what you're doing but you.

This attitude may be reinforced by the fact that when the researcher begins his task he may have only the most general ideas about which problems he hopes to tackle and in what ways he will approach them. Since he cannot immediately explain his research problem to the practitioners and may be some time going about exploring what is researchable in the agency, all sorts of misconceptions about his role, usually reflecting the anxieties of the practitioners about their own performance, can arise.

In one instance, one of the writers entered a social work agency in order to explore what was researchable and after being in the agency for several months, a questionnaire was answered by the social workers in which they were asked, among other things, to give their impressions of what the research worker was doing in the agency. At an early staff meeting the administrator explained that *exploration* was the research worker's function, and this was repeated by the researcher to all practitioners who individually asked him about his work. Despite this emphasis upon *exploration,* eight of the twenty-five social workers who answered the questionnaire mentioned that *evaluation* was a function of the worker's job. This was done in terms such as assessment, evaluation, and observation in relation to the adequacy of service and the achievement of agency goals. Two examples of such responses are presented below:

Mainly he seemed to be observing, asking questions on an informal level, and I thought that he was reading records and evaluating the work of the agency.

Gathering statistical information and studying what an agency such as ours does, what its good and bad points are.

The researcher, however, is not in a marginal position simply by virtue of the fact that he is placed there by the practitioner due to his distinctive role as an evaluator. His sense of marginality may also stem from his feelings about the means and ends of science and the means and ends of social action, both of which may hold some attraction for him but may also appear to be in opposition. As Tax has said,

Our action anthropology thus gets a moral and even missionary tinge that is perhaps more important for some of us than for others.[37]

Or as Towle suggests in her discussion of the relations between social scientists and social workers (whom she refers to as "scientific missionaries"),

Today, it looks as if the social scientist, in studying the missionary, risks becoming one.[38]

Whether or not one agrees with Towle's further comment that it may be necessary for the researcher to become a "missionary" in some measure

if he is to be an understanding and hence a useful collaborator,[39]

it is not difficult to understand the internal struggle which may be created when the researcher finds himself faced with the possibility of becoming a part of that which he is studying, thereby running the risk of losing the objectivity which he has been taught to value so highly.

DENIAL AND DISPLACEMENT

Up to this point we have concentrated upon the ways in which the formal organization of a clinical agency leads to strains in the relationship between researchers and practitioners. We now want to focus upon some of the reactions that take place because of the formally induced strains. The first reaction we will discuss is that of denial and displacement, a reaction in which the researcher is not merely isolated by the practitioner, but annihilated. Such a response obviously does not lead to a better working relationship between researcher and practitioner. When we take up the informal humor that develops in the relationship between researcher and practitioner, and the formal responses to strain that may develop, we will be dealing with reactions that do lead to better working relationships between researchers and practitioners.

By denial and displacement we refer to the practitioner's refusal to take the researcher or his findings seriously; rather, attention is called to the fact that the researcher is merely projecting. Simply put, the researcher who suggests that a particular clinical practice is defective may be told that it is his own personality that is defective.[40] In this way, the practitioner may ignore the researcher, or, at the very least, he may ignore some of the remarks that the researcher makes. He therefore attempts to eliminate the strains in his relationship with the researcher by creating a situation that permits him, in a sense, to deny the role of the researcher.

It is perhaps to be expected that certain professional groups, such as psychiatrists and social workers, should resort to this type of denial and displacement. They have, after all, been especially trained to observe personality functioning, and are not nearly so well trained to observe the functioning of a social organization.

We suspect, however, that this type of response does not take place too frequently. This is fortunate, for although it may effectively protect the practitioners from the threatening researcher, it also inhibits the researcher from making any kind of contribution to the clinical agency.

Apart from the professional self-restraint and general good sense characteristic of most practitioners, one reason why this kind of response does not take place too frequently is because of the administrator-researcher tie: any outright attempt to annihilate the role of the researcher becomes an attack upon the administration.

When denial and displacement do occur, however, they need not permanently inhibit the researcher. As long as he tries to understand the sources of these defenses and does not merely react to them as though they were personal attacks he may, in the long run, enhance his relationship with the practitioner. There are, after all, many matters of common interest to researchers and practitioners, and these may override defensiveness. Practitioners, moreover, have become more interested in social factors and social scientists have become more interested in psychological and psychopathological factors, and this convergence provides a base that should enable researchers and practitioners to overcome defensiveness from either side.

ONE-WAY HUMOR

One of the most noticeable reactions to the strains between practitioners and researchers is the informal humor that may develop between them. As we have observed it, the humor is not symmetrical—most of the humorous remarks are made by the practitioner and directed toward the researcher. It is our belief that this humor reflects the ambivalence of the practitioner toward the researcher, and that its one-sidedness reflects the researcher's marginal position within the clinical agency.

One way in which the humor manifests itself is in the somewhat sarcastic, but kindly manner in which the researcher is addressed. Examples of terms of address that are used are "Doctor" (in a social work agency) and "Professor."[41] The latter term may be related to the stereotype sometimes held of the researcher as an intellectual who is far removed from the real problems of the everyday world. Other humorous remarks of a similar nature refer to the "Ivory Tower" that the researcher occupies; to the fact that he "has his head in the clouds"; or to his "high falutin' gobbledygook."[42] These all serve to emphasize the fact that the researcher is different, and they reflect his marginal position within the agency.

Other humorous remarks that are directed toward the researcher are a reflection of the different jobs that are done by the practitioner and the researcher. The following three joking remarks, for example, all devalue the writing and publishing that the researcher does:

I've got an idea—why don't we all stop working and just write.

What are you doing with your time? Just writing?

[A practitioner made an especially perceptive comment.]
RESEARCHER: Gee, that's an interesting remark!
PRACTITIONER: Why don't you write another article on that?

Another species of humorous remarks reflects the practitioner's ambivalence toward the researcher's recording. In the lunchroom one day a social worker called out loudly and jokingly to one of the writers who was sitting alone at a table,

Hey, what are you doing there? Are you taking notes on group process?

At another time, during a conversation, a social worker in the group turned to one of the writers and said,

Now I hope you're not going to go along [to the administrator] and tell him what we said.

The writer replied,

That's just what I was going to do,

and everyone laughed loudly.

These jokes seem to indicate a fear on the part of the practitioners that their activities will be reported, and also a desire to gain recognition through having their work reported. A not uncommon remark that is jokingly interjected into an informal conversation with a researcher—"Are you taking all this down?"—would seem to reflect this ambivalence very well.

Perhaps the humorous remarks that have the greatest significance, however, are those expressed by the practitioners as part of their working relationship with the researchers. In this way the practitioners can release some of their hostility in an acceptable manner, and thus be in a better position to cooperate with the researchers. For example, one of the writers received a birthday card from some practitioners who were collaborating with him that was signed, "From your resistant researchers." Practitioners have also opened a research meeting with,

Well what magnificent ideas are we going to come up with today?

and they have said, in the course of a meeting with the researcher,

Boy, this is one of my resistant mornings.

In these ways the practitioners can jokingly express a degree of hostility toward the researcher or his work without actually upsetting their relationship with the researcher.

Radcliffe-Brown has pointed to the way in which joking develops between individuals who are in an ambiguous relationship to each other,[43] and R. L. Coser has added that in a hierarchical structure humor tends to be directed downward.[44] What we are saying is that there is a tendency for the humor to be directed not downward but sideways from those who play a more central role in an organization toward those whose role is peripheral. This humor, even though it is not reciprocal, clearly serves a social, as well as a psychological, function.[45] And we might expect that as the peripheral researchers come to play a more central role in a clinical agency there will be an increase in the reciprocity of the humorous exchanges.[46]

FORMAL RESPONSES TO STRAIN

The formal structure of an organization is of course not absolutely fixed, and various kinds of formal changes can and have been made in order to minimize the strains that we have discussed. For example, the use of research consultants is one way of providing "external structural supports"[47] for the researcher who occupies a marginal position within a clinical agency. In this way the researcher spends a certain part of his time in interaction with someone who shares his viewpoint, and he can gain

the encouragement he needs to persevere in his research tasks. This kind of formal provision would seem to be an especially valuable and necessary one for the lone researcher in a clinical agency.[48]

Another formal response to the potential strains we have discussed is the appointment of a professionally trained practitioner to the researcher's role.[49] In this way there may be less mistrust and more understanding between researcher and practitioner, but such an appointment does not necessarily eliminate all problems.

Another type of formal response is the use of "research-practitioners" who have the research focus of their job clearly spelled out to them before they start work.[50] This is a typical practice where a grant has been provided for a specific research or demonstration project, and insofar as practitioners are made aware of the research aspect of their job and insofar as the job draws practitioners with an interest in research, some of the difficulties we have discussed can be eliminated. The practitioner, indeed, may be the one who originates the research and who hires the social scientists, and under such circumstances there is also a better likelihood of minimizing the strains inherent in researcher-practitioner relationships.

A final type of response, which however takes us away from this paper's major focus upon researcher-practitioner relations within a clinical agency, is the creation of a research unit within an academic, rather than a clinical, setting. Under such an arrangement the practitioners may become the marginal men. But such an arrangement does serve to provide organizational support for abandoning one's traditional clinical role, so that, for example, psychiatrists will

> modify their methods of inquiry to the special requirements of social research.[51]

It should be clear, however, that the formal strains that arise in the relationship between practitioner and researcher in a clinical agency are not dissipated by the appointment of practitioner-trained researchers or research-oriented practitioners. This is because the goals of the researcher and practitioner differ, so that in their role relationship a certain amount of strain must be expected regardless of who plays these particular roles.

The validity of our argument becomes clear when we examine those situtations in which the same person plays both the role of researcher and of practitioner. If what we have said about the strains that arise in the relationship between researcher and practitioner is correct, then one would expect to discover strains within the person who plays a dual researcher-practitioner role. In other words, one would expect to find a role-conflict situation under these circumstances, and that is exactly what has been reported in the literature.

Perry and Wynne, for example, discuss the role of the clinical researcher in a research hospital. They point out that the clinical researcher faces

> conflict between his role as therapist and his role as researcher.

The role conflict is "built into his job."[52] Barnett discusses the difficulties of being both an anthropologist-researcher and an administrator with policy-making functions,[53] and Holmberg, who was the *patrón* of a Peruvian *hacienda* and who was a researcher, too, describes the difficulties of

> playing the dual role of God and anthropologist.[54]

The most complete account of the strains that are inherent in the dual researcher-practitioner role is superbly portrayed by Fox, in her study of a group of clinical investigators and their patients.[55] The clinical investigators or research physicians had the dual responsibility of caring for patients with little-understood diseases and of conducting research upon them. Fox deals with the stresses that come from this kind of dual responsibility and with the ways in which the clinical investigators tried to cope with these stresses. It quickly becomes clear that the major factor which underlies the stresses faced by the clinical investigators is the organization of their job—the fact that they have two roles to play, and that these roles are often at variance. As one of the clinical investigators said,

> We're caught in an eternal conflict between being physician and medical researcher.[56]

SUMMARY AND CONCLUSION

The relationship between researcher and practitioner may be plagued by a variety of problems, and personality factors are often cited as the core of these problems. On the one hand we hear of the neurotic anxiety of the practitioner when he is faced with research, and on the other hand we hear of the defective personality of the researcher who projects his own problems upon the clinical agency he is studying. Personality factors are not irrelevant, but they may often mask the nature of the role relationships between researcher and practitioner. It is the nature of this role relationship within a professional agency, and the strains that stem from this role relationship, that have been the primary focus of this paper.

The organizationally-structured strains in the relationship between researcher and practitioner are too frequently overlooked. For example, there has been practically no discussion of the related questions of credit for publication and anonymity in the relationship between researcher and practitioner.[57] It is of little wonder, therefore, that the question is only rarely discussed by researcher and practitioner before and during their research collaboration, and that this often becomes one of the chronic and insidious problems in the relationship.

Other aspects of the formal role relationship of researcher and practitioner that we have discussed are the evaluating nature of the researcher's role, and his special tie to the ad-

ministrator. On account of this, the practitioner feels that his work is being assessed by someone with a vested interest in discerning errors who is also in a position to report these errors to the administrator. In addition, the researcher's primary job is tangential to the practitioner's primary job, and they organize their time very differently—thus making it all the more difficult for them to understand each other and to collaborate effectively. As a member of the staff organization of the agency, the researcher finds himself in a marginal position, and this may intensify his ties to the administrator, and therefore add to the strain in his relationship with the practitioner.

Certain reactions to the strains between researcher and practitioner—denial and displacement on the part of the practitioner, the development of a one-way humor relationship, and various changes in the formal organization—have also been discussed. From this it becomes clear that although some strain is inevitable in the relationship between researcher and practitioner, it is also possible to move toward alleviating this strain through a direct recognition of its most important source: the social organization of the clinical agency.

NOTES

1. Many different variables are involved in the relationship between researcher and practitioner. Some of them are: the specific organizational setting; the composition of the researcher-practitioner group (e.g., the disciplines represented and the number from each discipline); the relative status of the discipline and the representatives of these disciplines; the source of support for the research and for the agency's clinical program; basic or applied research; length of time of the research project and the security of employment of the project members; the nature of the research being done; differences

in value and in personality organization of the researchers and practitioners. No one that we know of has systematically pursued the association of any of these variables to differences in the nature of the researcher-practitioner relationship. The following references, however, although they focus more upon interdisciplinary research within the social sciences than upon researcher-practitioner relations, do take note of some of the variables that are involved in collaborative efforts: Gordon W. Blackwell, "Multidisciplinary Team Research," *Social Forces,* XXXIII (May, 1955), 367–374; R. Richard Wohl, "Some Observations on the Social Organization of Interdisciplinary Social Science Reserach," *Social Forces,* XXXIII (May, 1955), 374–383; Margaret Barron Luszki, "Team Research in Social Science: Major Consequences of a Growing Trend," *Human Organization,* XVI (Spring, 1957), 21–24.

2. Margaret Barron Luszki, *Interdisciplinary Team Research: Methods and Problems,* National Training Laboratories, N.E.A., Washington, D.C., 1958.

3. Cf. Ozzie G. Simmons and James A. Davis, "Interdisciplinary Collaboration in Mental Illness Research," *American Journal of Sociology,* LXIII (November, 1957), 297–303. The major barrier to collaboration pointed to by Simmons and Davis is the difference in methodological approach—some had a "clinical" and some had a "quantitative" point of view.

4. Margaret Blenkner, "Obstacles to Evaluative Research in Casework: Part I," *Social Casework,* XXXI (February, 1950), 56.

5. Howard E. Mitchell and Emily H. Mudd, "Anxieties Associated With The Conduct of Research In A Clinical Setting," *American Journal of Orthopsychiatry,* XXVII (April, 1957), 314.

6. *Ibid.,* p. 320. Young has also pointed out that among other characteristics, researchers attribute problems in their relationships with practitioners to such personality characteristics of the practitioner as arrogance, narrowmindedness, and authoritarianism. See Donald Young, "Sociology and the Practicing Profession," *American Sociological Review,* XX (December, 1955), 647.

7. Urie Bronfenbrenner and Edward C. Devereux, "Interdisciplinary Planning for Team Research on Constructive Community Behavior," *Human Relations,* V (1952), 187–203; a major interdisciplinary problem was that the team members were initially person-centered rather than task-centered.

8. Since 1950 Russell Sage Foundation has spurred the development of effective researcher-practitioner relations across many fields of social science and professional practice. For a general report of the problems and successes of this program see *Annual Report 1958–1959* and *Annual Report 1959–1960,* Russell Sage Foundation, New York; see also Ralph L. Kolodny, "Research Planning and Group Work Practice," *Mental Hygiene,* XLII (January, 1958), 121–132; Hope Leichter and Judith Lieb, " Implications of a Research Experience with Caseworkers and Clients," *Journal of Jewish Communal Service,* XXXVI (Spring, 1960), 313–321.

9. Elizabeth Herzog, *Some Guide Lines For Evaluative Research,* Children's Bureau Publication, No. 375, 1959, 79.

10. *Evaluation And Mental Health,* Public Health Service Publication No. 413, U.S. Department of Health, Education and Welfare, Washington, D.C., 1955, p. 6.

11. "The Function and Practice of Research in Social Work," Social Work Research Group, May, 1955, 28.

12. Harold L. Wilensky and Charles N. Lebeaux, *Industrial Society and Social Welfare,* Russell Sage Foundation, New York, 1958, p. 20.

13. Stephen E. Fitzgerald, "Public Relations Learns to Use Research," *Public Opinion Quarterly*, XXI (Spring, 1957), 141–146.

14. Mary Wirth, *Social Service Review*, XXXIII (March, 1959), 102. Cf. Robert C. Angell, "A Research Basis for Welfare Practice," *Social Work Journal*, XXXV (October, 1954), 145–148, 169–171.

15. Kaspar D. Naegele, "A Mental Health Project in a Boston Suburb," in Benjamin D. Paul and Walter B. Miller (eds.), *Health, Culture and Community*, Russell Sage Foundation, New York, 1955, 317.

16. Otto Pollak, "Comments," *Social Service Review*, XXX (September, 1956), 298.

17. Rudolf Ekstein and Robert S. Wallerstein, *The Teaching and Learning of Psychotherapy*, Basic Books, New York, 1958, p. 7.

18. Melville Dalton, "Conflicts Between Staff and Line Managerial Officers," *American Sociological Review*, XV (June, 1950), 342–351.

19. Stuart Adams, "Status Congruency as a Variable in Small Group Performance," *Social Forces*, XXXII (October, 1953), 16–22; George C. Homans, "Status Among Clerical Workers," *Human Organization*, XII (Spring, 1953), 5–10; Gerhard Lenski, "Social Participation and Status Crystallization," *American Sociological Review*, XXI (August, 1956), 458–464; Gerd H. Fenchel, Jack H. Monderer, and Eugene L. Hartley, "Subjective Status and the Equilibration Hypothesis," *Journal of Abnormal and Social Psychology*, XLVI (October, 1951), 476–479; Irwin W. Goffman, "Status Consistency and Preference for Change in Power Distribution," *American Sociological Review*, XXII (June, 1957), 275–281; Roland J. Pellegrin and Frederick L. Bates, "Congruity and Incongruity of Status Attributes within Occupation and Work Positions," *Social Forces*, XXXVIII (October, 1959), 23–28.

20. Cf. Joseph W. Eaton and Robert J. Weil, "Psychotherapeutic Principles in Social Research," *Psychiatry*, XIV (November, 1951), 440–441.

21. Ekstein and Wallerstein, *op. cit.*, 6.

22. In one case we know of, the only recourse left to the researchers was to shift their interest from a comparison between experimental and control patients to a study of the resistance of the practitioners to the research project.

23. Florence Hollis, *Women in Marital Conflict*, Family Service Association of America, New York, 1949, 220–221. See also Margaret Blenkner, "Obstacles to Evaluative Research in Casework: Part II," *Social Casework*, XXXI (March, 1950), 99.

24. Martin Wolins, "Comments," *Social Service Review*, XXX (September, 1956), 345; see also Margaret Blenkner, "Part II," *op. cit.*, 98.

25. F. Stuart Chapin, *Experimental Designs in Sociological Research*, Harper, New York, 1947, pp. 158–169.

26. Ekstein and Wallerstein, *op. cit.*, 74–75.

27. Eleanor Gay, "Collecting Data by Case Recording," *Social Work*, III (January, 1958), 77.

28. Some discussions which refer to differences in attitudes or values of researchers and practitioners, or which discuss researcher-practitioner relations generally are: Donald Young, "Sociology and the Practicing Professions," *American Sociological Review*, XX (December, 1955), 641–643; Robert C. Angell, *op. cit.*; R. Richard Wohl, *op. cit.*; Lawrence K. Frank, "Research for What?" *Journal of Social Issues*, Supplement Series, No. 10, 1957; Mary E. W. Goss and George G. Reader, "Collaboration Between Sociologist and Physician," *Social Problems*, IV (July, 1956), 82–89; Jurgen Ruesch, "Creation of a Multidisciplinary Team: Introducing the Social Scientist to

Psychiatric Research," *Psychosomatic Medicine,* XVIII (March–April, 1956), 105–112; Erika Chance, *Families in Treatment,* Basic Books, New York, 1959; Yngvar Løchen, "Some Experiences in Participant Observation From a Norwegian Mental Hospital Study," paper presented at Eastern Sociological Society meetings, New York, April, 1960. See also Frank L. Sweetser, "Sociology and Urban Renewal," *Alpha Kappa Deltan,* XXVIII (Winter, 1958), 42–47; W. L. Slocum, "Sociological Research for Action Agencies: Some Guides and Hazards," *Rural Sociology,* XXI (June, 1956), 196–199; Robert W. Lamson, "The Present Strains Between Science and Government," *Social Forces,* XXXIII (May, 1955), 360–367.

29. This is not altogether unlike the way in which men seem to underestimate and women to overestimate the frequency of marital coitus. See Alfred C. Kinsey *et al., Sexual Behavior in the Human Female,* W. B. Saunders, Philadelphia, 1953, p. 349.

30. Researchers and practitioners can have a very different notion of how important a job writing up the final report is. As we point out further on, practitioners occasionally belittle the writing job, as in the phrase, "just writing."

31. Another problem of publication is the issue of censorship. Do any of the practitioners or administrators within the agency have the right to censor the researchers' publications? This issue is related to other variables, such as the type of agency involved and the source of research support. See Daniel J. Levinson, "The Mental Hospital as a Research Setting: A Critical Appraisal," in Milton Greenblatt, Daniel J. Levinson, and Richard H. Williams (eds.), *The Patient and the Mental Hospital,* The Free Press, Glencoe, Illinois, 1957, p. 641.

32. Mitchell and Mudd, *op. cit.,* 312. Cf. Paul C. Agnew and Francis L. K. Hsu, "Introducing Change in a Mental Hospital," *Human Organization,* XIX (Winter, 1960–61), 195–199.

33. William D. Schmidt, *The Executive and the Board in Social Welfare,* Howard Allen, Inc., Cleveland, 1959, pp. 35–36.

34. See Daniel J. Levinson, *op. cit.,* 633–649. Writing more generally about the position of the social sciences in medicine, Jaco points out the marginality of that position by indicating that most social scientists in medical schools are situated in low-status departments such as psychiatry, preventive medicine and public health, and nursing schools: E. Gartly Jaco, "Problems and Prospects of the Social Sciences in Medical Education," *Health and Human Behavior,* I (Spring, 1960), 29–34.

35. Lenski, in his discussion of status inconsistency (the lack of status crystallization), relates it to marginality. Gerhard E. Lenski, "Status Crystallization: A Non-Vertical Dimension of Social Status," *American Sociological Review,* XIX (August, 1954), 412.

36. Cf. Donald Young, *op. cit.*

37. Sol Tax, "The Fox Project," *Human Organization,* XVII (Spring, 1958), 18.

38. Charlotte Towle, "Implications of Contemporary Human and Social Values for Selection of Social Work Students," *Social Service Review,* XXXIII (September, 1959), 262.

39. *Ibid.* Unlike Towle, Gordon feels such a development is unfortunate. Noting that circumstances have favored "the moving into social work research of (researchers) who were already well identified with the aims, objectives and values of social work and most informed about it," and have discouraged "those from entering this field whose identification with social work was neutral or possibly negative" he warns that, "researchers may have become so much like social workers in general that their capacity to

contribute to the profession has been impaired." William E. Gordon, "The Future of Social Work Research," *Social Work,* III (October, 1958), 99–106.

40. This is similar to the practice of the researcher, that we have already discussed, to attribute the difficulties in his relationships with the practitioner to the practitioner's personality. The reader interested in material related to this tendency to explain problems of social organization by focusing upon psychological factors should consult: C. Wright Mills, *The Sociological Imagination,* Oxford University Press, New York, 1959, 8–11, 186–188, *et passim;* Robert N. Rapoport, "Notes on the Disparagement of 'Sociologizing' in Collaborative Research," *Human Organization,* XVI (Spring, 1957), 14–15; Alfred H. Stanton and Morris S. Schwartz, *The Mental Hospital,* Basic Books, New York, 1954, 39; Peter M. Blau, *The Dynamics of Bureaucracy,* University of Chicago Press, Chicago, 1955, 54–55. Personalities, of course, may be defective, and we do not mean to imply otherwise. Luszki, for example, points out that "often problems resulting from the individual personality are erroneously attributed to the discipline," Margaret Barron Luszki, *Interdisciplinary Team Research: Methods and Problems, op. cit.,* 50.

41. The marginality implied here becomes apparent when one considers that the researcher is placed in the highly ambiguous position of being a doctor without patients or a professor without a class.

42. Chris Argyris, "Creating Effective Research Relationships in Organizations," *Human Organization,* XVII (Spring, 1958), 35.

43. A. R. Radcliffe-Brown, *Structure and Function in Primitive Society,* The Free Press, Glencoe, Illinois, 1952, 90–104.

44. Rose Laub Coser, "Laughter Among Colleagues," *Psychiatry,* XXIII (February, 1960), 81–95.

45. See Rose Laub Coser, "Some Social Functions of Laughter," *Human Relations,* XII (1959), 171–182.

46. A beautiful illustration of the joking within a group of research physicians is given by Fox. In at least some of the illustrations the "researcher" seems to be joking about the physician's role; in more instances, the "physician" seems to be joking about the researcher's role. And even where it is not possible to specify the direction of humor of these researcher physicians, much of the humor does nevertheless reflect, and does tend to overcome, the role conflict they face. Renée C. Fox, *Experiment Perilous,* The Free Press, Glencoe, Illinois, 1959, 63–64, 76–82.

47. Robert N. Rapoport, *op. cit.,* 15. Cf. Jurgen Ruesch, *op. cit.,* 110.

48. See *Annual Report 1958–1959* and *Annual Report 1959–1960,* Russell Sage Foundation, New York.

49. "The Function and Practice of Research in Social Work," Social Work Research Group, May, 1955; Margaret Blenkner, "Part 1" *op. cit.,* 59.

50. Emily H. Mudd, "Knowns and Unknowns in Marriage Counseling Research," *Marriage and Family Living,* XIX (February, 1957), 78.

51. Joseph W. Eaton and Robert J. Weil, *op. cit.,* 452.

52. Stewart E. Perry and Lyman C. Wynne, "Role Conflict, Role Redefinition, and Social Change in a Clinical Research Organization," *Social Forces,* XXXVIII (October, 1959), 62–65.

53. H. G. Barnett, "Anthropology as an Applied Science," *Human Organization,* XVII (Spring, 1958), 9–11.

54. Allan R. Holmberg, "The Research and Development Approach to the Study of Change," *Human Organization*, XVII (Spring, 1958), 12–16.

55. Renée C. Fox, *op. cit.*

56. *Ibid.*, 62.

57. In Luszki's summarizing report of five conferences on the problems of interdisciplinary team research, involving one hundred and seven research workers, only four lines are devoted to the question of research publication, and even these are not specific to the researcher-practitioner relationship. Margaret Barron Luszki, *Interdisciplinary Team Research: Methods and Problems, op. cit.*, 215.

6. The Politics of Evaluation in Higher Education

Ernest R. House

Recently, in connection with evaluations conducted in higher education, I have found myself in shouting matches with vice-chancellors, have had my work censored, and have heard lawsuits mentioned. I have been in so much political trouble that I have begun seeing myself as the "Kojak" of the evaluation world. As I look around, I see my colleagues in similar difficulties. I think there are common causes for these troubles, causes that lie within the structure of colleges and universities themselves.

Much program evaluation in higher education revolves around special projects, often funded by outside agencies which demand an evaluation [2]. The immediate reason for the evaluation is the external official demand and innovators often wonder why they are evaluated when traditional programs, probably worse, are not. There is a deeper reason than the tie to outside funds. Innovations of any substance almost always involve high social and economic costs to those living in the system being changed. These costs have not been calculated by economists but they are substantial and felt intuitively by those involved. Of course, there are also benefits which may be difficult to calculate.

Two types of belief systems grow out of these projects and have heavy implications for evaluation—ideologies and sagas. An *ideology* is a unified, coherent, and shared-belief system that is used to appeal to important audiences and to coalesce the project staff. Ordinarily the ideology is presented in the project proposal. Needless to say, it is absolutely indispensable in securing the project funds because it says what the sponsors want to hear.

If you look closely at the ideology, you will find it contains much the same promises for projects the world over. The project offers to individualize instruction, increase student affect toward learning, cut costs, save talent loss, be widely accepted by educators everywhere, and produce the leading project of its type. In promising individual opportunity and societal efficiency, the ideology appeals both to educators and to those who control the funds.

Now the evaluator enters and seizes upon the project goals as stated in the proposal as standards by which to judge the project. There is, of course, no way in which the project can live up to its ideology so, when the evaluation results are in, two scenarios are possible. One possibility is protracted conflict between the project staff and the evaluator in which the staff tries to

Reprinted with permission from the *Journal of Higher Education*, Vol. XLV, No. 8, November 1974, pp. 618–27. Copyright © 1974 by the Ohio State University Press.

discredit the evaluation. The other possibility is that the evaluator scales down expectations by statements to the effect that, although the project has not quite achieved its goals, it is "on its way," "getting there," or in other ways exuding a positive aura. Which scenario occurs depends on the extent to which the evaluator has been socialized into the project by personal contacts with the staff and by his estimates of how hard they are trying.

There is another belief system with which the evaluator must contend—the *saga*. Burton Clark has explicated the development of the organizational saga as a critical factor in the development of Antioch, Reed, and Swarthmore Colleges [1]. The saga is a collective understanding, a story, of the unique accomplishment of the group. As it grows historically, it becomes embellished through telling and retelling so that it is imbued with affect and sentiment and contains mythical elements. It plays an important role in helping the individual rationalize his commitment to projects as well.

As part of the saga, anecdotes develop about the genius, character, and peculiarities of the strong central figure who is the base for almost all successful projects. If the saga develops slowly enough, it has a chance to seep into the social structure and become a part of the stable relationships among people in the project. Such a saga then becomes a powerful socializing force for the new initiates and a critical factor in sustaining the project over time. In fact, if the saga does not develop, the project's influence is likely to be short-lived.

Just as the ideology is necessary to gaining initial external support, the saga is necessary in maintaining internal support.

Into this political scene comes the evaluator, concerned in the simplicity of his existence with instrumentation, sampling, and other irrelevant issues. Soon he comes face to face with the "true believers" who have devoted themselves body and soul to *their* project. It is in the nature of the saga that it be so overpowering that the outside world seems like an illusion. The believers often see themselves as the lucky few in a routine world. They *know* the project is good, that it works, and they can only look upon the evaluator with his puny data-collection devices in disdain. Infidel that he is, what can he possibly tell them that will make any difference? In short, the belief system is nearly impermeable to conflicting data.

That is not the end of the matter. Roughly corresponding to the size of the project, feelings toward it in the university are likely to be highly politicized so that any negative information about it is likely to be seized upon by political enemies and widely publicized. Data become ammunition. Similar phenomena occur in the elementary and secondary schools but in miniature. The authority structure in the lower schools does not allow as much initiative as that in higher education. The looseness of the authority structure in higher education and the accepted autonomy of the faculty makes entrepreneurism much more common. In the lower schools, initiative is more likely to reside with the administrators and entrepreneurism is both less frequent overall and more the prerogative of administrators.

In spite of fears that the program will be cut back or eliminated as a result of the evaluation, this is seldom the case in fact. Universities and colleges have little stomach for such drastic actions, although amputations have become somewhat more frequent in these tight money times. Attrition is a more likely strategy for cutting back and a project receiving a bad evaluation is more likely not to expand further than to be terminated—if the evaluation has any effect at all. Reorganization or replacement of the executive officer are possibilities in extreme cases. Although terminations are considered rather infrequently, they remain a spectre of the program staff, of course.

However, it is not only the large institutions with many projects that have these difficulties. It is significant that Clark developed the idea of the saga with Antioch, Reed, and Swarthmore—small liberal arts colleges. Recently we have been approached by two such colleges to do an evaluation. Let me discuss one situation in detail. The college is one of moderate and good reputation, but it has been losing enrollment gradually over several years. In short, like all liberal arts colleges, it is in serious financial difficulty, the trouble dating back to the time the junior-college system was expanded in this particular state.

Being in financial trouble, the president of the college goes to his board of trustees—who are wealthy and influential businessmen whom the president knows well and many of

whom he has appointed to the board—and asks the board to help raise some money for the school. The board says, "How do we know the college is worth it? We wouldn't mind soliciting money from our friends if we thought the college was uniquely worth preserving." The president and the board go into a week-long retreat to define the "unique essence" of the college. Casting about for several days, they retrieve "competency-based" instruction. After all, one can only catch what lies out there and, besides, competency-based instruction looks as if it just might be something the federal government would like to fund. But the basic idea is to give the board a unique image for the college—something they can sell.

So far so good. Now comes step 3—*somebody has to tell the faculty*—for they had not told the faculty nor the students nor anyone anything about the new college image. The dean is selected to relay the message. Whether the dean was in uniform when he went into the faculty meeting, I do not know. When he came out, he was in flames. One thing liberal arts faculties do not like is reducing liberal education to competency-based skills. Another thing they do not like is a *fait accompli*. Now the faculty must organize into committees to work out the new college program. There is trouble. There is trouble. There is trouble.

Step 4—call in the evaluators. They can evaluate and measure the competency-based instruction; provide some much needed legitimacy; and, who knows, they may even know what competency-based instruction is. Step

5—the most incredible step of all— the evaluators respond! Next year we are applying for an NSF grant to evaluate a bear trap by sticking our leg in it. What the ending of this drama will be I do not know since it is still in progress. But I suspect that not all will be "smooth sailing." If the college is successful, it will develop a unique image, a saga of its own, and survive its time of troubles. If it is not successful, it may well go under financially. The evaluation is fraught with political difficulties for it is entangled with nothing less than the continued existence of the college itself. I suspect that similar dramas are being repeated all over the country as small colleges fall into financial crises.

One of my colleagues has recently undertaken an evaluation of a well-known Eastern women's college which has been concerned about its image. Wise in the ways of the world, he has insisted in negotiations that the final report be shared with faculty and students. After considerable reluctance on the part of the administration, the college finally agreed to his terms and he proceeded to collect data. In my last letter from him, he reported that the president of the college had become very anxious about the report and was trying to squelch it before a single word had been written.

Now, even though evaluators lack prudence, they are not dumb. Many of them have experienced repeatedly the types of problems I have enumerated and have formulated responses of their own. Stake's responsive evaluation [7], Scriven's goal-free evaluation [6], Rippey's transactional evaluation [5], and the many other evaluation models all have their own way of attacking these problems. Sometimes the approach is to focus on results rather than aspirations, to describe the project rather than compare it to its goals, to respond to the project staff rather than to written documents, and so on.

One of the most sophisticated evaluation approaches is Parlett and Hamilton's "illuminative" evaluation [4]. A few years ago Parlett evaluated two innovative projects at MIT. In a typical university authority structure, Parlett reported to an education committee of the university, which had program power over the projects, and also to the chancellor's office, which had financial power. The decision to be served was to make the projects a regular part of the curriculum, to continue them as experiments, or to discontinue them altogether. True to his evaluational disposition, Parlett refused to make final judgments and decisions in his report but concentrated his effort on "illuminating" the projects as best he could and providing the committee with an information base on which *they* would make the decisions.

Recently Moffett and Herrlitz have completed a study of this particular evaluation's effect on decision-making at the university [3]. The Parlett evaluation did raise the level of discussion in the committee considerably, mainly by revealing the inner workings and problems of the projects themselves. No longer were the projects "unexplored, privileged domains" hiding behind a defensive wall of official reports which presented overly optimistic accounts of the projects' progress. For their part the projects claimed no benefit from the evaluation study, that the study had no surprises for them, and that they had already addressed themselves to the problems outlined in the evaluations. Of course, the projects had communicated none of their shortcomings to the committee previously.

The committee itself was unwilling to arrive at such a radical decision as eliminating one of the projects. In fact, after months of discussion, it arrived at a typical nondecision resolution. It communicated its concerns to the projects without coming to a decision, resulting in both projects being continued as experimental. The projects themselves withdrew their requests to become part of the regular program and adjusted to the demands of the committee without formal action on the committee's behalf. Major internal changes were made by the projects in reaction to discussions with the committee and administration but not in reaction to the evaluation itself or its results.

While the evaluation raised the level of discussion about the projects within the committee, politics involving the projects' directors, the dropout rates of the projects, financial considerations, and gossip about one of the projects (confirmed by the evaluation) seemed to be more influential in the eventual resolution of the issues than was the evaluation. The investigators concluded that the decision-making process must be seen within the "complete context of policy, politics, judgments, and information" existing *prior* to the evaluation. Interestingly, after the evaluation the committee returned to its reliance on

official project reports which had proved so inadequate in the past.

Since both projects claimed that the evaluation had no major influence on their thinking or actions and since both claimed the whole process was of no value to them, the investigators also concluded that future evaluations be addressed to the project staff. But there is good reason to wonder under what conditions such evaluations can ever be internally useful to the project staff directly.

Consider the evaluation of a high-technology project we did recently for a major university. In the beginning we decided the evaluation should be immediately useful to the project staff so we would report periodically with brief written or oral reports to the project people themselves rather than write a final report at the end of the year. We also decided we would penetrate the veil of ideology and saga by using anecdotal information gained from the participants themselves, particularly those lower in the project, such as the teachers, and thus create counter stories that would rival the anecdotes floating through the system.

Although the project staff seldom challenged the veracity of our reports and sometimes changed several overt practices based on our information, they never seemed to like very much what we were doing. As in the MIT study, the project staff claimed to know already everything we found out and to have already addressed themselves to the problems. Far from being interested in the internal information that we conveyed to them, they seemed unimpressed. I got the impression that their idea of service consisted of our documenting to an outside audience (which we never reported to except through them) their successes. When we continued to uncover what we thought was a balanced picture containing many problems (like all projects), they were unenthusiastic.

All this was a low-key prelude to the climax at the end of the year. We were asked to write a final report, which we had never intended doing. So drawing on the only materials we had at hand, we constructed a narrative of what had happened the previous year. On seeing this (by their own admission containing nothing new or that they had not seen before), the project staff grew very irritated indeed and insisted on revisions and a highly limited circulation of the report although it was only a narrative containing no overall judgments of success or failure. After some heated discussions, some revisions were made and the circulation of the report was limited—though not as much as the project staff wished. The staff had written their own final official report, of course.

A few copies of our evaluation eventually made their way into the administrative structure of the university; and since the narrative proved to be highly readable and the project of great interest to the university, it has been passed from hand to hand. Although very long, it has been widely read. The last I heard, it was crashing around through the administrative underbrush like a wild beast on the loose in the forest.

In spite of being a self-proclaimed expert on the politics of evaluation, I was somewhat surprised at the intense reaction to an evaluation which I thought balanced and which project personnel admitted to being accurate. If the evaluation had been out-and-out negative, that would have been easier to understand. But, of course, as I now understand, the evaluation *was* intensely negative from the project staff's view—negative to their own public image. They had propagated an image of great accomplishment and success. Our report confirmed the rumors circulating that the project had some problems—as indeed do all innovative projects.

I have considered at length the supreme importance for innovation of people pursuing their careers and of innovative projects serving as primary vehicles for administrative promotion and advancement [2]. What I should now add is that not only does the upwardly mobile person need a project with which to build his reputation but the project ideally must be without blemish. Within our system as it operates the *appearance* of the project is as important as the project itself. This puts the evaluator on a collision course with the project staff. No matter how balanced the evaluation report, the evaluator is certain to uncover problems.

As long as knowledge of the problems is private, their discovery is simply disagreeable to the project personnel. Making these blemishes public is to damage the administrative entrepreneur's career so that he must always face the possibility of someone uncovering an inadequacy from his past—a man with a prison record. The administrator's career, and perhaps his personality, demand perfection or its appearance. Now I realize there are administrators, even some wholly committed to their own advancement, who are able to entertain and even make public their own mistakes. But my experience is that such people are rare. The evaluator must be in political trouble when uncovering flaws in the project.

Most of these difficulties trace back to a single principle. It is a truth so terrible in import that I fear to announce it. The principle is this: the people at the top of the system are no more competent than those at the bottom. Yet the structure is a hierarchical one in which it is assumed that those at the top command more wisdom, ability, and information than those at the bottom. Achieving a position at the top depends on personal influence, fortune, and a set of credentials. It is the latter that is most susceptible to defamation by evaluation.

An excellent set of credentials is used to justify why one man gets the job over another although the real reason may lie elsewhere. Credentials are necessary to legitimizing the system. At the same time the emphasis on credentialism as a major factor in promotion means the administrator must manufacture a highly positively skewed portrait of his past accomplishments. His documentation of his past performance bears about as much relationship to his actual performance as the professor's vita bears to his contribution to his field. In both cases it is essential in the hiring process to keep out any negative information since it will be used as a pretext for awarding the position to someone else, as anyone who has ever served on a search committee knows. This effect is intensified by the fact that any number of people could do the job adequately. Maintaining the appearance of a meritocracy requires finding reasons for eliminating job contenders. What place does evaluation that produces even moderately negative findings have in such a system?

Without pursuing the principle much further, let me point out one other manifestation in higher education: the conflict between boards of higher education and individual universities and the conflict between central university administrations and lower units. Boards of higher education often contend that individual colleges and universities are unable to evaluate programs and needs within the larger context since they are too vested in their own interests. What they ingenuously do not add is that they also have their own highly vested interest in conducting the evaluations themselves.

Again within this hierarchical division of labor it is assumed that greater competence lies at the top of the system than at the bottom. Again the converse may actually be true: greater evaluation expertise lies with the individual professors, especially in large universities. However, that does not prevent the board staff from doing evaluations nor should it. I would hope that this realization would prevent board staffs from doing simplistic evaluations. The vertical division of labor prevents the overall system from acute embarassment.

Although there are many issues in

the politics of evaluation in higher education I have not touched upon, let me bring this paper to an end by citing a positive example. I have been pleasantly surprised by an evaluation system our campus has implemented and one with which I have little to do, a factor which may contribute heavily to its success. Committees of prominent faculty members are selected to evaluate whole departments and units. They are given little structure or criteria on which to proceed. They must collect their own information and discover criteria on which to base their recommendations, which are then presented to the campus administration.

In debriefing committee members we have been impressed with how well the process has worked. Being respected colleagues, the judgment of these outside scholars is usually well received by members of the department. The evaluation committees also elicit criteria and information that the department members find credible to themselves. Major disadvantages are that it takes the time of prominent scholars and that there is a suspicion that the information will not be acted upon by the administration. The professors are happy that it circumvents the arbitrary evaluations they see emanating from the central administration. I would speculate that the procedure will generate only very conservative changes. This is a new procedure, the merits of which it is too early to evaluate but which may have some promise.

Let me conclude by saying that our universities have prided themselves as places for the generation and free exchange of ideas—and indeed they are, far more than are other settings. But they are not organized to receive critical feedback about themselves, and in this they are no different than any of our other institutions.

REFERENCES

[1] Clark, Burton R. "The Organizational Saga in Higher Education," *Administrative Science Quarterly*, 17 (June, 1972).

[2] House, Ernest R. *The Politics of Educational Innovation.* Berkeley: McCutchan Publishing Corporation, [1974].

[3] Moffett, Marian and Wolfgang Herrlitz. "A Study of Evaluation Models and Decision-Making." February 1974 (Mimeo).

[4] Parlett, Malcolm and D. Hamilton. *Evaluation as Illumination: A New Approach to the Study of Innovatory Programs,* Occasional Paper 9. Edinburgh, Scotland: Centre for Research in the Educational Sciences of Edinburgh, Scotland. University of Edinburgh, October 1972.

[5] Rippey, Robert M. (ed.). *Studies in Transactional Evaluation.* Berkeley: McCutchan Publishing Corporation, 1973.

[6] Scriven, Michael. "Goal-Free Evaluation." In Ernest R. House (Ed.), *School Evaluation: The Politics and Process.* Berkeley: McCutchan Publishing Corporation, 1973.

[7] Stake, Robert E. "To Evaluate an Arts Program," *The Journal of Aesthetic Education,* Fall 1973.

7. Program Management and the Federal Evaluator

Pamela Horst, Joe N. Nay, John W. Scanlon, and Joseph S. Wholey

In 1969, The Urban Institute completed an extensive study of federal evaluation and concluded that, "The most impressive finding about the evaluation of social programs in the federal government is that substantial work in this field is almost non-existent."[1] A limited resurvey of the field in 1972 revealed a quite different picture: funds committed to evaluation had mushroomed, many studies had been completed, and the use of large-scale social experimentation was increasing.[2]

This growth in evaluation has contributed information—often imperfect, sometimes incorrect—to today's arguments about the direction, method, and purpose of social programs. Without evaluation, many arguments would have remained at the level of polemic. There is no question that the presence of program evaluation has heightened the consciousness of federal program managers and policy makers to the fact that they may, from time to time, have to respond to queries about the effectiveness of their programs.

While evaluation has firmly established itself since 1969 in both the budget and the administrative rhetoric of the federal government, there is little evidence to show that evaluation generally leads to more effective social policies or programs. On the contrary, the experience to date strongly suggests that social programs have not been as effective as expected and have not improved in performance following evaluation. This situation can be phrased as a critical management problem which we see confronting government agencies:

> Why have those in charge of programs and those who evaluate them not been able to join their efforts in a way that leads more frequently to significant improvements in program performance?

Having been able both to observe and to participate in the development of federal program evaluation, we have chosen here to raise three propositions about the root causes of the above problem. If these causes are the crucial ones and if we can come to understand their true impact, federal program management and evaluation stand on the edge of a period of increasing success. If not, and the causes of these weaknesses continue to be ignored, then evaluation, program management, the programs themselves, and those the programs are intended to serve will all continue to suffer.

This paper elaborates on why the three root causes, when they exist, block further improvement of many programs. The idea of a "preassess-ment" of program evaluability is in-

Reprinted with permission from *Public Administration Review,* Vol. 34, No. 4, July/August 1974, pp. 300–308.

troduced as one tool for improving both program management and program evaluation. We begin with a discussion of the conventional treatment of evaluation problems and then present an alternative diagnosis and prescription. Although much of the material presented is addressed to federal managers and federal evaluators, we believe the problems and solutions discussed also hold for state and local government.

APPARENT CAUSES OF EVALUATION PROBLEMS—AND AN ALTERNATIVE STATEMENT

Most reviews made to determine what causes programs and their evaluations to be ineffective include one or more of the following conclusions:[3]

Evaluations are not planned to support decision making.

The timing, format, and precision of evaluation studies are not geared to user needs.

Evaluation findings are not adequately communicated to decision makers.

Different evaluations of the same program are not comparable.

Evaluation fails to provide an accumulating, increasingly accurate body of evidence.

Evaluation studies often address unanswerable questions and produce inconclusive results.

The first three apparent causes deal with aspects of evaluation use. They occur at the interface between the producers of evaluations and the prospective users of evaluation.

The second three apparent causes deal with the methods used by the evaluators in assessing the interven-

tions of the programs in society. They occur at the interface between the producers of evaluation and the program as it exists. They concern flaws in making measurements and comparisons and in drawing conclusions.

Our experience to date in studying the management problem—namely, the lack of significant improvement in program performance—and in watching various agencies attack the apparent causes of the problem has led us to conclude that these six statements largely refer to symptoms, rather than causes. We believe that the causes of the problem may more properly be described by one or more of the following three propositions concerning the program itself:

Lack of Definition: the problem addressed, the program intervention being made, the expected direct outcome of that intervention, or the expected impact on the overall society or on the problem addressed are not sufficiently well defined to be measurable.

Lack of Clear Logic: the logic of assumptions linking expenditure of resources, the implementation of a program intervention, the immediate outcome to be caused by that intervention, and the resulting impact are not specified or understood clearly enough to permit testing them.

Lack of Management: those in charge of the program lack the motivation, understanding, ability, or authority to act on evaluation measurements and comparisons of *actual* intervention activity, *actual* outcomes, and *actual* impact.

When one or more of these three

propositions is true, both the problem (lack of significant improvement in program performance) and the six apparent causes listed earlier can easily occur. In cases where the first two propositions hold, an enormous range of possibilities will present themselves as to which measurements and comparisons to make—with no criteria for making sound choices. In cases where the last proposition holds, even exceptionally high quality evaluation is not likely to be used well, if used at all. If a program suffers from one or more of these three flaws, there is a very low probability that evaluation information useful to program improvement can be produced. Thus the program may be "unevaluable" until the flaws are corrected.

A statement that the quality and value of evaluation are strongly affected by the degree to which these three conditions exist is not a startling finding. What has not been realized or acknowledged in the past, however, is that these three factors are not the responsibility of the evaluator. While the conventional apparent causes relate to how the evaluator does his job, these latter three propositions describe an organizational environment over which the evaluator typically has little control. Evaluators, more than any other group in an agency, will appear unable to complete their work successfully when these conditions exist, regardless of how they deal with the apparent causes.

WHY THE APPARENT CAUSES ARE SUSPECT

In the past few years, we have conducted a number of federal program evaluations and helped to develop evaluation planning systems for several federal agencies. In the course of our work, we have observed many attempts to treat the six apparent causes directly by improving the use and methodology of evaluation. These attempts include policy review and dissemination panels, letting contracts for methodology development, high level reviews of evaluation plans, task forces to select better questions for evaluation, better systems for collecting data, requiring program offices to submit advance descriptions of how evaluation findings will be used, and the tightening of contract selection and monitoring procedures to increase contractor responsiveness to agency needs. In some cases, the "solution" was reorganization: centralizing previously decentralized evaluation units. Since revenue sharing, talk of decentralizing a previously centralized evaluation office has gained popularity. In this case, the headquarters office would no longer be responsible for conducting national program evaluation, but instead would go into the business of building local evaluation capability.

As these proposed solutions were implemented, however, we have continued to talk with and work with participants in the process from the assistant secretary level, through the program level, and on down to the recipients of services. We find that the management problem—that is, the lack of significant improvement of program performance—continues to exist and the same apparent causes continue to be cited, whether there are high or low quality evaluation efforts.

Improvements in programs and in delivery of effective services remain far below the levels desired or expected. If the root causes of the problem lay within the evaluation process, we believe that these correctives would be showing some degree of success. Consequently this experience led us to search for alternative explanations and, finally, to the consideration of the three conditions stated above as root causes of the problem.

The Source of the Problem

The significance of the proposed causes can best be understood by contrasting the nature of the intervention that the social programs of today attempt to make in the society at large with the principal types of program interventions attempted in the past. Many older, classical government activities involved program interventions whose nature was clearly defined and agreed upon and which were described in detail in a body of law or regulation (e.g., Social Security). The implementation of such activities was largely an act of administration of the laws and regulations. Evaluation of success or failure of the act of implementation was primarily a matter of assessing compliance with the guiding laws and regulations. Discretion was at a minimum (at least over the short term). Arguments might take place about whether *goals* were adequate, but the *details of the program intervention* were determined in advance.

In contrast, many new missions that the federal government has been called upon to undertake (e.g., lowering hard core unemployment) involve problems in which the proper program intervention mechanism is not well understood, or defined, or in some cases even known. Since in these cases no one knows exactly what detailed program intervention will be of value, greater management discretion is allowed and exercised. While in some cases research may be undertaken or experiments may be made to increase understanding, more typically a purportedly successful type of program intervention is simply put into place and an agency or bureau is charged with making it into a successful operation. In this case, evaluation is expected to report to those in charge of a program on whether the use of discretion in choosing specific program intervention techniques was successful and perhaps to suggest modifications or alternatives.

The newer program areas are characterized by uncertainty and discretion: uncertainty as to the nature of the problem and what constitutes effective strategies of intervention, and discretion in how the problem and the intervention are defined and how the intervention is implemented. These conditions make sound and rapid evaluation all the more important to effective management. Consider, however, how today's program environments can disable evaluation through three factors: lack of definition, lack of a clear logic, and lack of management.

Lack of Definition

Examination of program legislation, regulations, policy manuals, plans, and budget to determine what a program intervention is can be very deceptive. What at first seems clear often evaporates when the test of measurability is applied. The language used turns out to be ambiguous precisely where it would have to be specific in order for evaluation to be useful. Three common forms of inadequate language are: the vaporous wish, local project packaging, and how-to-do-it rule making.

The vaporous wish is the eloquent but elusive language of goals put forward for most federal programs. Exactly what are the "unemployability," "alienation," "dependency," and "community tensions" some programs desire to reduce? How would one know when a program crossed the line, successfully converting "poor quality of life" into "adequate quality of life"? Would anyone recognize "improved mental health," "improved local capability," or "revitalized institutions"? The problems addressed by social programs are almost never stated so that institutions, people, or the relevant socioeconomic conditions could be classified according to the degree to which they are afflicted with a problem. It is very hard to propose a solution to a problem that is ill-defined or undefined. How much harder it is to evaluate the success of that proposed solution.

Next, there is the project packaging language which purports to describe the intervention activity to be planted in the field and the expected outcome for those directly served by that activity. As any experienced site visitor will attest, this language is often so annoyingly imprecise that it is difficult to tell what parts of a local operation are under discussion and even harder to distinguish compliance or assess performance. For example, project characteristics prescribed in various program guidelines include: "coordinative mechanism," "integrated services," a "range of modalities," "extended career ladders," "accessibility of services," "continuity of care," "multi-disciplinary teams," "outreach capability," etc. Projects should produce "upgraded job skills," "increased cultural enrichment," "increased personal autonomy," "improved family cohesion," etc. Rarely are useful measures or norms for these activities and outcomes provided.

How-to-do-it rule making is the third kind of language that is commonly found. Here the terms are very concrete and specific. We find guidance on factors like the qualifications of project directors, the contents of affiliation agreements with other local agencies, reporting relationships, the use of consultants, and accounting practices. This guidance appears to be definite and all inclusive. Closer examination shows that it usually tells how to run the part of a project which does not deal directly with the intervention into society. Guidance for the part of the project which actually produces effects in society is not provided.

When these three forms of language predominate, the intervention activities in the field may be diverse indeed. Our experiences examining field operations indicate that program packaging is generally skin deep and that very different project activities and definitions of outcome often parade under the same assumed program names. An examination of 20 projects in the same program will often reveal 20 very different program intervention designs, different in activity and purpose. This means that the program activity and objective, as implemented in the field, cannot be defined on a common base of measurable terms. It is often difficult to find any consensus among federal level policy makers as to what the definitional base should be. This lack of a common framework can disable management and evaluation efforts alike.

It is becoming clearer that many federal social programs are simply envelopes for a large federal investment in a problem area. A program may be deceptive in the sense that it has enough content to allow it to be described in the media, lobbied into existence, and established as a federal effort—and yet the program interventions are not spelled out in any detail. Many program administrators over the last decade have essentially received a program envelope with only vaporous wishes and money inside. Although more detailed definition may not have been necessary in order to spend the money, much more detailed definition is needed to evaluate the process and outcome.

If it is decided that certain programs should be further defined, who in an agency should be responsible for the tasks? It should not be left to the auditors or to the evaluators or to the information system people, because the choice of specific measurable definitions is not merely a technical task. The definition of what is to be measured in a program is central to policy making and program management. If there are many different ways

to measure the problem a social program purports to influence, this often means that there are many different problems. For many programs, no one has yet exercised the prerogative of selecting which specific set of social ills the program is trying to cure or the methods of cure. Legislation or regulations rarely make this choice, and the choice has policy implications since it further specifies program intent and intervention. One of the major factors in shaping and directing a program is carefully selecting what the program is going to do. The failure to define measurable interventions, outcomes, and impact for a program is a major policy making defect. Those in charge of the agency and the program, rather than the evaluators, should have primary responsibility for program definitions.

Lack of a Clear Logic of Testable Assumptions

Even if the policy makers or program managers have provided measurable definitions, there still may not be unanimity within a federal social program about design or logic. As a result, different evaluation efforts are often based on *different* assumptions linking program intervention with immediate outcome and ultimate program impact. The measures and data collection instruments used are those that seem most reasonable to the evaluator. In this context it is easy to understand why evaluation findings are often noncomparable. When there is no carefully determined framework to guide the program, there is, of course, no such framework for evaluation studies. Nor is there a framework for systematically accumulating knowledge of program performance. In fact, it becomes unclear what program performance means.

Program assumptions might be as simple as that "the transfer of money to school districts will raise the reading level of disadvantaged students" or that "the training of the unemployed will lower unemployment." Often the broad program charters from the Congress referred to earlier have caused clusters of competing assumptions to grow up in many social programs. One set of assumptions may be used for arguments with friends, for instance, and another for arguments with enemies. This may be good politics, but it makes for difficult evaluation design, since evaluation design should relate to the information needed to validate, refute, or modify a set of operating assumptions.

Without an adequate description of the assumptions governing the intervention of a program into society, it is more likely that evaluators will be asked to address unanswerable questions far removed from the actual activities taking place. To take a quite reasonable example, a program office might insist on funding an evaluation to assess the relative effectiveness of different drug treatment modalities. The evaluator may then find that these modalities do not represent pure, mutually exclusive approaches which are replicated in multiple local settings. He is likely to find, on the contrary, that a "halfway house" or a "therapeutic community" in one locale bears no resemblance in operating assumptions to others which go by the same name. After spending a lot of

money, time, and effort, the evaluator will be forced to tell the agency what types of programs are really out there, rather than how successful they are, and also that the only way to test the effectiveness of alternative assumptions of treatment is to implement a program-level experiment, or introduce planned and enforced variations into the program design. Those in charge of the program may feel that the evaluator has once again failed to answer their questions. There are many examples of evaluations being mounted to answer questions which bear no relationship to the program activity actually taking place in the field. This counterproductive practice results from the failure of the agency to describe carefully the program assumptions so that they can be implemented and tested.

Summing up, even when the intervention, expected outcome, and impact are defined in measurable terms, the more subtle questions of the logic linking (a) program expenditures to production of the intervention, (b) intervention to outcome, and (c) outcome to impact on the problem must still be considered. The use of the word "logic" here is not meant to imply that the linking assumptions are loose or tight, valid or invalid, defensible or stupid. All that is implied is that a program in reality is based on an interrelated set of assumptions about what is believed to happen (and sometimes why) when money is spent and the intervention made. The absence of statements of these assumptions might be expected to cause a problem for both program managers and evaluators. The evaluators often notice the absence first, however, because they must design tests of these assumptions. Tests cannot be designed for people who are unable to, or refuse to, state their assumptions.

Once again (as with measurable definitions) the statement of the logic of testable assumptions is a policy question, not one that should be decided by the evaluators. Evaluators should test the assumptions about what works. Those in charge should make the initial assumptions underlying the funding and operation of the program.

Lack of Management

To get at the significance of lack of management, it is important to realize that evaluation is useful only if it is, in fact, a tool of management. A manager has a variety of tools to employ that include direction of his line management, planning, budgeting, audit and financial control, administration (for that part of his activity that can be clearly defined and where a law or set of rules is used to guide program implementation), policy analysis, and evaluation. Evaluation is needed principally in support of policy analysis and management discretion. Evaluation performs the same function for management that audit and control do for budgeting and that compliance checks do for administration.

One way of understanding the role of evaluation as a management tool is to explore how a "textbook manager" might use evaluation in attempts to improve program performance and then to contrast that with the way evaluation more frequently is used.

Evaluators and the "textbook man-

ager" cooperate very well. When the policy decisions about program design are to be made, the evaluator asks the manager to specify the measurable definitions, the assumptions of the program linking these definitions, what kind of performance data would cause the manager to act, and the kinds of action the manager has the authority and willingness to implement. Armed with this guidance, the evaluator estimates the level of error associated with collecting the evidence, estimates the ranges of possible findings, and bounds the cost of the proposed evaluation. The evaluator is then equipped to provide a service not commonly rendered at present. He can advise management on the cost and feasibility of procuring evaluation evidence, and the manager can weigh these factors against the potential value of evidence for improving program performance. When the evaluation is finally commissioned, the evaluator has a clear basis for judging the best level of aggregation, precision, and delivery schedule because he has a user for the proposed evaluation. Many market surveys and internal evaluations are conducted this way in industry. When this kind of rational planning occurs, one does not generate evaluation studies in search of users and uses.

The utility of social program evaluation depends at least in part upon defining the decision context as well as the program design. The "textbook manager" has already defined his program in measurable terms and has indicated what it purports to accomplish. If evaluation is to contribute to program improvement, there must be at least a few decision areas where the manager will rely on program performance feedback (measures of impact, outcome, intervention activities), as well as on political pressures, popular approaches, or his own hunches and beliefs. Else why buy evaluation at all? The "textbook manager" knows in advance and can specify what level of evidence will prompt him to act at all, or cause him to select among alternative actions. Further, he has the authority to act.

Return with us now to reality, where the typical government administrators live. These administrators participate in continual agency debate over program issues, but the debates proceed in a language which means different things to different people. The debates are not centered on a measurable set of program descriptions nor are the assumptions guiding the program intervention made clear enough to be testable. In fact, most of the people in this world will go to great lengths to keep these two things ambiguous in order to expand their area for maneuver. The administrator is a decision maker—he does take action. As in "textbook" management, many of his actions are based on guesses about what is needed, shifting academic opinions and political support, and the demands of a set of higher level policy makers subject to continual turnover. Unlike the "textbook" management, however, the typical government administrator does not establish and test assumptions linking intervention activities to program performance. Typical government administration might be called "pseudo-management," be-

cause all its management activity takes place in a process that is not linked to actual program results. In its own terms, such "pseudo-management" is good if its activities remain acceptable to an ever-changing cast of characters at the policy level.

Evaluators and pseudo-managers operate independently of one another. There is no basis for communication between them. The pseudo-manager has no real use for evaluation and the evaluator can provide few, if any, services to assist in pseudo-management. In fact, sound evaluation results may present a clear and present danger to the pseudo-manager. In this environment, the evaluator can expect his work to have minimal impact. The problem for the evaluator is to distinguish pseudo-management from textbook management. On the surface it appears to us that pseudo-management predominates in social agencies; the potential for textbook management is yet unknown.

Our emphasis on identifying actual users of evaluation and on pre-specifying the decision context and uses of evaluation information may seem excessive. Yet the desired use of evaluation information determines not only how much it is worth but also the form and accuracy that it must have. And if those in charge of a program have no use for information about that program, then there is no real way to design an adequate evaluation for them. What this might mean may be demonstrated by an example.

Assume that a federal drug treatment program for heroin abusers defines outcome success in the following terms: the client reveals absence of heroin use six months after discharge from treatment, as tested by three randomly spaced urinalyses during the follow-up period and one urinalysis at the end of the six months. Those in charge of the program say that they require information about this outcome to assist in decisions about the following: allocation of technical assistance among drug treatment projects, reallocation of funds among projects, and assignment of headquarters staff to study problems associated with achieving a desirable outcome level. But suppose those in charge are challenged to specify in advance how decisions might vary with the range of possible evaluation findings. For example, will a task force convene for program redesign if national program cure rates average 5 per cent, 15 per cent, or 50 per cent? Will technical assistance be given to projects whose average cure rate falls below 5 per cent? Is there technical assistance to give? Can projects be closed down? Will a stated national objective of a 30 per cent cure rate be adjusted downward, if the actual average cure rate found is 15 per cent? This type of dialogue would permit the evaluator to assess the potential value of evaluation information by identifying plausible and practical uses for it and also permit the evaluator to assess the specific type and accuracy of the information required.

The level of validity and reliability required in measurable data should be an important factor used in analyzing the method of collection, the cost of data collection, and the methods and cost of data analysis before data collection efforts ever begin. The "conclu-

siveness" of data only takes on meaning in relation to particular actions the data may suggest. But as we saw earlier, if everything is left ambiguous, no one will know what level of evaluation findings would or should prompt action and therefore what level of validity and reliability are required in the evaluation data. This means that, in our example, drug program evaluations which show cure rates of 2 per cent, 5 per cent, 20 per cent, 50 per cent, and 75 per cent could all be dismissed by the pseudo-managers as "inconclusive" for decision making.

When a single individual does not have the authority to take or to elaborate on the kinds of action mentioned above, those individuals whose consensus is required must be found and consulted. The point is that management of a program is a policy matter. Evaluation cannot prescribe management actions. Rather, the needs of management should define evaluations.

THE CONSEQUENCES OF EVALUATING WHEN THESE CONDITIONS EXIST

Why should the evaluator worry about the soft, unmeasurable underbelly of social program goals, objectives, and activity; about the obscure logic of program assumptions; or about whether there is a management vacuum? If our analysis is correct, weaknesses in these areas can disable an evaluation effort while making the failure appear to be the evaluator's own doing.

If the agency evaluator, alone or with a contractor, attempts to carry out an evaluation of a program where these flaws exist, our experience indicates that there are two highly likely outcomes. First, the evaluator's attempt to define the program in measurable and logical terms will flounder. No available methodology can bridge the gap between the program as implemented in the field and the program as suggested by program goal statements. Thus the results of his evaluation are likely to be labeled "inconclusive," "abstract," or "an effort to develop methodology." Second, his findings will not be responsive to the information needs of those in charge of the program. He may produce the wrong information or information that is too imprecise or too sparse. Even if the evaluation is technically unimpeachable, those in charge of the program may find it irrelevant to their decision context, seeing no way to act upon the information.

We have suggested that the definition of measurable program design and of testable assumptions about how the program works is a major policy issue which should be resolved by policy makers and program managers within the discretionary boundaries of program legislation. Program policy making is not the job of the agency evaluator, and he should not undertake the task even if it is disguised as a "technical" choice of the proper program measures needed to conduct an evaluation.

Some Sources of Leverage

Is there a strategy that evaluators can adopt to return the jobs of policy making and program management to policy makers and evaluators—and

improve the utility and yield of evaluation (and program) dollars? Fortunately, some factors in the present federal environment may supply the leverage needed to force attention to the three conditions (lack of definition, lack of clear logic, and lack of management) that have proven costly to program effectiveness and evaluation.

First, there is less naiveté about federal social programs today. More awareness exists that attacking a vague problem with an unproven social, behavioral, or economic theory is not likely to bring success. Raising issues about program definitions and assumptions is now more likely to strike a responsive chord in this climate. Secondly, the federal budget is not expanding rapidly, and the present Administration and the Congress are placing more emphasis on accountability. Third, both the Congress and citizens are pushing for more effective delivery of public services, and more evidence of effectiveness.

The evaluator, with some help from high level policy makers and program managers, may be able to take advantage of these potential sources of leverage and use them to force the definition that makes evaluation possible. At least he may assure that his efforts are expended in areas where there is the best chance of success. The tool that we recommend he employ is a "preassessment of evaluability" for every program that is a candidate for evaluation.

PREASSESSMENT OF EVALUABILITY

We recommend a process of pre-evaluation design.[4] If conducted in proper detail, this process can provide what might be called a "rapid feedback evaluation" of the present status of a program and its information base, and can make clear whether a major evaluation effort is or is not warranted. In essence, the three root causes of problems in program evaluation can be transformed into a set of criteria for determining the evaluability of a public program. These criteria are expressed in the following questions:

Are the problems, intended program interventions, anticipated outcomes, and the expected impact sufficiently well defined as to be measurable?

In the assumptions linking expenditure to implementation of intervention, intervention to the outcome anticipated, and immediate outcome to the expected impact on the problem, is the logic laid out clearly enough to be tested?

Is there anyone clearly in charge of the program? Who? What are the constraints on his ability to act? What range of actions might he reasonably take or consider as a result of various possible evaluation findings about the measures and assumptions discussed above?

In a sense the criteria are sequential. Measurable definitions form a basis for the testable assumptions. Then both serve as a basis for the consideration of the range of decisions that those in charge of the program might make as a result of information about actual costs, interventions, outcomes, and impact.

In practice the evaluator will have to judge the degree to which the three criteria are satisfied for particular programs. The evaluator generally has several programs in his agency that can be evaluated at any one time. In initial planning, the evaluator should focus on testing each program against these three criteria, using the best information available from the programs themselves to assess how valuable each program may be. This assessment should be discussed directly with policy makers and program officials. The interaction between evaluator and program officials may assist policy makers and program officials to define the measures and specify the logic of assumptions that need to be tested.

The next task is to decide which programs meet all three criteria. Then programs that meet some criteria, or almost meet all criteria, may be sorted out. Finally, in most agencies, a third group of programs will emerge which satisfy few—if any—of the three criteria.

At this point the evaluator will have completed his own preassessment of the "evaluability" of the programs of his agency. It is almost useless to explore questions of use and methodology for programs that clearly do not meet the criteria. The next and final step is both a possible source of leverage for the evaluator and a somewhat risky business in many agencies.

CLEARLY NAMING THE PROBLEM FOR OTHERS

The evaluator has now created three lists of programs: "evaluable," "potentially evaluable with further program or management definition," and "not evaluable." Since these problems are now understood to involve policy and management questions, as well as evaluation design questions, the list has two uses.

First, the evaluator should evaluate only the programs that are evaluable. He should agree to help with the definitional problems of potentially evaluable programs. But he should not hesitate to name the nature of the problem. The evaluator should tell policy makers and program managers whether their programs are or are not evaluable, and why. Second, the evaluator should bring the serious problems on the list to the attention of the top level of the agency hierarchy so they will know which programs are or are not evaluable, and why.

These actions may be very risky things to do in many agencies, but it can prevent a lot of useless evaluation attempts and later recrimination. We believe that they would force improvements in program performance as well.

NOTES

1. Joseph S. Wholey, et al., *Federal Evaluation Policy* (Washington, D.C.: The Urban Institute, 1970).

2. Garth N. Buchanan and Joseph S. Wholey, "Federal Level Evaluation," in *Evaluation*, Vol. 1, No. 1 (Fall 1972), pp. 17–22.

3. For a concise overview of the literature in which these criticisms have been put forward, see Francis G. Caro (ed.), *Readings in Evaluation Research* (New York: Russell Sage Foundation, 1971), pp. 9–15. In our own work we have had access to unpublished internal assessments of evaluation efforts by several federal agencies; the majority of these note agency dissatisfaction with their evaluation product and identify many of these apparent causes as major influences.

4. See John D. Waller and John W. Scanlon, *Urban Institute Plan for the Design of an Evaluation* (Washington, D.C.: The Urban Institute, March 1973).

8. Between the Cup and the Lip

Carol H. Weiss

Evaluation research calls for research skills plus a diverse array of talents to facilitate the use of those skills in a basically inhospitable setting. Recognition of this fact came as a result of study by Columbia University's Bureau of Applied Social Research of 10 applied research projects. Seven of the projects were funded by NIMH, three by other federal agencies. While not all of them were specifically designed as program evaluations, all but one had an immediate or prospective evaluative orientation.

Selection of the NIMH projects was based largely on two criteria: first, that the project had paid serious attention to research and second, that key staff were accessible (though not necessarily with the original agency). The three non-NIMH projects were selected by the same criteria and also because of the interesting nature of their evaluative issues or designs.

All the programs were open, community programs. All attempted to deal in innovative ways with voluntary participants. None worked with the captive populations of hospital ward or classroom.

Nevertheless, the programs exhibited great differences. Some projects received a single grant to run a demonstration project and evaluate it, other grants were given exclusively for the applied research component. The grants varied greatly in size. The agencies varied greatly, too, from long-established formal organizations to new, innovative, and in some cases chaotic structures. The evaluated project in some agencies was a minor part of the agency's operation. In others it was the major "showcase" project. The quality of the applied research, to the continued glory of the normal curve, was fairly well distributed. Two of the researches were excellent. Two were, by any criteria, very poor. We did no systematic rating of research quality, but it appeared clear that the others bunched in the middle.

Our procedure was to interview all the actors in the applied research activity—primarily project administrators, practitioners, and researchers. We also spoke with the staff who had written the original proposal for support (not always one of the present actors); former administrators, practitioners, and researchers; members of lay boards who were involved with the project and the study; consultants; staff of the parent agency; nonprofessional staff; and members of agencies that were expected to take over and continue the demonstration project.

Condensed from a report by Dr. Weiss entitled "Organizational Constraints on Evaluation Research," which was supported by contract HSM-42-69-82 from the National Institute of Mental Health.
Reprinted with permission from *Evaluation,* Vol. 1, No. 2, 1973, pp. 49–55.

On occasion, we traveled hundreds of miles to see former staff members. We read original applications, applications for renewal, progress reports, final reports (when the study was concluded), and in a few cases papers and journal articles based on the study. We reviewed data collection instruments, code books, manuals of procedure, computer print-outs, internal reports, and memoranda. In one project, we attended an interviewer briefing session. Several times we observed program sessions.

Our informants were remarkably candid. We always pledged that we would take all possible steps to safeguard the anonymity of the person and the project, but even so, we were recurrently surprised at the frankness of their reports. Many people were clearly delighted to have someone to whom to tell their problems, ambitions, grievances, satisfactions, and thwarted hopes. Inasmuch as we explored multiple perspectives on the same events, and tried to double-check as systematically as possible, we believe that we reconstructed the life histories of the projects with fair accuracy.

A number of themes clearly emerged. Applied research, and evaluation research in particular, has to coexist with a program whose commitment is to helping people. If research is necessary to satisfy the requirements for funding by a federal agency or is otherwise mandated by the funder, or if it provides extra money, possibly relevant information, and some eclat to the agency, it is acceptable—but it is operating on the program's turf. At best, research

shares the attention of administrators and staff. At worst, it is resented, misunderstood, neglected, not given the conditions it needs to survive, or sabotaged.

The following sections deal with specific constraints on evaluation. The problems are real and serious, but ingenious evaluators, to some degree or other, have surmounted them. By emphasizing the constraints under which they work, we aim to direct attention to the improvement of the conditions, and thus the caliber, of applied research.

CONFLICTING PERCEPTIONS OF EVALUATION PURPOSES

Most projects showed some uncertainty about the purposes for which the evaluation was being conducted. Although they had submitted a proposal for research that had been accepted and funded, they were not clear about whose ends the evaluation was to serve: should the evaluation be of use to the program, to NIMH, or to the development of knowledge in the field? Evaluators, administrators, and program staff often had different purposes in mind. Some program administrators and staff saw evaluation as a ritual to secure funding, others viewed it as a potential guide to adaptations that would strengthen the program during its course, still others expected evaluation to provide "program vindicators" to justify the program and help obtain further funding. Evaluators, on the other hand, tended to see their role as assessing the effectiveness of the program after the demonstration period was over so that NIMH and other agencies could decide whether to continue, adopt, or advocate it elsewhere. A few evaluators also expected to make contributions to basic knowledge (for example, the dimensions of "mental health" and their intercorrelations), but agency conflicts over research design usually thwarted such hopes.

Disagreement over purpose had several unfortunate consequences. When administrators expected "formative" evaluation to aid ongoing program development and evaluators designed "summative" studies to render judgment on the program after its conclusion, administrators lost interest and withdrew support. The evaluation was seen as irrelevant, "for NIMH," or for some mythical future application of no immediate concern. Some evaluators who tried to provide "formative" research information had doubts that administrators genuinely wanted inputs from research during the program or, if they wanted them, knew how or were able to make use of them. One research director said:

> [The project administrator] said, "Educate me," but he didn't sit still. He believed in research, he thought it should be done, but he had no understanding of how he should back it up or administer a combined service-research program. When I reported findings . . . he listened to me (I don't think he did more than glance at anything I'd written), but he didn't do anything about implementing the results.

Because of lack of clear purpose, there was sometimes rigid adherence to the original research plan, even when changes in program had made it irrelevant. Opportunities were lost for contributing useful information to

decision-makers on the program-in-process.

In summative evaluation, of course, feedback of evaluative information is undesirable because it is likely to contaminate the program. The program should remain stable and well-defined, so that it is clear what stimuli brought about the observed outcomes. But many of the programs shifted, lurched about, and sought new directions. For example, one program that started as a referral source moved into the organization of recreational activities ("art in the alleys," one worker called it). Another shifted from group counseling to promotion of family planning and a series of recreational outings. In these cases, before-after outcome data are difficult to interpret, because the definition of "the program" associated with given outcomes is not clear. A phased series of shorter-term studies might have gauged intermediate effects and produced information useful for planning later stages of the program.

Where political, community, and staff pressures were altering the course of the program willy-nilly, more decision-oriented study of the system might have been of help. In a larger sense, too, it would be useful to know how communities respond to innovative programs, what pressures are brought to bear on the agency, and how the program reacts and changes. (We have barely begun to explore how innovations can be introduced into community delivery systems without being neutralized, co-opted, or disrupted.)

Regarding the preparation of final reports, when administrators and staff expected evaluation to legitimate the program, disagreements with evaluators arose. The fear of negative findings did not influence the research design, the selection of criterion measures, or the data collection. *But after the data were in,* administrators wanted to put the rosiest interpretation on evaluative findings; evaluators fought for the integrity of their data. As most outcome results showed that the program had had indifferent success, the conflict was sometimes bitter.

The eruption of dissension at the report-writing stage suggests that the relative autonomy given to evaluators (within the limits set by program priorities) to pursue their research was motivated less by respect for the integrity of research than by unsophistication about the possible effects of evaluation. Most program personnel apparently did not seriously entertain the notion that evaluation results might show their program in an unfavorable light. As this likelihood becomes better understood, there may be more interference with the planning and conduct of evaluation research.

EVALUATION'S PLACE WITHIN THE ORGANIZATIONAL STRUCTURE

The context within which evaluation proceeds has enormous consequences for the kind and quality of results produced. In most of our cases, evaluation was subordinate to the administrator; he controlled the evaluation funds, and the researcher was dependent upon him for approval of major decisions and often minor ones as well.

Most evaluators believed it essential for administrators to play a major role in defining the purposes for research; all of them recognized administrators' responsibility for formulating program goals (whose attainment evaluation would assess); but several felt that administrators should have less control over decisions (even essentially program decisions) when these affected research design, measures, size of sample, sources of data, and so forth. In their view, administrators had made some decisions that severely hampered evaluation, not so much out of defensiveness of their program as out of sheer ignorance. Three evaluators recommended that research money should go directly to researchers and not have to be filtered through the administrative layer. They believed that fiscal control would have strengthened their hand in negotiations. However, one research director who *did* have fiscal control of research funds entered an important qualifier: that *whoever* administers the budget, the research has to cope with the program-as-operated. He thought it might be better for the director of a center (if he were a data person) to get the grant so that he could control all facets of the situation.

RELATIONSHIPS BETWEEN EVALUATORS AND PRACTITIONERS

Tensions between evaluators and administrators, as we have seen, arose from differing expectations about the purposes of evaluation and the ends it was to serve, and from conflicts over control of funds and decisions affecting research.

There were differences between evaluators and program staff, too. Previous writings on researcher-practitioner relations have alerted us to four main potential sources of conflict: (1) personality differences, (2) role differences, (3) unclarity about boundaries of responsibility and procedures for reconciling boundary disputes, and (4) resentments over differential rewards.

In our study we found very few frictions that arose from, or were attributed to, differences in personality. There were several reports of *past* "personality conflicts," but in every case the individuals who were "hard to get along with" (usually researchers, but occasionally program staff as well) had left the project. Evidently these kinds of organizations tend to resolve disruptive disputes by extruding the offending individuals.

Role differences, on the other hand, were a significant feature. As one psychiatrist noted, there is a basic difference in stance between practitioners and evaluators:

Practitioners have to believe in what they are doing; evaluators have to doubt.

This difference in professional orientation also can be seen in the individual's orientation to the project. Practitioners are committed to a project; they invest enormous amounts of time and energy and their professional reputations in its success. Evaluators are committed to the acquisition of knowledge, and their careers are dependent on producing competent research whether the project succeeds or fails; thus, they are sometimes viewed as unsympathetic and perhaps basically critical of the project to which others are devoting their lives.

In a few projects practitioners resented what they saw as unfair rewards to evaluators. One project had different pay scales that favored the evaluators and even the clerical assistants in the evaluation unit. In other places, evaluators appeared to work fewer hours and to be less "busy" (sitting alone in an office reading or writing didn't look busy). There was some annoyance, too, that evaluation reports bore only the evaluators' names; they got "all the glory when practitioners had done all the work."

The issue that most frequently precipitated conflict was the collection of data. In many projects evaluators asked practitioners to turn in records on the people who participated in the program. One researcher reported the common experience:

Clinicians at all levels and the paraprofessionals, too, resist filling out records. We couldn't devise a reward system to motivate them. They don't see the usefulness of the records for them. They see it as an accountability system checking up on them. And the records don't adequately reflect how busy they are and how hard they work. There's just no pay-off for the average clinician. They were involved in developing the record system from the very beginning, so it's not a matter of the system being imposed.

As this quotation suggests, the remedy that has often been proposed, to mitigate conflicts between evaluators and practitioners—involving program staff in the conceptualization, design, and use of the study—is not a panacea. Several evaluators took great pains to involve program staff in the study, but the expected Eden did not arrive. Sometimes the program staff who had participated in the early conferences left the agency and new uninitiated workers came in; continuing discussions were necessary.

Even more commonly, the basic differences in orientation persisted. The clinician's emphasis on service to individuals made him very sensitive to particulars, to individual differences, to the complexities of the single case. If research showed that on the average, one type of input was associated with better or poorer outcomes, he distrusted the application of such statistical generalizations; he saw his own clinical judgment as a better guide than aggregate data on crude and over-simplified measures. With this perspective, he often resisted the intrusions into his time that evaluation required.

Observers of the perennial frictions that beset applied research have suggested that conflict would be reduced if researchers and practitioners received more similar training. Thus researchers with program experience would be more aware of, and responsive to, practitioners' perspectives and needs. One project in our study provided a clue to the utility of the prescription. The research director was a former chief of the psychiatric service, the senior researcher had been director of nursing service, and a third staff member had been a nurse in the same hospital. While they were personally respected and their research project was accepted by the service staffs, they

were no longer perceived as colleagues. According to one informant, "They have leaped the fence and gone over to the other side." Although they continued to attend staff meetings and retain good personal relationships, their interests, needs, and roles were different.

Not even the best will in the world can resolve all frictions between evaluators and practitioners. Apparently some disagreement is inevitable. But as several of the projects illustrated, this need not be a serious interference when there is clarity of function and structure, avoidance of incursions on others' domains, mutual respect and negotiation, and above all, consensus on the purposes that the study is to serve.

STAFFING OF EVALUATION

The one finding of our study that previous writing in the field had not prepared us for was the tremendous instability of evaluation staffs. Part-time directors were the rule rather than the exception. Turnover in evaluation staff at all levels was phenomenal. It was not uncommon for a three-year study to have had three or four different directors and three complete turnovers in research associates. To fill in the gaps, there was heavy reliance on outside consultants. Only two projects maintained the same research staff relatively unchanged over the course of the study.

Because of sporadic contact with administrators and program staff, the part-time evaluator may not be effective in seeing that requisite research conditions are maintained. In one project, far fewer patients entered the program than had been anticipated. Accordingly, the program staff decided to admit as patients the group that had formerly been designated as controls. Because he was not on the spot, the evaluator did not have a chance to argue the case for the control group. He did not even hear about the decision until over a week had passed and the move was practically irrevocable.

One reason for part-time research direction is evidently the difficulty in attracting full-time people to short-term assignments. Most able researchers are in demand and they are unwilling to move from one short-term project to another. They prefer the security of an academic (or other institutional) affiliation, and thus are able to give the project only a limited number of hours per week.

It was also suggested that the frustrations of applied research are often so great (particularly when the research staff is small and does not provide a supportive reference group) that evaluators need to return periodically to a congenial environment for sustenance and renewal.

Turnover in evaluation staffs is probably an even greater handicap. Second-level evaluation staff were subject to many of the same stresses that afflicted directors, and in addition, had to cope with the fact that directors were part-time or being replaced. Further, they did not foresee the kind of reward from a successfully completed study (for example, professional recognition and publication) that recompenses the director. With less autonomy and usually full-time exposure to project frictions, they had less

motivation to stay with the study. High turnover meant further recruitment and selection, re-training, loss of time for the study, and duplication of work. There were significant slowdowns while new staff learned their assignments.

With changes in evaluation staff, the development of relationships with administrators and practitioners had to begin anew. It took time to build mutual trust and understanding. It sometimes took time, too, for administrators to learn new vocabularies, for example when psychologists were replaced by sociologists.

Research consultants played an unexpectedly large role in the projects. Most project applications for funding were written before there was a resident staff, and consultants usually wrote the applied research section. In a fair number of cases, when funds came through, the consultant became the research director, at least on a part-time basis. But in others, he remained a consultant on call. In one project, the consultant effectively ran the evaluation from behind the scenes through his relationship with the project administrator, who kept the titular research director on short strings.

When a research director resigned, research consultants were called in to fill the gap. They sometimes took over supervision of the evaluation on a part-time basis for weeks or even months. They sometimes helped to recruit new research staff. If a new research director came on staff who neglected some aspect of the study that was of interest to the administrator, a consultant might be given the assignment to continue that part of the work.

Two striking themes emerged regarding consultants. First, they were generally recruited through an interpersonal network. They were friends or colleagues of the administrator, usually at a university, or were referred by friends or colleagues. Their relationship with the administrator tended to be close and personal, and because they were generally persons of greater reputation than the resident research director, the administrator often relied heavily on them. Second, many of them interpreted their responsibility only partly in professional research terms. They felt an obligation, too, to support the administrator personally, and sometimes the program staff as well. A cynic might suspect that the character of the relationship was an attempt to assure continuation of a remunerative arrangement that was dependent on the whim of the administrator. However, it appears that consultants recognized the extraordinary pressures under which the projects operated and honestly attempted to help reconcile program and evaluation demands (rather than insisting on evaluation priorities) in ways that eased the strain.

CHARACTERISTICS OF THE PROGRAM

The sins of the program are often visited on the evaluation. When programs are well-conceptualized and developed, with clearly defined goals and consistent methods of work, the lot of evaluation is relatively easy. But when programs are disorganized, beset with disruptions, ineffectively designed, or poorly managed, the

evaluation falls heir to the problems of the setting.

Generally, it appears that for the evaluation to be relevant, agreement on several prior issues is essential: (1) the goals of the program, (2) the nature of program service (and any variants thereof), (3) measures that indicated the effectiveness of the program in meeting its goals, (4) methods of selection of participants and controls, (5) allocation of responsibilities for participant selection, data collection, descriptions of program input, etc., (6) procedures for resolving disagreements between program and evaluation, and above all, (7) the decisional purposes that evaluation is expected to serve. Where evaluation gets started before such issues as these are resolved, it runs the risk of having to be rethought and redone in midstream.

TIMING OF EVALUATION

Meshing the time schedules of programs and their evaluation is sometimes a problem. Evaluation usually wants to take "Time 1" (before) measures prior to the start of service activities. One project wanted to train its service staff through supervised on-the-job experience. However, the evaluators had not yet administered the Time 1 measures; they objected to "contaminating" program participants through the service given by trainee-workers. In this case, evaluation prevailed and the workers were trained on clients of another agency, which turned out to be less than satisfactory. Somewhat more "give" in the time schedule may prevent collisions of this type.

Near the end of the project, time

pressures again became acute. Analysis was rushed, much data was left unanalyzed, interrelations among sets of data went unexplored. Because many of the programs were fixed-life demonstrations, staff began looking around for other jobs. There were several instances of evaluators leaving the job before the report was completed, although in every case they managed to complete the report on some basis (as part-time staff member, consultant, or on their own time). Some of the reports were late; several were "bare-bones" analyses with little attention to the interpretation of findings for future program development.

Perhaps the major timing issue is one we have already alluded to: when the project was over, very few people were interested in the evaluation report or its implications for action. There were a few exemplary agencies (particularly those with a continuing staff and responsibility for other programs of similar type) that gave evaluation results careful study and derived what they believed were useful lessons. A few evaluators published, or planned to publish, papers of interest to a professional audience. In other projects, the matter was left in the lap of the gods—or NIMH.

USE OF EVALUATION RESULTS ELSEWHERE

When the evaluation was developed with no clear concept of who was to use the results, the report often wound up in no-man's land. There were no obvious channels (other than articles in professional journals) through which information could reach prospective users in other sites. The federal agency that funded the project was sometimes expected to disseminate results, but there was skepticism that it would.

A few administrative and program personnel reported that they referred to evaluative findings in courses they gave at universities or in training sessions for state agencies or hospitals. One agency used the evaluation document as support for its lobbying for continuation of the program by a city agency (even though the data were, at best, inconclusive regarding program success). They believed that the report was of some use in legitimating the program, but they thought that "showing the program in action would have been a better sales device." Since the program had ended, evaluation was a second-best.

Several of the studies developed findings that appear to have general interest. One illustration: a study of neighborhood mental health satellite centers found that clients tended to come in with practical problems regarding unemployment, housing, welfare, and the like rather than "mental health problems," but there was suggestive evidence that they were indeed people who had greater emotional problems than others in the neighborhood. There is room for further study and interpretation of these data, but in general, better ways should be found to move the more provocative learnings from bulky, mimeographed final reports into the public arena.

A number of people suggested that NIMH should serve as a clearinghouse. They proposed not an unselective "garbage-in-garbage-out" information system, but a careful culling of applied research results to select important and valid findings for diffusion. One person noted that regional field staff should be well apprised of past results and should pass them along to prospective applicants to prevent duplication. Conferences were also suggested as a way to transfer knowledge, because in-person communication is more effective than written materials (particularly when the materials are—as they often are—unread).

Our review suggests that, while not all of the impediments can be planned away in advance, certain basic conditions should be present before evaluation grants are made. Among the most important prerequisites are: (1) clarity of purpose for the study, (2) a well-defined and relatively stable program, (3) administrative support, and

(4) an able research staff who give a substantial proportion of time to the study.

Also, not all evaluations need be devoted to answering the summative question: How well is the program meeting its goals? While programs are developing, there is room for research on shorter-term developmental issues that engage the program staff. Applied research that is focused on pressing informational needs will stand a better chance of being usable and used. There will still be resistance, particularly from those who find the status quo a comfortable and rewarding state. But such research may be better able to attract advocates who fight for its conclusions when decisions are being made.

9. *The Need for Research on the Communication of Research Results*

Floyd Mann and Rensis Likert

Research on problems of human relations differs from research in most other fields of science in a very important respect. In most fields of science it is not necessary for administrators or executives to have a comprehensive understanding of the research in order to utilize the results. All that has to be known is that the research has yielded a better method or a better product. Approval to substitute the new for the old can then be given. But in the field of human relations, effective use of the research findings cannot be obtained merely by an executive issuing an order.

Administrators must thoroughly understand the results of human relations research and their implications if their organizations are to use them. This requires both an intellectual understanding and an incorporation of the results into the administrator's attitudinal structure and behavioral patterns.

Research in human relations, therefore, requires a dual approach. First, studies need to be made of the dynamics of social organization; and second, research needs to be done on how the findings of such studies can be communicated so as to produce the required changes in attitudes and habits. The necessity of doing research on both human relations and organizational structure as well as on how to communicate the results of such research has been recognized in the Survey Research Center's long-range program of research on the fundamental problems of organizing human behavior.[1] This program has two dis-

This paper summarizes briefly some of the exploratory work being done at the Survey Research Center on the problems of communicating research findings. The general theory and the specific procedures on which this exploratory study has been done have been the product of the thinking of a number of persons both at the Center and in The Detroit Edison Company where the work was done. Everett Reimer, Frances Fielder and Theodore Hariton of the Center, and S. F. Leahy, Blair Swartz, Robert Schwab, and John Sparling of the Company all made important contributions to this study. The work of the members of the Research Center for Group Dynamics and the Tavistock Institute of Human Relations has also been drawn on heavily. The Survey Research Center and the Research Center for Group Dynamics are divisions of the Institute for Social Research.

The work reported here is one of a number of studies being done by the Center under its long-range program of research in human relations in organization. Both The Detroit Edison Company and the Office of Naval Research contributed to the support of this particular company-wide study.

Reproduced by permission of the Society for Applied Anthropology from *Human Organization*, Vol. 11, No. 4, 1952.

tinct phases. The first consists of the discovery of the factors associated with a high level of group motivation, productivity, and individual satisfaction in group situations. The second phase of the program calls for the translation of these findings into the every-day operation of organization in order to test their nature further and to discover the most effective procedures and principles for utilizing them.

During the first half of 1948, an extensive body of data was collected in The Detroit Edison Company through a company-wide study of employee and supervisory attitudes and opinions. The main objectives of this study were:

1. To determine what satisfactions employees engaged in a wide range of occupations, and supervisors at all levels, obtain from their work situations.

2. To determine the interrelationship between the supervisory or managerial philosophies and behavior on the one hand, and the attitudes and behavior of subordinate supervisors and employees on the other.

3. To study the relationship between organizational structure and interpersonal relations.

4. To explore different techniques for communicating findings from human relations research and for translating research findings into administrative action. (This article summarizes some of our exploratory findings concerning this fourth objective.)

In attempting to discover the best techniques for the effective communication of research findings, we made use of a number of psychological and sociological principles concerning motivation, attitude and behavior change, and group structure.

From the very beginning of the study we endeavored to apply the principles of participation. For example, we involved in study planning all persons who would many months later have the major responsibility for making administrative use of the survey findings. This was done in a number of different ways and with varying intensity at different levels within the organization. Since the top executives would have a greater voice in the way the findings were utilized than supervisors at intermediate levels, we devoted more effort to involving top management than intermediate management. Some of the specific procedures used at this stage were: (a) individual conferences with members of top management to learn what they felt their major problems were, and on which they would like data from the study, and (b) chains of conferences starting at the top of the organization and going on down to the employees, explaining the purposes of the study, answering any questions which might be raised about the whole project, and asking for suggestions as to what should be included in the study. Throughout the whole project—during both the collection and the analysis-interpretation phases—steps were taken to keep company personnel informed as to what was going on and what would be happening next.

In many research projects a real effort is often made at the outset to secure widespread participation. The need for clearly defining the specific objectives of the study frequently accomplishes this indirectly. More often than not, however, as the study progresses, less and less attention is paid to participation. Efforts at joint consideration usually cease by the time the study reaches the analysis-interpretation phase. Thus at the end of the usual study, the traditional form of consultant-client relationship is firmly established and the researchers place a weighty volume, including the complete analysis and extensive recommendations, in the hands of those who were interested in the research.

Instead of allowing participation to decrease as the study progressed, not only did we attempt to keep employees and supervisors at all levels—and especially top management—involved, but we increased the involvement during the analysis-interpretation phase as much as possible. For example, we did not write any reports containing a set of recommendations based solely on *our* analysis of the data. We recognized that company executives, supervisors, and employees at all levels possessed knowledge of the company's operation and history which would have to be focused on the data if the most adequate interpretation was to be obtained. Our procedure was to present the data showing the attitudes of employees and the practices of supervisors and to ask the men concerned with each set of data to help us study them and interpret them with us. We, of course, did not wait to look at the data until we sat down with company personnel, but studied them carefully in advance in order that our thinking in these meetings could be as

constructive as possible. Often company officers also studied the data prior to the meeting.

THE PROCESS OF PRESENTING THE FINDINGS

The specific process which we have used in involving the total structure—from top management down to the employee—in the analysis of the survey findings developed in the following way:

As the initial data for the organization as a whole became available, members of the Survey Research Center and members of the Company's personnel staff met to review the over-all figures and to plan in general what the first steps should be in getting the findings of the survey back into the Company. The members of this group agreed that if the data were to be put to use it would have to be done by the line—not the staff—organization and that data should be introduced at the top and not into the middle of the structure.

The data for the Company as a whole and for a few major departments were then discussed with the two top officers of the Company—the president and the executive vice-president. These two men were asked to help interpret the data and to help plan a program for a gradual introduction of the survey findings into the Company. At this meeting—after a lengthy discussion about the tentative meaning of the data and the possible next steps—it was agreed that a series of meetings should be held to present to small groups of top officers the survey findings for their departments. It was also agreed that the meetings with these officers should include the president and executive vice-president, as well as the major executives for whose departments the data were being presented. Representatives from the Survey Research Center and the Company's Personnel Department were also included in the meeting.

When these meetings were held, the data presented provided a comparison between the attitudes of the employees in the departments being considered and the Company as a whole. Large charts were used to show how the attitudes of all employees in the Company compared with the attitudes of the employees in the specific departments for which the major executives attending the meeting were responsible. Only departments having employees whose attitudes might be expected to be comparable were examined in a given meeting.

In these meetings the executives were asked to help us interpret the data and to decide what further analyses of the data should be made to help them in formulating plans for constructive administrative actions. They participated not only in exploring the meaning of the data but also in planning the next steps for the introduction of the over-all findings to the next lower level of management. Through these group discussions it was usually decided that the results for each major executive group and the data for each department within each executive group should be taken to the department heads for further joint planning and analysis.

One or two planning sessions were held with each major executive before these group meetings with his de-

partment heads were undertaken. In these planning sessions, tentative objectives of these future meetings with the department heads were considered, and technical questions concerning the procedures used in collecting and processing the data were discussed fully so that the executive could present and discuss all but the most detailed technical questions concerning the data. The objective of these planning sessions was to equip the executive who was calling the meeting to handle his meeting without assistance from the staff of the Survey Research Center or the personnel staff of the Company.

Each executive then met with his department heads to examine the survey findings, which were analyzed by departments. The same general joint analyzing and planning session was then gone through by this group as had occurred in the meetings with the president and executive vice-president.

In subsequent meetings each department head in turn held meetings with his division heads. For these meetings the survey data were available, analyzed by divisions and even sections. This process has been repeated right on down to the first-line supervisor and in some instances to the employees in his work group.

OBSERVATIONS CONCERNING
THIS PROCESS

Our experiences in these meetings—some 200 of them—have suggested factors which we believe are important for securing maximum acceptance and utilization of survey results in any operating organization.

Some of the major points emerging are:

1. A High Degree of Participation and Personal Involvement Is Important

Personal involvement not only decreases the barriers to the utilization of data; it increases the probability that the results will be understood and emotionally accepted. It also yields positive motivation to apply the results.

The series of meetings we have just described are consistent with motivational theory on several counts. The process consists of involving, through participation in research planning and analysis, the total line structure from top management down to the employees. The involvement of all individuals and groups who are likely to be affected by the findings must *start* at the very beginning of the project and *increase* as the project reaches the analysis stages. To wait until research results are available before attempting to secure participation is likely to lead to rejection of the results.

A high degree of personal involvement in the analysis and interpretation was obtained through having each supervisor who was engaged in any managerial or supervisory activity participate in two kinds of meetings. First, there was one or more meetings in which he participated as a subordinate with his associates and under the leadership of his chief, and secondly, there was one or more meetings where he participated as the chief of his group and conducted the meeting with his own immediate subordinates. This latter compelled him to be familiar enough with the techniques used in the collection of the data and the over-all results so that he would have a good understanding of it.

In many instances, as managers and supervisors participated in the analysis, they gained simultaneously a new awareness of the importance of the human problems of management, and a feeling of responsibility for initiating constructive action to solve such problems. They also tended to gain through discussions with their superiors and subordinates a somewhat better idea of what they could do to help solve these problems.

It is important to note that part of the personal involvement achieved was obtained from following a procedure which differs substantially from that often used by the outside expert who has a fund of information available. Instead of assuming the role of outside experts and telling company officers and executives what to do, we *asked* persons at all levels of management to *help us* analyze the data. We recognized that their knowledge of company operations made them experts whose help we needed to interpret the data adequately. This action thus made the interpretations which emerged theirs rather than ours.

2. Group Forces Are Important in Facilitating Attitude Changes and Redefinitions of Situations

The procedure employed here involved working with groups rather than with individuals alone. Lewin[2] and his students[3] have emphasized the power of the interacting forces exerted by group members on one another. Participation in group discussions and group decisions concerning future action sets into motion pressures for action which are more effective than when individuals alone are concerned. Through working with groups we attempted to make use of these continuing group forces.

We found that the group situation seemed to be important for several reasons:

a. Through group discussions the findings could be examined in a broader perspective because the group brought to the data experience that was richer and more varied than that of any one individual. The research data stimulated discussion which tended to bring into the open the relevant information each member of the group had about a specific problem and its causes. Often important information or unrecognized problems, which some members of the group had long known, were in this way brought into focus and dealt with constructively.

b. Group discussions, by allowing the pooling and exchange of this wider range of information, also provided the psychological situation in which superiors and subordinates at all levels could discuss possible solutions and thus give each other new and improved ways of not only viewing, but also of solving their problems.

c. The discussion of the research data by groups compelled all members of the group to recognize openly the existence of the problems revealed by the data. Important and serious problems which had long been bothersome were brought to light in an atmosphere and relationship which led to constructive attempts to solve them.

d. Group discussions also helped

supervisors at all levels—especially the new group members in organizational families—to learn what was expected of them by the group concerning their relationship with subordinates, associates and their own chief.

e. Group decisions concerning the next steps put powerful pressure, in the form of reciprocal expectations, on each member to carry out the decisions agreed to by the group.

It is important to note that in many instances these groups were considering problems of inter-personal and inter-group relations which had been disturbed for some time and which were emotionally loaded. Problems, which had been avoided because they were extremely difficult, were frequently brought out in the open by data. The objective impartiality of the findings helped the members of the group to approach these problems in a constructive problem-solving way. This body of evidence, therefore, provided each superior and his immediate subordinates with a chance to assess their organization's long and short suits in human relations skills. Employees' attitudes and feelings came to be facts, not things to be disregarded because they appeared to be too difficult to handle or did not clamor for immediate attention.

3. It Is Important to Recognize the Hierarchical Structure of an Organization; It Is Also Essential to Understand and Utilize the Power Structure as Perceived by the Members of the Organization

The sequence of meetings described above is consistent with what is known about the sociological and psychological implications of the hierarchical structure of American business organizations. Our data showed how different persons in the organization perceived the power roles of other persons in the line and in staff groups. As a rule, the particular set of managerial practices and beliefs found within a department—the managerial culture of an organizational unit—was determined primarily by the line rather than the staff. Moreover, the people at the top of each organizational unit—particularly if they were perceived as competent and powerful—were found to exercise more influence on the organization than any other persons within it. In addition to carrying out direct orders, their subordinates also endeavored to do what they felt their superior desired, even on matters on which he had made no specific request. For these reasons, the series of meetings were started at the top of the line organization and worked down. We found that in those departments where the people at the top took a genuine interest in the findings, studied them and tried to apply them, that the data were discussed more adequately and used more constructively in working out action steps than where such interest was lacking. If the immediate line supervisor evidenced a concern about developing a better understanding of human relations problems, so did his subordinates. Higher levels of line management, by taking an interest in the factors affecting the morale of the non-supervisor employees, thus in a sense changed the environment within which supervisors at lower levels operated.

It is important to mention that these sequences of meetings moved at different rates and developed in different ways in different departments. The flexibility of the general procedure was such that it could be geared to the operating problems and the psychological atmosphere which varied from department to department. We found that each supervisor in analyzing the data with his own group gave special emphasis to three or four specific points which seemed the most crucial to the problems that his group was facing. We also found that these groups did not dwell at length on those aspects of the survey findings which indicated where they were doing a good job but, after taking account of their assets, moved rather quickly to a consideration of their problems.

We found that the chain of accountability which we had expected would become operative through the structuring of meetings with organizational families—that is, the supervisor and his subordinates considering the survey findings together—was not sufficient to result in the maximum utilization of data. At the outset, we assumed that as the sequence of meetings moved down the structure, and different groups considered the findings and came to some tentative conclusions and proposals for action, that these results would be reported back up to the higher levels which had already considered the data. We found this did not happen unless specific meetings were scheduled for this reporting back up the structure. The survey findings were much more fully utilized in those departments where the sequence of meetings was organized so that as the findings and discussions worked down the organization, the results on action taken were reported back up, than in those departments where the process went but one way—down. When top management was sufficiently interested to want to know how the results were interpreted and what action was taken, supervisors at lower levels were motivated to use the research results more effectively.

4. Participation in the Form of Self-Analysis Is More Likely to Be Followed by Changes Than if the Analysis Is Made by an Outsider

Like most of the other points we have made in this paper, this point and the specific procedures we used to implement this point are not new. Clinical psychologists are well aware of the importance of self-analysis for bringing about change.[4]

Some of the factors we have found to be particularly important are as follows:

a. Objective survey data facilitate thorough and critical self-evaluations. The discussions concerning the problems of a particular organizational family were started from and centered around objective measurements about the situation. This resulted in keeping the discussions in a more objective and problem-solving atmosphere than if the group had been considering less accurately based information. There were relatively few statements or interpretations made by the outsiders to which an individual or a group could take exception. At times the accuracy of some of the data was questioned, but an examination of other relevant information led with few exceptions to

a recognition that the results were substantially correct.

b. The researcher can, by maintaining his role as researcher and being careful not to be drawn into the expert role, sidestep many of the individual and group protective mechanisms which are set into action during any real evaluation of the self or the organization in which the self is deeply involved. In the group of meetings we described no outside expert told any person what the data meant or what their problems were. The interpretations were worked out by the members of the groups themselves, with the Survey Research Center representative present to answer technical questions which the group leader could not answer about the data, their limitations, or the survey methods used in collecting the findings. The Center representative also answered questions on what additional tabulations and analyses could be prepared if the group was interested in getting further information. The researcher did not take the role of expert and make interpretations. As indicated earlier, he did sometimes ask questions for his own information and occasionally to focus attention on a specific problem area.

c. Timing and pacing is important in facilitating the acceptance of the data and gaining recognition of the need to act upon them. In those situations in which the survey results were quite different from what had been expected, we found it was necessary to proceed very cautiously—preferably letting the individuals who were surprised set the tempo. This meant letting the group pace itself in the speed with which it considered the different aspects of the findings, and also in determining the depth to which the analysis and interpretation of the data would go at any one meeting. These two factors were important in that they tended to reduce the number of times that resistances arose because the group members were not yet prepared to understand or ready to accept certain findings as facts.

d. It is important that the results be presented in a positive atmosphere. Every survey yields data showing that there are many excellent points about a given operation, as well as results indicating where certain things can be improved. It is useful to emphasize first the results which show what is being done well. Even when results are being presented on where the operation can be improved, it is important that the discussion be oriented toward what the data suggest are ways to improve the operation. Emphasis on the possible *means* of improving enlists interest and consideration, while concentration on weaknesses or failures produces an avoidance reaction.

e. Arbitrary insistence that the data are accurate, which is an implicit demand that the other individual make an immediate redefinition of the situation, only serves to increase the emotional resistance and the amount of time ultimately required before the findings are accepted and utilized. Examination of other relevant evidence was often helpful. We also found it best to give the individual ways to save face—let him explore all of the different possible meanings which the findings might be assumed to have—before going ahead. One of the most important things that an outsider can effectively do is to provide the individual with the motivation to reexamine his psychological field and see if there are not even better interpretations to the perceptual clues he has been getting and piecing together in a particular pattern which satisfies him.

f. Presenting the results in simple non-technical language and in graphical presentation form is also important. Use of easily understood materials facilitates self-analysis by making the group realize that the data deal with its situation and are not something belonging to the research organization.

In closing we would like to underline our conviction that effective human relations research in everyday organizational situations requires skills in interpersonal relations on the part of social science research teams. From the work we have done so far, it also appears that the interpersonal skills required to do research successfully in ongoing, operating organizations are based on the same fundamental principles as those required in communicating to others the results of human relations research. It is, therefore, our judgment that research on these principles is an essential part of any program of research on human relations.

NOTES

1. Likert, Rensis. "A Program of Research on the Fundamental Problems of Organizing Human Behavior." Survey Research Center publication, 1947.

2. Lewin, Kurt. "Group Decision and Social Change." In Newcomb and Hartley: *Readings in Social Psychology.* New York: Holt and Company, 1947; and Lewin, Kurt. *Resolving Social Conflicts.* New York: Harper and Brothers, 1948.

3. Festinger, Leon, et al. *Theory and Experiment in Social Communication.* Research Center for Group Dynamics, 1950.

4. Rogers, Carl. *Counseling and Psychotherapy.* Boston: Houghton Mifflin, 1942.

PART III
METHODOLOGICAL ISSUES:
MEASUREMENT AND DESIGN

Use of the scientific method in obtaining information distinguishes evaluative research from general evaluation processes. The basic methodological principles that apply to evaluative research are the same as those used in traditional scientific inquiry. The situations with which the evaluative researcher is confronted, however, are such that the methods of social research must be applied in specialized fashion. The papers in this section are addressed to the methodological issues posed by evaluative research.

Greenberg offers a thorough and balanced presentation of the essentials of evaluation methodology, with emphasis on application to public health problems. Particularly valuable is his treatment of the various levels of evaluation, ranging from measures of ultimate objectives to measures of inputs and program operations.

It is reasonable that evaluative research should be structured so that its conclusions are unbiased. Lerman claims that much evaluative research in the delinquency treatment field has been designed in ways that exaggerate actual program effectiveness. Some programs are successful only because they can be selective in accepting clients, and only those who complete treatments are considered for evaluation purposes. Lerman argues, then, that in evaluative research the population studied should include those who drop out or are pushed out of programs.

Campbell recognizes that because social reform programs are conducted in a political arena, honest evaluation is often impossible. Yet, situations arise in which administrators have a serious interest in evaluative research and are in a position to structure programs so that evaluative research can be conducted. He suggests a number of ingenious ways in which experimental designs can be adapted for evaluation purposes. Particularly valuable are his recommendations for the use of time series data.

The challenge of applying evaluative research methods to complex, large-scale programs is addressed by Freeman and Sherwood. Citing their early experiences with Boston's antipoverty program, they point out that in spite of serious obstacles, subjects sometimes can be randomly assigned to nontreatment or alternate treatment groups. In addition to concerning himself with program effectiveness, the evaluative researcher must deal with the efficiency of programs and their accountability, that is, the manner in which programs are actually implemented. Exposure of subjects to multiple programs is identified as a particularly difficult problem for evaluative researchers who are asked to sort out the effects of individual programs.

Because creative practitioners will take innovative programs in unanticipated directions, Deutscher warns against basing evaluations on the official goals expressed in program statements. So that they learn what is actually intended, Deutscher advises evaluators to interact extensively with policy makers and practitioners. He recommends process analysis through participant observation as a way of finding out what is actually attempted and of identifying likely unintended results.

Controlled experiments are the most powerful devices available for evaluative research; yet, they are politically and administratively difficult to utilize in the context of an action program. Rossi urges that this additional dilemma be dealt with through a two-phased strategy. Correlational designs should be used first for rough screening. Experimental research then should be conducted on the more promising programs.

10. Evaluation of Social Programs

B. G. Greenberg

1. INTRODUCTION

Governmental programs which provide social and educational services to the public are generally costly in terms of money and manpower. Public administrators of such programs have the responsibility to account for their accomplishments not only because of the scarcity of these resources but the sometimes dreadful consequences which can result to the people from poorly administered services. In health, educational, and welfare activities the damage caused by inadequate service is often irreversible. It may be too late for the victims of poorly designed or inefficiently administered programs to have deficiencies corrected at a subsequent date. Public accountability requires advance planning such that, for the resources available, the best possible program is implemented at the outset both in design and performance.

The procedure by which programs are studied to ascertain their effectiveness in the fulfillment of goals is referred to as evaluation. It is the kind of follow-up one takes for granted in a field like medicine. One would not look with favor upon the physician who failed to prescribe the correct medication for the given specific ailment or who was lax in determining the merits of this therapy. Therein lies the crux of the problem of evaluation—follow-up of therapy pursuant to a correct diagnosis.

Although evaluation is defined as measurement of accomplishment with respect to a program's particular target, meaningful study of this scoring operation requires a look at the whole process of social programming. Programming starts much before establishment of the goals which are later evaluated. It would be a sterile exercise in statistical methodology to single out one discrete process, called evaluation, and to study it without considering the framework within which it is embedded.

To what avail is the result of program evaluation if wrong targets had been chosen at the outset of the service?

In statistical terms, this is equivalent to asking, "To what avail is the result of complex multivariate analysis if the basic data were invalid or the wrong variables had been chosen for study"?

Both situations might be statistically valid from a methodological point of view but meaningless to the community of persons interested in application of the results. In the present paper brief mention will be made as to how statistical methods can be used to study the whole range of prob-

This investigation was supported (in part) by Public Health Service Fellowship 1-F3-GM37,750 from the National Institute of General Medical Sciences.

Reprinted with permission from *Review of the International Statistical Institute,* Vol. 36, No. 3, 1968, pp. 260–277.

lems that occur in social programming. The emphasis devoted to evaluation as a special tool will then fit into its proper place rather than overshadow other important phases of the programming operation.

To illustrate the process in programming, reference will be made to programs in public health and medicine. The principles involved are generic and transference to other fields should be relatively simple.

2. STATISTICAL METHODS IN PROGRAMMING

The programming operation consists roughly of five stages listed below and described thereafter in limited detail.

1. Measurement of need through community diagnosis.
2. Program design and setting of goals.
3. Measurement of service.
4. Evaluation of goal fulfillment.
5. Cost-benefit analyses and other input-output studies.

Phase 1. Diagnosis

A public program is provided because there is felt need for the services rendered. Such need might be taken for granted because of tradition at the time government is instituted (e.g. education and police protection), or the need established as a result of new demands by the public and/or interested groups. Regardless of the origin, it behooves the public official to design the program purposefully by measuring the needs in the community. This measurement process in public health is termed *community diagnosis*. [1]

The process of diagnosis involves the compilation of a community profile in as complete and precise a manner as possible. Thus, in estimating the need for a family planning or counselling program in the community, study should be made of fertility patterns, family size, birth rates, death rates, marriages, and hospital admissions for abortion and complications of abortion. In addition, surveys should be made regarding the knowledge, attitudes, and practices of family planning. This is by no means an all-inclusive listing of variables that need to be studied. The important thing is to study these indices in different geographic and demographic units that can be readily identified to learn where the need is concentrated.

Foolish would be the administrator who inaugurated a family planning service for the distribution of intrauterine devices, say, where the knowledge and attitudes of the group were not appropriate to the use of these contraceptive methods. It would take him up to the time of evaluation to realize that a more meaningful objective in such circumstances would probably have been an education campaign among school children to prepare them to accept the use of these methods.

The sources of information used in compiling the community profile include: routine statistical data obtained by registration procedures (e.g. birth, death, and marriage certificates); morbidity reports; censuses and other demographic studies; special surveys of the population for knowledge, attitudes, and behavior patterns: surveys of special groups (doctors, hospitals, insurance companies) and other sources containing information about social and economic factors.

To establish a community diagnosis of needs, some standards or norms must be available. The physician strongly suspects an individual's blood pressure is abnormal because there is available to him data on what supposedly normal, healthy individuals manifest on this characteristic. Lacking norms in community diagnosis, arbitrary rules have to be introduced to decide, say, that the death rate from a disease is too great, or that the illiteracy rate is too high. These rules (or lack of rules) call into play more subjectivity and personal judgment than when accepted standards exist.

To overcome the usual objection to arbitrary judgments, let us go back and consider how or when an individual is judged to be sick.

Initially, we might agree that a person is ill when he cannot continue to perform efficiently his usual role or occupation. This concept of change in role performance does nothing for the person born blind, deaf, or otherwise congenitally malformed. So, we enlarge the category of illness by allowing for the individual who differs physically or mentally from 95 per cent, 99 per cent, or 99.9 per cent of the remainder of his appropriate group. whether the figure of tolerance is 95 per cent or 99.9 per cent is arbitrary and is dependent upon the severity of the disease and what one is going to do about it. For high blood pressure, we might be willing to call an individual deviant if he falls into the upper 5 per cent group. For blindness, we might employ only the upper 1 per cent or 2 per cent with regard to loss of vision.

Both of these rules for diagnosing illness, viz. change in role performance and deviation from central tendency, involve an arbitrary element in their definition.

How does this information help us in community diagnosis?

First of all, we need to recognize that an arbitrary norm or standard may not be any less useful or functional merely because of its subjectivity. The level at which a death rate is tolerable (provided one accepts the notion of non-immortality) may not be scientifically and objectively deduced but any relatively low figure can be valuable by serving as a target at which to aim. Fortunately, there is in most fields a body of empirical knowledge available to help in setting realistic goals from a study of the community profile. For instance, if some other community has succeeded in achieving a given level, evidence exists that a goal at that level is attainable. Similarly, the presence or absence of a condition in individuals leads one to assume that perhaps the entire community (or 98 per cent, or 95 per cent) can achieve this same desirable state.

At any rate, one must accept the fact that diagnosis is based upon norms and standards which are subjective. Moreover, these standards are used as a basis for establishing goals and this process is discussed in the next stage of programming.

Phase 2. Program Design and Objectives

Based upon the statistical information collected for the community profile in diagnosis, a program should be designed with specific aims and targets such as the reduction of a death rate to a given level or the vaccination of p per cent of the population. The setting of goals gives direction to evaluation and is more important from a statistical point of view than the detailed plans for rendering the service. There are two problems that arise in choosing program goals.

a) Should the goal or objective be one which is attainable within one year, five years, or twenty-five years?

Using the family planning program once more as an illustration, should the purpose be to attain long-range population stability, a lower birth rate, or simply the immediate widespread use of recommended contraceptive devices?

In certain social and economic planning, the custom has developed to operate within a so-called five-year plan. This has real merit on one hand but its universal use tends to defer answering unequivocally the evaluation question for a period of five years.

A suggested way of examining the advantages and disadvantages of using in evaluation immediate, intermediate, and long-range goals will be discussed in Phase 4, Evaluative Activities. Further discussion will be deferred until then.

b) Having selected a particular set of time-dependent goals, there still remains a degree of arbitrariness with respect to the level stipulated, as discussed in the preceding phase on diagnosis.

How low is low?

Should a nation strive for a popula-

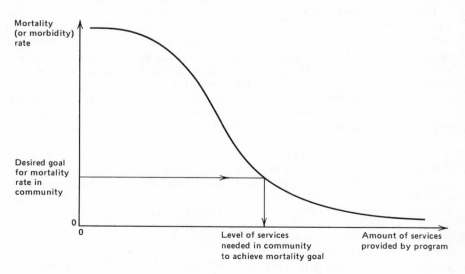

FIG. 1. A hypothetical dosage-response relationship curve depicting how the arbitrary selection of a desired mortality rate can be converted into program needs.

tion growth rate of 1 per cent, 2 per cent, or 4 per cent per year?

Should the annual death rate from tuberculosis be lowered to 100, 10, or 0 per 100,000 persons?

In addition to the points mentioned previously, it is helpful for the administrator in choosing a level to envision the relationship that probably exists between amount of services and resultant benefits. This may be expressed in the form of a dosage-response curve such as the one shown in Figure 1. In this hypothetical formulation, the level of services on the abscissa might refer to the total amount of money spent for control of the disease (viz. money for tuberculin testing and immunization against tuberculosis plus the treatment of active cases and follow-up of all contacts). The response or ordinate scale in the graph would represent the tuberculosis mortality rate. The curve is based upon a model which attempts to relate input to output.

Although the specific dosage-response curve may not be known or formalized for a particular problem, it is still helpful to realize the existence of this kind of relationship. Even crude notions about the shape of the curve have led to the establishment of accepted standards. From such curves, quotas in terms of level of services have been established in public health which serve as convenient guides. For example, there exists a recommended number of health service personnel per 10,000 persons served, number of home visits per nurse per week, number of sanitary inspections per month, and a host of others. These are based upon the assumption that the

specified amount of personnel and their activity will likely result in some desirable condition.

Similarly, in education, it is possible to plot the number of pupils per teacher on the abscissa and educational achievement on the ordinate scale. From this, one might be able to decide upon the optimal size of a class.

Standards and quotas can be established from a dosage-response curve by using something like the principle of optimal return. A point is selected on the ordinate where the rate of change in the slope is at a critical point. This is usually slightly above the origin but higher than the point where the lower tail on the right is flat and elongated (or its converse if high values on the ordinate are the desirable goal).

An important contribution to program evaluation can be made by administrators who accumulate data from which dosage-response curves or input-output surfaces can be estimated. Even a rough clue as to the relationship involved can serve as a guide to future planners. This is a plea for public officials to make available data which can thus be used to relate input to output.

Phase 3. Measurement of Services (Input)

Along with the setting of goals during the previous stage, quotas and guidelines are established to measure progress at periodic intervals. To learn whether the quotas are being filled service providers must keep an account of their activities.

For example, a family planning program should specify the expected number of clinic visits per month.

Each clinic must keep records to measure its progress against this quota and gauge its own progress from month to month. Furthermore, the program administrator can study all clinics during any one month to analyze why differing clinics vary in filling their quotas.

This means that counts must be recorded by the service providers or their helpers. To facilitate this recording in the field and so as not to interfere with the service itself, labor saving devices are commonly used. These take the form of precoded questionnaires, portable punch cards, mark-sensing devices, or even tape recorders. In the latter case, the material is coded or converted into usable form by a clerk or the person himself at a later time. However it is done, the basic data are compiled from records initiated by the program personnel.

The results of these compilations are called Service Statistics. They permit a statistical description of the services, the characteristics of those receiving and those rendering the service, the place and time of the service, how the recipient's needs were brought to light, and other features about the operations involved.

These descriptions are of value to the program director and other supervisors as well as to the service personnel themselves. These pieces of information, plus comparable data on financial costs, constitute the denominators that measure input discussed below in the input-output studies (cf. Phase 5).

Phase 4. Evaluation (Output)

This is the focal point of our discus-sion. To be of any value, the assessment assumes that suitable targets were selected during the design stage. In the present phase, an attempt is made to answer statistically what portion of the goal has been reached and how much of this can be credited to the program.

Before considering the formal mechanics involved in an evaluative scheme, much good can come from a pre-evaluation overview. This early appraisal, let us call it quasi-evaluation, starts by examining the details of a program even before service is rendered or data are collected. From this investigation one might be able to predict a likely outcome of the program using both a knowledge of the subject matter and general management science.

For example, most health programs require early community and physician involvement in planning the service if it is to be successful. When a newly proposed health program ignores or pays little attention to the element of involvement, predictions of a probable poor outcome may be justified.

Listed below are several items into which an experienced public administrator would likely inquire during this pre-evaluation review.

1. Organizational chart outlining the areas of responsibility, channels of communication, and ground rules for decision making by members of the staff.

2. The staffing of positions, proposed qualifications of personnel, plans for continued employment, promotion, incentives, and staff morale.

3. Plans for funding the program initially and in later stages of development.

4. Relationships with professional groups and other community agencies in both horizontal and vertical directions.

5. Built-in designs for supervision, quotas and quality control measures.

Early appraisal of a program using these general rules of management may avert a failure which true evaluation would require several months or years to detect.

Looking now at true evaluation, the inevitable, crucial questions to be answered are how much of the objective is being reached, and whether such accomplishment is due solely to the social program or to other concomitant and frequently uncontrollable forces in the community.

A consideration of these questions will be undertaken in Section 3. Before considering the statistical aspects discussed in that section, however, it is well to reflect upon the kinds of goals that can be evaluated.

Evaluation of accomplishment and, in fact, all output can be measured on a time scale which extends from immediate results to long-range and ultimate goals. Ultimate goals may be specific, such as lowered mortality, or they may be vague and refer to such concepts as increased levels of well-being or healthful living.

The possible outcomes for health programs on this time scale are illustrated in Table 1. Immediate goals are based upon increments in knowledge about health and disease, improved attitudes towards the adoption of recommended health practices, and

finally, adoption of the suggested pattern of behavior. Some of the immediate goals can be scored or measured almost spontaneously and usually most of them are affected within a period of not more than about six to twelve months.

The intermediate goals concentrate on the early benefits that are supposed to be derived from the recommended health practice. If the health practice is vaccination, for instance, the intermediate goal would be less disease. If the program consists of family planning services, the intermediate goal would be a significant decline in the crude birth rate or age-specific fertility rates.

During the intermediate phase, there may also be other changes, more subtle in nature, taking place which reflect less discomfort and deprivation among members of the community. Less disease, for instance, should be responsible for lower absence from school and industry as well as reduced hospitalisation for that diagnostic condition. This means that the evaluation might be based upon an indirect, correlated response variable when measurement of the direct effect is too costly or imprecise.

Both the direct and indirect intermediate changes require longer periods of time to appear than the immediate responses. A three-to-five year period is not unreasonably long to wait before intermediate effects are detectable.

The long-range goals focus upon the eventual reduction of disability and death. Such effects may require ten or more years before being discernible.

The output goals listed in Table 1

TABLE 1. A LISTING OF INPUT AND OUTPUT VARIABLES
WHICH ARE ESSENTIAL IN A PROGRAM OF EVALUATION

	Output (True evaluation)		
Input (Quasi-evaluation)	*Immediate Goals* Increase in knowl- edge, improved attitudes and practices.	*Intermediate Goals* More positive health and im- proved status.	*Long-Range Goals* Reduction in morbidity and mortality.

                                                                   → ULTIMATE

	Immediate Goals	*Intermediate Goals*	*Long-Range Goals*

1. *Administrative pattern*
  a. Organizational chart
  b. Personnel staffing
	Reduced
	*d*issatisfaction
		Reduced
		*d*isease
			Reduction
			in *d*eath

c. Funding plans
  d. Relationships with
     other agencies (hori-
     zontal and vertical)
  e. Built-in quality con-
     trol measures
	Reduced
	*d*isinterest
		Reduced
		*d*iscomfort and
		*d*eprivation
			Reduced
			*d*isability

2. *Service statistics*
  a. Operations analysis
     of services provided
     including crossclassi-
     fication by charac-
     teristics of services,
     recipients, and pro-
     viders of service   OTHER OUTPUT

  b. Feedback and feed   1. Accompanying favorable effects in community other
     forward operations   than among recipients of service
     including compari-   2. Untoward side effects
     son with standards
     and quotas

FINAL INDEX   Efficiency = $\dfrac{\text{Output (in terms of goal fulfillment)}}{\text{Input (in terms of dollars, services and/or personnel time)}}$

are all characterised by reductions in undesirable states. This is because the diagnosis of needs was upon those same states and it is easier to measure deviations from health than to characterize well-being or positive health. All of the undesirable states listed in Table 1 start with the letter *d,* viz., disinterest, discomfort, disease, disability, and death. This mnemonic device is convenient in the field of health because data sources are expressible in the same letter, viz., doctors, dispensaries, departments of health and statistics, and domiciles.

    In selecting a goal for evaluation,

success can be more rapidly ascertained by using an immediate goal. This has the obvious disadvantage of assuming that subsequent developments will continue favorably. For example, a family planning program can be judged an early success if sufficiently large numbers of females accept and practice contraception for the first time. To achieve a reduction of the birth rate or an eventual stable rate of population growth, however, the program will require not only the continued usage of contraception by these early clients but also an unending introduction of new clients in each cohort of females.

Another limiting feature about choice of an immediate goal is that changes from *before* to *after* are sometimes more difficult to detect. An intermediate goal involving reduction of the birth rate or death rate is relatively easy to ascertain in countries where there is dependable registration of vital events. On the other hand, detecting changes in knowledge or attitude may require highly sensitive measurement devices which are not available. Even changes in patterns of behavior are sometimes difficult to quantify when information must be based upon interviews and household surveys [2]. For example, in a program to improve mental hygiene in the home, how does one measure the emotional climate and stress in the home to see if changes have occurred?

Fortunately, the choice of goal in evaluative activities is neither restricted nor unique. The evaluator is not necessarily limited to studying one target alone but can examine a whole series of timed sequences. Fur-

thermore, at any one time period, a recommended safeguard is to look at cause-related variables of an indirect nature to detect changes in the status quo. This is a kind of insurance to protect the sensitivity of the evaluation.

Expert opinion is often valuable in helping to decide the levels of success deemed feasible and realistic for a given community with specified resources. Owing to the fact that the level chosen for any target will be subjective, guidance by persons with experience in other communities is most helpful.

Finally, the evaluator must reckon with the existence of unanticipated effects regardless of the kind of outcome to be studied. Some of these accompanying side effects are favorable and might even overshadow in importance the main purpose of the program. Thus, in a family planning program based upon the insertion of intrauterine devices, physical examination of the women might lead to early detection of uterine abnormalities. Similarly, the use of contraceptive pills has been suggested as being valuable in preventing some forms of uterine cancer [9]. The latter finding has been challenged [10] but it illustrates how a beneficial side effect could be important in assessing the full worthwhileness of any program.

On the other side of the coin, there are genuinely untoward results that are also possible. Using the contraceptive pill again to illustrate the point, a suspected harmful effect is the premature development of blood clots and thromboembolic phenomena [7], [11].

The two possibilities, good and bad, highlight the need for all agencies engaged in any kind of social program to be on the alert for accompanying side effects. Changes in the status quo of a dynamic, interwoven system of culture will result in many waves other than the one focused on the targeted variable. If it is possible to assign a value judgment to the desirable and undesirable effects, the difference between the two might be considered as a kind of net output.

A discussion of more technical statistical problems in evaluation will be resumed in Section 3.

Phase 5. Input-Output Studies

This stage is concerned with an analysis of the benefits versus the costs, and is referred to as cost-benefit analysis, dosage-response curve, or an input-output study. The principle is simple in concept but difficult in application.

The basic idea is to construct a model of how the important variables function within the social system involved. Given an input or service as measured in Phase 3, we try to relate it to possible outcomes or output as measured in Phase 4. The input might be expressed in terms of money, personnel, facilities employed, or any combination of them.

The most frequently encountered type of problem involving input-output is one in which the input is arbitrarily fixed and the aim is to maximize the output. Thus, an administrator may be told that he has X millions of dollars to spend for a program and his goal is to prevent the largest number of deaths or disease under this restriction.

Another way of considering the input-output method of approach is to inquire how much input is required to produce a given level of output. For example, how much does it cost to prevent a case of tuberculosis, or to achieve a year of birth prevention in a woman?

Or, how many clinic visits are required to prevent one birth?

The answers to these questions become guidelines for the future. Thus, early experience in family planning confirmed that the insertion of intrauterine devices in approximately five eligible women would prevent one birth that year. Now, rightly or wrongly, this is frequently used as a rule of thumb in planning future programs of contraception.

The efficiency of competing social programs, determined by the ratio of output to input (or its reciprocal), can also be measured in this phase. This is a kind of operations analysis which is common to the military, growing quickly in industry, but only slowly seeping into social programming. Where skilled personnel are scarce, the time has come in which output-input studies are indispensable tools of administration and where the most important input variable should be personnel time.

Thus, suppose in a family planning clinic one obstetrician and two nurses can prevent one thousand conceptions per year. Is this more efficient than the half-time of an obstetrician and four nurses, or some other combination that involves health visitors and health educators?

Efficiency in social programs is not any less desirable than efficiency in industry!

3. STATISTICAL DESIGN OF EVALUATIVE STUDIES

Evaluation of a social program is more closely related to and identified as a research endeavour than as a service function. This does not mean that service-oriented social programs have any less obligation to encourage and promote evaluative activities nor does it imply that some other unit in government which is more research-oriented has the responsibility for evaluation. A well-designed social program incorporates plans for evaluation at the outset of the operation.

Evaluation as a research type of operation does imply that the personnel involved in it should be free of any service functions. Separation of the two roles is not because of possible conflicts of interest—namely, that service personnel might consciously or subconsciously try to make a program appear favorable. One should assume that service personnel will want to know the program's true strengths and where the deficiencies, if any, lie. To assure that this assumption holds, the point should be stressed again and again with service personnel that the evaluation is not a means of checking on their loyalty or ability nor is it being used as a kind of personnel grading scheme.

The separation of staff for the two functions is to avoid a conflict in role at the time of rendering service. Persons gathering information for evaluation should be concentrating solely on that aspect and none other.

The separation of roles does not necessarily require that two distinct staffs must be maintained, one purely for service functions and the other only for evaluation. The same personnel might be used for both activities by alternating their roles between service and evaluative functions. Not all staff should be required to rotate duties in this way but certainly all should be free to elect to do so.

The scheme for evaluation does not differ in principle from the usual experiment and resembles quite closely the clinical trial of a drug or the field trial of a vaccine. Methodology for such experimentation can be found in most statistical textbooks or reference can be made to [5].

The basic design stipulates that one portion of the sampled population be allocated to the experimental treatment (i.e. the social program) and the remainder assigned to a comparison or control treatment, or placebo, and that this allocation should be done at random. After the passage of adequate time for the criterion event to develop, measurements are taken to ascertain changes in the response variables. Differences in response between the two groups are tested to determine their statistical significance before generalizing the observations for the larger population or universe.

The methods are simple enough in principle but difficult to apply in the case of field studies involving groups of human subjects. Let us consider five broad classes of statistical problems that almost always arise in this context.

1. The first problem concerns the experimental units which are to be allocated to the differing treatments. Experimental units are supposed to be relatively equivalent to one another at the outset or, if not, to have covariables attached to them which can be adjusted so that equivalence prevails

statistically if not physically. This requirement creates a host of problems in evaluation of social programs because the experimental units will frequently be whole communities.

a) How can a set be constructed which contains truly equivalent communities available for study?

b) Can allocation be done at random within this set, especially if some communities are not ready or willing to accept the social program?

c) Can program officials justify the denial, during the length of time necessary for evaluation, of the supposed benefits of a social program to, let us say, one-half of the communities that are ready for it?

d) Will there be cross-communication between the two treatment groups which invalidates the original separation for the experiment?

These questions are not unfamiliar to the specialist in experimental design because they arise whether the testing program involves animals, human subjects, or entire communities. Some partial replies to these questions are presented herewith in the same sequence as above.

a) Experimental design recognizes that no two experimental units are truly identical and especially if the unit is a living organism. In one sense, each such unit is a population unto itself. On the other hand, all that experimental design requires is that the two groups should be as much alike as possible with respect to the more important variables, or adjustable in these variables by an analysis of covariance. One of the roles of randomization is to balance the effects of the uncontrollable forces of variation.

In some cases, the evaluator can take the whole community and divide it randomly into equivalent portions by using an unrelated or supposedly neutral variable. This might be done roughly by letters of the alphabet for family name, by Social Security numbers, or by certificate number in the register of births, deaths, and marriages. An example of this type of allocation in evaluating a piece of health education literature is illustrated in [6]. Where such division is possible, the design comes closest to constituting allocation at random with equivalence of the experimental and comparison groups.

Where division of the community on some neutral category is not possible, a geographic classification or subdivision of the community is the next best scheme for generating experimental units. The least satisfactory and most questionable procedure is to classify the community into time periods, such as "before" and "after" the program.

When the community has been subdivided into constituent geographic regions, these smaller areas constitute experimental units available for allocation. To safeguard against unforeseen possibilities, the principle of replication is used as a kind of insurance. Rather than a single experimental and a single control area, it is much wiser to have 3 to 5 or more small areas or communities in the experimental program and a like number in the comparison group.

If it is possible to pair the constituent communities based upon a few major characteristics, considerable gain can be achieved by assigning at random one of each pair to the experimental program. No loss is sustained if the pairing was, in fact, unnecessary. A helpful reference in pairing may be found in Cochran [1].

In the act of pairing two supposedly equivalent communities, attention should be focused upon trends rather than on the status quo. For example, consider a family planning program with a goal of lowering the overall birth rate. Suppose we observe two communities, A and B, which have practically identical birth rates plus a few other vital features which are similar at time t_0.

Is this sufficient evidence to pair the two communities?

It is equally important to study the historical developments in the two communities which brought them to the point of having identical birth rates. Thus, the graph in Figure 2 shows that the two communities may have arrived at the common point by different paths and that this trend during the next five years might continue. That being the case, it would be folly to assume that the future birth rates in the two communities would be equivalent in the absence of any special program. In other words, the communities should be equivalent in terms of expected future characteristics rather than simply their present status.

b) Within the broad geographic area to be covered by the program, only those communities which are ready and willing to accept the program should be considered eligible for the randomization process. This might entail assistance to some communities in order to prepare them for

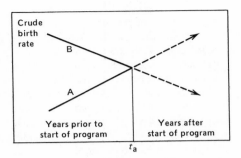

FIG. 2. Hypothetical graph of the crude birth rates in two communities before and after the start of an experimental program at time t_0.

the program and then if they are assigned to a control comparison group, to risk loss of their faith and cooperation.

This problem is not unrelated to item (c) discussed immediately below. One solution is to avoid a true placebo but to substitute, in its stead, a comparison social program where the goal of evaluation is to learn which program is better or more efficient. Another solution is the proper indoctrination of the communities beforehand so that they are prepared to accept various experimental designs like switch-over trials, latin squares and randomized blocks, which provide each participant community with a sampling of all the programs over a period of time. For such designs, a standard text on experimental design, such as Cochran and Cox [3], can be useful here.

c) A social program is usually being evaluated because its effectiveness may be in doubt. If a program is still experimental and has not been established as being worthwhile, temporary denial of its services to a community should not be penalizing or prejudicial. This argument will, unfortunately, not carry much weight in convincing community leaders that it is just as good to be a control area. They will still feel, and perhaps rightly so, that any program providing social service must have more positive values than negative ones. The only solution is to resort to experimental designs which provide all communities with a variety of treatments at different times. As mentioned above, good designs are available for this purpose and appropriate ones can even measure residual and carry-over effects as the treatments change during the different time periods.

d) Cross-communication between communities, or groups within one community, will inevitably occur and especially when the social program has an educational or learning aspect. Evidence of cross-communication is, of course, an accompanying beneficial side effect because it means the program is affecting more than the direct recipients.

An interesting side experiment can be carried out if distances between experimental and control groups within each pair are used as an additional variable to measure the degree of cross-communication. Thus, suppose program differences are practically non-existent where the two communities in the pair are adjacent to one another but the program differences increase with the distances separating each pair. Not only can cross-communication be substantiated here but an attempt made to estimate

its spatial relationship. Cross-communication can sometimes be established by time comparisons as well as by space comparisons.

If cross-communication is present and can not be related to time or distance between pairs of communities, what effect does this have upon the evaluation scheme?

Cross-communication tends to diminish true differences between experimental and control groups and therefore lowers the probability of rejecting the null hypothesis. If the null hypothesis is rejected despite the presence of cross-communication, the estimate of program effectiveness is obviously a minimal one. To maintain the power of the evaluation procedure efforts should be made to minimize cross-communication if it can not be measured.

2. The second type of problem in experimental design involving social programs is concerned with the difficulty of confounding the merits of the program with the personnel involved. In any service regimen the testing procedure consists of evaluating the program in the hands of specified personnel rather than the program per se.

The surest way to untangle the confounding is to rotate personnel so that every worker spends an equal amount of time on each treatment or within the framework of the experimental design. Again, this principle is simple in concept but difficult to implement. Service personnel can not be moved about as pieces in a chess game. Moreover, the effectiveness of service personnel frequently depends upon the close, personal relationships they attain over long periods of time and they resent frequent interruptions of this relationship. The evaluation must strike a compromise here in order to have as much staff rotation as possible under the circumstances.

Staff rotation does not solve all of the problems in this category. Service personnel often express a preference for or are better skilled in one kind of service than another. If evaluation is to ascertain the effectiveness of the program when serviced by the average type of employee in the field, the service personnel should not be assigned to that particular treatment for which they express a preference. Those assigned to each treatment should represent a cross-section of interest, motivation, and ability for that particular regimen. In spite of the foregoing, personnel should not be forced to render service relating to a particular treatment to which they are strongly opposed.

An interesting example in the field of medicine will illustrate this problem and the solution adapted. In gastrectomy for duodenal ulcer, some surgeons testified as to the superiority of operation type 1, and others did likewise for operation type 2. Each school of surgery had compiled reams of evidence reporting on the percentage of successes achieved by its own type of operation. The data from the two groups were not comparable, randomization had not been practised, and no valid inferences could be drawn about the relative merits of the two types of operation.

A clinical trial was thereupon designed to answer the question as to which type of operation would be superior if a group of young, uncom-

mitted surgeons could be taught to perform both operations equally well. The surgical plan which was devised required each participant surgeon to be available for both types of operation and each case was determined by a random selection procedure.

There was a small clique of older surgeons, however, who insisted upon performing only the single operation which they felt was superior and they would be unavailable for rotation. The participation and co-operation of this senior group was necessary to make the trial feasible and acceptable to surgeons elsewhere. Rotation being out of the question for them, and probably wisely so, each type of operation was controlled so as to have an identical number of these "committed" surgeons in addition to uncommitted ones performing both types of operation. Comparisons between the two types of operation could be made within the committed group, the uncommitted group, and the total.

3. The third statistical problem involves a decision about the timing of measurements to be taken after the start of the program. In addition to the base or initial measurements which might be available from the community diagnosis stage, the question arises whether subsequent measurements should be taken more than once and, if so, how often?

Also, how long after the start of a program should the final observations be made for evaluative purposes?

There is no panacea to this problem. Some clues as to the relative merits of repeated measurements, and their frequency, can be obtained from the literature of growth studies [12].

In these types of studies, however, repeated measurement is likely to have little or no effect upon subsequent development. In community studies, on the other hand, the measurement process might become intertwined with the regimen itself and this in turn may influence program participation and/or effectiveness.

To facilitate the taking of periodic measurements without unduly influencing the program, observations can be conducted upon small samples of the population receiving the services of each program. By periodic sampling of non-overlapping segments, costs are reduced and observations are less likely to be autocorrelated. In some cases it is also possible to use successive samples with partial replacement of the units sampled, and this method is discussed by Patterson [8].

By taking periodic observations, also, changes in the differences between treatment groups are more likely to be identified and traceable. The timing of the maximum differential effect between programs is thereby ascertainable. This is important because many social programs produce a small initial improvement which blossoms to a peak, eventually declines, and may disappear altogether. By spacing the observations over time in discrete non-overlapping samples, type II errors can be minimized as well as learning if program accomplishments are temporary or more permanent.

A natural guide for the timing of final observations is, of course, the type of goal selected for evaluation. Goals with an immediate effect require early observation. Similarly, it

would be foolish to expect any rapid change in a criterion based upon a goal far out to the right of the time scale displayed in Table 1.

To sum up the recommendations regarding the timing of measurements, the first approximation should be based upon the nature of the goal to be evaluated. Having judged the expected time of its fulfillment, small, discrete samples should be selected for observation starting no later than one-half this expected time and extending to at least twice the expected period.

4. The next statistical problem in evaluation concerns the mechanics involved in making the observations. In principle, the observer should be unaware as to which service program that particular community had been receiving.

The basic notion of a "double blind" field trial is at stake because complete concealment is obviously impossible. In fact, whenever an experiment is based upon an activity in which service is rendered to human subjects, concealment of treatment identification is impossible from both the experimental unit and the service provider. In medicine, for instance, it is literally impossible to conceal from either the recipient or the donor the nature of the services rendered in psychiatric counselling, surgery,[2] nursing care, prenatal obstetric care, and others.

In social programs involving the community, one might argue rather convincingly that an integral portion of the program is the community's involvement and awareness of it. Psychological and motivational benefits might be inextricably combined with the service and this total package is what should be evaluated. In this case, any attempt to conceal the knowledge from the community that the program was underway or to mask its identity would, in fact, be wrong.

Regardless of the steps taken to conceal, or not, the nature of the program from the community, it is absolutely imperative that final measurements on the criterion or response variables should be made by unbiased observers who are unfamiliar with the identity of the program. One way of promoting this is to select observers who were not involved in providing the service in that particular community. This procedure reaffirms the principle of separating the staff roles discussed at the beginning of this section.

5. Finally, the question of sampling and the applicability of tests of significance face the statistician-evaluator. Social programs generally are based upon whole communities consisting of large numbers of people. If tests of significance are appropriate here, the sampling errors are probably negligible in comparison to the magnitude of the non-sampling errors.

In most cases of program evaluation, there is likely to have been sampling involved either in space or time, or both. Therefore, even if the whole city or state is participating in the program under evaluation, one can consider it as a sample from a universe which is time-oriented in its repetitiveness. That is, the question being posed is whether the program will continue to be effective next year, and the next one after that, and so on.

This approach to the sampling problem makes sense statistically although it is not a realistic appraisal of life. The program will inevitably change during the following years as the population migrates, ages, and its diagnosis undergoes modification. Similarly, the service personnel and administrators will change with time and all of them, whether desired or not, were part of the program that was evaluated.

As a kind of insurance policy, however, it is probably wiser to test for statistical significance when in doubt about the appropriateness of doing so. The risk of reaching a wrong conclusion by accepting the null hypothesis is not increased very much by testing because the sampling errors will usually be negligible. To compensate, of course, there is a reduction in the chance of erroneously rejecting the null hypothesis.

As in other uses of significance testing, the statistician must stress with the program administrator that testing is not in any way related to validating the social importance of changes wrought by the service. The distinction between sampling errors and importance of an effect is no less necessary in social programming than in other statistical operations.

4. ASSESSMENT PROCEDURES WHEN EVALUATION IS NOT CONTROLLED

As discussed in the previous section, valid evaluation of a social program demands the same exactitude as any controlled clinical trial including random allocation of treatments, use of placebo controls or comparison groups, double blind features and significance testing of differences observed in the response variables. These requirements are more difficult, and sometimes impossible, to fulfill in dealing with communities as experimental units and where social programs based upon rendering service constitute the experimental regimen. These difficulties, real as they are, must not preclude the effort by program administrators to attempt good evaluative designs nor ever to justify no evaluation at all. If any of the desiderata are relaxed, the evaluator must try to ascertain the risks of permitting such deviation and its possible effect upon any inferences.

For instance, let us suppose that random assignment is impossible in a specific program evaluation. The investigator should take every precaution to measure how paired communities differ and, at least, try to correct for any imbalance. Techniques such as analysis of covariance, age adjusted and standardized rates, and similar tools are helpful [4]. *This does not imply that analysis of covariance corrects or adjusts for lack of randomization.* Systematic designs and the use of communities which volunteer for only one regimen are non-random and no amount of statistical manipulation will overcome this defect. It is some comfort, nevertheless, to know that initial differences were at least adjusted statistically by use of a device like a standardized rate.

Likewise, suppose concurrent control or comparison communities were not included in the evaluation design at the time services were implemented either because of oversight or difficulty in procuring them. A frequently used method, unsatisfactory as it is, is to use each community as its own control over time. In this way, several points from the past are selected to establish a trend so that expected values without the program might be forecast for the community. In this procedure, owing to the absence of randomly allocated placebo controls, several adjacent and distant communities without the program should also be examined in the same way. The degree of change over time in the non-program areas provides some expectation of what might have happened in the study community if it did not have the program. If the trends in the two classes of communities are similar, it would certainly appear that the service program was not primarily responsible for observed changes.

Another approach to the use of a community as its own control is to classify the services rendered according to characteristics of its recipients. Then, changes within the study community should be concentrated among those groups receiving the most service. By dividing the community into groups according to the amount of service received by each segment, one is essentially using segments of the community to serve as controls. This is a type of internal control.

An illustration will help to elucidate this point. Consider the plight of a city in South America which was faced with a large and rapidly increasing problem of abortion. Hospital admissions caused by complications resulting from abortion induced for non-medical reasons were almost 25,000 cases per year.[3]

Owing to the rapidly rising rate of hospital admissions, family planning programs were started in several health districts throughout the city. Control health districts seemed impractical because census studies showed that the populations migrated frequently not only within the city but back and forth between city and farm. Not only would cross-communication be severe but the calculation of rates of hospital admissions with this diagnosis for each district would be quite invalid. The denominators needed for such health district rates would be complete guesswork.

After the start of the family planning programs, the hospital admissions with this diagnosis for the total city started to decline about 4–5% per year for each of the first two years. The decline was even greater when measured against the expected number of cases from a projected trend line based upon previous years.

Was the family planning program entitled to take credit for this decline?

The use of other cities for comparative purposes, as suggested above, would not have sufficed because there were also changes during this same period of time in the definitions of and requirements for eligibility for hospitalization and other services under the country's National Health Service. These changes were not implemented uniformly through the country and the whole pattern was mixed up.

Hence, the only internal controls possible were obtained by subdividing the community according to the characteristics of those using the family planning service. The age distribution of the females using the service could be reliably and validly determined from good records that were

available in all the clinics. Alongside this distribution of service recipients were placed the data on hospital admissions for Years 0, 1, and 2, classified by age. Again, such data were fairly accurately determined from the hospital records. (The data on hospital admissions for this diagnosis for Year 0 could be either the expected number of admissions in Years 1 and 2 based upon the previous trend or the figure could be the actual annual number of admissions in the one or two years prior to the start of the program.) Thus, the proposed data table might look like the one shown in Table 2.

The statistical analysis would measure how the service recipients were correlated by age with the changes in hospital admission rates. As shown in Table 2, changes in the hospital admission rates are measured by the ratio of observed admissions to expected admissions. Obviously, in addition to the "ratio" of the hospital admissions, attention could also be focused on the "difference" in the numbers of hospital admissions.

Simple statistical procedures involving ranks and other nonparametric procedures would be useful in relating the changes reflected in the last three columns with the three columns measuring the beneficiaries of the service. Intuitively one would expect that the age group receiving the greatest amount of service should reflect the maximum gain. This expectation is based upon certain plausible assumptions about equal need and viability at various age groups.

From a technical point of view, minor adjustments in the proposed tabulation need to be taken into ac-

TABLE 2. PROPOSED TABULATION OF SERVICES AND HOSPITAL ADMISSIONS,
CLASSIFIED BY AGE, FOR YEARS PRIOR TO AND
AFTER START OF THE PROGRAM

Age Group (years)	Number of Recipients of Service by Year			Hospital Admissions by Year					
				Number			Percent Changes		
	Year 1	Year 2	Years 1 & 2	Year 0	Year 1	Year 2	$\frac{Year\ 1}{Year\ 0}$	$\frac{Year\ 2}{Year\ 0}$	$\frac{Years\ 1\ \&\ 2}{2 \cdot Year\ 0}$
15–19									
20–24									
25–29									
30–34									
35–39									
40 and over									
Total									

count to adjust for movement or graduation from one age group to another as the program develops in time from Year 0 to Year 2. Alternatively, a cohort method of analysis based upon year of birth rather than age could be used to handle this problem satisfactorily.

In the suggested tabulation and analysis, the service recipients and the hospital admissions were classified by age of mother or year of her birth. One should do identical analyses with all other variables which are reliably measured both in terms of services received and hospital admissions. In the present situation, this would certainly include marital status, number of living children, and birth parity of the mother since both sets of records were adequate for these variables. Other demographic variables which are always worth considering are race, sex, occupation, education, and level of income. In the case of medical and health data, additional variables that are frequently available include height, weight, other physical features, blood groupings, blood pressure, personality type, smoking habits, dietary patterns, and others.

In the analysis of data in the recommended form, let us suppose that the family planning service had been concentrated among married mothers with three or more children and who were 20–29 years of age, from a low socio-economic group. Let us further suppose that this was the very group which experienced the greatest decline in hospital admissions for complications of nonmedically induced abortions.

Does this relationship prove that the family planning service was responsible for the decline in hospitalization?

Unfortunately, it does not! We can not associate probability inferences to any statement rejecting the null hypothesis in this type of observational data or analytic survey. On the other hand, we would probably be willing to cast aside any notions of a causal relationship if the association between the two variables did not show up in the data. The argument would be that since this group of women who had so much service did not show any improvement in the rate of hospitalization, whereas other groups of females did show improvement, it seems reasonable to conclude the family planning service was ineffectual in reducing hospitalization.

One may question the wisdom of conducting this unilateral approach which does not prove the existence of a causal relationship but which can be helpful in disproving it.

Why do it?

The answer depends upon the purpose of the analysis and what decisions are to be based upon it. If the aim is to establish scientific evidence that a program did indeed cause some desirable effect, the evaluation must be along the lines of the controlled field trial with random allocation and all the other details. This is the limita-

tion resulting from our existing knowledge of the scientific method and the requirements currently accepted to establish causal relationships.

If, however, the aim is to recommend to health administrators what kinds of programs are likely to be effective, the need for scientific proof is not as stringent. The association of the two variables, hospital admissions and services received, in specific demographic groups does tend to lend credence to a causal relationship in a way which is quantitatively immeasurable. This belief is subjective but if enough persons of recognised authority accept the idea, there would seem to be sufficient ground to base health programs upon the relationship. After all, deferral of a social program while waiting for the scientific proof to appear can be a disastrous decision in some fields of application. The decision maker must reckon with the loss caused by a wrong decision in either direction. Nowhere is this more beautifully illustrated than in the present controversy regarding lung cancer and cigarette smoking.

NOTES

1. The activity may be denoted by other designations in different fields of application.

2. In surgery, sham operations are sometimes performed to mask the identity of the treatment from the subject. This masking effect is particularly important in those areas where the psychological impact is likely to be as important, if not more, as the physiological benefit. This practice in surgery raised an ethical and moral issue which needs to be considered and resolved in every case of its usage on each subject.

3. If one assumes that there was at least one satisfactory or successful abortion for each one requiring hospitalization, the size of this particular city was such that somewhere between one-fourth and one-half of all pregnant women were having abortions

performed. No one would question that this is a high rate of nonmedically induced abortion.

REFERENCES

[1] Cochran, W. G. (1953) Matching in analytical studies. *American Journal of Public Health,* 43, 684–691

[2] Cochran, W. G. (1955) Research techniques in the study of human beings. *The Milbank Memorial Fund Quarterly,* XXXIII, 121–136

[3] Cochran, W. G., Cox, G. M. (1957) *Experimental designs;* second edition. New York, Wiley

[4] Greenberg, B. G. (1953) The use of analysis of covariance and balancing in analytical surveys. *American Journal of Public Health,* 43, 692–699

[5] Greenberg, B. G. (1965) Biostatistics. Chapter 4 in *Preventive medicine for the doctor in his community;* third edition; by Leavell, H. R. and Clark, E. G. New York, McGraw-Hill

[6] Greenberg, B. G., et al. (1953) A method for evaluating the effectiveness of health education literature. *American Journal of Public Health,* 43, 1147–1155

[7] Oral contraceptives and thromboembolism (1967). Editorial in *The Lancet,* 1, 827

[8] Patterson, H. D. (1950) Sampling on successive occasions with partial replacement of units. *Journal of the Royal Statistical Society,* Series B, 12, 241–255

[9] Pincus, G., Garcia, C. R. (1965) Studies on vaginal, cervical, and uterine histology. *Metabolism,* 14, 344–347

[10] *Report on oral contraceptives.* (1966) Food and Drug Administration, Washington, D.C. Report of the task force on carcinogenic potential, Appendix 2, 21

[11] Risk of thromboembolic disease in women taking oral contraceptives. A preliminary communication to the Medical Research Council by a Subcommittee. (1967) *British Medical Journal,* 2, 355–359

[12] Tanner, J. M. (1951) Some notes on the reporting of growth data. *Human Biology,* 23, 93–159

11. Evaluative Studies of Institutions for Delinquents: Implications for Research and Social Policy

Paul Lerman

Evaluative research is usually undertaken for the purpose of gathering evidence of a program's success in achieving its avowed goals.[1] This approach can be questioned, however, unless a more basic question has first been answered in the affirmative: Is there any empirical evidence that the program under consideration is more likely to be associated with success than with failure? It is not sufficient merely to assume that assessing success is the relevant evaluative problem. One must be willing to face the possibility that the program is associated with high rates of failure. Instead of the success of a program, it might be more relevant to evaluate its failure.

This point of view can be applied to any program of interest to social workers. It is especially appropriate in studying institutions that seek to transform delinquents into law-abiding youths. This paper will provide evidence that supports the following conclusion: Regardless of the type of program investigated, residential institutions for delinquents (under 18 years of age) are characterized by high rates of potential failure. On the basis of this evidence, it will be argued that researchers interested in evaluating new programs should focus on the problem of whether (and how) failure rates have been reduced—not whether an institution can claim success. In addition, this paper will propose that the issue of humanitarianism be considered apart from the ideologies of treatment and success.

WHAT IS ORGANIZATIONAL FAILURE?

It has become virtually a custom in the delinquency field to measure the success of correctional organizations by determining whether boys released from custody have refrained from known law violations.[2] From an evaluative perspective this approach is quite misleading. Boys released from a residential institution who are not "renoticed" by the legal system *might* be regarded as successes, but it still must be demonstrated that their success is attributable to the organization. Boys can be successful in this respect for many reasons that have little to do with their residential experiences. It is the task of evaluative research to demonstrate that the organization was actually responsible for the boys' achievement.[3]

The crucial difference between potential and actual organizational success becomes even clearer when the boys who *are* renoticed are examined. Residential organizations will not readily agree that renoticed boys constitute evidence of the organizations' *actual* failure to rehabilitate. Rather, they argue (and correctly so) that the

Reprinted with permission of the author and the National Association of Social Workers, from *Social Work*, Vol. 13, No. 3, July 1968, pp. 55–64.

failure may be due to many factors—some of which may be beyond the power of the institution to control. Without further evidence, it is no less unfair to attribute the failures to the organization than to credit it with the successes. But organizations cannot claim unnoticed boys as their successes without also claiming renoticed boys as their failures. Again, it is the task of evaluative research to demonstrate that the organization was responsible for the boys' failure or success.

At the stage of formulating the evaluative problem to be investigated, interest is in estimating *potential* organizational failures. To carry out this purpose, *all the boys whom the organization cannot reasonably claim as evidence of success must be identified.*

Recontact with the criminal justice system constitutes one measure of potential failure. Although this is a crude measure, it is difficult to deny its social utility. If it is granted that there is social utility in assessing failure by indications of renewed delinquent activity, it is still appropriate to question the usual measure utilized in evaluation studies. Most delinquency studies rely on recidivist data—the reinstitutionalization of released boys. This type of measure implies that boys who are known to the police and/or courts but who were not reinstitutionalized should be counted as successes, which is a dubious practice. Sophisticated criminologists are well aware that indications of delinquency or criminality decrease in reliability as the level of enforcement takes one further away from the offense itself. Sellin, the dean of American criminology, states this position as follows:

The difficulty with statistics drawn from later stages in the administrative process is that they may show changes or fluctuations which are not due to changes in criminality but to variations in the policies or the efficiencies of administrative agencies.[4]

In classifying boys as potential successes or failures, it is important that one avoid confounding the issue of renewed delinquent behavior with discretionary reactions to that behavior by court personnel. Whenever possible, studies must be analyzed to obtain indications of failure regardless of whether boys were reinstitutionalized. In brief, the notion of counting as successes boys whose behavior indicates that the institution has probably failed is rejected.

The importance of making these distinctions explicit can be highlighted by reviewing the results of a major current study.[5] For the past 6½ years the California Youth Authority's research department has been continually engaged in evaluating the Community Treatment Project, in which since September 1961 first-commitment youths have been randomly assigned to experimental services in their own communities or to a control situation that involves residence in an institution away from home. As of March 31, 1966, 241 in the experimental group and 220 in the control group had been paroled to Sacramento and Stockton, the two major sources of the sample; the former had been on parole for an average of 16.4 months and the latter for an average of 17.9 months. As of May 1967, 33 percent of the experimentals and 55 percent of the controls had violated parole (i.e., the boys' parole was officially revoked, they were recommitted, or they had received an unfavorable discharge from the youth authority). A more detailed analysis sustains this difference, but regardless of the refinement, the findings are quite misleading about the behavior of the two groups.

The difference in parole violation figures suggests that the experimentals as a group were less delinquent in their behavior than the controls, but this is not the case. As a matter of fact, the experimentals had more known delinquent offenses per boy than the controls (2.81 to 1.61).[6] When the seriousness of the offenses is considered, then the rates for "low serious" offenses are 1.56 per boy for the experimentals and .52 for the controls; for "medium serious" offenses, .61 per boy for the experimentals and .45 for the controls; and for "high serious" offenses, .64 per boy for both groups.[7] The authors present convincing evidence that the parole officers of the experimentals were much more likely to know about their boys' offenses than the parole officers of the controls.[8] In effect, they argue that the delinquent *behavioral output* was probably the same, but that the *rate of being noticed* was different.

The report could go a step further: It could demonstrate that the noticed offenses were reacted to differently by the experimental and control organizations. The parole violation rates differ because the modes of reacting to and handling the offenses are different. Table 1 compares the experimental and control groups by the seriousness of the offenses officially known; using known offenses as the base, the table then indicates the proportion of parole vio-

lations for each offense category for experimentals and controls. The table attempts to answer the following questions: Are noticed offenses of varying degrees of severity more or less likely to be judged parole violations when committed by the experimental group?

As the table clearly shows, the chance that an experimental boy's offense will be handled by revocation of parole is lower than for a control boy if the offense is low or moderate in seriousness; experimentals are judged similarly to the controls *only* when the

TABLE 1. RATES OF PAROLE
VIOLATION PER OFFENSE CATEGORY
FOR EXPERIMENTALS AND
CONTROLS, CALIFORNIA
COMMUNITY TREATMENT PROJECT

Seriousness of Offense[a]	Experimentals		Controls	
	Number	Rate	Number	Rate
Low	376	.02	114	.17
Medium	146	.10	100	.40
High	156	.37	140	.44

[a]Seriousness-of-offense ratings are those used in the CTP study, but they have been trichotomized to highlight the trends. The low category includes California Youth Authority ratings 1–2, medium includes ratings 3–4, and high includes ratings 5–10.

SOURCE: Marguerite Q. Warren, Virginia V. Neto, Theodore B. Palmer, and James K. Turner, "Community Treatment Project: An Evaluation of Community Treatment for Delinquents," CTP Research Report No. 7 (Sacramento: California Youth Authority, Division of Research, August 1966). (Mimeographed.) These rates do not appear in the report but are easily derived by using Tables 6 and 15.

offenses are of high seriousness. It is difficult not to conclude that the experimental boys have a lower parole violation rate because offenses of low and medium seriousness are evaluated differently by adults according to organizational context.

Instead of the misleading conclusion derived from using only parole violation differences, it appears that the potential rates of failure of the two programs are similar (at this point in time). The behavioral outputs of the experimentals and controls are probably the same; however, the experimentals' parole agents notice more of this behavior and therefore give the impression that the experimentals are more delinquent. But even though the behavior of experimentals attracts more notice, it is not evaluated in the same way as the behavior of the controls. This important study may have exercised excellent control over the random selection of boys; unfortunately, the ideology of treating boys in the community spilled over into the postexperimental phase. The experimental and control groups appear to differ in the behavior of the parole agents with respect to revocation of parole—not in the delinquent behavior of the boys.

In addition to officially noticed delinquent actions that are not regarded as parole violations, there is another measure of potential failure that has been disregarded: boys who do not "complete treatment." The following section will describe this additional source of measurement; a subsequent section will then provide data from published and unpublished studies that highlight the importance of measuring *all* the potential failures.

COUNTING ALL OUTCOMES

Before measurement of this other type of failure is discussed, the social bookkeeping of institutions must be understood. The literature on delinquency reveals a curious bookkeeping habit: Boys who do not complete treatment are usually *not counted* in evaluations of organizational effectiveness. These boys are treated statistically as if they never existed; in a sense they are dealt with as Orwellian "no-persons." It is difficult to think of such outcomes as successes, but organizations do not like to count them as failures. Therefore, these boys are set aside and ignored. If this group were small, this accounting fiction might be accepted; unfortunately, it is not. The rate of no-persons in an institutional population can exceed 30 percent. Discarding a third of an agency's budget as nonaccountable would never be tolerated; should one tolerate discarding a third of its clients?

The problem of how to count boys who are labeled as not completing treatment is especially acute in the private sector. Although private institutions for delinquents are heavily subsidized by public funds, they have been permitted an enormous amount of discretion in controlling the population they treat, especially with regard to intake and maintenance. These agencies choose the boys who will enter into residence and those who will remain in residence and complete treatment (and, of course, those who will not do so). By contrast, most public institutions, unless they are special experimental programs, are forced to accept into residence all boys the private institutions reject at intake; even if the boys do not "work out," they are usually maintained in the institution, since there are few if any other places that will take them. State training schools rarely have reason to use the classification "not completing treatment."

One private residential center in New York State studied by the author controls its population to the extent of rejecting seventeen boys for every one accepted for residential treatment. This institution (hereafter referred to as "Boysville") considers many nonpsychological factors in exercising discretion at intake, i.e., age, previous record, ethnicity, space in the cottages. Having exercised this population control at intake, Boysville then proceeds to use its freedom to reject boys who "resist treatment." An unpublished study by the author of Boysville found that 31 percent (51 out of 164) of the boys in the study sample released from the institution were classified as not completing treatment. Most of these boys (40) were sent to state training schools. The average length of their stay at the private institution was sixteen months, far exceeding the customary remand period of ninety days. Had these boys been sent to nearby "Statesville" at intake, their average stay would have been only nine months.

This outcome was not unique to the specific time chosen for the Boysville study. The administrative staff was so surprised by the findings that they examined their records for a different time period. This unusual replication—conducted surreptitiously—revealed an almost identical rate of boys classified as not completing treatment released from the institution (33 percent).

Nor is this problem unique to private nonsectarian organizations in New York State; it is just more acute at Boysville. A study of Highlights, a special public organization located in New Jersey, reveals that 18 percent of the population released did not complete treatment.[9] A study of another special public program located in Michigan reveals a rate of 18 percent.[10] An unpublished study of a sectarian residential treatment center in New York State disclosed a rate of 25 percent.[11] Street, Vinter, and Perrow comment that in one treatment institution "many boys were screened out in the first three months."[12] These organizations share one characteristic: each exercised control at intake and was also able to "get rid of" boys who were "untreatable." In a less sophisticated period these boys might have been called "incorrigible."

This shift in semantic labels should suggest to the researcher the need to seek his own definition of this outcome. It is suggested that boys classified as not completing treatment have been granted "dishonorable discharges" from the institution, whereas those who have completed treatment are released as "honorably discharged." Only the latter boys can reasonably be conceived of as contributing to an organization's potential success. Redefining boys not completing treatment as dishonorably discharged permits counting of *all* the boys admitted to an institution in evaluating its success. Once this is done, it is clear that institutions yield two types of potential failures:

1. *Internal potential failures*—boys released from residential institutions via the route of a dishonorable discharge.

2. *External potential failures*—boys released with an honorable discharge who later engage in criminal or delinquent violations.

Internal failures can easily be identified in the everyday records of residential institutions. However, the type of discharge will not be stamped on the folders. Of the fifty-one boys in the Boysville sample who did not receive the usual honorable discharge—release to aftercare—forty were reinstitutionalized in state training schools, five were sent to mental hospitals, and six were purportedly "released to the community," but were actually runaways who could not be found. All these boys are classifiable as dishonorably discharged; they should be counted as the institution's potential internal failures. Certainly it is unreasonable to view them as potential successes.

ADDING UP FAILURES

The profound differences that can ensue when *all* boys regardless of discharge status are counted are clearly shown in Table 2. When internal failures are taken into account, the minimum estimate of the total potential failures of Boysville is 54 percent. (If this group of boys had been followed for a longer period of time, there is little doubt that the total failure rate would have been higher.) If the usual custom of "not counting" internal failures in either the numerator or the denominator had been followed, the estimate would have been 34 percent.

TABLE 2. POTENTIAL FAILURES OF BOYSVILLE RESIDENTIAL TREATMENT CENTER BY TWO COUNTING METHODS (PERCENTAGE)

Type of Failure	All Boys Released (n = 164)	Honorable Discharges Only (n = 113)
Internal	31	0
External[a]	23	34
Total	54	34

[a] Refers to boys officially rated as having violated the law between six and twenty-four months after their release to one of the five boroughs of New York City. Institutional records and the state files at Albany furnished the data.

Which social bookkeeping method is used obviously matters; the distinction is not just academic.

Although Boysville differs in many ways from its public neighbor, Statesville, the total potential failure rates for the two institutions are quite comparable for similar postrelease periods. The major difference between them is that Boysville's potential failure rate is derived from both internal and external sources; Statesville has an internal failure rate of only 3 percent. The total rates are similar even though Boysville and Statesville differ in their relative power to control intake and maintenance of population in addition to treatment modalities.

Is this estimate of comparable failure rates a unique finding? Reanalysis of the best evaluation study available in the literature indicates that it is not.[13] In Table 3 data obtained from Weeks's comparison of Highfields, a special public program, and Annandale, a typical state training school—both of which are located in New Jersey—are presented.

TABLE 3. COMPARISON OF
POTENTIAL FAILURES OF
TWO NEW JERSEY PUBLIC
INSTITUTIONS
(PERCENTAGE)

Type of Failure	Highfields (n = 229)	Annandale (n = 116)
Internal	18	3
External[a]	34	59
Total	52	62

[a] The external failures include all law violators, both institutionalized and noninstitutionalized, who have been released for at least eight months.

SOURCE: H. Ashley Weeks, *Youthful Offenders at Highfields* (Ann Arbor: University of Michigan Press, 1958), pp. 46–50, 52, 60. This table does not appear in Weeks but is derived from data appearing in the cited pages.

The rates of total potential failures differ by only 10 percent. However, the two institutions differed in their treatment services; Highfields boys worked away from their residence, received "guided group interaction," and stayed only four months; Annandale boys were incarcerated on a routine twenty-four-hour basis and stayed twelve months. The similarity

of the failure rates is even more striking when the initial differences between the populations are taken into account: Annandale boys were more likely to have come from urban centers rather than suburban towns, were more likely to be Negro, and had longer and more intense careers as delinquents; Highfields boys tended to be younger and to have completed more years of schooling. In addition to these initial population differences, Highfields was composed of first offenders only; although the Annandale sample was also composed of first offenders, the institution itself contained knowledgeable multiple offenders. Annandale had little control over the maintenance of membership and initial recruitment, while Highfields had a great deal.

Furthermore, the two populations were exposed to different types of parole (or aftercare) services. Highfields parole officers encouraged boys to enlist in the armed services; twenty-seven Highfields boys and only seven Annandale boys entered the armed forces and thus were removed from the risk of failure. Also, Highfields boys, unlike their peers from Annandale, were discharged from postprogram supervision "within only a few months after their release."[14] More Annandale than Highfields boys were actually reinstitutionalized because of parole violations; had these boys not been under longer supervision they might not have been so easily renoticed. In general, Weeks presents an image of the Highfields population as more advantaged before, during, and after treatment. Despite these differences, the total potential failure rates are not too dissimilar and in both cases involve a majority of the boys.

COMPARABILITY OF CONTROL GROUPS

In investigating potential failure, it is not necessary to measure boys "before" and "after." Attempting to assess attitudinal change that can be attributed to an organizational experience is a complex affair; if the potential rates of failure are high, there is scant justification for expending money, personnel, and creative energy in this direction. However, there is one feature of the usual approach to evaluation that cannot be set aside so easily in assessing potential failure: if two organizations are being compared, then it is crucial that the population of boys be quite similar. The Highfields study by Weeks exhibits sensitivity to this requirement; unfortunately, a more recent study indicates that this sensitivity has not yet been translated into a norm of evaluative research.

In 1965, Jesness released a study, sponsored by the California Youth Authority, that attempted to compare "outcomes with small versus large living groups in the rehabilitation of delinquents."[15] The design of the study called for random assignment of 10–11-year-old boys at Fricot Ranch to either the experimental twenty-boy lodge or the control fifty-boy lodge. For unknown reasons, random processes did not appear to be operating in the actual assignments. Instead of being comparable, the two populations were discovered to have significant background differences: the experimentals were 73 percent white and the controls only 55 percent, 35 percent of the experimentals and 50 percent of the controls came from the poorest homes, and 67 percent of the experimentals were from households in which the father was the main provider as compared with only 52 percent of the controls.[16]

Using revocation of parole as a measure of failure, Jesness found that the experimentals were less likely to fail than the controls up until after thirty-six months of exposure to parole. The rates are as follows: 32–48 percent after twelve months, 42–58 percent after fifteen months, and 61–70 percent after twenty-four months. After thirty-six months the rates were virtually the same—76 and 78 percent respectively.[17] Jesness concludes that the "effects of the experimental program tend to fade as the exposure period increases."[18] This may be so, but it seems even more likely that the higher failure rates of the controls reflect the fact that they were actually a higher-risk group at the outset of parole, since the group was comprised of more Negroes and Mexican-Americans and came from poorer homes than the experimentals (and probably poorer neighborhoods, too). Unless Jesness presents evidence that these critical background variables, when used as analytical controls, do not change the differential outcomes after twelve or fifteen months of parole exposure, his inference cannot be accepted. These background variables, for which Jesness does not control, have usually been strongly associated with delinquency and recidivism and these, not the institutional experiences, probably account for the differences in failure. In the language of multivariate analysis, Jesness' findings on early failure are probably spurious (i.e., the result of a third, uncontrolled variable).

INSTITUTIONAL INTERESTS

Organizational personnel have a major stake in any evaluative outcome. They want to be associated with potential success, not failure. Researchers are not likely to have a similar stake in the outcome. Although researchers do not purposefully seek to devalue people or organizations, their motto is much more likely to be: "Let's find out the truth and let the chips fall where they may." Their reference group is the scientific community and their ethics are ideally guided accordingly. Administrators, on the other hand—the persons who hire researchers—usually want the evaluators to demonstrate that their operations are successful and worthy of the external community's moral and financial support. Rather than deny this conflict of interest, one ought to be aware of its existence and make sure that biases do not influence empirical studies and written reports.

Biases influenced by organizational interests are especially likely to develop when researchers give up their independence and seek ways to demonstrate program success. Consider the evaluative study of Wiltwyck reported by William and Joan McCord.[19] Employed as the institution's resident psychologists, the McCords seemed so eager to prove its success that they defined one type of *failure* as "partial success." Table 4 presents the data as reported by the McCords for Wiltwyck and "New England State School."

From the McCord text it is learned that "partial success" refers to boys who actually appeared in court for law violations but were not reinstitutionalized; "complete failures" were both noticed and reinstitutionalized. The McCords do not seem to be bothered by this odd use of labels, for they claim that Wiltwyck had a *combined* success rate of 71 percent whereas New England, a state institution, had a rate of only 53 percent. A fair appraisal of the data would suggest that there is no appreciable difference between these institutions in potential success, using this writer's definition; the 5 percent difference—in favor of New England—is small. If all law violations are counted as potential failure, regardless of court disposition, it appears that *both* institutions are characterized by high external failure.

A subtle form of bias can be found in a study reported by Black and Glick.[20] The population of primary interest was

TABLE 4. SUCCESSES AND FAILURES AS REPORTED BY WILLIAM MCCORD AND JOAN MCCORD (PERCENTAGE)

Type of Outcome[a]	Wiltwyck (n = 65)	"New England State" (n = 228)
Complete success	43	48
Partial success	28	5
Complete failure	29	33
Don't know	0	13

[a] For definitions of categories *see* text.

SOURCE: William McCord and Joan McCord, "Two Approaches to the Cure of Delinquents," in Sheldon Glueck, ed., *The Problem of Delinquency* (Boston: Houghton Mifflin Co., 1959), pp. 735–736.

composed mainly of Jewish boys sentenced to Hawthorne Cedar Knolls School, a sectarian-sponsored residential treatment institution. Both researchers were regular employees of the Jewish Board of Guardians, the sponsoring agency. In a monograph reporting their results, the investigators describe the selection of their sample as follows: "For purposes of this study the followup period was computed from the date of discharge from aftercare."[21] Not surprisingly, Black and Glick report that Hawthorne Cedar Knolls had a higher success rate than a neighboring state school. They excluded from their sample not only all of the internal failures, but also all of the external failures occurring during the period of aftercare. Since the bulk of post-release failures take place within the first two years, the researchers thus eliminated the chance of finding many failures. In effect, all this study can hope to describe is the potential success rate of an unknown population that has been selectively screened for boys who might be failures. Since the researchers have gone to such lengths to minimize their potential failures, it is reasonable to conclude that they were unwilling to face up to the possibility that their organization, like the state school, is characterized by a high rate of internal and/or external failure.

IMPLICATIONS FOR A HUMANITARIAN POLICY

The consistent finding that treatment programs have not yet been proved to have an appreciable impact on failure rates should not be misinterpreted. For even though institutions for delinquents are probably not highly successful—regardless of treatment type—there is no reason to go back to harsher methods of child handling. It can be argued, rather, that even when boys are kept for only four months and treated with trust (as at Highfields), there is no evidence that this "coddling" will yield greater failure rates.

The case for a humanitarian approach needs to be divorced from any specific mode of treatment. People can be nice to boys with and without engaging in psychotherapy. This point is implicit in the recent work by Street, Vinter, and Perrow.[22] But we should not delude ourselves into adopting the unsubstantiated position that a humanitarian organization for delinquent boys yields lower rates of potential failures. With our present state of knowledge, it makes more sense to advocate a more humanitarian approach on the ground that it does not increase the *risk* of potential failure.

If it is decided to advocate humanitarianism in its own right, the social policy issue becomes much clearer. Given the fact that social work is still unable to influence appreciably the rates of failure of institutions for court-sentenced delinquents, should not ways be sought to make the total criminal-delinquent system more humane? In the name of treatment, boys have actually been sentenced for two and a half years (as at Boysville) for offenses that might bring an adult a sentence of only thirty, sixty, or ninety days. Surely it is time that youths were dealt with as humanely, and with similar regard for equity and due process of law, as adults.[23]

If lighter sentences do not increase

the risk of failure, then why not be more humane and equitable? Keeping boys in the community is undoubtedly a lighter sentence than sending them away. But California has found that this probably does not increase the risk of failure. Actually, the California Community Treatment Program has evolved a series of graded punishments. If youngsters in this program misbehave or do not obey the youth officer, they are *temporarily* confined. During the first nineteen months of the program, 57 of 72 experimental cases were placed in temporary confinement a total of 183 times; this was an average of three times each, with an average length of stay of twelve days per confinement.[24] As earlier analysis disclosed, the risk of post-program failure is not increased by using this kind of approach. It is even conceivable— although this has not been demonstrated—that keeping these boys out of all long-term institutions in itself constitutes treatment and that this treatment may have a payoff much later, when the boys become adults. Spending less time in an all-delinquent community might yield more conforming adults.

Even if communities are not willing to follow the California community approach, one can still argue for shorter "lock-ups." Highfields kept first offenders for only four months, yet the risk of failure was not increased. As long as society is still determined to "teach boys a lesson" by locking them up (or sending them away), why not extend the idea of shorter confinements to a series of graded punishments for offenses? Adults are sentenced for thirty, sixty, or ninety days—why not children? Perhaps we might even come to advocate taking the institutional budgets allocated for food, beds, and clothing (based on lengthy stays) and spending them on boys and their families in their own homes. It is doubtful whether this would add to the risks, but the program would be a great deal more fun to study and run than the old failures.

Whether one embraces the perspective offered here, it is certainly time to address the problem of social accountability, regardless of the type of program. Social welfare institutions are too heavily subsidized, indirectly and directly, for social workers not to take the responsibility for knowing what has happened to the people served. A good start can be made by keeping track of all the people not completing treatment, discontinuing service, dropping out of programs, and running away. Rigorous and nondeceptive social bookkeeping may yield discomforting facts about agency success and reputation. It is hoped that we will be aware of defensive reactions and remind ourselves that we entered social work to serve *people* in trouble—not established agencies, ideologies, and methods.

NOTES

1. Herbert H. Hyman, Charles R. Wright, and Terence K. Hopkins, *Application of Methods of Evaluation: Four Studies of the Encampment for Citizenship* (Berkeley and Los Angeles: University of California Press, 1962), pp. 3–88.

2. For example, *see* Bernard C. Kirby, "Measuring Effects of Treatment of Criminals

and Delinquents,"*Sociology and Social Research,* Vol. 38, No. 6 (July–August 1954), pp. 368–375; Vernon Fox, "Michigan Experiment in Minimum Security Penology,"*Journal of Criminal Law and Criminology,* Vol. 41, No. 2 (July–August 1950), pp. 150–166; William McCord and Joan McCord, "Two Approaches to the Cure of Delinquents," in Sheldon Glueck, ed., *The Problem of Delinquency* (Boston: Houghton-Mifflin Co., 1959); Bertram J. Black and Selma J. Glick, *Recidivism at the Hawthorne Cedar Knolls School,* Research Monograph No. 2 (New York: Jewish Board of Guardians, 1952); H. Ashley Weeks, *Youthful Offenders at Highfields: An Evaluation of the Effects of the Short-Term Treatment of Delinquent Boys* (Ann Arbor: University of Michigan Press, 1958).

3. This type of research demands careful attention to design to provide evidence that the experimental program had a greater impact on attitudes and values that, in turn, influenced postrelease behavior. This requires control groups and "before-after" measures. At the level of evaluative research herein referred to, in which *potential* outcomes are being assessed, attitudinal measures before and after are *not* necessary. As noted later on, comparability of groups continues to be important at *all* levels of evaluative research. *See* Hyman, Wright, and Hopkins, *op. cit.,* for a general statement of the problems. *See* Weeks, *op. cit.,* for the best-detailed example of evaluative research regarding institutions for delinquents.

4. Thorstein Sellin, "The Significance of Records of Crime," in Marvin E. Wolfgang, Leonard Savitz, and Norman Johnston, eds., *The Sociology of Crime and Delinquency* (New York: John Wiley & Sons, 1962), p. 64.

5. Marguerite Q. Warren, Virginia V. Neto, Theodore B. Palmer, and James K. Turner, "Community Treatment Project: An Evaluation of Community Treatment for Delinquents," CTP Research Report No. 7 (Sacramento: California Youth Authority, Division of Research, August 1966). (Mimeographed.)

6. *Ibid.,* p. 64.

7. *See ibid.,* Table 15, p. 68. For an explanation of the ranking of offenses by seriousness on which these figures are based, *see* Table 1 of this article.

8. *Ibid.,* p. 65.

9. Weeks, *op. cit.*

10. Fox, *op. cit.*

11. Personal communication from Robert Ontell, former study director of Mobilization For Youth's Reintegration of Juvenile Offenders Project, 1962.

12. David Street, Robert D. Vinter, and Charles Perrow, *Organization for Treatment: A Comparative Study of Institutions for Delinquents* (New York: Free Press, 1966), p. 196. This information is presented in a parenthetical comment about "Inland," a private institution. How many of the boys released as not completing treatment are actually excluded or included in this study is difficult to estimate. This study focuses on the attitudes of institutionalized boys about their experiences in residence. It would have been extremely valuable to know whether the screened-out boys differed in their responses to the attitudinal questions. It would also have been valuable to know whether the runaways also differed. Such information might have provided evidence that the attitudinal measures had validity. Presumably boys "resisting treatment" (i.e., those who were screened out or ran away) should have responded differently to questions about themselves and the institutional staff. These kinds of missing data are quite central to the argument concerning the institutional "effectiveness" of Inland.

13. Weeks, *op. cit.,* pp. 41–62.

14. *Ibid.,* p. 61.

15. Carl F. Jesness, "The Fricot Ranch Study: Outcomes with Small vs. Large Living Groups in the Rehabilitation of Delinquents," Research Report No. 47 (Sacramento: California Youth Authority, Division of Research, October 1, 1965). (Mimeographed.)

16. *Ibid.*, p. 52.

17. *Ibid.*, pp. 85–90.

18. *Ibid.*, p. 89.

19. McCord and McCord, *op. cit.* The Wiltwyck sample is composed only of Negro boys between the ages of 8 and 12 (at intake) who presented no "deep-seated psychiatric problems." "New England," on the other hand, is much more heterogeneous and has older boys. The data regarding the Wiltwyck sample can be found in Lois Wiley, "An Early Follow-up Study for Wiltwyck School." Unpublished master's thesis, New York School of Social Work, 1941.

20. Black and Glick, *op. cit.*

21. *Ibid.*, p. 4.

22. *Op. cit.*

23. *See* David Matza's insightful description of youthful appraisals of the juvenile court system in the discussion of the "Sense of Injustice," in Matza, *Delinquency and Drift* (New York: John Wiley & Sons, 1964).

24. Marguerite Q. Grant, Martin Warren, and James K. Turner, "Community Treatment Project: An Evaluation of Community Treatment of Delinquents," CTP Research Report No. 3 (Sacramento: California Youth Authority, Division of Research, August 1, 1963), p. 38. (Mimeographed.)

12. Reforms as Experiments

Donald T. Campbell

The United States and other modern nations should be ready for an experimental approach to social reform, an approach in which we try out new programs designed to cure specific social problems, in which we learn whether or not these programs are effective, and in which we retain, imitate, modify, or discard them on the basis of apparent effectiveness on the multiple imperfect criteria available. Our readiness for this stage is indicated by the inclusion of specific provisions for program evaluation in the first wave of the "Great Society" legislation, and by the current congressional proposals for establishing "social indicators" and socially relevant "data banks." So long have we had good intentions in this regard that many may feel we are already at this stage, that we already are continuing or discontinuing programs on the basis of assessed effectiveness. It is a theme of this article that this is not at all so, that most ameliorative programs end up with *no* interpretable evaluation (Etzioni, 1968; Hyman & Wright, 1967; Schwartz, 1961). We must look hard at the sources of this condition, and design ways of overcoming the difficulties. This article is a preliminary effort in this regard.

Many of the difficulties lie in the intransigencies of the research setting and in the presence of recurrent seductive pitfalls of interpretation. The bulk of this article will be devoted to these problems. But the few available solutions turn out to depend upon correct administrative decisions in the initiation and execution of the program. These decisions are made in a political arena, and involve political jeopardies that are often sufficient to explain the lack of hard-headed evaluation of effects. Removing reform administrators from the political spotlight seems both highly unlikely, and undesirable even if it were possible. What is instead essential is that the social scientist research advisor understand the political realities of the situation, and that he aid by helping create a public demand for hard-headed evaluation, by contributing to those political inventions that reduce the liability of honest evaluation, and by educating future administrators to the problems and possibilities.

For this reason, there is also an attempt in this article to consider the political setting of program evaluation, and to offer suggestions as to political postures that might further a

The preparation of this paper has been supported by National Science Foundation Grant GS1309X. Versions of this paper have been presented at the Northwestern University Alumni Fund Lecture, January 24, 1968; to the Social Psychology Section of the British Psychological Society at Oxford, September 20, 1968; to the International Conference on Social Psychology at Prague, October 7, 1968 (under a different title); and to several other groups.

From *American Psychologist*, Vol. 24, No. 4, April 1969, pp. 409–429, with modifications. Copyright 1969 by the American Psychological Association. Reprinted by permission.

truly experimental approach to social reform. Although such considerations will be distributed as a minor theme throughout this article, it seems convenient to begin with some general points of this political nature.

POLITICAL VULNERABILITY FROM KNOWING OUTCOMES

It is one of the most characteristic aspects of the present situation that *specific reforms are advocated as though they were certain to be successful*. For this reason, knowing outcomes has immediate political implications. Given the inherent difficulty of making significant improvements by the means usually provided and given the discrepancy between promise and possibility, most administrators wisely prefer to limit the evaluations to those the outcomes of which they can control, particularly insofar as published outcomes or press releases are concerned. Ambiguity, lack of truly comparable comparison bases, and lack of concrete evidence all work to increase the administrator's control over what gets said, or at least to reduce the bite of criticism in the case of actual failure. There is safety under the cloak of ignorance. Over and above this tie-in of advocacy and administration, there is another source of vulnerability in that the facts relevant to experimental program evaluation are also available to argue the general efficiency and honesty of administrators. The public availability of such facts reduces the privacy and security of at least some administrators.

Even where there are ideological commitments to a hard-headed evaluation of organizational efficiency, or to a scientific organization of society, these two jeopardies lead to the failure to evaluate organizational experiments realistically. If the political and administrative system has committed itself in advance to the correctness and efficacy of its reforms, it cannot tolerate learning of failure. To be truly scientific we must be able to experiment. We must be able to advocate without that excess of commitment that blinds us to reality testing.

This predicament, abetted by public apathy and by deliberate corruption, may prove in the long run to permanently preclude a truly experimental approach to social amelioration. But our needs and our hopes for a better society demand we make the effort. There are a few signs of hope. In the United States we have been able to achieve cost-of-living and unemployment indices that, however imperfect, have embarrassed the administrations that published them. We are able to conduct censuses that reduce the number of representatives a state has in Congress. These are grounds for optimism, although the corrupt tardiness of state governments in following their own constitutions in revising legislative districts illustrates the problem.

One simple shift in political posture which would reduce the problem is the shift from the advocacy of a specific reform to the advocacy of the seriousness of the problem, and hence to the advocacy of persistence in alternative reform efforts should the first one fail. The political stance would become: "This is a serious problem. We propose to initiate Policy A on an experimental basis. If after five years there has been no significant improvement, we will shift to Policy B." By making explicit that a given problem solution was only one of several that the administrator or party could in good conscience advocate, and by having ready a plausible alternative, the administrator could afford honest evaluation of outcomes. Negative results, a failure of the first program, would not jeopardize his job, for his job would be to keep after the problem until something was found that worked.

Coupled with this should be a general moratorium on ad hominum evaluative research, that is, on research designed to evaluate specific administrators rather than alternative policies. If we worry about the invasion-of-privacy problem in the data banks and social indicators of the future (e.g., Sawyer & Schechter, 1968), the touchiest point is the privacy of administrators. If we threaten this, the measurement system will surely be sabotaged in the innumerable ways possible. While this may sound unduly pessimistic, the recurrent anecdotes of administrators attempting to squelch unwanted research findings convince me of its accuracy. But we should be able to evaluate those alternative policies that a given administrator has the option of implementing.

FIELD EXPERIMENTS AND QUASI-EXPERIMENTAL DESIGNS

In efforts to extend the logic of laboratory experimentation into the "field," and into settings not fully experimental, an inventory of threats to experimental validity has been assembled, in terms of which some 15 or 20 experimental and quasi-experimental designs have been evaluated (Campbell, 1957, 1963; Campbell & Stanley, 1963). In the present article

only three or four designs will be examined, and therefore not all of the validity threats will be relevant, but it will provide useful background to look briefly at them all. Following are nine threats to internal validity.[1]

1. *History:* events, other than the experimental treatment, occurring between pretest and posttest and thus providing alternate explanations of effects.

2. *Maturation:* processes within the respondents or observed social units producing changes as a function of the passage of time per se, such as growth, fatigue, secular trends, etc.

3. *Instability:* unreliability of measures, fluctuations in sampling persons or components, autonomous instability of repeated or "equivalent" measures. (This is the only threat to which statistical tests of significance are relevant.)

4. *Testing:* the effect of taking a test upon the scores of a second testing. The effect of publication of a social indicator upon subsequent readings of that indicator.

5. *Instrumentation:* in which changes in the calibration of a measuring instrument or changes in the observers or scores used may produce changes in the obtained measurements.

6. *Regression artifacts:* pseudo-shifts occurring when persons or treatment units have been selected upon the basis of their extreme scores.

7. *Selection:* biases resulting from differential recruitment of comparison groups, producing different mean levels on the measure of effects.

8. *Experimental mortality:* the differential loss of respondents from comparison groups.

9. *Selection-maturation interaction:* selection biases resulting in differential rates of "maturation" or autonomous change.

If a change or difference occurs, these are rival explanations that could be used to explain away an effect and thus to deny that in this specific experiment any genuine effect of the experimental treatment had been demonstrated. These are faults that true experiments avoid, primarily through the use of randomization and control groups. In the approach here advocated, this checklist is used to evaluate specific quasi-experimental designs. This is evaluation, not rejection, for it often turns out that for a specific design in a specific setting the threat is implausible, or that there are supplementary data that can help rule it out even where randomization is impossible. The general ethic, here advocated for public administrators as well as social scientists, is to use the very best method possible, aiming at "true experiments" with random control groups. But where randomized treatments are not possible, a self-critical use of quasi-experimental designs is advocated. We must do the best we can with what is available to us.

Our posture vis-à-vis perfectionist critics from laboratory experimentation is more militant than this: the only threats to validity that we will allow to invalidate an experiment are those that admit of the status of empirical laws more dependable and more plausible than the law involving the treatment. The mere possibility of some alternative explanation is not enough—it is only the *plausible* rival hypotheses that are invalidating.

Vis-à-vis correlational studies, on the other hand, our stance is one of greater conservatism. For example, because of the specific methodological trap of regression artifacts, the sociological tradition of "ex post facto" designs (Chapin, 1947; Greenwood, 1945) is totally rejected (Campbell & Stanley, 1963, pp. 240–241; 1966, pp. 70–71).

Threats to external validity, which follow, cover the validity problems involved in interpreting experimental results, the threats to valid generalization of the results to other settings, to other versions of the treatment, or to other measures of the effect:[2]

1. *Interaction effects of testing:* the effect of a pretest in increasing or decreasing the respondent's sensitivity or responsiveness to the experimental variable, thus making the results obtained for a pretested population unrepresentative of the effects of the experimental variable for the unpretested universe from which the experimental respondents were selected.

2. *Interaction of selection and experimental treatment:* unrepresentative responsiveness of the treated population.

3. *Reactive effects of experimental arrangements:* "artificiality"; conditions making the experimental setting atypical of conditions of regular application of the treatment: "Hawthorne effects."

4. *Multiple-treatment interference:* where multiple treatments are jointly applied, effects atypical of the separate application of the treatments.

5. *Irrelevant responsiveness of measures:* all measures are complex, and all include irrelevant components that may produce apparent effects.

6. *Irrelevant replicability of treat-*

ments: treatments are complex, and replications of them may fail to include those components actually responsible for the effects.

These threats apply equally to true experiments and quasi-experiments. They are particularly relevant to applied experimentation. In the cumulative history of our methodology, this class of threats was first noted as a critique of true experiments involving pretests (Schanck & Goodman, 1939; Solomon, 1949). Such experiments provided a sound basis for generalizing to other *pretested* populations, but the reactions of unpretested populations to the treatment might well be quite different. As a result, there has been an advocacy of true experimental designs obviating the pretest (Campbell, 1957; Schanck & Goodman, 1939; Solomon, 1949) and a search for nonreactive measures (Webb, Campbell, Schwartz, & Sechrest, 1966).

These threats to validity will serve as a background against which we will discuss several research designs particularly appropriate for evaluating specific programs of social amelioration. These are the "interrupted time-series design," the "control series design," "regression discontinuity design," and various "true experiments." The order is from a weak but generally available design to stronger ones that require more administrative foresight and determination.

INTERRUPTED TIME-SERIES DESIGN

By and large, when a political unit initiates a reform it is put into effect across the board, with the total unit being affected. In this setting the only comparison base is the record of previous years. The usual mode of utilization is a casual version of a very weak quasi-experimental design, the one-group pretest-posttest design.

A convenient illustration comes from the 1955 Connecticut crackdown on speeding, which Sociologist H. Laurence Ross and I have been analyzing as a methodological illustration (Campbell & Ross, 1968; Glass, 1968; Ross & Campbell, 1968). After a record high of traffic fatalities in 1955, Governor Abraham Ribicoff instituted an unprecedentedly severe crackdown on speeding. At the end of a year of such enforcement there had been but 284 traffic deaths as compared with 324 the year before. In announcing this the Governor stated, "With the saving of 40 lives in 1956, a reduction of 12.3% from the 1955 motor vehicle death toll, we can say that the program is definitely worthwhile." These results are graphed in Figure 1, with a deliberate effort to make them look impressive.

In what follows, while we in the end decided that the crackdown had some beneficial effects, we criticize Ribicoff's interpretation of his results, from the point of view of the social scientist's proper standards of evidence. Were the now Senator Ribicoff not the man of stature that he is, this would be most unpolitic, because we could be alienating one of the strongest proponents of social experimentation in our nation. Given his character, however, we may feel sure that he shares our interests both in a progressive program of experimental social amelioration, and in making the most

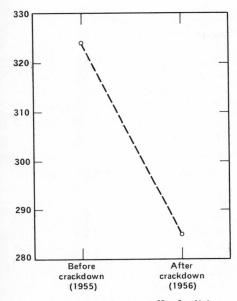

FIG. 1. Connecticut traffic fatalities.

hard-headed evaluation possible of these experiments. Indeed, it was his integrity in using every available means at his disposal as Governor to make sure that the unpopular speeding crackdown was indeed enforced that make these data worth examining at all. But the potentials of this one illustration and our political temptation to substitute for it a less touchy one, point to the political problems that must be faced in experimenting with social reform.

Keeping Figure 1 and Ribicoff's statement in mind, let us look at the same data presented as a part of an extended time series in Figure 2 and go over the relevant threats to internal validity. First, *History*. Both presentations fail to control for the effects of other potential change agents. For instance, 1956 might have been a particularly dry year, with fewer accidents due to rain or snow. Or there might have been a dramatic increase in use of seat belts, or other safety features. The advocated strategy in quasi-experimentation is not to throw up one's hands and refuse to use the evidence because of this lack of control, but rather to generate by informed criticism appropriate to this specific setting as many *plausible* rival hypotheses as possible, and then to do the supplementary research, as into weather records and safety-belt sales, for example, which would reflect on these rival hypotheses.

Maturation

This is a term coming from criticisms of training studies of children.

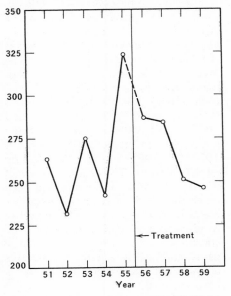

FIG. 2. Connecticut traffic fatalities. (Same data as in Figure 1 presented as part of an extended time series.)

Applied here to the simple pretest-posttest data of Figure 1, it could be the plausible rival hypothesis that death rates were steadily going down year after year (as indeed they are, relative to miles driven or population of automobiles). Here the extended time series has a strong methodological advantage, and rules out this threat to validity. The general trend is inconsistently up prior to the crackdown, and steadily down thereafter.

Instability

Seemingly implicit in the public pronouncement was the assumption that all of the change from 1955 to 1956 was due to the crackdown. There was no recognition of the fact that all time series are unstable even when no treatments are being applied. The degree of this normal instability is the crucial issue, and one of the main advantages of the extended time series is that it samples this instability. The great pretreatment instability now makes the treatment effect look relatively trivial. The 1955–56 shift is less than the gains of both 1954–55 and 1952–53. It is the largest drop in the series, but it exceeds the drops of 1951–52, 1953–54, and 1957–58 by trivial amounts. Thus the unexplained instabilities of the series are such as to make the 1955–56 drop understandable as more of the same. On the other hand, it is noteworthy that after the crackdown there are no year-to-year gains, and in this respect the character of the time series seems definitely to have changed.

The threat of instability is the only threat to which tests of significance are relevant. Box and Tiao (1965) have an elegant Bayesian model for the interrupted time series. Applied by Glass (1968) to our monthly data, with seasonal trends removed, it shows a statistically significant downward shift in the series after the crackdown. But as we shall see, an alternative explanation of at least part of this significant effect exists.

Regression

In true experiments the treatment is applied independently of the prior state of the units. In natural experiments exposure to treatment is often a cosymptom of the treated group's condition. The treatment is apt to be an *effect* rather than, or in addition to being, a cause. Psychotherapy is such a cosymptom treatment, as is any other in which the treated group is self-selected or assigned on the basis of need. These all present special problems of interpretation, of which the present illustration provides one type.

The selection-regression plausible rival hypothesis works this way: Given that the fatality rate has some degree of unreliability, then a subsample selected for its extremity in 1955 would on the average, merely as a reflection of that unreliability, be less extreme in 1956. Has there been selection for extremity in applying this treatment? Probably yes. Of all Connecticut fatality years, the most likely time for a crackdown would be after an exceptionally high year. If the time series showed instability, the subsequent year would on the average be less, *purely as a function of that instability*. Regression artifacts are probably the most recurrent form of self-deception in the experimental social reform literature. It is hard to make them intuitively obvious. Let us try again. Take any time series with variability, including one generated of pure error. Move along it as in a time dimension. Pick a point that is the "highest so far." Look then at the next point. On the average this next point will be lower, or nearer the general trend.

In our present setting the most striking shift in the whole series is the upward shift just prior to the crackdown. It is highly probable that this caused the crackdown, rather than, or in addition to, the crackdown causing the 1956 drop. At least part of the 1956 drop is an artifact of the 1955 extremity. While in principle the degree of expected regression can be computed from the autocorrelation of the series, we lack here an extended-enough body of data to do this with any confidence.

Advice to administrators who want to do genuine reality-testing must include attention to this problem, and it will be a very hard problem to surmount. The most general advice would be to work on chronic problems of a persistent urgency or extremity, rather than reacting to momentary extremes. The administrator should look at the pretreatment time series to judge whether or not instability plus momentary extremity will explain away his program gains. If it will, he should schedule the treatment for a year or two later, so that his decision is more independent of the one year's extremity. (The selection biases remaining under such a procedure need further examination.)

In giving advice to the *experimental* administrator, one is also inevitably

giving advice to those *trapped* administrators whose political predicament requires a favorable outcome whether valid or not. To such trapped administrators the advice is pick the very worst year, and the very worst social unit. If there is inherent instability, there is no where to go but up, for the average case at least.

Two other threats to internal validity need discussion in regard to this design. By *testing* we typically have in mind the condition under which a test of attitude, ability, or personality is itself a change agent, persuading, informing, practicing, or otherwise setting processes of change in action. No artificially introduced testing procedures are involved here. However, for the simple before-and-after design of Figure 1, if the pretest were the first data collection of its kind ever publicized, this publicity in itself might produce a reduction in traffic deaths which would have taken place even without a speeding crackdown. Many traffic safety programs assume this. The longer time-series evidence reassures us on this only to the extent that we can assume that the figures had been published each year with equivalent emphasis.[3]

Instrumentation changes are not a likely flaw in this instance, but would be if recording practices and institutional responsibility had shifted simultaneously with the crackdown. Probably in a case like this it is better to use raw frequencies rather than indices whose correction parameters are subject to periodic revision. Thus per capita rates are subject to periodic jumps as new census figures become available correcting old extrapolations.

Analogously, a change in the miles per gallon assumed in estimating traffic mileage for mileage-based mortality rates might explain a shift. Such biases can of course work to disguise a true effect. Almost certainly, Ribicoff's crackdown reduced traffic speed (Campbell & Ross, 1968). Such a decrease in speed increases the miles per gallon actually obtained, producing a concomitant drop in the estimate of miles driven, which would appear as an inflation of the estimate of mileage-based traffic fatalities if the same fixed approximation to actual miles per gallon were used, as it undoubtedly would be.

The "new broom" that introduces abrupt changes of policy is apt to reform the record keeping too, and thus confound reform treatments with instrumentation change. The ideal experimental administrator will, if possible, avoid doing this. He will prefer to keep comparable a partially imperfect measuring system rather than lose comparability altogether. The politics of the situation do not always make this possible, however. Consider, as an experimental reform, Orlando Wilson's reorganization of the police system in Chicago. Figure 3 shows his impact on petty larceny in Chicago—a striking *increase!* Wilson, of course, called this shot in advance, one aspect of his reform being a reform in the bookkeeping. (Note in the pre-Wilson records the suspicious absence of the expected upward secular trend.) In this situation Wilson had no choice. Had he left the record keeping as it was, for the purposes of better experimental design, his resentful patrolmen would have clobbered him with a crime wave by

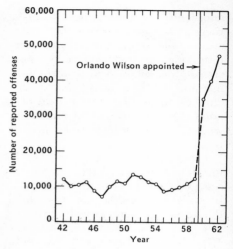

FIG. 3. Number of reported larcenies under $50 in Chicago, Illinois, from 1942 to 1962 (data from *Uniform Crime Reports for the United States,* 1942–62).

deliberately starting to record the many complaints that had not been getting into the books.[4]

Those who advocate the use of archival measures as social indicators (Bauer, 1966; Gross, 1966, 1967; Kaysen, 1967; Webb et al., 1966) must face up not only to their high degree of chaotic error and systematic bias, but also to the politically motivated changes in record keeping that will follow upon their public use as social indicators (Etzioni & Lehman, 1967). Not all measures are equally susceptible. In Figure 4, Orlando Wilson's effect on homicides seems negligible one way or the other.

Of the threats to external validity, the one most relevant to social experimentation is *Irrelevant Responsiveness of Measures.* This seems best discussed in terms of the problem of generalizing from indicator to indicator or in terms of the imperfect validity of all measures that is only to be overcome by the use of multiple measures of independent imperfection (Campbell & Fiske, 1959; Webb et al., 1966).

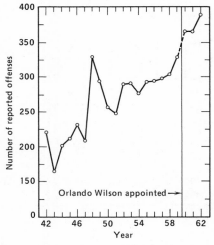

FIG. 4. Number of reported murders and nonnegligent manslaughters in Chicago, Illinois, from 1942 to 1962 (data from *Uniform Crime Reports for the United States,* 1942–62).

For treatments on any given problem within any given governmental or business subunit, there will usually be something of a governmental monopoly on reform. Even though different divisions may optimally be trying different reforms, within each division there will usually be only one reform on a given problem going on at a time. But for measures of effect this need not and should not be the case. The administrative machinery should itself make multiple measures of po-

tential benefits and of unwanted side effects. In addition, the loyal opposition should be allowed to add still other indicators, with the political process and adversary argument challenging both validity and relative importance, with social science methodologists testifying for both parties, and with the basic records kept public and under bipartisan audit (as are voting records under optimal conditions). This competitive scrutiny is indeed the main source of objectivity in sciences (Polanyi, 1966, 1967; Popper, 1963) and epitomizes an ideal of democratic practice in both judicial and legislative procedures.

The next few figures return again to the Connecticut crackdown on speeding and look to some other measures of effect. They are relevant to the confirming that there was indeed a crackdown, and to the issue of side effects. They also provide the methodological comfort of assuring us that in some cases the interrupted time-series design can provide clear-cut evidence of effect. Figure 5 shows the jump in suspensions of licenses for speeding—evidence that severe punishment was abruptly instituted. Again a note to experimental administrators: with this weak design, *it is only abrupt and decisive changes that we have any chance of evaluating.* A gradually introduced reform will be indistinguishable from the background of secular change, from the net effect of the innumerable change agents continually impinging.

We would want intermediate evidence that traffic speed was modified. A sampling each year of a few hundred five-minute highway movies (random as to location and time) could have

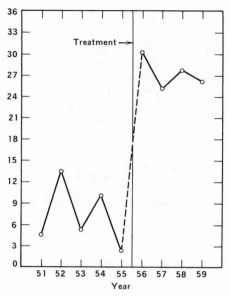

FIG. 5. Suspensions of licenses for speeding, as a percentage of all suspensions.

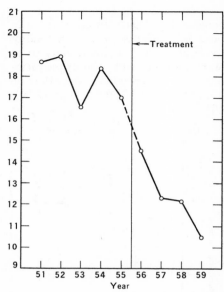

FIG. 6. Speeding violations, as a percentage of all traffic violations.

provided this at a moderate cost, but they were not collected. Of the public records available, perhaps the data of Figure 6, showing a reduction in speeding violations, indicate a reduction in traffic speed. But the effects on the legal system were complex, and in part undesirable. Driving with a suspended license markedly increased (Figure 7), at least in the biased sample of those arrested. Presumably because of the harshness of the punishment if guilty, judges may have become more lenient (Figure 8) although this effect is of marginal significance.

The relevance of indicators for the social problems we wish to cure must be kept continually in focus. The social

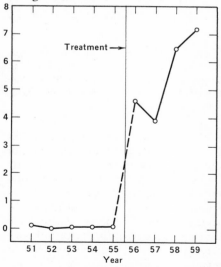

FIG. 7. Arrested while driving with a suspended license, as a percentage of suspensions.

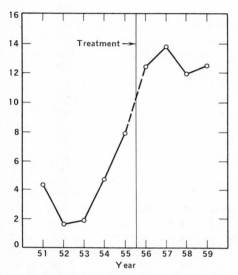

FIG. 8. Percentage of speeding violations judged not guilty.

indicators approach will tend to make the indicators themselves the goal of social action, rather than the social problems they but imperfectly indicate. There are apt to be tendencies to legislate changes in the indicators per se rather than changes in the social problems.

To illustrate the problem of the irrelevant responsiveness of measures, Figure 9 shows a result of the 1900 change in divorce law in Germany. In a recent reanalysis of the data with the Box and Tiao (1965) statistic, Glass (Glass, Tiao, & Maguire, 1969) has found the change highly significant, in contrast to earlier statistical analyses (Rheinstein, 1959; Wolf, Lüke, & Hax, 1959). But Rheinstein's emphasis would still be relevant: This indicator change indicates no likely improvement in marital harmony, or even in marital stability. Rather than reducing them, the legal change has made the divorce rate a less valid indicator of marital discord and separation than it had been earlier (see also Etzioni & Lehman, 1967).

CONTROL SERIES DESIGN

The interrupted time-series design as discussed so far is available for those settings in which no control group is

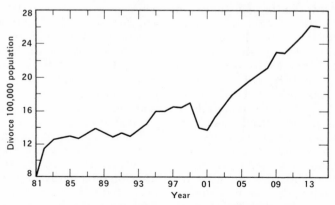

FIG. 9. Divorce rate for German Empire, 1881–1914.

possible, in which the total governmental unit has received the experimental treatment, the social reform measure. In the general program of quasi-experimental design, we argue the great advantage of untreated comparison groups even where these cannot be assigned at random. The most common of such designs is the nonequivalent control-group pretest-posttest design, in which for each of two natural groups, one of which receives the treatment, a pretest and posttest measure is taken. If the traditional mistaken practice is avoided of matching on pretest scores (with resultant regression artifacts), this design provides a useful control over those aspects of history, maturation, and test-retest effects shared by both groups. But it does not control for the plausible rival hypothesis of *selection-maturation interaction*—that is, the hypothesis that the selection differences in the natural aggregations involve not only differences in mean level, but differences in maturation rate.

This point can be illustrated in terms of the traditional quasi-experimental design problem of the effects of Latin on English vocabulary (Campbell, 1963). In the hypothetical data of Figure 10B, two alternative interpretations remain open. Latin may have had effect, for those taking Latin gained more than those not. But, on the other hand, those students taking Latin may have a greater annual rate of vocabulary growth that would manifest itself whether or not they took Latin. Extending this common design into two time series provides relevant

evidence, as comparison of the two alternative outcomes of Figure 10C and 10D shows. Thus approaching quasi-experimental design from either improving the nonequivalent control-group design or from improving the interrupted time-series design, we arrive at the control series design. Figure 11 shows this for the Connecticut speeding crackdown, adding evidence from the fatality rates of neighboring states. Here the data are presented as population-based fatality rates so as to make the two series of comparable magnitude.

The control series design of Figure 11 shows that downward trends were available in the other states for 1955–56 as due to history and maturation, that is, due to shared secular trends, weather, automotive safety features, etc. But the data also show a general trend for Connecticut to rise relatively closer to the other states prior to 1955, and to steadily drop more rapidly than other states from 1956 on. Glass (1968) has used our monthly data for Connecticut and the control states to generate a monthly difference score, and this too shows a significant shift in trend in the Box and Tiao (1965) statistic. Impressed particularly by the 1957, 1958, and 1959 trend, we are willing to conclude that the crackdown had some effect, over and above the undeniable pseudo-effects of regression (Campbell & Ross, 1968).

The advantages of the control series design point to the advantages for social experimentation of a social system allowing subunit diversity. Our ability to estimate the effects of the speeding crackdown, Rose's (1952) and Stieber's

(1949) ability to estimate the effects on strikes of compulsory arbitration laws, and Simon's (1966) ability to estimate the price elasticity of liquor were made possible because the changes were not being put into effect in all states simultaneously, because they were matters of state legislation rather than national. I do not want to appear to justify on these grounds the wasteful and unjust diversity of laws and enforcement practices from state to state. But I would strongly advocate that social engineers make use of this diversity while it remains available, and plan cooperatively their changes in administrative policy and in record keeping so as to provide optimal experimental inference. More

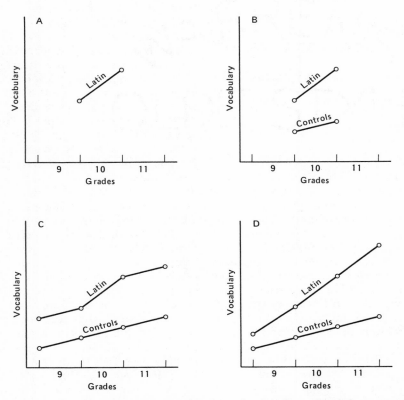

FIG. 10. Forms of quasi-experimental analysis for the effect of specific course work, including control series design.

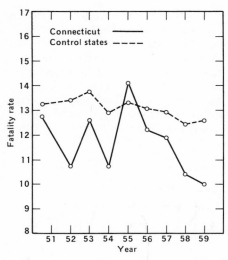

FIG. 11. Control series design comparing Connecticut fatalities with those of four comparable states.

important is the recommendation that, for those aspects of social reform handled by the central government, a purposeful diversity of implementation be envisaged so that experimental and control groups be available for analysis. Properly planned, these can approach true experiments, better than the casual and ad hoc comparison groups now available. But without such fundamental planning, uniform central control can reduce the present possibilities of reality testing, that is, of true social experimentation. In the same spirit, decentralization of desion making, both within large government and within private monopolies, can provide a useful competition for both efficiency and innovation, reflected in a multiplicity of indicators.

One further illustration of the interrupted time series and the control series will be provided. The variety of illustrations so far given have each illustrated some methodological point, and have thus ended up as "bad examples." To provide a "good example," an instance which survives methodological critique as a valid illustration of a successful reform, data from the British Road Safety Act of 1967 are provided in Figure 11A (from Ross, Campbell, & Glass, 1970).

The data on a weekly-hours basis are available only for a composite category of fatalities plus serious injuries, and Figure 11A therefore uses this composite for all three bodies of data. The "Weekend Nights" comprises Friday and Saturday nights from 10:00 P.M. to 4:00 A.M. Here, as expected, the crackdown is most dramatically effective, producing initially more than a 40 per cent drop, leveling off at perhaps 30 per cent, although this involves dubious extrapolations in the absence of some control comparison to indicate what the trend over the years might have been without the crackdown. In this British case, no comparison state with comparable traffic conditions or drinking laws was available. But controls need not always be separate groups of persons, they may also be separate samples of times or stimulus materials (Campbell & Stanley, 1966 pp. 43–47). A cigarette company may use the sales of its main competitor as a control comparison to evaluate a new advertising campaign.

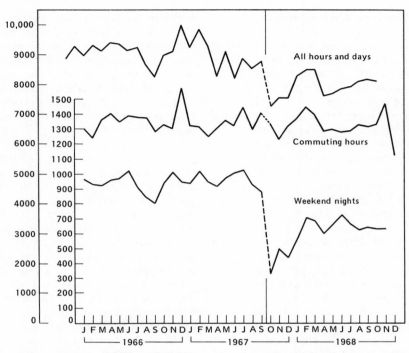

FIG. 11A. British traffic fatalities plus serious injuries, before and after Breathalyser crackdown of October 1967 (seasonally adjusted).

One should search around for the most nearly appropriate control comparison. For the Breathalyser crackdown, commuting hours when pubs had been long closed seemed ideal. (The "Commuting Hours" figures come from 7:00 A.M. to 10:00 A.M. and 4:00 P.M. to 5:00 P.M. Monday through Friday. Pubs are open for lunch from 12:00 to 2:00 or 2:30, and open again at 5:00 P.M.)

These commuting hours data convincingly show no effect, but are too unstable to help much with estimating the long-term effects. They show a different annual cycle than do the weekend nights or the overall figures, and do not go back far enough to provide an adequate base for estimating this annual cycle with precision.

The use of a highly judgmental category such as "serious injuries" provides an opportunity for pseudo effects owing to a shift in the classifiers' standards. The overall figures are available separately for fatalities, and these show a highly significant effect as strong as that found for the serious injury category or the composite shown in Figure 11A.

More details and the methodological problems are considered in our fuller presentation (Ross, Campbell, & Glass, 1970). One further rule for the use of this design needs emphasizing. The interrupted time series can provide clear evidence of effect only where the reform is introduced with a vigorous abruptness. A gradually introduced reform has little chance of being distinguished from shifts in secular trends or from the cumulative effect of the many other influences impinging during a prolonged period of introduction. In the Breathalyser crackdown, an intense publicity campaign naming the specific starting date preceded the actual crackdown. Although the impact seems primarily due to publicity and fear rather than an actual increase of arrests, an abrupt initiation date was achieved. Had the enforcement effort changed at the moment the Act was passed, with public awareness being built up by subsequent publicity, the resulting data series would have been essentially uninterpretable.

REGRESSION DISCONTINUITY DESIGN

We shift now to social ameliorations that are in short supply, and that therefore cannot be given to all individuals. Such scarcity is inevitable under many circumstances, and can make possible an evaluation of effects that would otherwise be impossible. Consider the heroic Salk poliomyelitis vaccine trials in which some children were given the vaccine while others were given an inert saline placebo injection—and in which many more of these placebo controls would die than would have if they had been given the vaccine. Creation of these placebo controls would have been morally, psychologically, and socially impossible had there been enough vaccine for all. As it was, due to the scarcity, most children that year had to go without the vaccine anyway. The creation of experimental and control groups was the highly moral allocation of that scarcity so as to enable us to learn the true efficacy of the supposed good. The usual medical practice of introducing new cures on a so-called trial basis in general medical practice makes evaluation impossible by confounding prior status with treatment, that is, giving the drug to the most needy or most hopeless. It has the further social bias of giving the supposed benefit to those most assiduous in keeping their medical needs in the attention of the medical profession, that is, the upper and upper-middle classes. The political stance furthering social experimentation here is the recognition of randomization as the most democratic and moral means of allocating scarce resources (and scarce hazardous duties), plus the moral imperative to further utilize the randomization so that society may indeed learn the true value of the supposed boon. This is the ideology that makes possible "true experiments" in a large class of social reforms.

But if randomization is not politically feasible or morally justifiable in a given setting, there is a powerful quasi-experimental design available that allows the scarce good to be given to the most needy or the most deserv-

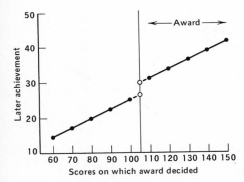

FIG. 12. Tie-breaking experiment and regression discontinuity analysis.

ing. This is the regression discontinuity design. All it requires is strict and orderly attention to the priority dimension. The design originated through an advocacy of a tie-breaking experiment to measure the effects of receiving a fellowship (Thistlethwaite & Campbell, 1960), and it seems easiest to explain it in that light. Consider as in Figure 12, pre-award ability-and-merit dimension, which would have some relation to later success in life (finishing college, earnings 10 years later, etc.). Those higher on the pre-measure are most deserving and receive the award. They do better in later life, but does the award have an effect? It is normally impossible to say because they would have done better in later life anyway. Full randomization of the award was impossible given the stated intention to reward merit and ability. But it might be possible to take a narrow band of ability at the cutting point, to regard all of these persons as tied, and to assign half of

them to awards, half to no awards, by means of a tie-breaking randomization.

The tie-breaking rationale is still worth doing, but in considering that design it became obvious that, if the regression of premeasure on later effects were reasonably orderly, one should be able to extrapolate to the results of the tie-breaking experiment by plotting the regression of posttest on pretest separately for those in the award and nonaward regions. If there is no significant difference for these at the decision-point intercept, then the tie-breaking experiment should show no difference. In cases where the tie breakers would show an effect, there should be an abrupt discontinuity in the regression line. Such a discontinuity cannot be explained away by the normal regression of the posttest on pretest, for this normal regression, as extensively sampled within the nonaward area and within the award area, provides no such expectation.

Figure 12 presents, in terms of column means, an instance in which higher pretest scores would have led to higher posttest scores even without the treatment, and in which there is in addition a substantial treatment effect. Figure 13 shows a series of paired outcomes, those on the left to be interpreted as no effect, those in the center and on the right as effect. Note some particular cases. In instances of granting opportunity on the basis of merit, like 13a and b (and Figure 12), neglect of the background regression of pretest on posttest leads to optimistic pseudo-effects: in Figure 13a, those receiving the award do do better in later

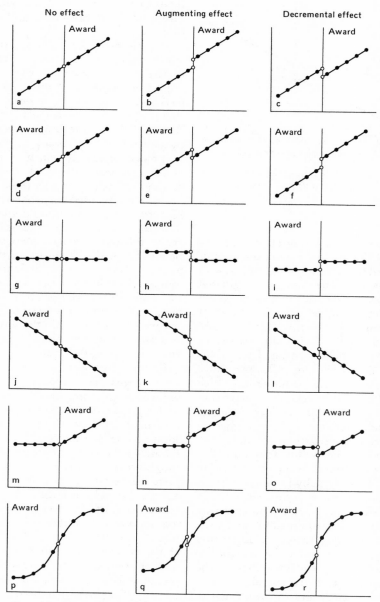

FIG. 13. Illustrative outcomes of regression discontinuity analyses.

life, though not really because of the award. But in social ameliorative efforts, the setting is more apt to be like Figure 13d and e, where neglect of the background regression is apt to make the program look deleterious if no effect, or ineffective if there is a real effect.

The design will of course work just as well or better if the award dimension and the decision base, the pretest measure, are unrelated to the posttest dimension, if it is irrelevant or unfair, as instanced in Figure 13g, h, and i. In such cases the decision base is the functional equivalent of randomization. Negative background relationships are obviously possible, as in Figure 13j, k, and l. In Figure 13, m, n, and o are included to emphasize that it is a jump in intercept at the cutting point that shows effect, and that differences in

slope without differences at the cutting point are not acceptable as evidences of effect. This becomes more obvious if we remember that in cases like m, a tie-breaking randomization experiment would have shown no difference. Curvilinear background relationships, as in Figure 13p, q, and r, will provide added obstacles to clear inference in many instances, where sampling error could make Figure 13p look like 13b.

As further illustration, Figure 14 provides computer-simulated data, showing individual observations and fitted regression lines, in a fuller version of the no-effect outcome of Figure 13a. Figure 15 shows an outcome with effect. These have been generated[5] by assigning to each individual a weighted normal random number as a "true score," to which is added a weighted independent "error" to gen-

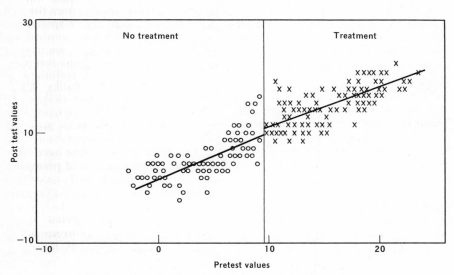

FIG. 14. Regression discontinuity design: No effect.

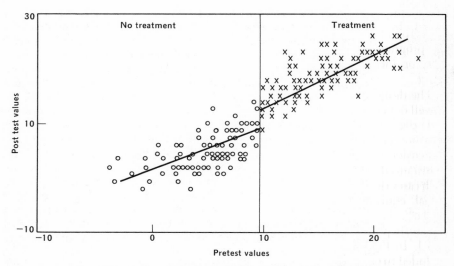

FIG. 15. Regression discontinuity design: Genuine effect.

erate the "pretest." The "true score" plus another independent "error" produces the "posttest" in no-effect cases such as Figure 14. In treatment-effect simulations, as in Figure 15, there are added into the posttest "effects points" for all "treated" cases, that is, those above the cutting point on the pretest score.

This design could be used in a number of settings. Consider Job Training Corps applicants, in larger number than the program can accommodate, with eligibility determined by need. The setting would be as in Figure 13d and e. The base-line decision dimension could be per capita family income, with those at below the cutoff getting training. The outcome dimension could be the amount of withholding tax withheld two years later, or the percentage drawing un-

employment insurance, these follow-up figures being provided from the National Data Bank in response to categorized social security numbers fed in, without individual anonymity being breached, without any real invasion of privacy—by the technique of Mutually Insulated Data Banks. While the plotted points could be named, there is no need that they be named. In a classic field experiment on tax compliance, Richard Schwartz and the Bureau of Internal Revenue have managed to put together sets of personally identified interviews and tax-return data so that statistical analyses such as these can be done, without the separate custodians of either interview or tax returns learning the corresponding data for specific persons (Schwartz & Orleans, 1967; see also Schwartz & Skolnick, 1963).

Applied to the Job Training Corps illustration, it would work as follows: Separate lists of job-corps applicants (with social security numbers) would be prepared for every class interval on per capita family income. To each of these lists an alphabetical designation would be assigned at random. (Thus the $10.00 per week list might be labeled *M;* $11.00, *C;* $12.00, *Z;* $13.00, *Q;* $14.00, *N;* etc.) These lists would be sent to Internal Revenue, without the Internal Revenue personnel being able to learn anything interpretable about their traineeship status or family income. The Internal Revenue statisticians would locate the withholding tax collected for each person on each list, but would not return the data in that form. Instead, for each list, only the withholding tax amounts would be listed, and these in a newly randomized order. These would be returned to Job Corps research, who could use them to plot a graph like Figures 10 or 11, and do the appropriate statistical analyses by retranslating the alphabetical symbols into meaningful base-line values. But, within any list, they would be unable to learn which value belonged to which person. (To insure this effective anonymity, it could be specified that no lists shorter than 100 persons be used, the base-line intervals being expanded if necessary to achieve this.)

Manniche and Hayes (1957) have spelled out how a broker can be used in a two-staged matching of doubly coded data. Kaysen (1967) and Sawyer and Schechter (1968) have wise discussions of the more general problem.

What is required of the adminis-trator of a scarce ameliorative commodity to use this design? Most essential is a sharp cutoff point on a decision-criterion dimension, on which several other qualitatively similar analytic cutoffs can be made both above and below the award cut. Let me explain this better by explaining why National Merit scholarships were unable to use the design for their actual fellowship decision (although it has been used for their Certificate of Merit). In their operation, diverse committees make small numbers of award decisions by considering a group of candidates and then picking from them the N best to which to award the N fellowships allocated them. This provides one cutting point on an unspecified pooled decision base, but fails to provide analogous potential cutting points above and below. What could be done is for each committee to collectively rank its group of 20 or so candidates. The top N would then receive the award. Pooling cases across committees, cases could be classified according to number of ranks above and below the cutting point, these other ranks being analogous to the award-nonaward cutting point as far as regression onto posttreatment measures was concerned. Such group ranking would be costly of committee time. An equally good procedure, if committees agreed, would be to have each member, after full discussion and freedom to revise, give each candidate a grade, A+, A, A−, B+, B, etc., and to award the fellowships to the N candidates averaging best on these ratings, with no revisions allowed after the averaging process. These ranking or rating units, even if not comparable from committee to committee in range of talent, in number of persons ranked, or in cutting point, could be pooled without bias as far as a regression discontinuity is concerned, for that range of units above and below the cutting point in which all committees were represented.

It is the dimensionality and sharpness of the decision criterion that is at issue, not its components or validity. The ratings could be based upon nepotism, whimsey, and superstition and still serve. As has been stated, if the decision criterion is utterly invalid we approach the pure randomness of a true experiment. Thus the weakness of subjective committee decisions is not their subjectivity, but the fact that they provide only the one cutting point on their net subjective dimension. Even in the form of average ratings the recommended procedures probably represent some slight increase in committee work load. But this could be justified to the decision committees by the fact that through refusals, etc., it cannot be known at the time of the committee meeting the exact number to whom the fellowship can be offered. Other costs at the planning time are likewise minimal. The primary additional burden is in keeping as good records on the nonawardees as on the awardees. Thus at a low cost, an experimental administrator can lay the groundwork for later scientific follow-ups, the budgets for which need not yet be in sight.

Our present situation is more apt to be one where our pretreatment measures, aptitude measures, reference ratings, etc., can be combined via multiple correlation into an index that correlates highly but not perfectly with the award decision. For this dimension there is a fuzzy cutoff point. Can the design be used in this case? Probably not. Figure 16 shows the pseudo-effect possible if the award decision contributes any valid variance to the quantified pretest evidence, as it usually will. The award regression rides above the nonaward regression just because of that valid variance in this simulated case, there being no true award effect at all. (In simulating this case, the award decision has been based upon a composite of true score plus an independent award error.) Figure 17 shows a fuzzy cutting point plus a genuine award effect.[6] The recommendation to the administrator is clear: aim for a sharp cutting point on a quantified decision criterion. If there are complex rules for eligibility, only one of which is quantified, seek out for follow-up that subset of persons for whom the quantitative dimension was determinate. If political patronage necessitates some decisions inconsistent with a sharp cutoff, record these cases under the heading "qualitative decision rule" and keep them out of your experimental analysis.

Almost all of our ameliorative programs designed for the disadvantaged could be studied via this design, and so too some major governmental actions affecting the lives of citizens in ways we do not think of as experimental. For example, for a considerable period, quantitative test scores have been used to call up for military service or reject as unfit at the lower ability range. If these cutting points, test scores, names, and social security numbers have been recorded for a number of steps both above and below the cutting point, we could make elegant studies of the effect of military service on later withholding taxes, mortality, number of dependents, etc.

This illustration points to one of the threats to external validity of this design, or of the tie-breaking experiment. The effect of the treatment has only been studied for that narrow range of talent near the cutting point, and generalization of the effects of military service, for example, from this low ability level to the careers of the most able would be hazardous in the extreme. But in the draft laws and the requirements of the military services there may be other sharp cutting points on a quantitative criterion that could

also be used. For example, those over 6 feet 6 inches are excluded from service. Imagine a five-year-later follow-up of draftees grouped by inch in the 6 feet 1 inch to 6 feet 5 inches range, and a group of their counterparts who would have been drafted except for their heights, 6 feet 6 inches to 6 feet 10 inches. (The fact that the other grounds of deferment might not have been examined by the draft board would be a problem here, but probably not insurmountable.) That we should not expect height in this range to have any relation to later-life variables is not at all a weakness of this design, and if we have indeed a subpopulation for which there is a sharp numerical cutting point, an internally valid measure of effects would result. Deferment under the present system is an unquan-

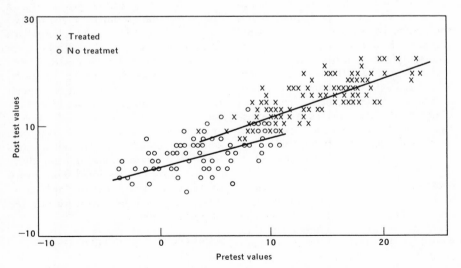

FIG. 16. Regression discontinuity design: Fuzzy cutting point, pseudo treatment effect only.

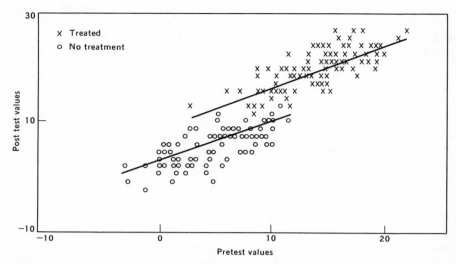

FIG. 17. Regression discontinuity design: Fuzzy cutting point, with real treatment plus pseudo treatment effects.

tified committee decision. But just as the sense of justice of United States soldiers was quantified through paired comparisons of cases into an acceptable Demobilization Points system at the end of World War II (Guttman, 1946; Stouffer, 1949), so a quantified composite index of deferment priority could be achieved and applied as uniform justice across the nation, providing another numerical cutting point.

In addition to the National Data Bank type of indicators, there will be occasions in which new data collections as by interview or questionnaire are needed. For these there is the special problem of uneven cooperation that would be classified as instrumentation error. In our traditional mode of thinking, completeness of description is valued more highly than comparability.

Thus if, in a fellowship study, a follow-up mailed out from the fellowship office would bring a higher return from past winners, this might seem desirable even if the nonawardees' rate of response was much lower. From the point of view of quasi-experimentation, however, it would be better to use an independent survey agency and a disguised purpose, achieving equally low response rates from both awardees and nonawardees, and avoiding a regression discontinuity in cooperation rate that might be misinterpreted as a discontinuity in more important effects.

RANDOMIZED CONTROL GROUP EXPERIMENTS

Experiments with randomization tend to be limited to the laboratory and agricultural experiment station. But this certainly need not be so. The randomization unit may be persons, families, precincts, or larger administrative units. For statistical purposes the randomization units should be numerous, and hence ideally small. But for reasons of external validity, including reactive arrangements, the randomization units should be selected on the basis of the units of administrative access. Where policies are administered through individual client contacts, randomization at the person level may be often inconspicuously achieved, with the clients unaware that different ones of them are getting different treatments. But for most social reforms, larger administrative units will be involved, such as classrooms, schools, cities, counties, or states. We need to develop the political postures and ideologies that make randomization at these levels possible.

"Pilot project" is a useful term already in our political vocabulary. It designates a trial program that, if it works, will be spread to other areas. By modifying actual practice in this regard, without going outside of the popular understanding of the term, a valuable experimental ideology could be developed. How are areas selected for pilot projects? If the public worries about this, it probably assumes a lobbying process in which the greater needs of some areas are only one consideration, political power and expediency being others. Without violating the public tolerance or intent, one could probably devise a system in which the usual lobbying decided upon the areas eligible for a formal public

lottery that would make final choices between matched pairs. Such decision procedures as the drawing of lots have had a justly esteemed position since time immemorial (e.g., Aubert, 1959). At the present time, record keeping for pilot projects tends to be limited to the experimental group only. In the experimental ideology, comparable data would be collected on designated controls. (There are of course exceptions, as in the heroic Public Health Service fluoridation experiments, in which the teeth of Oak Park children were examined year after year as controls for the Evanston experimentals [Blayney & Hill, 1967].)

Another general political stance making possible experimental social amelioration is that of *staged innovation.* Even though by intent a new reform is to be put into effect in all units, the logistics of the situation usually dictate that simultaneous introduction is not possible. What results is a haphazard sequence of convenience. Under the program of staged innovation, the introduction of the program would be deliberately spread out, and those units selected to be first and last would be randomly assigned (perhaps randomization from matched pairs), so that during the transition period the first recipients could be analyzed as experimental units, the last recipients as controls. A third ideology making possible true experiments has already been discussed: randomization as the democratic means of allocating scarce resources.

This article will not give true experimentation equal space with quasi-experimentation only because excellent discussions of, and statistical consultation on, true experimentation are readily available. True experiments should almost always be preferred to quasi-experiments where both are available. Only occasionally are the threats to external validity so much greater for the true experiment that one would prefer a quasi-experiment. The uneven allocation of space here should not be read as indicating otherwise.

MORE ADVICE FOR TRAPPED ADMINISTRATORS

But the competition is not really between the fairly interpretable quasi-experiments here reviewed and "true" experiments. Both stand together as rare excellencies in contrast with a morass of obfuscation and self-deception. Both to emphasize this contrast, and again as guidelines for the benefit of those trapped administrators whose political predicament will not allow the risk of failure, some of these alternatives should be mentioned.

Grateful Testimonials

Human courtesy and gratitude being what it is, the most dependable means of assuring a favorable evaluation is to use voluntary testimonials from those who have had the treatment. If the spontaneously produced testimonials are in short supply, these should be solicited from the recipients with whom the program is still in contact. The rosy glow resulting is analogous to the professor's impression of his teaching success when it is based solely upon the comments of those students who come up and talk with him after class. In many programs, as in

psychotherapy, the recipient, as well as the agency, has devoted much time and effort to the program and it is dissonance reducing for himself, as well as common courtesy to his therapist, to report improvement. These grateful testimonials can come in the language of letters and conversation, or be framed as answers to multiple-item "tests" in which a recurrent theme of "I am sick," "I am well," "I am happy," "I am sad" recurs. Probably the testimonials will be more favorable as: (*a*) the more the evaluative meaning of the response measure is clear to the recipient—it is completely clear in most personality, adjustment, morale, and attitude tests; (*b*) the more directly the recipient is identified by name with his answer; (*c*) the more the recipient gives the answer directly to the therapist or agent of reform; (*d*) the more the agent will continue to be influential in the recipient's life in the future; (*e*) the more the answers deal with feelings and evaluations rather than with verifiable facts; and (*f*) the more the recipients participating in the evaluation are a small and self-selected or agent-selected subset of all recipients. Properly designed the grateful testimonial method can involve pretests as well as posttests, and randomized control groups as well as experimentals, for there are usually no placebo treatments, and the recipients know when they have had the boon.

Confounding Selection and Treatment

Another dependable tactic bound to give favorable outcomes is to confound selection and treatment, so that in the published comparison those receiving the treatment are also the more able and well placed. The often-cited evidence of the dollar value of a college education is of this nature—all careful studies show that most of the effect, and of the superior effect of superior colleges, is explainable in terms of superior talents and family connections, rather than in terms of what is learned or even the prestige of the degree. Matching techniques and statistical partialings generally undermatch and do not fully control for the selection differences—they introduce regression artifacts confusable as treatment effects.

There are two types of situations that must be distinguished. First, there are those treatments that are given to the most promising, treatments like a college education which are regularly given to those who need it least. For these, the later concomitants of the grounds of selection operate in the same direction as the treatment: those most likely to achieve anyway get into the college most likely to produce later achievement. For these settings, the trapped administrator should use the pooled mean of all those treated, comparing it with the mean of all untreated, although in this setting almost any comparison an administrator might hit upon would be biased in his favor.

At the other end of the talent continuum are those remedial treatments given to those who need it most. Here the later concomitants of the grounds of selection are poorer success. In the Job Training Corps example, casual comparisons of the later unemployment rate of those who received the training with those who did not are in general biased against showing an advantage to the training. Here the trapped administrator must be careful to seek out those few special comparisons biasing selection in his favor. For training programs such as Operation Head Start and tutoring programs, a useful solution is to compare the later success of those who completed the training program with those who were invited but never showed plus those who came a few times and dropped out. By regarding only those who complete the program as "trained" and using the other as controls, one is selecting for conscientiousness, stable and supporting family backgrounds, enjoyment of the training activity, ability, determination to get ahead in the world—all factors promising well for future achievement even if the remedial program is valueless. To apply this tactic effectively in the Job Training Corps, one might have to eliminate from the so-called control group all those who quit the training program because they had found a job—but this would seem a reasonable practice and would not blemish the reception of a glowing progress report.

These are but two more samples of well-tried modes of analysis for the trapped administrator who cannot afford an honest evaluation of the social reform he directs. They remind us again that we must help create a political climate that demands more rigorous and less self-deceptive reality testing. We must provide political stances that permit true experiments, or good quasi-experiments. Of the several suggestions toward this end that are contained in this article, the most important is probably the initial theme: Administrators and parties must advocate the importance of the problem rather than the importance of the answer. They must advocate experimental sequences of reforms, rather than one certain cure-all, advocating Reform A with Alternative B available to try next should an honest evaluation of A prove it worthless or harmful.

MULTIPLE REPLICATION IN ENACTMENT

Too many social scientists expect single experiments to settle issues once and for all. This may be a mistaken generalization from the history of great crucial experiments in physics and chemistry. In actuality the significant experiments in the physical sciences are replicated thousands of times, not only in deliberate replication efforts, but also as inevitable incidentals in successive experimentation and in utilizations of those many measurement devices (such as the galvanometer) that in their own operation embody the principles of classic experiments. Because we social scientists have less ability to achieve "experimental isolation," because we have good reason to expect our treatment effects to interact significantly with a wide variety of social factors many of which we have not yet mapped, we have much greater needs for replication experiments than do the physical sciences.

The implications are clear. We should not only do hard-headed reality testing in the initial pilot testing and choosing of which reform to make gen-

eral law; but once it has been decided that the reform is to be adopted as standard practice in all administrative units, we should experimentally evaluate it in each of its implementations (Campbell, 1967).

CONCLUSIONS

Trapped administrators have so committed themselves in advance to the efficacy of the reform that they cannot afford honest evaluation. For them, favorably biased analyses are recommended, including capitalizing on regression, grateful testimonials, and confounding selection and treatment. *Experimental administrators* have justified the reform on the basis of the importance of the problem, not the certainty of their answer, and are committed to going on to other potential solutions if the one first tried fails. They are therefore not threatened by a hard-headed analysis of the reform. For such, proper administrative decisions can lay the base for useful experimental or quasi-experimental analyses. Through the ideology of allocating scarce resources by lottery, through the use of staged innovation, and through the pilot project, true experiments with randomly assigned control groups can be achieved. If the reform must be introduced across the board, the interrupted time-series design is available. If there are similar units under independent administration, a control series design adds strength. If a scarce boon must be given to the most needy or to the most deserving, quantifying this need or merit makes possible the regression discontinuity analysis.

NOTES

1. This list has been expanded from the major previous presentations by the addition of *Instability* (but see Campbell, 1968; Campbell & Ross, 1968). This has been done in reaction to the sociological discussion of the use of tests of significance in nonexperimental or quasi-experimental research (e.g., Selvin, 1957; and as reviewed by Galtung, 1967, pp. 358–389). On the one hand, I join with the critics in criticizing the exaggerated status of "statistically significant differences" in establishing convictions of validity. Statistical tests are relevant to at best 1 out of 15 or so threats to validity. On the other hand, I join with those who defend their use in situations where randomization has not been employed. Even in those situations, it is relevant to say or to deny, "This is a trivial difference. It is of the order that would have occurred frequently *had* these measures been assigned to these classes solely by chance." Tests of significance, making use of random reassignments of the actual scores, are particularly useful in communicating this point.

2. This list has been lengthened from previous presentations to make more salient Threats 5 and 6 which are particularly relevant to social experimentation. Discussion in previous presentations (Campbell, 1957, pp. 309–310; Campbell & Stanley, 1963, pp. 203–204) had covered these points, but they had not been included in the checklist.

3. No doubt the public and press shared the Governor's special alarm over the 1955 death toll. This differential reaction could be seen as a negative feedback servosystem in which the dampening effect was proportional to the degree of upward deviation from the prior trend. Insofar as such alarm reduces traffic fatalities, it adds a negative component to the autocorrelation, increasing the regression effect. This component should probably be regarded as a rival cause or treatment rather than as artifact. (The regression effect is less as the positive autocorrelation is higher, and will be present to some degree insofar as this correlation is less than positive unity. Negative correlation in a time series would represent regression beyond the mean, in a way not quite analogous to negative correlation across persons. For an autocorrelation of Lag 1, high negative correlation would be represented by a series that oscillated maximally from one extreme to the other.)

4. Wilson's inconsistency in utilization of records and the political problem of relevant records are ably documented in Kamisar (1964). Etzioni (1968) reports that in New York City in 1965 a crime wave was proclaimed that turned out to be due to an unpublicized improvement in record keeping.

5. J. Sween & D. T. Campbell, Computer programs for simulating and analyzing sharp and fuzzy regression-discontinuity experiments. In preparation.

6. There are some subtle statistical clues that might distinguish these two instances if one had enough cases. There should be increased pooled column variance in the mixed columns for a true effects case. If the data are arbitrarily treated as though there had been a sharp cutting point located in the middle of the overlap area, then there should be no discontinuity in the no-effect case, and some discontinuity in the case of a real effect, albeit an underestimated discontinuity, since there are untreated cases above the cutting point and treated ones below, dampening the apparent effect. The degree of such dampening should be estimable, and correctable, perhaps by iterative procedures. But these are hopes for the future.

REFERENCES

Aubert, V. Chance in social affairs. *Inquiry,* 1959, 2, 1–24.
Bauer, R. M. *Social indicators.* Cambridge, Mass.: M.I.T. Press, 1966.

Blayney, J. R., & Hill, I. N. Fluorine and dental caries. *The Journal of the American Dental Association* (Special Issue), 1967, 74, 233–302.

Box, G. E. P., & Tiao, G. C. A change in level of a nonstationary time series. *Biometrika,* 1965, 52, 181–192.

Campbell, D. T. Factors relevant to the validity of experiments in social settings. *Psychological Bulletin,* 1957, 54, 297–312.

Campbell, D. T. From description to experimentation: Interpreting trends as quasi-experiments. In C. W. Harris (Ed.), *Problems in measuring change.* Madison: University of Wisconsin Press, 1963.

Campbell, D. T. Administrative experimentation, institutional records, and nonreactive measures. In J. C. Stanley (Ed.), *Improving experimental design and statistical analysis.* Chicago: Rand McNally, 1967.

Campbell, D. T. Quasi-experimental design. In D. L. Sills (Ed.), *International Encyclopedia of the Social Sciences.* New York: Macmillan and Free Press, 1968, Vol. 5, 259–263.

Campbell, D. T., & Fiske, D. W. Convergent and discriminant validation by the multitrait-multimethod matrix. *Psychological Bulletin,* 1959, 56, 81–105.

Campbell, D. T., & Ross, H. L. The Connecticut crackdown on speeding: Time-series data in quasi-experimental analysis. *Law and Society Review,* 1968, 3 (1), 33–53.

Campbell, D. T., & Stanley, J. C. Experimental and quasi-experimental designs for research on teaching. In N. L. Gage (Ed.), *Handbook of research on teaching.* Chicago: Rand McNally, 1963. (Reprinted as *Experimental and quasi-experimental design for research.* Chicago: Rand McNally, 1966.)

Chapin, F. S. *Experimental design in sociological research.* New York: Harper, 1947.

Etzioni, A. "Shortcuts" to social change? *The Public Interest,* 1968, 12, 40–51.

Etzioni, A., & Lehman, E. W. Some dangers in "valid" social measurement. *Annals of the American Academy of Political and Social Science,* 1967, 373, 1–15.

Galtung, J. *Theory and methods of social research.* Oslo: Universitetsforloget; London: Allen & Unwin; New York: Columbia University Press, 1967.

Glass, G. V. Analysis of data on the Connecticut speeding crackdown as a time-series quasi-experiment. *Law and Society Review,* 1968, 3 (1), 55–76.

Glass, G. V., Tiao, G. C., & Maguire, T. O. Analysis of data on the 1900 revision of the German divorce laws as a quasi-experiment. *Law and Society Review,* 1969, in press.

Greenwood, E. *Experimental sociology: A study in method.* New York: King's Crown Press, 1945.

Gross, B. M. *The state of the nation: Social system accounting.* London: Tavistock Publications, 1966. (Also in R. M. Bauer, *Social indicators.* Cambridge, Mass.: M.I.T. Press, 1966.)

Gross, B. M. (Ed.) Social goals and indicators. *Annals of the American Academy of Political and Social Science,* 1967, 371, Part 1, May, pp. i–iii and 1–177; Part 2, September, pp. i–iii and 1–218.

Guttman, L. An approach for quantifying paired comparisons and rank order. *Annals of Mathematical Statistics,* 1946, 17, 144–163.

Hyman, H. H., & Wright, C. R. Evaluating social action programs. In P. F. Lazarsfeld, W. H. Sewell, & H. L. Wilensky (Eds.), *The uses of sociology.* New York: Basic Books, 1967.

Kamisar, Y. The tactics of police-persecution oriented critics of the courts. *Cornell Law Quarterly,* 1964, 49, 458–471.

Kaysen, C. Data banks and dossiers. *The Public Interest,* 1967, 7, 52–60.

Manniche, E., & Hayes, D. P. Respondent anonymity and data matching. *Public Opinion Quarterly,* 1957, 21 (3), 384–388.

Polanyi, M. A society of explorers. In, *The tacit dimension.* (Ch. 3) New York: Doubleday, 1966.

Polanyi, M. The growth of science in society. *Minerva,* 1967, 5, 533–545.

Popper, K. R. *Conjectures and refutations.* London: Routledge and Kegan Paul; New York: Basic Books, 1963.

Rheinstein, M. Divorce and the law in Germany: A review. *American Journal of Sociology,* 1959, 65, 489–498.

Rose, A. M. Needed research on the mediation of labor disputes. *Personnel Psychology,* 1952, 5, 187–200.

Ross, H. L., & Campbell, D. T. The Connecticut speed crackdown: A study of the effects of legal change. In H. L. Ross (Ed.), *Perspectives on the social order: Readings in sociology.* New York: McGraw-Hill, 1968.

Ross, H. L., Campbell, D. T., and Glass, G. V. Determining the social effects of a legal reform: The British "Breathalyser" crackdown of 1967. *American Behavioral Scientist,* 1970, 13, 493–509.

Sawyer, J., & Schechter, H. Computers, privacy, and the National Data Center: The responsibility of social scientists. *American Psychologist,* 1968, 23, 810–818.

Schanck, R. L., & Goodman, C. Reactions to propaganda on both sides of a controversial issue. *Public Opinion Quarterly,* 1939, 3, 107–112.

Schwartz, R. D. Field experimentation in sociological research. *Journal of Legal Education,* 1961, 13, 401–410.

Schwartz, R. D., & Orleans, S. On legal sanctions. *University of Chicago Law Review,* 1967, 34, 274–300.

Schwartz, R. D., & Skolnick, J. H. Televised communication and income tax compliance. In L. Arons & M. May (Eds.), *Television and human behavior.* New York: Appleton-Century-Crofts, 1963.

Selvin, H. A critique of tests of significance in survey research. *American Sociological Review,* 1957, 22, 519–527.

Simon, J. L. The price elasticity of liquor in the U.S. and a simple method of determination. *Econometrica,* 1966, 34, 193–205.

Solomon, R. W. An extension of control group design. *Psychological Bulletin,* 1949, 46, 137–150.

Stieber, J. W. *Ten years of the Minnesota Labor Relations Act.* Minneapolis: Industrial Relations Center, University of Minnesota, 1949.

Stouffer, S. A. The point system for redeployment and discharge. In S. A. Stouffer et al., *The American soldier. Vol. 2, Combat and its aftermath.* Princeton: Princeton University Press, 1949.

Suchman, E. A. *Evaluative research: Principles and practice in public service and social action programs.* New York: Russell Sage, 1967.

Sween, J., & Campbell, D. T. A study of the effect of proximally auto-correlated error on tests of significance for the interrupted time-series quasi-experimental design. Available from author, 1965. (Multilith)

Thistlethwaite, D. L., & Campbell, D. T. Regression-discontinuity analysis: An alternative to the ex post facto experiment. *Journal of Educational Psychology,* 1960, 51, 309–317.

Walker, H. M., & Lev, J. *Statistical inference.* New York: Holt, 1953.
Webb, E. J., Campbell, D. T., Schwartz, R. D., & Sechrest, L. B. *Unobtrusive measures: Nonreactive research in the social sciences.* Chicago: Rand McNally, 1966.
Wolf, E., Lüke, G., & Hax, H. *Scheidung und Scheidungsrecht: Grundfrägen der Ehescheidung in Deutschland.* Tübingen: J. C. B. Mohr, 1959.

13. *Research in Large-Scale Intervention Programs*

Howard E. Freeman and Clarence C. Sherwood

Dissatisfaction with the social order and zealous efforts at community change have characterized the personal and academic lives of social scientists since their emergence as an identifiable group on the American scene.[1] In many ways, of course, the various disciplines and the persons that hold membership in them have changed markedly over the last several decades: the influence of visionary clergymen, guilt-ridden do-gooders, and political radicals—dedicated to projecting their own humanitarian views in the guise of scientific inquiry—has pretty well diminished.[2]

But the social scientist has expanded his role in the modification of community life and in the amelioration of social pathologies. He puts forth theories on which action programs may be based; he serves as expert and consultant to policy-makers; and he uses his research repertoire to guide program development. There are outstanding examples of such influence: the work of Stouffer and his associates on military problems, the studies of learning psychologists on educational practices, the manifesto of Clark and other social scientists in connection with the Supreme Court's integration decision, and most recently, the document of Ohlin and Cloward on delinquency programs.[3] Certainly much of social

science activity is directed at understanding "basic" processes, but, whether by intent or not, social scientists serve as agents of social change; and, if one is willing to extrapolate from shifts in occupational settings, it appears that there is an increasing number of them who know full well the social-change potential of their work.[4]

Over the years social scientists, at least a small number of them, have been engaged in still another type of activity, the evaluation of health, education and welfare programs and interventions—in some instances by means of experimental designs that include control groups and pre-post-test measures. But up until recently the impact of their work and the findings of their studies on social policy and on community life has been minimal. This is so in spite of the fact that for 15 years or more there has been increased emphasis—particularly at the Federal level—on demonstration-research programs.

On paper, at least, there has been much concern with the assessment of therapeutic and rehabilitation efforts. Virtually all of the demonstration programs supported by public funds in the health and welfare field and many of the projects sponsored by philanthropic foundations include a require-

This paper draws heavily on material presented by the authors in separate papers at the 1964 Meetings of the American Statistical Association, Chicago, Illinois.

Reprinted with permission from *The Journal of Social Issues,* Vol. 21, No. 1, 1965, pp. 11–28.

ment that the worth of the effort be assessed. For the most part, however, the evaluation requirement has remained a formality; granting agencies have tended to overlook it in their frenzy to implement programs intuitively believed worthwhile; statements and often elaborate designs for evaluation in demonstration-research programs have been included in proposals as a ritual with full knowledge that the commitment would not be met; and researchers have, on occasion, found it expeditious to accept evaluation assignments and then redirect the resources to another type of study.

Further, a significant proportion of studies that are actually initiated are not carried to completion. In part the failure to undertake and particularly to complete experimental investigations is related to the barriers put forth by practitioners. There is no need to underscore the difficulties of undertaking research when the co-operation of practitioners and flexibility on their part is necessary for the development and implementation of an adequate design; conflict between clinician and scientist pervades all fields and the difficulties that medical researchers have in undertaking experiments with human subjects are minimal in comparison with evaluation efforts in the community.[5] Also, of course, many social scientists engaged in evaluation studies regard them as a dilettante activity and their interest in such work continues only so long as they think they are testing a theory of concern to them or believe their work will provide scholarly publications or economic affluence.

As a consequence, adequately conceived efforts have in fact been undertaken only rarely and the sheer infrequency of completed investigations is a major reason for the minimal impact of evaluation research on social policy. Certainly it is difficult to point to many instances in which programs actually have been modified, expanded or terminated because of evaluation findings.

The multi-billion dollar "War on Poverty" has intensified the demand for a concerted attempt to undertake broad-scale action-research demonstrations, and to engage in knowledge-seeking efforts evaluated in terms of effect—rather than merely in terms of whether or not the program proves workable administratively or whether or not so-called "experts" approve of it. Certainly, without efforts in this direction, literally billions of dollars may be spent without anyone knowing what works and, what is perhaps more frightening, without our being any better equipped to contribute to the next round of mass change efforts.

This situation would not be so serious if the social sciences had a significant reservoir of findings on which to base broad-scale intervention programs or had a wealth of experience in how to go about evaluating community-wide action programs in ways that provide "hard" findings on their worth. It also would not be so serious were there the opportunity to earn new methodological wrinkles or to develop a strategy for rendering the results of evaluation studies into a potent force in the determination of action programs and social policy. But we suddenly have a mandate to participate in massive social change, via community-wide efforts projected to restructure health and welfare activities and to reorient the efforts of practitioners. Despite the failure to work out methods and, most important, a strategy to influence policy on small-scale action programs, we now have been thrust into a prominent role in massive efforts designed to have an impact on virtually all community members and indeed on the very social order. It is simply not possible to retreat from this assignment, any more than it is for all physicists to avoid participation in the development and improvement of destructive devices.

The opportunity to participate carries with it great responsibility; our posture and pronouncements are likely to affect markedly the shape of future health and welfare programs and indeed of all community life. Although many individuals, for a variety of reasons, have decried so-called centralized programs of planned change and have expressed alarm over their control by public bodies and large foundations, there is little doubt that this is the direction that health and welfare activities are taking; and, the recent national election is clearly an overwhelming mandate for these efforts to continue.[6]

Perhaps those of us located in professional schools or employed directly by community-based programs are most sensitive to the stakes involved, but it is obvious that the comprehensive and massive character of projects sponsored by organizations such as the President's Committee on Juvenile Delinquency and Youth Crime, The Ford Foundation, and now the Office of Economic Opportunity are likely to rock the very foundations of our social system. If these observations are valid, we must rapidly accumulate an adequate technical repertoire for the task and explicate the conditions that must be met in order for our work to have social policy potential and to meet the.demands of our times. It is essential that we understand better the environment in which we are being called upon to work; have a clearer understanding of the conceptual issues involved in measuring the impact of broad-scale programs; and recognize the knotty methodological problems that one encounters when participating in action-research demonstrations. In this paper we address ourselves to these issues and use portions of Action for Boston Community Development's (ABCD) delinquency action-research program to illustrate notions advanced in this paper.

THE RESEARCH ENVIRONMENT

Since many social scientists have at one point or another been involved with large bureaucracies operating on a crash basis, certain rather obvious preliminary observations can be made most briefly. It is important to point out that dependence upon the legislative branch of our government or to whims of foundations for funds and the necessity to involve and obtain the cooperation of politically and ideologically antagonistic parties in local communities have and will continue to produce a considerable degree of disorder in most of the massive programs. The development of adequate staffs, personnel policies, and long range planning by community-based mass programs is difficult—some maintain almost impossible—given the condition of being affluent one minute and poverty-stricken the next and given the fleeting support of the various political forces involved. The shape, size, and goals of programs appear to change from day-to-day, and one of the difficulties of evaluation research in these settings stems from the high degree of organizational and interorganizational chaos.

Even in those efforts in which the over-all objectives remain relatively stable, the number of specific programs is large. Moreover most programs consist of a complex of multiple stimuli imposed over an extended period of time, and the goals of the individual programs are diverse. The situation is much too complex to fit the classical independent-dependent variable model. Therefore, action-research needs to be developed in terms of a series of staged inputs and outputs.

The juvenile delinquency action research demonstration project at ABCD which seeks to deal with this problem provides an illustration. It is based on three sets of variables: the dependent variable of the project is juvenile delinquency; more specifically defined as law-violating behavior of 12 through 16 year old males residing in specific areas of Boston. The second set of variables are referred to as the intermediate variables; according to the three-step hypothesis, changes in the intermediate variables should produce desired change in the dependent variable. The third set are referred to as program variables: these are the specific interventions by which it is hoped to produce changes in one or more of the intermediate variables.

A brief description of one of the programs, the "Week-End Ranger

Camp," may make the ABCD delinquency model clearer. At a regular summer-camp site, boys on probation participate each week-end in a series of activities such as discussion groups, council meetings, and work and recreational activities (the program variables). The model specifies that, as a result of these programs, shifts will occur in anomie, alienation and social values (the intermediate variables). The increased engagement of delinquent boys with the values and structural system of the society is held to lead to a reduction in delinquency (the dependent variable). In order to evaluate the program, the overall design specifies that local probation offices in parts of the City of Boston provide lists of names of boys eligible by reason of age, residence and other criteria for participation in the program. These boys were asked to come to the probation offices and participate in a study. At the office, the boys were pretested on several attitude measures—i.e., anomie, alienation and value scales. An attempt has been made to build procedures into the program which appear to have some hope of changing the attitudes of these youth and ultimately, according to the model, their on-the-street social behavior as well. After pretesting, the youth were randomly divided into two groups and the members of one group were invited to participate in the week-end program. The members of the other group were designated as ineligible for the program.

In order to undertake appropriately the evaluation of a mass program, it is necessary to develop an action-research design that includes a description of the interrelated elements: it must specify the ways the intermediate changes are expected to be produced, and provide hypotheses about the relationships between these changes and the dependent variable. Further, the design must outline the ways to determine, if such intermediate changes do occur, whether or not they are followed by the desired changes in the dependent variable.

A proper evaluation of the implementation of such a model requires not only knowing that certain effects were obtained but also knowing with some degree of probability that the effects were substantively related to a particular set of stimuli. Consequently, one major problem confronting efforts to evaluate programs of this type is that of controlling the stimuli. Major strides toward the accumulation of definitive knowledge about the effects of programs will not be made until we are able to think through and develop procedures for handling the problem of what constitutes the stimuli. The basic question is what is it that should be repeated if the program appears to work?

There are two related but nevertheless operationally separate issues here. One is the design of the stimulus or intervention. The other—and perhaps the more difficult one—is the problem of monitoring the intervention. Even if one begins with very definite and clear cut intentions to conduct and evaluate "repeatable" programs, it is possible to underestimate grossly the difficulties which are involved in both designing and monitoring programs with the goal of repeatability in mind. It is clear that this problem cannot be satisfactor-

ily resolved simply by reducing it to a process of spelling out procedures in great and specific detail, as difficult as even that may be.

In an attempt to deal with this problem, the approach at ABCD has been to move toward the development of principles rather than procedures, toward a set of theoretical concepts or ideas which trace the dynamics of how it is expected that the program will have the desired effects, i.e., towards a theory which logically interrelates a set of principles and procedures with desired outcomes. If such an impact model is sufficiently worked out, a set of working principles becomes available upon which practitioners can draw not only for the design of programs but also to make practical decisions about day-to-day program situations.

But unless the social science researcher participates, indeed leads the dialogue and bargaining required for the development of an impact model—including the identification of goals, the description of input-output variables, and the elaboration of a rationale that specifies the relationship between input variables and goals— these tasks are likely to remain undone. Once the impact model is formulated, the researcher must continue to remain within the environment, like a snarling watchdog ready to oppose alterations in program and procedures that could render his evaluation efforts useless.

It is only fair and from our view unfortunate to note that the researcher can expect little help or guidance from the funding groups in these tasks. In part this is related to the lack of structured expectations of outcome on the part of these groups, but also because of an effort to maintain as non-directed a posture as possible in the light of accusations of authoritarian control over the programs, or the theories that underlie them, in individual cities. The various President's Committee on Delinquency projects illustrate this point well. From city to city, though the legislation directs attention to the reduction of youth crime and the amelioration of related problems, considerable latitude has been allowed individual cities not only in program development but in evaluation design. Thus, not only are there variations in whether one is concerned with area-crime rates, the police contacts of individual youths, or the reduction of deviant though not necessarily illegal behavior, but some cities apparently have not felt a need to be particularly concerned with any phenomenon of this sort. Unless the situation changes, the researcher is naive to expect that sanctions from above are going to provide him with much support in the specification of objectives, the identification of the intermediate variables (i.e., the goals of specific programs) or the outlining of the theoretical links between these intermediate variables and the over-all objectives.

The researcher has three choices: he can follow Hyman's recommendation and try to guess the intermediate and over-all goals, and later be told that the ones he selected were not relevant at all;[7] he can insist that program persons provide them in which case he should bring lots of novels to the office to read while he waits, or he can participate or even take a major responsibility for the development of the action framework.

There is little likelihood of developing evaluation designs for these massive programs by either second-guessing the action people or by insisting upon their coming up with an appropriate and explicit flow-chart. Indeed, if the researcher is going to act responsibly as an agent of social change through his evaluation research, it probably is mandatory for him to engage himself in program development.[8] The task would be much easier if the sponsors of these massive programs would establish and enforce a requirement that the necessary specifications be part of any application and renewal of applications and that sanctions be exercised to prevent slippage.

Furthermore, the task would become more manageable if the sponsors provided a minimal set of outcome variables—uniform measurement would be most valuable for long-range program planning. It is most difficult, indeed probably impossible, to compare the various delinquency prevention efforts of the last three years, the various mental health reorganization attempts over the past ten years and, unless there are marked changes in policy, only limited likelihood of making city-to-city comparisons in the economic, educational, and occupational rehabilitation programs now underway as part of the poverty package. Given the lack of structured directions by the government and foundation granting programs, and the lack of commitment to evaluation research on the part of many practitioners on the local level, it is not easy to manipulate the environment so the researcher can undertake his task.

Again, we must acknowledge that

the researcher has not always partici-pated in these evaluation studies en-thusiastically and with a full sense of commitment; to argue that the prob-lems of evaluation research are solely due to the actions of others is as ludi-crous as the general who maintained that the high V.D. rate among his troops was due to the promiscuity of the civilian population. Participation within the action environment obli-gates the researcher to bring to bear his substantive knowledge in the design of programs; to be a positive influence in their development and to recommend or condemn program plans or at least forcefully report and interpret findings from other research that have a bearing on program development. This we often fail to do. If we did exercise our responsibility, we probably would have built into these massive efforts more attempts to use physical means such as brighter street lights to prevent delinquency and have exerted more pressure for coercive programs such as forced literacy training as a condition of probation and parole in contrast with increased numbers of therapeutic communities and the burgeoning of street-worker projects.[9]

CONCEPTIONS OF EVALUATION

In order to influence social policy, findings from social-action experi-ments must provide a basis for the effi-cient allocation of financial and human resources in the solution of social prob-lems. It is this notion of the efficient allocation of resources that is the key to the whole problem of planning and choosing among social-action pro-grams.

Traditionally service has been viewed—and in a vague way measured—in terms of that which is offered such as counseling, guidance, therapy, advice and the like. Good service is therefore that which is offered in a professional manner by a qualified person who in turn is supervised by a qualified supervisor. But service needs to be viewed not only in terms of pro-cess but of impact as well. In the final analysis, success must be viewed in terms of outcome rather than in terms of the supposed quality of the proce-dures used. The implications of this shift in view are considerable:

1. It forces those responsible for program design to clearly specify their objectives, to define what it is they are trying to achieve, what specific changes they are trying to effect. At the very least, it requires them to co-operate in efforts to operationalize what they have in mind;

2. It shifts the emphasis from "pro-cedure as an end" to "procedure as a means." Program personnel must then consider the relationship between the procedures it recommends and the de-fined outcomes that have been chosen;

3. It leads to a reconsideration of the whole notion of cost of service. Currently, we are in the grip of the proponents of the "per capita cost of service" point of view. If programs were to compete on the basis of how much it costs to achieve one unit (how-ever that may be defined) of desired outcome, the ultimate selection of programs would be very different;

4. And, finally, this view forces the inclusion of solid, empirical research into the over-all planning and program operation, because the decisions as to the optimum allocation of the re-

sources available can, within this view, only be made on the basis of empirical evidence.

The first requirement of evaluation research is the determination of efficacy. Evaluation research efforts must, therefore, seek to approximate the experimental model as much as possible—we do not do so often enough and some of the so-called evaluation designs of the current mass programs have completely forgone an experimental or quasi-experimental approach. Admittedly, there is a limit to the extent controlled experiments can be conducted within these programs. Nevertheless it is possible in most instances to make use of at least rudimentary or quasi-designs to approximate the conditions of the before-after and/or pre-post test designs, be it through randomization or statistical procedures.

The situation is exceedingly complex because of the previously discussed need to evaluate a series of input-outputs rather than just examining specific independent-dependent variable relationships. The kinds of massive efforts going on are of a linked input-output type and it is necessary to assess the efficacy of each of the specific programs, to measure the interactions among programs, and to tie together by means of relational analysis the impact that changes due to sub-programs have on the over-all program objectives. For example, an educational program may be designed to improve reading and this must be assessed, but if the over-all objective of the community project is to reduce school dropouts, the relationship between reading improvement and drop-outs must also be demonstrated.

Of the many problems confronting the utilization of experimental models, the linking issue seems to be the most difficult. There is too great a tendency to use assumed reflectors of change rather than direct measures of desired change, such as shifts in attitudes toward Negroes when the program is concerned with reducing discrimination. The problem is most serious when attitude scales are used as substitutes for measures of overt behavior. Most of us are aware of the limited correlations often found between attitudes and behavior, but as a recent paper points out, the situation may be worse than that: reanalysis of several studies suggests that changes in attitudes may be *inversely* correlated with changes in behavior. Thus, if one may extrapolate, reducing prejudice may indeed lead to increasing discrimination.[10] Use of attitudinal reflectors instead of the direct behavioral measures specified in an impact model may therefore render impossible the linking process.

Given the size of community efforts under the poverty program, assessing the efficacy of each sub-program in every city is pretty well impossible. Even assuming the availability of research funds, the problem of obtaining necessary professional manpower renders this unworkable. Consequently, a more practical approach would be to sample programs in various cities and this raises knotty problems because of the already-made observations of the linked input-output character of these programs. Sampling must be attempted in terms of the selection of linked programs and the sampling unit needs to be a sub-system of linked programs, analytically if not actually distinct. For example, if one of the goals of a day-care program is to free unmarried mothers so they may receive literacy training to be eligible for employment counseling and training, this "sub-system" of programs must constitute the sampling unit. It is worth emphasizing again that in order to sample such linked programs, it is necessary to have explicit statements of the goals and linkages of the various parts of the community-wide efforts and emphasize the need for well formulated conceptual frameworks (impact models) for current efforts.

But, we have no alternative to experimental evaluation. Should we demand less in terms of the treatment of community problems than we call for in the provision of medical care for ourselves or our pets? Despite the problems of limited sampling and of validity and reliability in assessing consumer goods, many of us read *Consumer Reports* before making major purchases and a few of us even query our physician about the efficacy of his intended therapies. We reject notions of "intuitive reasonableness" and "impressionistic worth" and seek out comparative assessments in making many personal decisions and we have the responsibility to insist on such evaluation in these mass programs as well.

At the present time even the most basic aspects of these community-wide programs are open to question. Many of the mass efforts, for example, are heavily committed to community organization programs and to the stimulation of expressive actions on the part of the so-called deprived populations. These programs have, as in the case of New York City's Mobilization for Youth, been a major source of controversy and yet, despite the resources expended and the conflict occasioned by them, at present they cannot be condemned or condoned in terms of objective evidence.[11] It is possible to mass opinions pro and con but such major issues cannot be settled on the basis of evidence though it is thirty years ago that community experiments were attempted by a social scientist in Syria.[12]

It is possible, despite the difficulties, to conduct reasonably well-controlled experiments in the community, even ones which require the cooperation of a number of individuals and agencies. At ABCD it has been found possible to institute studies with the random allocation of subjects to treatment and non-treatment groups. These designs usually must be modified because not all of those randomly selected for the experimental groups agree to participate in the programs and therefore the exposed and the unexposed populations do not constitute truly random samples from the same population. In addition, it is possible to obtain the necessary co-operation for rather extensive pre-testing of both experimental and control youth. It is likely that some version of a pre- posttest design is going to be necessary in such experiments because of this element of voluntary self-selection to participate on the part of the experimental group. Thus we are eventually going to have to (and because of this co-operation we will be able to) rely on covariance adjustments to bring the experimental and control groups back into line.

It is worth noting, however, that a main reason we were able to get support for the randomization procedures was because of the limited number of openings in the programs. But there is still great public resistance to and a considerable lack of understanding about randomization. This problem is likely to be even more serious in the case of really massive programs in which there appears to be room for everybody. This is likely to be particularly true where randomization to non-treatment groups is involved.

Furthermore, in addition to the ever present abhorrence of "denial of service" there is a very strong proclivity on the part of practitioners to believe that they know which type of person will benefit most from a particular program. Therefore, co-operating practitioners designate more people for a program than there are openings only with great reluctance. There is a related tendency for practitioners to want the most deserving youth to receive the opportunity to participate in special programs. Unfortunately, in many programs, it is impossible to determine the extent to which these two tendencies are operating in the selection of candidates for the program. But if only the most deserving are selected—even from among say probationers—the possibility of program impact may be lessened because both the experimental and the control subjects may fare very well according to the outcome criterion. Another problem is that when the selection is left to the personal preference of the practitioners the representativeness of the demonstration population relative to some larger population will be unknown.

There are two lessons here of relevance to the evaluation of anti-poverty programs. One is that random allocation to treatment and *non*-treatment groups is not likely to be possible frequently. But, random allocation to alternative treatments is feasible more of the time. This means, however, if such an approach is to be carried out well, the alternative treatments should be thought through very carefully so that at a minimum they are different and not camouflaged versions of the same basic idea. The impact model—the set of theoretical concepts or ideas which trace the dynamics of how it is expected that the program will have its desired effects—again rears its annoying head, and in turn a hard look at what the goals, the outcome variables, of such programs are and how to measure them will be required.

The second is that these broad scale anti-poverty programs are not likely to be well-off with regard to knowledge of the representativeness of population treated; it is necessary to face the problem of self-selection, for participation and thus extensive pre-testing with sound instruments is going to be essential if anything resembling definitive findings is to emerge. Not only should there be common use of some of the same instruments across similar programs within communities but also across similar programs between communities. For the first time we might have some cross-country comparative material concerning the populations being reached and the changes being observed.

Accountability is the second requirement of evaluation research. By accountability we refer to evidence that there is indeed a target population that can be dealt with by means of a program; that this population is important either because of its size or the intensity of pathology; and that the project program for the target population actually is undertaken with *them*.

It is not enough to evaluate efficacy—the outcomes of programs. The massive efforts now underway need to be evaluated in terms of accountability as well. While one might be accused of being inhuman for saying it, given the needs, there is little excuse for sanctioning action programs that affect insignificant portions of the population. One of the aspects of accountability is the estimation of the incidence and prevalence of problems. Oftentimes programs are developed to deal with problems that exist in the minds of practitioners or because of stereotypes held by the public. To cite one illustration, consider drug-addiction; despite newspaper and public alarm, the incidence in many urban centers is so low that on accountability grounds these efforts hardly merit the attention of so many or the utilization of extensive research resources to evaluate them. If small-size programs use up all the potential clients and thus there are no cases left for assignment to control groups, then only under very unusual circumstances may the researcher be justified in collaborating in their evaluation or even attempting to do so. If the programs are of a large-scale type, then the denial of services or at least the provision of "ordinary" treatment to a few for control purposes and subsequent estimation of worth is entirely necessary.

Accountability, however, has to do with more than the number of clients served and the size of the potential

aggregate of them. Evaluation researchers, in addition to a responsibility for determining efficacy, must deal with the implementation of the prescribed process. In many instances we have engaged in outcome studies without having any knowledge of whether or not what program people maintain is going on actually takes place. It is clear that in many of the sub-programs being implemented as part of these massive efforts—even when evaluation studies of the finest design are accompanying them—we are estimating the utility of programs that never get off the ground; evaluating programs in which volunteers do no more than sign up for week-end educational camping programs in which kids have a good time and do nothing more than play ball or eat marshmallows around the fireside. To say a program fails when it is not truly implemented is indeed misguided, and the evaluation researcher's responsibility here is one of providing evidence and information that permits an accounting of what took place as well as what was the result.

Finally, what we hardly ever worry about, to our knowledge, is efficiency.[13] The various specific programs that are linked together on these massive packages differ extensively in target groups, use of scarce resources and duration. At the risk of being ludicrous, suppose *neither* individual psychotherapy *nor* group psychotherapy has any impact on the lives of persons but the former costs ten times that of the latter; given such a situation there is little doubt where one should put his money. In certain fields of medicine and in certain areas of welfare there is literally no way, given the community's ideological outlook, to cease all treatment even if no efforts are efficacious. But without being too cynical, even when we know this is the case, we refuse to employ a concept of efficiency. Suppose short-term treatment institutions for delinquent offenders do no better than long-term ones, if they are more economical is this not something that the evaluation researcher has a responsibility to take into account?[14]

In terms of all programs, the efficient one is that which yields the greatest per unit change not the one that can be run at the least cost per recipient. What costs the most, takes the longest, and involves the greatest amount of manpower in gross terms may have the greatest net efficiency.[15] Decisions on the continuance of various programs beyond trial-demonstration periods require that we think in these terms. In most evaluation efforts we fail to relate units of change to economic, or manpower or time expenditures.

We contend that concepts of *accountability* and *efficiency* as well as *efficacy* need to be implemented in order for evaluation research to be undertaken properly. Admittedly, we ought to seek out efficacious programs. But these programs are or at least should be accountable in order for policy and program persons to make rational decisions, and we must also concern ourselves with efficiency of operations.

PROBLEMS OF MEASUREMENT

In previously discussing the impact model notion, we have suggested that in the design of these community programs the premise is that certain changes will be followed by other changes. Programs are designed to expose members of a target population to procedures that hopefully will produce changes in the individual or his environment. These individual or environmental changes are expected to produce improved behavior, for example less law violation on the part of the individual in the ABCD delinquency project. It is hoped that a significantly greater proportion of the experimentals in each program than their controls will experience the desired change and those experiencing such change, whether they are experimentals or controls, will manifest a reduction in law-violating behavior. It should be reemphasized that the hypothesis asserts a relationship between two sets of changes, not between two static conditions.

The problem of obtaining reasonably reliable change measures precedes the problem of relating change measures, since attempting to relate sets of unreliable change scores does not appear to be too promising a game to play. There has been, of course, a long-standing concern for the problem of the reliability of scores. Interest in the reliability of *change* scores is somewhat more recent and is only now receiving attention among statisticians and psychometricians.[16] Problems arising out of the mathematically demonstrated greater unreliability of change scores relative to the reliability of the scores from which they were derived and problems arising out of demonstrated regression to the mean tendencies in test-re-test situations are likely to remain central as well as difficult issues for those who are brave or foolish enough to pursue this change problem.

The problem of the measurement of the relationship between sets of change scores involves serious statistical and mathematical difficulties. Measurements of each variable at a minimum of three points in time are required to provide some estimate of the shape of the curves involved. Two of the problems involved are: (1) the relationship between the shapes of the curves—the change curve for the intermediate variable and the change curve for the dependent variable—and (2) the question of the time lag throughout the series and between the two sets of changes. When are the presumed effects of the program on the intermediate variable expected to take place: while the program is going on or after participation in the program has terminated? And for how long are the effects supposed to last? How long a time is expected to lapse between the changes in the intermediate variable and their presumed effects on the dependent variable? What are their relative rates of change? These and similar questions are directly related to some very practical issues such as the amount of success a project can possibly have during some specified demonstration period. If there is considerable lag or the rate of change in the dependent variable is relatively low, much of the effects of the demonstration may take place after the cut-off point for the evaluation of the project. Again the need for a theoretically-based impact model is, it seems to us, underscored.

Of the many other problems which beset efforts to conduct and evaluate

large-scale action programs, there are two more that should be noted. One is the problem of the meaning of change in the dependent variable—in our case, a reduction in law-violating behavior—and the other is the problem which arises from the fact that members of the target population may, in fact undoubtedly will, be involved with more than one of the programs and such multiple involvement is non-random.

The first decision made at ABCD concerning the definition of change in the dependent variable was that we could not use comparisons over time of area rates of delinquency as a basis. ABCD's aims were to change behavior, not to move law-violating people out of an area and non-violating people into it. Therefore an area delinquency-rate comparison over time was rejected as a basis for measuring change since wide variations in delinquency rates may occur over time simply because of changes in the constituency of the population. It was decided that a reduction in law-violating behavior would have to be measured in terms of the behavior of a specified population—that is, a cohort of individuals. The same issue confronts the Office of Economic Opportunity's community-action programs and the decision on evaluations must be the same.

Another major problem in defining how change in the dependent variable is to be measured is that of shifts in the character of the target population such as the known relationship between age and delinquency. Beginning around 10 or 11, age-specific delinquency rates increase rather sharply up into and through the late teens. Therefore to simply compare a given individual's behavior at age 15 with his behavior at age 14, 13, 12 and so on would lose sight of the fact that the probability of a delinquent act increases as he gets older. If a cohort of 15 year olds committed the same number of delinquent acts at age 15 as they did at age 13, for example, this might not look like a reduction—and in terms of absolute numbers it is not—but in terms of what might have been expected of them it is. Therefore, within the framework of ABCD's approach, a reduction of law-violating behavior must be defined in terms of a comparison of an observed measure with an expected measure. That is, a prediction instrument is required to provide an estimate of the law-violating behavior which would have occurred had there been no intervention.

A very similar problem will arise if efforts are made to take a hard look at the possible effects of various components of large-scale community efforts to deal with poverty. For example, employability—which is central to most of the poverty proposals—is also a function of age. It is quite well known that the great bulk of the very difficult to employ 16 to 21 year-olds begins to disappear into the job market and from the unemployment rolls as they approach their middle twenties. Therefore, if evaluations of community programs dealing with this particular segment of the population are based upon observations of their employment history subsequent to exposure to one or more anti-poverty programs, the success observed may be much more apparent than real. What is needed is a measure of their employment status and prospects at some point in time as compared with estimates of what would have been the case at that same point in time had there been no intervention.

A second issue that requires comment is that of multiple-exposure to programs. This has presented the ABCD project with distinct methodological difficulties. It is likely to be an even greater problem for any effort to evaluate the effects of anti-poverty programs. Two tendencies combine here, we believe, to aggravate the problem. One is the inclination on the part of practitioners to want to shower programs on the members of the target population. The other is the sheer amount of money that is involved and the resulting large number of programs that are likely to be conducted. This is an extremely important issue if we are serious in our desire to ultimately acquire knowledge concerning the most efficient allocation of human and financial resources. For if the members of the target population participate in a number of different programs and even if desired change occurs and is measured, a way must be devised to sort out the relative contributions of the different programs to the outcome. Otherwise, in order to produce the same results again the whole menagerie of programs would have to be repeated even though only a relatively few of the programs may have actually contributed to the desired outcome. Again, a prediction instrument appears to be indispensable to the solution of this problem. Individuals must be grouped according to the programs they have participated in—in our approach, according to the intermediate variable changes they have experienced—and then the groups compared on the differences between observed dependent variable and expected dependent variable behavior.

CONCLUDING COMMENTS

These remarks, though not entirely original, of course, may prove relevant for researchers who have occasion to participate in the evaluation of community-wide programs. The need to become engaged in the action environment, to look at a linked input-output system, to develop impact models, and to insist on experimental designs, and the necessity to assess efficiency and to recognize the accountability function in evaluation are, to our minds, key points and ones, not well-documented in our methods books and not always held to by persons participating in the evaluation of these massive efforts.

But we would like to feel that we have communicated more than some specific observations—that we have conveyed the potential and importance of the evaluation researcher's role and the sense of conviction, commitment, and responsibility required. At no other point in time have we had so great an opportunity to have an impact on the social order; if we are to realize our potential within our current stance as social scientists, however, we need more than additional technical innovations. An outlook, an ideology almost a morality if you will, must be developed in order to function appropriately as agents of social change.

NOTES

1. Howard Odum, *American Sociology,* New York: Longmans Green, 1951.

2. Maurice Stein, *Sociology on Trial,* New York: Prentice-Hall, Inc., 1963.

3. Richard A. Cloward and Lloyd E. Ohlin, *Delinquency and Opportunity,* Glencoe, Illinois: The Free Press, 1960 and Kenneth B. Clark, ed., "Desegregation in the Public Schools," *Social Problems,* 2 (April, 1955)—entire issue.

4. E. Sibley, *Education of Sociologists in the United States,* New York: Russell Sage Foundation, 1963.

5. R. C. Fox, *Experiment Perilous: Physicians and Patients Facing the Unknown,* New York: The Free Press of Glencoe, Inc., 1959.

6. John R. Seeley, "Central Planning: Prologue to a Critique," in Robert Morris, ed., *Centrally Planned Change: Prospects and Concepts,* New York: National Association of Social Workers, 1964, pp. 41–68.

7. Herbert Hyman, *Applications of Methods of Evaluation for Studies of Encampment for Citizenship,* California: University of California Press, 1962.

8. Howard E. Freeman, "The Strategy of Social Policy Research," in The Social Welfare Forum 1963, New York: Columbia University Press, 1963, pp. 143–156.

9. Admittedly, the evidence about the latter two approaches is fragmentary but nevertheless hardly in the direction to encourage the current expansion efforts. See Charles Perrow, "Hospitals: Goals, Structure and Technology," in James March, ed., *Handbook of Organizations,* Chicago: Rand McNally, 1964 and Walter B. Miller, "The Impact of a Total-Community Delinquency Control Project," *Social Problems,* 10 (Fall, 1962), pp. 168–191.

10. Leon Festinger, "Behavioral Support for Opinion Change," *Public Opinion Quarterly,* 28 (Fall, 1964), pp. 404–417.

11. Roland L. Warren, "The Impact of New Designs of Community Organizations," paper presented at the annual meetings of the National Social Welfare Assembly, November 30, 1964, New York City.

12. Stuart C. Dodd, *A Controlled Experiment on Rural Hygiene in Syria,* Beirut, Lebanon Republic: American Press, 1934.

13. An illustration of a study that does consider this problem is Julius Jahn and Margaret Bleckner, "Serving the Aged" (Methodological Supplement—Part I), New York: Community Service Society of New York, 1964.

14. Howard E. Freeman and H. Ashley Weeks, "Analysis of a Program of Treatment of Delinquent Boys," *American Journal of Sociology,* 62 (July, 1956), pp. 56–61.

15. Clarence C. Sherwood, "Social Research in New Community Planning Organizations," paper read at National Conference of Social Welfare, Cleveland, 1963.

16. C. W. Harris, *Problems in Measuring Change,* Madison: University of Wisconsin Press, 1963.

14. Toward Avoiding the Goal Trap in Evaluation Research

Irwin Deutscher

It is the purpose of this paper to devise means which may be helpful in implementing two values. If one does not concur in either of them, much of the paper will make no sense. If one does concur in both values, some of the paper may make some sense. First, it is desirable to determine the consequences of deliberate efforts to alter ongoing social processes—education, health, welfare, or whatever—and to do so in as detached a manner as is possible. A corollary to this value is that it is desirable to understand the new processes which lead to the new consequences. This determination of consequences and understanding of processes is what I intend by the phrase "program evaluation." The second value is that the major criterion of the success of program evaluation ought to be the extent to which it is taken into account in altering program policy, administration, or practice.

A CUE FROM
ORGANIZATIONAL THEORY

I take as my point of departure, a cue provided by organizational theory and developed by Robert Bogdan (1972).

From monographs published in the Chicago tradition during the early decades of this century to more recent organizational analyses, such as those by Becker et al. (1968), Gouldner (1968), and Blau (1955), it seems that organizations are rarely what they pretend to be. The distinction between the formal and the informal or the stated and the real is made in various ways, but it is always made. Organizational theory suggests that the structure, the processes, and the goals of any organization must be assumed to vary in fact from their descriptions in form. Perrow (1961), for example, distinguishes between official goals and operative ones. How organizations are built, what they do, and the consequences of this structure and process are frequently quite different from formal or public statements about such matters. In exploring how "original goals become bastardized," Bogdan observes that goal displacement is a key concept (Merton, 1957; Michels, 1959; Clark, 1956), while efforts to understand how organizations change their goals find the idea of goal succession most useful (Sills, 1957; Blau and Scott,

Revision of a paper read at the annual meeting of the American Sociological Association, Montreal, August, 1974. This paper was first drafted while the author was studying under a special post-doctoral fellowship from the National Institute of Mental Health at the University of California, San Diego. I am grateful for useful criticism and suggestions from Shirley S. Angrist, Alan P. Chesney, Robert A. Beauregard, Alan Dale, William J. Filstead, Paul Goldstein, Thomas A. Heberlein, Roxanne Hiltz, and Walter Williams.

1961; Thompson and McEwen, 1958).

I have emphasized the likelihood of discrepancy between formal goals and actual goals, because it is at that point that these observations from organizational theory become central to program evaluation.[1] As long ago as 1960, Etzioni noted the need for policy research to take account of the "illusory quality" of organizational goals. It is the contention of this paper that a sometimes unwarranted and frequently unrealistic emphasis on program goals persists in evaluation research. It persists (1) partly because we live in an achievement oriented society and therefore tend to assume that there is no better way to judge the merits of an organization than by evaluating its output; (2) partly because of the demands of funding agencies (if one hopes to obtain funds for a program, one must be able to specify in advance precisely what it intends to achieve); and (3) partly as a consequence of intimidation of program personnel by evaluators who assume that it is necessary to isolate precise and measurable goals in order to provide indexes of the "success" of a program.

Peter Rossi reflects this position when he writes that ". . . any program which does not have clearly specified goals cannot be evaluated without specifying some measurable goals. This statement is obvious enough to be a truism" (Rossi and Williams, 1972: 18). I find the statement neither obvious nor true. Rather, it reflects what in my review of the theoretical and methodological literature in evaluation research, I have come to think of as the goal trap. Taking the opposite position

from Rossi, Schulberg and Baker (1968) argue that there are two basic models of evaluation, goal attainment and systems. They suggest that the systems model provides a much better opportunity for implementation of the research findings. Although I applaud their search for alternatives to the goal-attainment model, I do not concur in the belief that systems analysis is the only one. In this paper I will suggest another.

In moving from organizational theory to a discussion of the goal trap, I would conclude with Bogdan (1972: 37) that

> It might be useful to think of a large number of organizational types as expressive rather than instrumental: they allow societies to act out their beliefs which may be unworkable in reality. Measures of success may serve the myth of the instrumental nature of organizations as well as myths societies hold in regard to the nature of certain problems.

THE GOAL TRAP

Unlike most traps, this one snares the trapper as well as the victim. It is to be expected that funding agencies should be as much a captive of our societal achievement orientation as anyone else, and this is as true outside of government as within. In these post-McNamara years of rational program accounting, it becomes necessary to know not only how money is being spent, but what the precise benefits of that expenditure are. It is not enough for competent and well-intended people to purport to be doing good, no matter how well they account for their expenditures. It is also necessary to know how much good they are doing. Efforts to deal with that question trap both the program people and the funding agencies.

In order for a proposed program to be funded, it must state clearly what it intends to do, how long it will take, how much of what kinds of personnel are needed, and how much it will cost. Let us leave aside, for the moment, proposals to continue ongoing programs and concentrate on proposals to create novel, innovative types of interventions. It is with the evaluation of such new programs that I am primarily concerned, and it is precisely such programs which are least likely to be specific about what they are attempting to do, how they intend to go about it, how much it will cost, etc. To the extent that their staff and management are creative and the program is indeed something new and different, there must inevitably be a great deal of flexibility—of winging it as the program and its problems develop. Competent program people understand this. Sometimes they also understand precisely what they are trying to do, but are rarely able to articulate it in the manner funding agencies require.

As a result of these conditions, program people feel that they must lie to funding people in order to meet the criteria required for a proposal to be funded. Sometimes they never intend to do what the proposal claims, but more often they begin by trying and end up by doing something that seems worthwhile to them even though it has nothing to do with the proposal which was funded. One of the officers in the

job training program evaluated by Bogdan is openly cynical (1972: 35–36).

> You know what they do with a proposal after [a training program] gets started, they turn it face down on the desk and never look at it. . . . Just as long as you write a nice neat package, just as long as it looks like it's going to work all right. They just assume it works that way. Write how many hours the trainees are going to do this, how much they are going to do that. Just a lot of bull shit. But they can pay people to write these things up. . . .

The result of such phony proposals is phantom programs. As Freeman and Sherwood put it (1965): "To say that a program fails when it is not truly implemented is indeed misguided." Hyman and Wright (1967) echo: "Taking the word for the deed, an evaluator may try to observe the effects of a nonexistent treatment. . . . Where a program has no input, no output . . . can ensue." And Rossi, discussing support for schools under Title I, notes "the problem of 'non-projects' " (Rossi and Williams, 1972: 40). Carol Weiss has argued over the years that "Among the many reasons for the negative pall of evaluation results is that studies have accepted bloated promises and political rhetoric as authentic program goals" (1973: 44; see also Weiss, 1971: 138). It is a foolish evaluator indeed who attempts to study a program in terms of the goals which it proposed in order to get funded. Such an evaluation is most likely to show no effect as well as to alienate all parties involved. I prefer to believe, however, that evaluators do not generally fall into the goal traps created by the demands of funding agencies; they are more likely to fall into those of their own making.

If it is necessary to provide an accounting for the effectiveness of a program, the evaluator usually feels that he must identify goals so that he can measure the extent to which the program appears to be achieving them. In fact, many distinguished evaluation researchers define program evaluation, as Rossi has, in terms of measurement of program goals (e.g., Brooks, 1965; Greenberg, 1968; Suchman, 1969). Most recently, Bernstein and Freeman (1973: 51) insist that "the crux of evaluative research is the assessment of the degree to which the program . . . has achieved its specified goals. . . ." Jones and Borgatta (1972: 41) argue that, unless objectives are stated in terms of measurable changes in intended directions, "evaluation research is not feasible." Frequently then, the first task attempted by the evaluator is to specify measurable program goals. This may not be unreasonable, except that just as frequently, program people do not think in terms of specific measurable goals. They are trying to make the sick healthy, or the poor rich, or the ignorant wise. Furthermore, they may believe that their experience, their commitment, and their competence combine to provide them with an opportunity to achieve such desirable ends. And they may be correct, a matter to which I will return in the discussion of avoiding the goal trap.

In pursuit of a clearcut evaluation design and the selection of appropriate measuring instruments, the evaluator is relentless in his quest for specific

goals. He has to have something to measure, and it must be something that is measurable. He scans the proposal; he interviews the administrator; he may even "have to observe some programs in order to identify what the objectives are" (Cain and Hollister, 1972: 114). From such sources he evolves program goals. If they are not immediately apparent, he hounds program people: "Is this a goal?" "or this?" "or this?" As Freeman and Sherwood have put it (1965), those responsible for program design must be "forced" to specify clearly their objectives. Reflecting on an earlier draft of this paper Goldstein (1974) views the commitment to achievement from the perspective of the sociology of knowledge.

> We live in the age of rationalism, of cause and effect, of getting the job done, of accomplishing. This is an overriding societal ethic. It is somehow indecent not to have a goal. In everyday life a really terrible thing to say about someone is that they don't have any goal in life. Everybody and everything has to have a goal. Or at least an articulated one to conceal the frenzy and confusion that lies just below the surface. Evaluation is a means to measure goals, a goal in and of itself, and a stimuli to force articulation of goals.

Program people may resist at first, but eventually intimidated by the evaluators' relentless pursuit of something he can measure, they will break down and weakly allow that such and such may be a goal: "I guess you could say that is one of our goals." The end result of this process is that, more often than not, the program is evaluated in terms of marginal goals which are unlikely to be achieved (if for no other reason, because no one is very serious about them) and are likely to be denied their legitimacy when the evaluator finally reports that the program does not seem to make any difference.

It may be that there are some kinds of programs where the goals are eminently clear, and all interested parties are in accord regarding them. Pamela Krochalk, for example, has suggested to me that the goals of job training programs are perfectly clear. She is echoed by Peter Rossi (Rossi and Williams, 1972: 18):

> Not all social welfare programs suffered to the same extent from ambiguity in the setting of goals. At the one extreme, manpower retraining programs were among the most clearly defined: A manpower retraining program is effective to the extent that it manages to impart marketable occupational skill.

But it was just such programs which Bogdan was studying when he drafted his provocative query on the theoretical viability of organizational goals (1972), and he provides a wide range of quantitative estimates of the success of the program. These estimates are all accurate enough even though some indicate tragic failure while others indicate massive success. The difference derives from subtle differences in the definition of program goals. Lerman (1968), although discussing delinquency control programs, makes the same point as Bogdan: "It all depends on how you count"! Goldstein, Hull, and Ostrander (1973) raise a series of related questions about job training. For example, if people are well trained for jobs that do not exist, is the pro-

gram a success? Finally, Campbell considers some of the distorting factors that can occur in the definition of success of a training program (1969).

Before turning to ways of avoiding the goal trap, let me make an observation on the somewhat different consequences that can arise from the imposition of goals on ongoing programs (in contrast with innovative, experimental, or otherwise novel ones). Bogdan (1972: 32), hitting close to home, says that measures of success are like the programs for professional meetings; they are something concrete in spite of the fact that they are largely irrelevant to what goes on. Although this may be true for novel programs, the reverse is possible for ongoing programs; the imposed measure of success can become the program's goal! Becker and his colleagues (1968) have documented the manner in which academic grades become transformed from a means of measuring academic success to ends in themselves. The prime aim of college students becomes, not to get educated, but to make reasonably good grades. In an interview (Salasin, 1973: 12), Campbell has argued that the goals of people and of organizations can be changed when quantitative criteria of success are demanded. He suggests, for example, that the McNamara PPBS system may have been self-sabotaging: "By requiring quantitative statements of goals and quantitative reporting on how well they were met, PPBS probably increased rather than decreased the dishonesty of annual reports."

Campbell's prime example is the imposition of the criterion of a body count in Vietnam in an effort to overcome the typically inflated estimates of enemy dead. The result of this neat quantitative index was to encourage the creation of bodies. Campbell suggests that this emerges as a new military goal. Lt. Calley was engaged in the legitimized military goal of getting bodies to count. Measures of success can and do become reified.

TOWARD AVOIDING THE GOAL TRAP

If the results of program evaluations are to be taken into account by practitioners, administrators, or policy makers, those results cannot be derived from phantom programs or spurious goals. Rossi (1969: 99) mentions the "wonderfully varied ways in which practitioners and administrators welch on evaluation."

> Most often of all, it is "discovered" (after finding negative results) that the "real" goals of the social action program in question were not the goals that were being evaluated in the research after all.

Although tinged with a bit of sarcasm and implying that it is the program people who are at fault, Rossi's point is essentially true. In a more constructive vein, Carol Weiss (1973: 40) states that "one of the reasons that evaluations are so readily disregarded is that they address only official goals." She goes on to suggest that it might be useful to assess other than official goals if the evaluation is to be taken seriously by decision makers. Evaluations must be credible—they must make sense to those who could act upon them. If evaluations are not credible and thus not taken into account in decision-making processes, then there is no sense in doing them. Avoiding the goal

trap increases the probability of credible and useful evaluation research.

It is not necessary to abandon goals and their measurement in order to avoid the goal trap; it is only necessary to avoid spurious goals and invalid measures. In this section I will suggest three ways in which the trap may be avoided, all of which retain to some degree the notion of achievement. In terms of current ideologies of evaluation, my three suggestions are presented in order from the most distant to the most familiar. It follows that they are presented in reverse order of their most immediate feasibility.

Input-Output vs. Social Process

The ideal method of avoiding the goal trap is to find alternative ways of thinking about evaluation—ways that do not hinge on measureable output and thus do not demand the identification of specific goals. Although it would require a terrible wrenching of our customary ways of thinking, it might be desirable to view success or failure in terms of process rather than of input and output. As Angrist puts it (1973: 15): "The input-output model is not enough; what we need to keep track of is what happens in the black box." By "process," I do not intend the distinction sometimes made in evaluation research between studying a program's output and studying the functioning of the program organization. It is in this inaccurate sense that Cain and Hollister (1972: 110), for example, define process analysis as "mainly administrative monitoring." Nor do I intend by "process analysis" the procedure of systems analysis that is sometimes usefully employed in the study of organizations. What I do intend is that we alter the syntax of our evaluation questions, shifting from the past tense, "What happened?" to the present progressive, "What is happening?"

This syntactic shift carries with it a methodological shift. Exploring the relationship between input and output involves analysis of the relationship between independent and dependent variables. Exploring the process involves analysis of an ongoing social act—one that is seen as constantly in flux and constantly amenable to new definitions of the social situation. The act has no end except perhaps the mortality of the actor.[2] Herbert Blumer (1956) has provided a theoretical groundwork for such process analysis, and I have tried to elaborate his position as a basis for understanding attitudinal and behavioral change (1973, Chs. 11 and 13). It is precisely such change that I believe most intervention programs are all about. There are pressing methodological questions that accompany this theoretical position, and the methodological solutions remain largely to be worked out. I believe the problems are soluble if not solved, and I am addressing them in my current evaluation research. I am not alone in this task.[3]

Some cues close to home for the evaluation researchers can be found in the critique provided by Weiss and Rein which addresses broad-aim programs (1969), Guttentag's (1973) plea for attention to neglected intervening processes, or the more general cautionary advice provided by Mushkin (1973).[4] Scholars who customarily deal with developmental processes easily detect the inherent problems of output

analyses in evaluation research. McDill, McDill, and Sprehe (1972: 159) relegate to a footnote, this critical comment by H. Zimiles (1970).

> His indictment has to do with a lack of knowledge base concerning the cognitive growth of young children which fosters an emphasis on "outcome" evaluation rather than "processual" evaluation, i.e., assessment of the cognitive processes and related personality variables which mediate and support the child's intellectual functioning at any given point in time.

Even the interrupted time series design, one of the quasi-experimental approaches advocated by Campbell (1969), takes into account the processual quality of social change. Another useful cue is provided by the concept of marginality which, as important as it is to comparative evaluations, seems to be taken seriously by no one but a few economists.[5] Glennan provides a simple, persuasive, and graphic argument for the need to follow a program through time in an effort to determine at what point its incremental increases become marginal. His provision of a second hypothetical program, which is discovered to be a slow starter with massive payoffs at later stages, illustrates the dramatic errors that are possible when programs are viewed with an inadequate time perspective (Glennan, 1972: 192–193). As the examples in this paragraph suggest, process analysis need not be qualitative. In fact, Chomie and Hudson (1974) point out that epidemiology provides a model for quantitative process analysis. Nevertheless, my emphasis in this section will be on process analysis as implemented through the methodology of participant observation.

Campbell, employing the term "process analysis" as I do, comments on the Weiss and Rein position. I think the comment is important, because it raises an issue about what constitutes experimentation.

> Let me discuss process evaluation in general. What we need first are some clear-cut examples. At present, those such as Weiss and Rein who hold up process evaluation as an alternative may be making an argument in favor of common sense knowing, in which case I agree with them. Or, they may be arguing that we should not pretend we can do outcome evaluation when we can't, in which case I agree with them. But if they are arguing for an alternative that is as good as or superior to experimental design, then I've got to wait for an example to see whether or not I feel it would have been strengthened with more attention to experimental design (Salasin, 1973: 10).

I fail to understand what the logic of experimental design has to do with whether or not one chooses to undertake output (variable) analysis or process analysis. My emphasis on social process and the suggestion to seek alternative methodologies to conventional variable analysis in no way implies an abandonment of experimental methodology. I know of no better logic for establishing the fact that a program makes a difference from no program at all or from other programs.

There is, however, a difference between experimental methodology—a logic of procedure—and current ex-

perimental techniques. Although present techniques seem to imply the manipulation of static variables, employing doubtful measures of unlikely goals, this is not inherent in the logic of experimentation. One can think experimentally in any effort to establish causation by comparing any two or more phenomena through time. The data employed in those comparisons can be of any type. Max Weber employed experimental logic in his turn of the century comparative studies of religion, using ethnographic and historical data. Furthermore, as Weber illustrates, such designs need not be post-factum. One may entertain hypotheses concerning the expected nature of the world without a given historical event (such as the existence of the Protestant ethic) and then seek out comparative societies that did not experience that event. Such societies may be located at some distant point in space or in time.

Campbell's call for "clear-cut examples" of process analysis is partly answered in the references cited in footnote three. There is, however, a genre of evaluation research that tends to be ignored by evaluators, because (I suspect) it is not labeled "program evaluation." I have in mind such monographs as the Becker, Geer, and Hughes evaluation of undergraduate education (1968) or the Wieder evaluation of an addict rehabilitation program (1973). The remaining two suggestions for avoiding the goal trap assume a commitment to outcomes. Both would automatically be subsumed under process analysis although they can be pursued independently.

Being Attentive to the Unintended

If we do alter our syntax and ask what is happening rather than what happened, are we not dealing with a loaded question? After all, when we ask what happened and test a null hypothesis, our very methods force us to consider the likelihood that nothing happened. In fact, this is frequently the conclusion reached from rigorously designed evaluation research. Process analysis does pose a loaded question! It assumes that any effort to intervene in ongoing social processes will somehow and to some degree alter those processes. Programs, as we know them, comprise such deliberate efforts to intervene. This assumption renders nonsensical a question like "did anything happen?" and rules out as logically and empirically impossible a conclusion, such as "nothing happened." By assuming that something is changing as a consequence of the program, our major research effort shifts from preordained goals to the discovery of processual consequences. One evaluation researcher states this assumption in a context of the constraints of organizational structure (Angrist, 1975).

> At times . . . I despair and conclude that nothing helps, no remedy cures, no program changes people, no spending is justified. At such times, I mentally review what as social scientists we well know: that specific social contexts do have noticeable consequences. We take for granted . . . that social classes, ethnic and religious groups differentially shape their members; that prisons and mental hospitals mold their inmates; that boarding schools, colleges, and sororities influence their recruits; that organizational structure constrains its functionaries.

The quest for program consequences can follow the conceptual guidelines provided by Merton (1957). When we ask, "what is happening?" we are guided by several corollaries to the question: What is happening that was intended? What is happening that was not intended? Furthermore, what unintended consequences of the program were also unanticipated. It is these unanticipated consequences of the program that demand the greatest sensitivity of the evaluator. The unintended may be anticipated, but the unanticipated must be mysterious.

I cannot at this time provide any systematic guidelines for the discovery of *unanticipated* consequences, but the New Jersey Income Maintenance Experiment illustrates how *unintended* consequences can inform program evaluation. Rossi (1974) describes how the gravest concerns of dubious congressmen are related to fears that income maintenance will result in a loss of interest in work on the part of those being maintained. Apparently there is little disagreement concerning the intended consequence of income maintenance; it is the unintended ones that are troublesome.[6] The investigators appropriately addressed themselves to such issues, for example, by testing the hypothesis that there is no difference between the experimental and control groups in earned income after the introduction of minimum income levels into the experimental group. The failure to find sufficient evidence to reject this null hypothesis ought to help relieve the anxieties of opponents to the program. This evaluation of unintended consequences is more likely to have an impact on policy than would an evaluation of the intended consequences. A fringe benefit from the point of view of program proponents is that the testing of null hypotheses concerning undesirable consequences of a program reverses the burden of proof. For a change the conservative bias of tests of significance is working on the side of program advocates instead of against them. It is, as Rossi puts it, a case of "No bananas again," but this time it is the good guys who do not like bananas.

Although rarely giving them much emphasis, evaluation researchers sometimes reflect awareness of one or another kind of unintended program consequences. Cain and Hollister (1972: 128–129) write of "third party effects"—those that affect others than the intended population. They mention negative as well as positive third party effects in youth training and job training programs. Greenberg (1968) discusses "side-effects" of contraceptive devices and drugs—both desirable and undesirable. Herberline (1973: 3–4) considers "second order unplanned effects" of flood control efforts. While Suchman (1969: 44) was concerned with unanticipated negative consequences, Mushkin (1973: 33) writes of our neglect of the "side-benefits" inherent in some programs and Angrist (1973) elaborates on desirable but unintended program consequences of the introduction of evaluation research itself—the matter of reactivity, which, important as it is, cannot be considered here.

Well over a decade ago, Hyman and Wright (1962) saw as one of the "major aspects" of evaluation research, "The conceptualization and measurement of . . . unanticipated relevant outcomes." A few years later they continue to argue the importance of such outcomes, employing Rieken's evaluation of a summer work camp as an example (Hyman and Wright, 1967). Nor do they believe it impossible to anticipate the unanticipated.

> Familiarity with previous studies of similar action programs and general scientific knowledge about the area involved—whether delinquency, attitudinal change, or voting behavior—can unlock the door to many of the relevant conceptualizations of unexpected results.

Houston (1972: 61) observes that, "Evaluation studies are notorious for appending to negative results the assertion that effects were unquestionably produced, but that no provision was made for their measurement." He recommends pilot studies and fractional designs that permit examination of a large number of factors. But it is Campbell who seems to pursue the problem and its solution with the greatest deliberation. He suggests (1971: 54) that criticism focused "on past ameliorative efforts, such as slum clearance, high-rise tenements, aid to dependent children, automation, and the like, can generate an explicit list of noxious values, possible pernicious side-effects to be measured just in case they might be among the effects of a specific program." In a more recent interview, Campbell says

> I think if we regularly made it our

business to interview the opponents of every new program . . . we could get a list of feared undesirable side-effects. . . . By interviewing the people who oppose the program, brainstorming with them about possible indicators of their fears, we could do much better than we do now about setting in motion indicators that might pick up some of the anticipatable, understandable side-effects. (Salasin, 1973: 12.)

For several years Michael Scriven (1972) has been urging educators to employ "goal-free evaluation." Although Scriven remains committed to outcome research, he argues against a focus on other peoples' predetermined objectives. His argument parallels that in this section in that it hinges on the need to determine the consequences of an intervention and whether or not those consequences have been defined as program goals. Scriven goes so far as to suggest that the evaluator is better off if he does not know what the specific program intentions are. Such ignorance permits the unbiased discovery of the fact that what programs intend is actually happening. As far as Scriven is concerned, goals are an appropriate criterion only in the evaluation of a proposal, never in the evaluation of a program.

Although a shift in thinking from "goals" to "processes" might be the most desirable solution to the goal trap and a greater emphasis on unintended program consequences would be helpful, there is another possible solution that does not require such a great departure from our conventional modes of thinking about program evaluation. Let us consider in the concluding section of this paper the possibility of negotiating various alternative scenarios in a search for more meaningful program goals.

Negotiating a Scenario

Suppose that, rather than intimidating practitioners or administrators into confessing their goals (since they frequently cannot articulate them anyway), the evaluator joined with these people in a mutual effort to search out reasonable program goals and reasonable methods for assessing them? On the basis of his experience with the New Jersey Negative Income Tax Experiment and his resulting concern about reactivity, Kershaw (1972: 226) reasonably recommends that, "Getting as many local people as possible to lose interest in the operation should be a primary goal." I am suggesting the reverse. I am not proposing the old-fashioned social work game of conning people into feeling that they own part of the operation—that it is theirs, when in fact, they do not own it at all, and it isn't theirs. That kind of deception may be useful in temporarily gaining needed cooperation, but what is proposed here is a mutual endeavor, in which in fact, all parties have serious input. Such a negotiation can result in the identification of goals which all parties find acceptable and thus improve the probability that the results of the evaluation will also be acceptable to all parties. And, as Carol Weiss has pointed out (1971: 141), there are fringe benefits.

Not only does their participation [administrators and practitioners] help in the definition of evaluation goals and the maintenance of study procedures, but it may help change the image of evaluation from "critical spying" to collaborative effort to understand and improve.

To those who insist that there can be no negotiating of reality, that it is the *real* goals that must be assessed rather than the results of some political process, I would point out that "the decisions about program design . . . have usually been based upon [among other things] political bargaining" (Glennan, 1972: 188). Mushkin (1973: 32) writes that "objectives of social programs often are clouded by compromises along the path toward legislative enactment." Weiss has argued that the creation of programs and their evaluation is inherently the consequence of extensive give and take.

Perhaps more important is the fact that much of what we consider to be "reality" is the consequence of negotiations among interested parties. Different parties to a program (staff, clientele, funders, administrators, evaluators) may entertain very different conceptions of the reality of the program goals (Krause and Howard, 1973: 1, 16; Weiss, 1974: 680). Recent introduction into the common parlance of the phrase "plea bargaining" has made it clear that what crimes were committed by what persons is a matter that is negotiated between the defense and the prosecution with the assistance of the judge. Criminologists have long been aware of this element in the social creation of criminal statistics (Newman, 1966: 76–330). The same order of social construction of data has been documented in clinic records (Garfinkel, 1967: 186–207), suicide (Douglas, 1967), medical statistics (Rysman, 1973), welfare data (Beck,

1970), and generally in any kind of official statistics (Kitsuse and Cicourel, 1963).

It would be a mistake to consider these as instances of fudging data. Those data are a negotiated reflection of a social order which they are at least in part responsible for creating. They are accurate. They do reflect reality. There are, of course, other sets of equally accurate data dealing with the same kinds of phenomena which also reflect reality, but then there are many realities. The negotiating of medical diagnoses has been documented in dealings between doctor and patient in a tuberculosis sanitarium (Roth, 1963) as well as in psychiatric interviews, both in America (Scheff, 1968) and in Britain (Morgan and Herne, 1973) in which careful bargaining on the precise nature of the diagnosis appears to occur. In many areas, reality is little more than what interested parties can agree it is. Why not in the area of defining goals for the evaluation of programs?

The germ of the idea of negotiation is found from time to time in the literature. Rossi has suggested (1969: 98–99) that action alternatives be developed for both contingencies—positive and negative findings. He believes that the development of such action alternatives enhances the commitment on the part of administrators and practitioners to alternative plans of action. Glennan (1972: 191) observes that planning decisions are the result of a complex bargaining process and that this is the way it should be. He too proposes a contingency analysis before the start of an evaluation: "If the evaluator and the planner were to sit down and ask what will happen if the results show one thing as opposed to another, the quality of evaluation would improve, its relevance would increase, and its results would be more likely to be used" (p. 215).

The transition of these ideas from the application of evaluations to the discovery of goals is made by Cain and Hollister (1972) who refer to "search-evaluation." They argue that the first stages of an evaluation must involve a search for the objectives of the program: "The attempts to follow the usual dogma of evaluation, starting with the definition of a single objective —or a hierarchy of objectives—for the program, are bound to fail" (p. 114). Harper and Babigian propose an extensive negotiation aimed at the decision-making process. They begin by exploring with the administrator the whole range of possible recommendations as the first step in designing the evaluation. They then struggle together to find reasonable answers to such questions as

> What kinds of data or information will lead to one or another of these decisions? and how does the evaluator obtain the best data that will enable the administrator to decide between making no change and making one of several possible changes? (Harper and Babigian, 1971: 152)

If we extend their limited concept of an evaluator-administrator interaction so that it includes other relevant parties and if we extend the negotiable issues to include program goals and their measurement, then what follows is precisely what I mean by negotiating scenarios.

The administrator and the evaluator should imagine themselves doing the evaluation and think through to its end—conjuring up possible sets of data or results and then making imaginary decisions based on the imaginary but alternative sets of data. (Harper and Babigian, 1971: 152)

These cues suggest to me that it is desirable for the evaluator to begin to locate what program people are trying to do by watching them do it and listening to them talk about it—*in situ!* There is a cumulating body of evidence from sociolinguistics that, if one listens to people talk about what they are doing while they are doing it, chances of understanding the activity are maximized. An example of this principle applied to evaluation can be found in Wieder's study of a halfway house for drug addicts (1973).[7]

Experienced and competent practitioners (and I do not imply that all practitioners fall into that category) can be assumed to know what they are trying to do even though they may not be able to articulate those goals. Part of the evaluator's task then is to discover what in fact is being attempted. After watching and listening he will begin to speculate about what is happening and can then begin to engage practitioners, administrators, clients, or policy makers in a dialogue in an effort to negotiate the reality of the situation. Alternative scenarios can be drawn employing different conceptions of goals, different measuring devices, and alternative conclusions. Such scenarios can be negotiated one by one with the program people until reasonable agreement is reached as to goals, means of measuring them, and the credibility of alternative conclusions. This kind of involvement, as difficult and time-consuming as it may be, will go a long way toward increasing the probability that practitioners, administrators, and policy makers will seriously take into account the findings of evaluation research. And that, after all, is what it is all about.

NOTES

1. I do not intend to suggest that this is the only relevant facet of organizational theory in program evaluation. Systems analysis, for example, provides useful guidelines for tracing organizational processes. Such concepts as feedback loops provide built-in assurance that the evaluator will consider the reactive elements of the evaluation per se in the functioning of the program. However, as I have argued elsewhere (1975), it is toward social psychological theory that one must turn for guidelines in most program development.

2. I say, "perhaps," since the influence of an actor and his actions generally transcends his death. As an extreme example, it may be that the most immortal action of the suicide is his suicide.

3. For a Blumer perspective on the closely related problems of social indicators, see Kisiel (1974). Program evaluators who are attempting to spell out such a methodology include Dale (1971), Fry (1973), Krause and Howard (1973), Allerhand (1971), Scriven (1972), Chomie and Hudson (1974), and Filstead (1970a, 1970b). The logic and applications of the basic methodology of participant observation is dealt with in the extensive writings of Blanche Geer and Howard Becker some of which are found in Becker (1970). See also Glaser and Strauss (1967), Filstead (1974), Schatzman and Strauss (1973), and Bogdan and Taylor (1975).

4. I suspect that Robert A. Dentler's "The Phenomenology of the Evaluation Researchers" might inform this discussion, but I have not been able to obtain a copy and it remains unpublished since Rossi and Williams chose not to include it in their volume containing papers from the conference where it was presented (Rossi and Williams, 1972). Rossi discusses the Dentler paper on pp. 36–38.

5. Alan Dale informs me that there is "quite a bit going on in Europe in this area" (1974).

6. In an earlier historical review, Rossi (1972: 17) observes that the grounds for attacks on New Deal programs frequently had to do with "negative side-effects."

7. Extensive references and some discussion of this issue can be found in Chapter 7 of Deutscher (1973). A comprehensive review of modern literature on sociolinguistics has been provided by Grimshaw (1973 and 1974).

REFERENCES

Allerhand, Melvin E.   1971   "The Process Outcome Research Model: An Alternative to Evaluation Research." in Richard O'Toole (ed.), *The Organization, Management, and Tactics of Social Research.* Cambridge, Mass.: Schenkman.
Angrist, Shirley S.   1975   "Evaluation Research: Possibilities and Limitations." *Journal of Applied Behavioral Science* (in press, quotes are from typescript draft).
Beck, Bernard.   1970   "Cooking Welfare Stew." In Robert W. Habenstein (ed.),

Pathways to Data: Field Methods for Studying Ongoing Social Organizations. Chicago: Aldine Publishing Company.

Becker, Howard S.   1970   *Sociological Work: Method and Substance.* Chicago: Aldine Publishing Company.

Becker, Howard S., Blanche Geer, and Everett C. Hughes.   1968   *Making the Grade: The Academic Side of College Life.* New York: John Wiley and Sons.

Bernstein, Ilene H. and Howard E. Freeman.   1973   "A Review of Evaluation Research: The State of the Art, Methodological Practices, and Dissemination of Research Findings." Presented at the American Sociological Association Meetings, New York. Published in *Academic and Entrepreneurial Research: The Consequences of Diversity in Federal Evaluation Studies.* New York: Russell Sage Foundation, 1975.

Blau, Peter.   1955   *The Dynamics of Bureaucracy.* Chicago: University of Chicago Press.

Blau, Peter and W. Richard Scott.   1961   *Formal Organizations.* San Francisco: Chandler Publishing Co.

Blumer, Herbert.   1956   "Sociological Analysis and the Variable." *American Sociological Review* 21: 683–690.

Bogdan, Robert.   1972   "Organizational Goals and Success Measurement in a Job-Training Program." Syracuse: Syracuse University, Center on Human Policy, Mimeographed.

Bogdan, Robert and Stephen Taylor.   1975   *An Introduction to Qualitative Research Methods.* New York: John Wiley.

Brooks, Michael P.   1965   "The Community Action Program as a Setting for Applied Research." *Journal of Social Issues* 21: 29–40.

Cain, Glen G. and Robinson G. Hollister.   1972   "The Methodology of Evaluating Social Action Programs." In Peter H. Rossi and Walter Williams, pp. 109–137.

Campbell, Donald T.   1969   "Reforms as Experiments." *American Psychologist* 24: 409–429. [Reprinted in this volume, No. 12, pp. 172–204]
1971   "Methods for the Experimenting Society." Presented at the Eastern Psychological Association, Washington, D.C., Mimeographed (Forthcoming in *American Psychologist*).

Caro, Francis G.   1971   *Readings in Evaluation Research.* New York: Russell Sage Foundation.

Chomie, Peter W. and Joe Hudson.   1974   "Evaluation of Outcome and Process." *Social Work* 19: 682–687.

Clark, Burton.   1956   "Organizational Adaptation and Precarious Values." *American Sociological Review* 21: 327–336.

Dale, Alan.   1971   "The Alpha Company: A Study of an Organizational Effectiveness Programme." Working Paper, London Graduate School of Business Studies.
1974   Personal Communication.

Deutscher, Irwin.   1973   *What We Say/What We Do: Sentiments and Acts.* Glenview, Ill.: Scott, Foresman and Company.
1975   "Social Theory and Program Evaluation: A Metatheoretical Note." Presented at the American Sociological Association Meetings, San Francisco.

Douglas, Jack D.   1967   *The Social Meaning of Suicide.* Princeton: Princeton University Press.

Etzioni, Amitai.   1960   "Two Approaches to Organizational Analysis." *Administrative Science Quarterly* 5: 257–278.

Filstead, William J.   1970a   "A Suggested Framework for Studying the Natural History of Personal Problems." Unpublished Paper, Lutheran General Hospital, Department of Psychiatry, Park Ridge, Ill.
      1970b   "The Clinical Perspective: Assumptions, Priorities, and Blindspots." Unpublished Paper, Lutheran General Hospital, Department of Psychiatry, Park Ridge, Ill.
      1974   "The Promises and Problems of Qualitative Methodology." Delivered to the Department of Sociology, American University, Washington, D.C.
Freeman, Howard E. and Clarence C. Sherwood.   1965   "Research in Large-Scale Intervention Programs." *The Journal of Social Issues* 21: 11–28. [Reprinted in this volume, No. 13, pp. 205–220]
Fry, Lincoln L.   1973   "Participant Observation and Program Evaluation." *Journal of Health and Social Behavior* 14: 274–278.
Garfinkel, Harold.   1967   *Studies in Ethnomethodology.* Englewood Cliffs, N.J.: Prentice-Hall (Chapter 6): 186–207.
Glaser, Barney G. and Anselm L. Strauss.   1967   *The Discovery of Grounded Theory: Strategies for Qualitative Research.* Chicago: Aldine Publishing Co.
Glennan, Thomas K., Jr.   1972   "Evaluating Federal Manpower Programs: Notes and Observations." Pp. 187–220 in Peter H. Rossi and Walter Williams (1972).
Goldstein, Paul.   1974   Personal Communication, March 8.
Goldstein, Paul, Donald Hull, and Susan Ostrander.   1973   "The Evaluation of Urban Ameliorative Projects: Case Studies and Integrating Framework." Presented at the North Central Sociological Association Meetings, Cincinnati.
Gouldner, Alvin W.   1968   "Organizational Analysis." Pp. 400–428 in Robert Merton, et al. (eds.), *Sociology Today.* New York: Basic Books.
Greenberg, B. G.   1968   "Evaluation of Social Programs." *Review of the International Statistical Institute* 36: 260–277. [Reprinted in this volume, No. 10, pp. 137–158]
Grimshaw, Allen D.   1973   "On Language in Society: Part I." *Contemporary Sociology* 2: 578–585.
      1974   "On Language in Society: Part II." *Contemporary Sociology* 3: 3–11.
Guttentag, Marcia.   1973   "Subjectivity and Its Use in Evaluation Research." *Evaluation* 1: 60–65.
Harper, Dean and Hartouton Babigian.   1971   "Evaluation Research: The Consequences of Program Evaluation." *Mental Hygiene* 55: 151–156.
Heberlein, Thomas A.   1973   "The Three Fixes: Technological, Cognitive, and Structural." Presented at the Water and Community Conference, Seattle, Mimeographed.
Houston, Tom R., Jr.   1972   "The Behavioral Sciences Impact-Effectiveness Model." Pp. 51–65 in Peter Rossi and Walter Williams (1972).
Hyman, Herbert H., Charles R. Wright, and Terence K. Hopkins.   1962   *Applications of Methods of Evaluation: Four Studies of the Encampment for Citizenship.* Berkeley: University of California Press.
Hyman, Herbert H. and Charles R. Wright.   1967   "Evaluating Social Action Programs." Pp. 741–782 in Paul F. Lazarsfeld, et al. (eds.), *The Uses of Sociology.* New York: Basic Books.
Jones, Wyatt C. and Edgar F. Borgatta.   1972   "Methodology of Evaluation." In Edward J. Mullen, et al. (eds.), *Evaluation of Social Intervention.* San Francisco: Jossey-Bass, 39–54.
Kesiel, Gerry.   1974   "Some Theoretical Problems in the Development and Use of

Social Indicators." Presented at the VIIIth World Congress of Sociology, Toronto.

Kershaw, David N.   1972   "Issues in Income Maintenance Experimentation." Pp. 221–245 in Peter Rossi and Walter Williams (1972).

Kitsuse, John L. and Aaron V. Cicourel.   1963   "A Note on the Use of Official Statistics." *Social Problems* 11: 131–139.

Krause, Merton S. and Kenneth I. Howard.   1973   "Program Evaluation in the Public Interest: A New Research Methodology." Presented at the Society for Psychotherapy Research, Philadelphia.

Lerman, Paul.   1968   "Evaluative Studies of Institutions for Delinquents: Implications for Research and Social Policy." *Social Work* 13: 55–64. [Reprinted in this volume, No. 11, pp. 159–171]

McDill, Edward L., Mary S. McDill, and J. Timothy Sprehe.   1972   "Evaluation in Practice: Compensatory Education." Pp. 141–185 in Peter Rossi and Walter Williams (1972).

Merton, Robert K.   1957   *Social Theory and Social Structure.* Glencoe, Ill.: The Free Press.

Michels, Robert.   1959   *Political Parties.* New York: Dover Press.

Morgan, Susan and Peter Herne.   1973   "What Have You Got to Lose: Notions of Negotiation and Power in Agent-Client Decisions." Unpublished Paper, Department of Sociology, University of Massachusetts at Boston.

Mushkin, Selma J.   1973   "Evaluations: Use with Caution." *Evaluation* 1: 31–35.

Newman, Donald J.   1966   *Conviction: The Determination of Guilt or Innocence Without Trial.* Boston: Little, Brown & Co. (Part III).

Perrow, Charles.   1961   "The Analysis of Goals in Complex Organizations." *The American Sociological Review,* 26: 854–866.

Rossi, Peter.   1969   "Evaluating Educational Programs." *The Urban Review* 3: 17–18.

1972   "Testing for Success and Failure in Social Action." Pp. 11–49 in Peter Rossi and Walter Williams (1972).

1974   "No Bananas Again: The Non-Results of the New Jersey Income Maintenance Experiment." Presented at Colloquia on Evaluation of Policy-Oriented Social Programs, University of California, Los Angeles.

Rossi, Peter and Walter Williams.   1972   *Evaluating Social Programs: Theory, Practice, and Politics.* New York: Seminar Press.

Roth, Julius A.   1963   *Timetables: Structuring the Passage of Time in Hospital Treatment and Other Careers.* Indianapolis: Bobbs-Merrill.

Rysman, Alexander.   1973   "Ill?" in Jack D. Douglas (ed.), *Social Problems in a Revolutionary Age.* New York: Random House.

Salasin, Susan.   1973   "Experimentation Revisited: A Conversation with Donald T. Campbell." *Evaluation* 1: 7–13.

Schatzman, Leonard and Anselm L. Strauss.   1973   *Field Research: Strategies for a Natural Sociology.* Englewood Cliffs, N.J.: Prentice-Hall.

Scheff, Thomas J.   1968   "Negotiating Reality: Notes on Power in the Assessment of Responsibility." *Social Problems* 16: 3–17.

Schulberg, Herbert C. and Frank Baker.   1968   "Program Evaluation Models and the Implementation of Research Findings." *American Journal of Public Health* 58: 1248–1255. [Reprinted in this volume, No. 3, pp. 54–63]

Scriven, Michael.   1972   "Prose and Cons about Goal Free Research." *Evaluation*

Comment: The Journal of Educational Evaluation, Center for the Study of Evaluation, UCLA, 3: 1–5.

Sills, David L.   1957   *The Volunteers.* Glencoe, Ill.: The Free Press.

Suchman, Edward A.   1969   "Evaluating Educational Programs." *The Urban Review* 3: 15–17. [Reprinted in this volume, No. 2, pp. 48–53]

Thompson, James and William McEwen.   1958   "Organizational Goals and Environment." *American Sociological Review,* 23: 23–31.

Weiss, Carol H.   1971   "Utilization of Evaluation: Toward Comparative Study." Pp. 136–142 in Francis Caro (1971).

    1973   "Where Politics and Evaluation Research Meet." *Evaluation* 1: 37–45.

    1974   "Alternative Models of Program Evaluation." *Social Work* 19: 675–681.

Weiss, Robert S. and Martin Rein.   1969   "The Evaluation of Broad-Aim Programs: A Cautionary Case and a Moral." *The Annals of the American Academy of Political and Social Science* 385: 133–142. [Reprinted in this volume, No. 16, pp. 253–262]

Wieder, D. Lawrence.   1973   *Language and Social Reality: The Case of Telling the Convict Code.* The Hague: Mouton

Zimiles, H.   1970   "Has Evaluation Failed Compensatory Education?" In J. Hellmuth (ed.), *Disadvantaged Child,* Vol. 3, New York: Brunner/Mazel.

15. Boobytraps and Pitfalls in the Evaluation of Social Action Programs

Peter H. Rossi

I: INTRODUCTION

If one were to measure success by the popularity of evaluation research, then empirical social research has certainly arrived. Perhaps, the best example of this popularity lies in the legislation authorizing the present War on Poverty in which the agencies involved are specifically directed to set aside funds for evaluation research. Other ameliorative programs may not give as much formal recognition to such activity, but nevertheless seek social researchers to add to their staffs for this purpose or attempt to get social research centers to provide evaluations of their programs.

There are other measures of success besides popularity. If one were to measure success by the proportion of evaluation researches which are conducted with powerful enough designs to render unequivocal evaluation statements, then empirical social research does not appear to be a smashing success. For a variety of reasons—some substantive, others related to the present state of development of research methodology, and still others concerned with the "politics" of evaluation—there are very few evaluation researches which have the elegance of design and clarity of execution which would achieve widespread admiration among social researchers.

The purpose of this paper is to explore some of the main reasons why evaluation research is hard to do well and to suggest some ways in which these difficulties can be overcome. Providing much of the materials on which this paper has been based have been the experiences with such research of the National Opinion Research Center over the past few years. However, I venture that the experiences of other research centers and of individual researchers has not been very different: At least my informal, but undoubtedly highly biased, survey would indicate strong similarities between our experiences and theirs.

In principle, the evaluation of action programs appears to be most appropriately undertaken through the use of experimental designs. All the elements which would strongly recommend such research designs are usually present: The program involved is something which is added to the ongoing social scene by purposive social action as opposed to events which are not under the control of some individual or agency. Because an action program is under someone's control, the construction of experimental and control groups is, in principle, possible. Furthermore, the program is usually not designed to cover an entire population, but only some portion of it so that some of a target population would not be

Reprinted with permission of the author from the 1966 Social Statistics Section, Proceedings of the American Statistical Association, pp. 127–132.

covered, making it possible to think in terms of control groups. Thus, in principle, it is not difficult to design an extremely elegant program of experiments to evaluate the effectiveness of the usual action program. Controlled experiments, however, are not frequently used in evaluation research. For example, there is not a single evaluation research being carried out on the major programs of the War on Poverty which follows closely the model of the controlled experiment.

II: ACTION PROGRAMS AND THE CONTEMPORARY SCENE

There can be little doubt that the present historical period is one in which there is considerable groping for new and presumably more effective treatments for a variety of presumed ills. We have rediscovered the poor, suddenly become intensely aware that Negroes are an incredibly disadvantaged group, become worried over the plight of the aged, and concerned about a presumed wasteage of brainpower. We also have enough national income to allocate some part of our resources to new programs designed to correct some of the obvious faults in our society.

However, there is an ironic twist to developing a heavy conscience in this historical period. This is because we cannot ordinarily expect that the new treatments we can devise will produce massive results. It appears as if we are in much the same position in the treatment of diseases. The introduction of modern medicine and modern sanitation procedures into a country which has had neither can very dramatically reduce morbidity and mor-

tality, as experiences in some of the emerging nations indicate. But, in the United States of today, each new gain in morbidity and mortality can be expected to be smaller and more difficult to achieve. Providing potable water is much easier to achieve, and more dramatic in its impact on morbidity and mortality, than any attempt we can make to lower the incidence of lung cancer, especially if we try it through lowering levels of smoking in individuals.

Similarly with respect to our social ills. Dramatic effects on illiteracy can be achieved by providing schools and teachers to all children: Achieving a universally high enough level of literacy and knowledge, so that everyone capable of learning can find a good spot in our modern labor force, is a lot more difficult. Hence, the more we have done in the past to lower unemployment rates, to provide social services, etc., the more difficult it is to add to the benefits derived from past programs by the addition of new ones. Partly, this is because we have achieved so much with the past programs and partly this is because the massive efforts of the past have not dealt with individual motivation as much as with benefits to aggregates of individuals.

In part, the concern of contemporary practitioners in the applied fields with evaluation arises out of their increased methodological sophistication. But, in even larger measure, it arises out of the expectation—held at some level or other—that massive effects are not to be expected from new programs and the new treatments are going to be increasingly expensive in terms of time and money. The problem of evaluation in this historical period is that the new treatments can be expected to yield marginal improvements over present treatments and that cost-to-benefit ratios can be expected to rise dramatically. Hence, there is considerable interest in research but considerable apprehension over what it will show concerning the effects of programs.

To illustrate, let us consider the case of Project Headstart: We have apparently wrung most of the benefits we can out of the traditional school system. Although everyone would agree that universal schooling for children up to approximately age sixteen has been a huge success, as opposed to a system of no schooling or of schooling mainly for those who pay for it themselves, there still remains considerable room for improvement, especially in the education of the poor and otherwise disadvantaged. A supplementary pre-school program bringing such children more into parity with those better off because of family background sounds like an excellent program. But, it is hardly likely to produce as much benefit as the introduction of universal elementary schooling did, especially since it is designed to do the job that a full-time institution, the family, neglected to do for one reason or another.

Effective new treatments which produce more than equivocal results are expensive. For example, each trainee at a Job Corps camp costs somewhere between five and ten thousand dollars a year (depending on which estimates you hear), as compared to considerably less than one thousand dollars per year in the usual public high school. Yet a year in a Job Corps Training Center is not going to be five to ten times more effective than a year in a public high school.

Paradoxically, the costs of evaluation are also expensive for these new programs. If effects can be expected to be small, greater precision is needed in research to demonstrate such effects unequivocally. This is another reason why I stressed the controlled experiment as the ideal evaluation research design: Its ability to detect effects is quite powerful compared to alternative methods.

Although as social scientists we can expect the new social programs to show marginal effects, the practitioner does not ordinarily share our pessimism— at least, not when he faces the Congressional Appropriating Committee. Hence, the claims made in public for the programs are ordinarily pitched much higher, in terms of expectation of benefits, than we could realistically expect with the worst of research and much better than we could expect with the best of research. Thus it turns out that one of the major obstacles to evaluation research is the interests in the maintenance of a program held by its administrators. Their ambivalence is born of a two horned dilemma: On the one hand, research is needed to demonstrate that the program has an effect; on the other hand, research might find that effects are negligible or non-existent.

III: COMMITMENT TO EVALUATION

The will to believe that their programs are effective is understandably strong among the practitioners who administer them. After all, they are committing their energies, careers and ideologies to programs of action and it is difficult, under such circumstances, to take a tentative position concerning outcomes. Hence, most evaluation researches which are undertaken at the behest of the administrators of the programs involved are expected to come out with results indicating that the program is effective. As long as the results are positive (or at least not negative) relationships between practitioners and researchers are cordial and sometimes even effusively friendly. But, what happens when it comes out the other way?

A few years ago, the National Opinion Research Center undertook research with the best of sponsorships on the effect of fellowships and scholarships on graduate study in the arts and sciences fields. It was the sincere conviction, on the part of the learned societies which sponsored the research, that such fellowships and scholarships were an immense aid to graduate students in the pursuit of their studies and that heavily supported fields were thereby able to attract better students than fields which were not well supported. The results of the study were quite equivocal: First, it did not appear that financial support had much to do with selection of a field for graduate study. Secondly, it did not appear that graduate students of high quality were being held back from the completion of their graduate programs by the lack of fellowships or scholarships: Those who were committed found some way to get their Ph.D.'s, often relying on their spouses to make a capital investment in their graduate training. The equivocal nature of the results was quite disappointing to the sponsors whose first reaction was to question the adequacy

of the study's methodology, leading to the coining of a National Opinion Research Center aphorism that the first defense of an outraged sponsor was methodological criticism. The findings affected policy not one whit: The sponsoring groups are still adamantly claiming more and more in the way of financial support for graduate students from the federal government on the grounds that such support materially affects the numbers of talented students who will go to graduate study beyond the B.A., and, furthermore, materially affects the distribution of talent among various fields of study.

Relations between the sponsoring learned societies and our researchers have been cool (if not distant) ever since. The learned societies believe their problem has been badly researched, and the researchers believe that their results have been badly ignored.

Sometimes both the researcher and the practitioner suffer from the will to believe leading to evaluation research containing the most lame sets of qualified results imaginable. Perhaps the best example can be gleaned from the long history of research on the effects of class size on learning. The earliest researches on this topic go back to the beginnings of empirical research in educational psychology and sociology in the early twenties. Since that time there is scarcely a year in which there has not been several dissertations and theses on this topic, not to mention larger researches done by more mature scholars. The researches have used a variety of designs ranging from the controlled experiment to correlational studies, the latest in the series being the results on this score obtained by

James Coleman in his nationwide study of schools conducted for the Office of Education under the Civil Rights Act of 1964. The results of these studies are extremely easy to summarize: By and large, class size has no effect on the learning of students, with the possible exception of classes in the language arts. But, the net results of more than two hundred researches on educational ideology and policy has been virtually nil. Every proposal for the betterment of education calls for reductions in the size of classes, despite the fact that there is no evidence that class size affects anything except possibly the job satisfaction of teachers. Even the researchers in presenting their results tend to present them apologetically, indicating the ways in which defects in their research designs may have produced negative findings as artifacts.

In fact, I do not know of any action program that has been put out of business by evaluation research, unless evaluation itself was used as the hatchet to begin with. Why is this the case? Why do negative results have so little impact? The main reason lies in the fact that the practitioners, first of all (and sometimes the researchers), never seriously entertained in advance the possibility that results would come out negative or insignificant. Without commitment to the bet, one or both of the gamblers usually welch.

The ways by which welching is accomplished are myriad. It is easy to attack the methodology of any study: Methodological unsophisticates suddenly become experts in sampling, questionnaire construction, experimental design, and statistical analysis, or borrow experts for the occasion. Further replication is called for. But, most often it is discovered that the goals of the program in terms of which it was evaluated are not the "real" goals after all. Thus, the important goals of school systems are not higher scores on multiple choice achievement tests, but better attitudes toward learning, a matter which the researcher neglected to evaluate. Or, the goals of a community organization in an urban renewal area were not really to affect the planning process but to produce a commitment to the neighborhood on the part of its residents while the planning took place.

Perhaps the best example of how "real" goals are discovered after goals that were evaluated were found to be poorly attained can be found in the work of a very prominent school administration group. This group, fully committed to the educational modernities of the forties and fifties, found to its surprise that whether or not a school system adopted its programs had little to do with the learning that students achieved. Hence, they dropped achievement tests as a criterion of the goodness of a school or school system and substituted instead a measure of how flexible the administration was in adopting new ideas in curriculum, producing an evaluation instrument which, in effect, states that a school system is good to the extent that it adopts policies that were currently being advocated by the group in question.

IV: ASSURING POSITIVE RESULTS

Given unlimited resources, it is possible to make some sort of dent in almost any problem. Even the most sodden wretch on skid row can be brought to a semblance of respectability for some period of time (provided that he is not too physically deteriorated) by intense, and expensive, handling. But, to make an impact on the denizens of all the skid rows in all of our great cities requires methods that are not intensive and are not expensive case by case. There is not sufficient manpower or resources to lead each single skid row inhabitant back to respectability, if only for a short period.

Yet, many action programs, particularly of the "demonstration" variety, resemble the intensive treatment model. They are bound to produce results if only because they maximize the operation of the Hawthorne and Rosenthal effects, but cannot be put into large scale operation because either manpower or resources are not available. Hence, programs which work well on the initial run on a small scale with dedicated personnel can be expected to show more positive results than the production runs of such programs with personnel not as committed to the program in question.

The distinction I want to make in this connection is that between "impact" and "coverage." The *impact* of a technique may be said to be its ability to produce changes in each situation to which it is applied, while the *coverage* of a technique is its ability to be applied to a large number of cases. Thus, face-to-face persuasion is a technique which has high impact as a means of getting people to come in for physical examinations, but its coverage is relatively slight. In contrast, bus and subway posters may have low impact in the sense of producing a desired effect each time someone is exposed, but large

coverage in the sense that many people can be exposed to bus and subway posters very easily.

An extremely effective technique for the amelioration of a social problem is one which has both high impact and high coverage. Perhaps the best example of such techniques can be found in medicine whose immunizing vaccines are inexpensive, easy to administer and very effective in reducing the incidence of certain diseases. It does not seem likely that we will find vaccines, or measures resembling them in impact and coverage, for the ills to which action programs in the social field are directed. It is more likely that we will have action programs which have either high impact or high coverage, but not both. The point I want to emphasize here is that it is a mistake to discard out of hand programs which have low impact but the potentiality of high coverage. Hence, programs which show small positive results on evaluation and which can be generalized to reach large numbers of people can, in the long run, have an extremely significant cumulative effect.

Examples of such programs in the social action field do not easily come to mind. But perhaps an illustration from the field of public health can be cited appropriately: Over the past few decades public health information specialists have been plagued by the fact that their most effective techniques have low coverage and their best mass techniques have little impact. Evaluation research after evaluation research has indicated that it is possible to raise the level of an individual's health knowledge and utilization of health facilities if you can get him to come to a course of lectures on the topic. In contrast, public health information campaigns utilizing the mass media have been shown to have minute effects. Yet, the information of the American population concerning health matters has appreciably increased over the past two decades. It is apparently the case that while no one campaign was particularly effective, their cumulative effects were considerable.

V: THE CONTROL GROUP PROBLEM

The key feature of the controlled experiment lies in the control exercised by the experimenter over the processes by which subjects are allocated to experimental and control groups. In a well-designed experiment, such allocations are made in an unbiased fashion. But, there are many ways in which a well thought out plan can go awry.

Perhaps the major obstacle to the use of controlled experiments in evaluation research is a political one. The political problem is simply that practitioners are extremely reluctant to allow the experimenters to exercise proper controls over the allocation of clients to experimental and control groups. For example, the proper evaluation of a manpower retraining program requires that potential trainees be separated into experimental and control groups with a contrast being made between the two groups at a later time. This obviously means that some potential clients, who are otherwise qualified, are barred arbitrarily from training— an act which public agencies are extremely reluctant to authorize.

In part, the political problem arises because researchers have not thought through sufficiently the problem of what constitutes a control or non-experimental experience. The logic of experimental design does not require that the experimental group not undergo *some* sort of treatment, it merely requires that the experimental group not be given the treatment which is being evaluated. In short, we have not been ingenious enough in inventing placebo treatments which are realistic enough to give the public official the feeling that he is not slighting some individuals at random. For example, a placebo treatment for a job retraining program may be conceived of as some treatment designed to help men get jobs but which does not involve retraining and, over which the training program should demonstrate some advantage. Perhaps testing and intensive counseling might be an acceptable placebo for a control group in an experimental evaluation of job training. Or, a placebo treatment for the evaluation of a community mental health center might be referrals to general practitioners for the kinds of treatment they either administer themselves or provide referrals to.

Even in the best circumstances and with the best of sponsors, the carrying out of controlled experiments can run into a number of boobytraps. There is, for example, the case of an evaluation research all set to go and well designed but whose program did not generate enough volunteers to fill up either the experimental or the control groups. Under these circumstances, the administrator opted to fill up the experimental groups abandoning all attempts at segregating the volunteers into experimental and control groups.

Or, there is the example of a well designed research on the effectiveness of certain means of reaching low income families with birth control information whose design was contaminated by the City Health Department setting up birth control clinics in areas which had been designated as controls!

Or, there is the risk that is run in long range experimental designs that the world may provide experiences to control, which would duplicate in some essential fashion, the experimental treatment. Thus, Wilner *et al.,* in the evaluation of the effects of public housing, unfortunately undertook their research in a period when the quality of the general housing stock in Baltimore was being improved at so fast a rate that the contrast in housing conditions between experimental and control groups had greatly diminished by the end of the observational period.

In sum, it is not easy either to obtain sufficient consent to undertake properly controlled experiments or to carry them out when such consent is obtained.

VI: A STRATEGY FOR EVALUATION RESEARCH

There are a number of lessons to be drawn from the various sections of this paper which hopefully could go some distance toward devising a strategy for the conduct of evaluation research. While it is true that in a Panglossian best of all possible worlds, the best of all possible research designs can be employed, in a compromised real world, full of evil as it is, it is necessary to make do with what is possible

within the limits of time and resources. The problem that faces us then is how can we set up the conditions for doing as best a job we can and produce research which is as relevant as possible to the judgment of the effectiveness of social policy programs.

Although the idea of evaluation research has gained wide acceptance, we are a long way from a full commitment to the outcomes of evaluation research. It is part of the researcher's responsibility to bring to the practitioner's attention that in most cases the effects of action programs are slight and that there is more than an off-chance possibility that evaluation will produce non-positive results. The policy implications of such findings have to be worked out in advance; otherwise the conduct of evaluation research may turn out to be a fatuous exercise.

Secondly, we have a long way to go in devising ways of applying controlled experiments to problems of evaluation. Political obstacles to the use of controls often make it hard to get acceptance of such designs, and the difficulty of maintaining controls in a non-sterile world makes full-fledged experimental designs relatively rare in use.

Earlier in this paper, I suggested that we take a lesson from medical research and search for the social analogues of placebos to be administered to our control groups. There are other directions in which experimental designs should go: For example, considering the high likelihood that treatments have small effects, we need very powerful designs to demonstrate positive results. But because power costs money, it is worthwhile considering research designs which evaluate several types of experimental treatments simultaneously so that the outcomes will be more useful to the setting of program policy. To illustrate: it is considerably more worthwhile to have the results of an experimental evaluation which provides results on several types of job corps camps than on job corps camps in general. Looking at the differential effectiveness of several job corps camps provides more detailed and better information for the improvement of job corps programs than would a gross evaluation of the program all told.

This paper has stressed the model of the controlled experiment as the desired one for evaluation research. But, it is abundantly clear that for a variety of reasons, controlled experiments are rarely employed as evaluational devices and that they are difficult to employ. Most frequent are some sort of quasi-experiments in which the control groups are constructed by methods which allow some biases to operate and correlational designs in which persons subjected to some sort of treatment are contrasted with persons who have not been treated, controlling statistically for relevant characteristics.

The important question which faces the evaluation researchers is how bad are such "soft" evaluational techniques, particularly correlational designs? Under what circumstances can they be employed with some confidence in their outcomes?

First of all, it seems to me that when it is massive effects that are expected and desired, "soft" techniques are almost as good as subtle and precise ones. To illustrate, if what is desired as the outcome of a particular treatment is

complete remission of all symptoms in each and every individual subject to treatment, then it is hardly necessary to have a control group. Thus if a birth control technique is to be judged effective *if and only if* it completely eliminates the chance of conception in an experimental group, then the research design is vastly simplified. The question is not whether those who use the method have less children than those who do not, but whether they have any children at all, a question which can be easily decided by administering the technique to a group and counting births (or conceptions) thereafter.

The obverse of the above also holds. If a treatment which is to be tested shows no effects using a soft method of evaluation, then it is highly unlikely that a very precise method of evaluation is going to show more than very slight effects. The existence of complex and large interaction effects which suppress large differences between a group subject to a treatment and statistical control groups seems highly unlikely. Thus if children participating in a Head Start program show no gain in learning ability compared to those who did not participate in the program, holding initial level of learning constant, then it is not likely that a controlled experiment in which children are randomly assigned to experimental and controlled groups is going to show dramatic effects from Head Start programs.

Of course, if a correlational design does show some program effects, then it is never clear whether selection biases or the program itself produce the effects shown.

This means that it is worthwhile to

consider soft methods as the first stage in evaluation research, discarding treatments which show no effects and retaining those with opposite characteristics to be tested with more powerful designs of the controlled experimental kind.

Although ex post facto designs of a correlational variety have obvious holes in them through which may creep the most insidious of biases, such designs are extremely useful in the investigation of effects which are postulated to be the results of long acting treatments. Despite the fact that it is possible that cigarettes cause cancer, the evidence from ex post facto studies of the correlation between cigarette smoking and lung cancer can hardly be ignored, even though the evidence is not pure from the viewpoint of a purist. Similarly, NORC's study of the effects of Catholic education on adults, despite all our efforts to hold constant relevant factors, can still be easily produced by self selection biases that were too subtle for our blunt instruments to

detect. We have nevertheless gained a great deal of knowledge concerning the order of effects that can be expected, were a controlled experiment extending over a generation conducted. The net differences between parochial school Catholics and public school Catholics are so slight that we now know that this institution is not very effective as a device for maintaining religiosity and that furthermore the effects we found are quite likely to have been generated by selection biases.

From these considerations a strategy for evaluation research is beginning to emerge. It seems to me to be useful to consider evaluation research in two stages—a Reconnaissance Phase in which the soft correlational designs are used to screen out those programs it is worthwhile to investigate further; and an Experimental Phase in which powerful controlled experimental designs are used to evaluate the differential effectiveness of a variety of programs which showed up as having sizable effects in the first phase.

PART IV
CASE MATERIALS

This final section consisting of reports on specific evaluation studies is intended to complement the general papers in previous sections. The case materials illustrate the application of general principles and the field experiences of researchers in conducting evaluation studies. Some of the case materials deal with the circumstances surrounding evaluation projects. These papers deal with the rationale for use of particular evaluation strategies in the situations described. The political and social policy context of evaluation projects is also illustrated in some of these cases. Other papers in this section are reports of completed evaluations. Studies are included of interventions in a variety of institutional sectors.

The evaluation component of an ambitious early antipoverty program was studied by Weiss and Rein. The complex, community-wide intervention was to be evaluated through an experimental study emphasizing implications for adolescents. Not only were the evaluators frustrated in their efforts to complete their research, but their strategy deflected them from attention to the intervention itself. The authors argue that the use of an experimental design for evaluation of a highly fluid and complex intervention was inappropriate. A case is presented for a qualitative, process-oriented approach to evaluation of interventions of this kind.

Klerman et al. provide an account of their experiences in addressing methodological issues in the evaluation of a program for pregnant teenage girls. Particularly noteworthy are the evaluators' struggles to find adequate control and comparison groups and to respond to significant changes over time in the experimental program.

Caro analyzes a case in which strong experimental research dominated a weak innovative service program for the elderly. He uses the example to argue for a "phased" evaluation strategy. "Soft," unobtrusive research approaches would be used to gauge roughly the viability of new programs. Sophisticated experimental research would be used only after new programs were well established and the initial evaluation had yielded promising results.

The National Income Transfer experiment sponsored by the Office of

Economic Opportunity is among the most important recent large-scale interventions concerned with a major social policy issue. Rossi and Lyall show how unanticipated external political issues jeopardized the project's field operations and undermined the credibility of its findings. The case illustrates the hazards of early participation of investigators in policy debates, the fragile basis on which researchers promise confidentiality, and the difficulty of timing major experiments so that their results can have a maximum impact on social policy deliberations.

How a process evaluation can contribute to the explanation of program failure is illustrated by Fry and Miller. Using participant observation techniques, the authors studied a skid row mission in which an innovative alcoholism treatment program was attempted. Fry and Miller trace over time the interactions of organizations, practitioners, and clients in the attempt to implement a program based on uncertain treatment technologies and questionable success criteria. The study points to a range of sociological and clinical issues that must be dealt with in program planning if innovative treatment programs are to have any chance for success.

Chapin's research on the effects of public housing is of particular interest as an early example of evaluative research. The paper is concerned with Chapin's experimental work on the social implications of housing in the period between 1935 and 1940. Measures of general adjustment, social participation, and social status were used to compare those residing in public housing projects with controls who continued to live in "slums."

An experimental study that challenges the conventional wisdom that police patrol is an effective component of a crime control program is reported by Kelling and associates. A thirty-two square mile area with a population of 150,000 was divided on a matching basis into areas in which preventive patrol was eliminated, held at its usual level, and intensified for a period of one year. The project is noteworthy in showing that substantial experimentation with an important aspect of police practice is feasible. The research is also significant for the measurement of results not only on crime and arrests but also on community attitudes, traffic accidents, police response time, and patterns of use of time by police.

Two papers deal with the effects of the Head Start program, a pre-school education program for children from low-income families. The first by Cicarelli summarizes the results of a study concerned with the psychological and intellectual impact of the program. A sample of first-, second-, and third-grade students who had participated were compared to a matched sample of nonparticipants. Evans then comments on the debate that followed release of the study. A participant in the design of the study, he defends the areas in which its methodology was criticized. Evans argues that to reject the findings of the study by pointing to methodological defects is unproductive. Rather, efforts should be made to implement the program more effectively.

The merits of two evaluations of the OEO Legal Services Program are debated in articles by Champagne and Berk. Champagne describes in some detail the two studies conducted by private consulting firms under contract with federal agencies. The evaluations of individual legal services projects were based on interviews with project staff, board members, and other pertinent community representatives. Effectiveness ratings of individual projects were made by interdisciplinary teams based on the evaluation data. Ratings of the evaluation teams were compared to effectiveness ratings made by spokesmen for significant community groups. Berk takes serious issue with the evaluations. He acknowledges that the evaluations established that the programs were implemented in a manner roughly consistent with what was intended. Berk points out, however, that the evaluations deal only with opinion; actual practices were not examined. Berk develops a framework for an adequate evaluation and systematically analyzes the two studies. The exchange concludes with a reply by Champagne who defends the evaluations on several counts.

Actual accomplishments of new towns in meeting human needs were studied by Burby, Weiss, and Zehner. New communities were compared with matching conventional communities on three dimensions: (1) objective characteristics of facilities and services, (2) performance of service system, and (3) resident satisfaction with the quality of facilities and services. An impressive array of specific measures is used for each dimension.

An experimental study of home versus hospital treatment of heart attack victims is reported by Mather et al. The project is significant as a large, general community intervention dealing with a life threatening issue. (Twelve percent of those randomly assigned to home or hospital care died within twenty-eight days of inclusion in the project.) The researchers indicate how they conducted a controlled study after taking into account treatment desires of patients, their relatives, and family doctors.

Use of the interrupted time series design in the evaluation of the effect of legal reform is illustrated by Ross, Campbell, and Glass. Their study concerns the use by police in England of a device to measure blood alcohol as a way of discouraging driving under the influence of alcohol. Automobile casualty rates were used to measure effects of the new law enforcement procedures. Control conditions were approximated by separating casualty rates for commuting hours during which bars and pubs were closed from those for weekend nights. The case shows how effective evaluation sometimes can be done in the absence of experimental controls.

16. The Evaluation of Broad-Aim Programs: A Cautionary Case and a Moral

Robert S. Weiss and Martin Rein

There is an approach to the evaluation of programs of social action which seems so sensible that it has been accepted without question in many quarters. The underlying assumption of the approach is that action-programs are designed to achieve specific ends, and that their success can be measured by the extent to which these ends were reached. The approach leads often to a study-design in experimental form, in which there is identification of the aspects of the situation or target population which are to be changed, the measurement of their state before introduction of the program, and the measurement of their state again after completion of the program. To support the argument that changes in criteria were the result of the introduction of the program, there may be measurement of criteria at two points in time in a control or comparison situation which does not receive the program.

On the basis of much observation, we believe that this very plausible approach is misleading when the action-programs have broad aims and unstandardized forms. We believe it may well be effective when a number of individuals are subjected to the same interventive stimulus and when the expected outcome is clear-cut and truly something anticipated. An example would be inoculation with a flu vaccine: the same thing can be done to a large number of subjects, and the expected outcome—freedom from influenza—can be clearly stated in advance. But there are many social-action programs, including most truly ambitious social-action programs, which do not have these characteristics. They are concerned first with the impact of the program on a situation, and only secondarily with the impact of the program on individuals. They are liable to take very different forms in different situations. And it is not at all clear at the outset what would be the consequences of a successful program. An example might be the Model Cities planning program. Here the program was concerned primarily with changing the relationship of members of a local community to the process of urban planning. The effect that this might have on individual members of model neighborhoods was not a primary concern of the program. The form taken by the planning program was dependent on the nature of the local situation, the character of the federal official assigned to supervise the

This article is a revision of a paper given at the American Academy of Arts and Sciences Conference on Evaluation of Social Action Programs, May 2–3, 1969, organized by the Academy's Committee on Poverty under a grant from the Ford Foundation.

Reprinted with permission from the authors and *The Annals of the American Academy of Political and Social Science*, Vol. 385, September 1969, pp. 133–142.

program, the characters of citizens who became involved in the program, and many other factors. The form of programs was neither determined by the federal agency which sponsored them nor identical from place to place. Finally, the consequences of a successful planning program might include community backing for the plan, or might include acceptance of the plan by a federal reviewing body, or might include a sense of increased political participation in the model neighborhood, but there was no reason to begin with the assumption—nor, for that matter, to say at any later time—that any one of these criteria, or any other criterion, singly or in combination, might serve as a measure of the succcess of the program. Or, to put it another way, there might be many different kinds of success, and putting one of them before another would be entirely arbitrary. Our belief is that when action-programs are more like Model Cities planning and less like inoculation with a flu vaccine, an experimental model for evaluating effectiveness is apt to be a mistake.

EVALUATING THE BROAD-AIM PROGRAM

The following is a case study of one instance of the use of an experimental approach to evaluate a broad-aim program. Our opinion is that the case described is more nearly typical of such ventures than not. We think that the failures and frustrations were consequences of the absence of fit between the research design and the actual research problem. The men involved were well-trained, industrious, and committed to the project. Their error

was in overconscientiousness, if it was anywhere; they adopted a methodology because it was sound, not recognizing that it was inappropriate.

Let us call the action-program the Neighborhood Benefit Program. Its aim was to change existing community institutions—the social agencies, the schools, the employment services—which because of tradition, and perhaps lack of imagination, were wedded to the status quo. The changed institutions, it was hoped, would be of greater service to a wide range of groups within the community, but especially to underprivileged youth. The federal agency which funded the program required that there be some documentation of the extent to which the study had been successful: they insisted, as a condition of funding, that the program evaluate itself.

The federal agency, perhaps in reaction against the impressionistic, cheerfully positive progress reports which were traditionally produced by action-programs, recommended that the evaluation study be as methodologically rigorous as possible. In addition, the agency made it clear that the program should be construed as a demonstration of the usefulness of programs of its type, rather than as having importance for its own sake. Therefore, the research group should give its attention primarily to generalizable assessments of the worth of the type of program, rather than to more particular assessments of just what had gone right and what had gone wrong in this one instance.

The sociologists who were obtained to staff the research group were entirely sympathetic to the aims of rigor and generality. They were trained in tough-minded scientific method, and their aim was to contribute to the development of general knowledge. Indeed, in the methodological climate of that time, it would have been difficult, though not entirely impossible, for the administrators of the program to have found competent research people whose priorities were toward a more qualitative, more case-oriented research style. But even if it had been possible to locate research personnel of this bent, the federal directive was clearly more sympathetic to the more rigorous approach.

One of the first concerns of the research group was the development of criteria of successful programs, and one of their first difficulties was that institutional change seemed difficult to assess, and that individual change could take what at first appeared to be an endless variety of forms. The study of institutional change was rejected as unfeasible because there were so many institutions at issue—the schools, the playgrounds, the job-finding agencies, and still others—that the interviewing and observation required for studying them would have exhausted all the staff time available—and more. In addition, there was every reason to believe that the staff of at least some of the institutions whose change was a Neighborhood Benefit Program aim would be resistant to a study sponsored by a parallel, and possibly rival, community agency. Finally, the research staff had been trained in the more rigorous methodologies of survey research and experimental measurement, rather than in the softer methods of field research. It was decided that the subject of study should be youth living in the area of Neighborhood Benefit

Association concern, and that any change in their attitudes or behavior which suggested better adaptation to their society would be taken as an indication of the program's success.

Altogether, some three hundred different individual-measurements were planned, ranging from measurements of attitudes toward the society to actual school-attendance records. The directors of the study were determined that the measurements should have maximum validity, reliability, and discriminating power, and so they spent a great deal of time in developing scales, or in locating scales in the existent literature, which would produce, with some trustworthiness, the quality of measurement that they wanted.

The next problem which presented itself was the necessity of deciding which individuals living within the target area had, in fact, been exposed to the Neighborhood Benefit Program. Was it anyone who had participated in any one of the activities sponsored by the Neighborhood Benefit Program? But it was not always easy to determine who had participated. What about the students who had been exposed to a school-enrichment program, in the sense that they had dutifully sat in a school auditorium while a number of speakers talked about the job-market? What about the youth who came only once to a playground and left without doing more than lean against a swing? And what about the youth who had never taken part in these programs, but whose father had found a job by means of the Neighborhood Benefit Program? Clearly, deciding who had participated would be difficult. Nevertheless, the research group developed forms to be filled out by manpower specialists and supervisors of playgrounds, and hoped that somehow the resulting data would be useful. As it turned out, this was not the case. Matching names on the forms with names on interview blanks was too great a job, and given the small proportion of participants, among all residents of the district, in any particular program—and the very different impacts of different programs—the energy required hardly seemed justifiable.

A related problem was that of evaluating the relative effectiveness of each of the large number of efforts planned by the Neighborhood Benefit Program. If school-enrichment and playground-enrichment affected the same children, how could one decide which results should be associated with which change-attempt? One proposal made by the research group was that different change attempts should be introduced into different districts of the metropolitan area: for example, a change in the schools in one district and a change in playgrounds in another. The administrators of the Neighborhood Benefit Program, concerned with the endless problems of attempting to achieve change in functioning institutions, found the idea charming, but unrealistic. The research group was required to define its task as that of evaluating the net impact on youths living in the target area—whether there was evidence that they had actively participated in the program or not—of the Neighborhood Benefit Program, taken as a whole.

The design which finally emerged, after acceptance of the net-impact formulation by the research group, was that of a questionnaire study of the effects on young people of the presence of the program in their area. The study anticipated the collection of data from a sample of about 1,500 young people in the target area, and from another sample of about 500 young people in a similar area in a neighboring city. This represented about a 25 percent sample of eligible youths in the two cities.

Fully 90 percent of the youths in the sample were located and interviewed, a remarkable response rate when one considers that a good proportion of the young people were not in school and not regularly at home. A great deal of information was collected from and about respondents: each respondent was given, not only an extensive questionnaire, but also a personal interview, and, in addition, information about him was obtained from his school.

Development of the data-collection instruments and actual collection of base-line (preprogram) data absorbed the first year of the project. Because the collection of data after completion of the action-program would utilize already developed instruments, and because the action-program had three years to run, the research group had a good deal of time for other work before it would have to mobilize itself to see what changes the Neighborhood Benefit Program had brought into being. During this interim period, the research group gave great attention to an analysis of data which was intended to establish where the youths were before the program was introduced. These data were treated by the research group simply as very interesting survey data. They examined the distribution of behaviors, beliefs, attitudes, and experiences by age, sex, race, and status in school. Some of their findings were interesting, but, of course, they had no greater relationship to the functioning of the Neighborhood Benefit Program than any set of findings from any study of a low-income area would have had.

The research group launched a few small studies in addition to the major effort just described. They hired a small team of participant-observers to go out and talk with neighborhood residents. The observers produced a set of rather journalistic materials which managed to suggest something of the style of life in the neighborhood, but nothing more. The research group also developed a study focused on the characteristics of problem youth in the district, in which they made a concerted attempt to identify and interview those young people whom their neighbors believed to be the most troublesome in the area. The research group then developed comparison data by studying the young people who were believed to be the most promising in the area. But the problem youths turned out to be just as difficult when filling out questionnaires as in other contacts with authorities, and there was much doubt regarding the validity of their responses. In addition, the issues to which the study found itself addressed turned out to be unrelated to any possible effect of the Neighborhood Benefit Program. And so, with distrust growing regarding the validity of the data, and increasing recognition that it would not contribute to evaluation in any event, the study was given less and less attention, and, finally, without any decision being made, was shelved.

By the end of the second year of the evaluation project, it had become clear to the administrators of the Neighborhood Benefit Program that they could expect little help from the research group for their own tasks. From the perspective of the administrators, the evaluation-research group seemed to be studying interesting questions—actually they could not be entirely certain exactly what the research group really was studying—but their work seemed to be in the realm of basic research, and to have rather little to offer to anyone who had to decide what to do in a given situation. Even this absence of applied usefulness would not have been disturbing to the administrative group, except that there seemed to be little information regarding evaluation either. The administrators, it turned out, found it difficult to keep in mind that the report on the evaluation could be prepared only after the end of their efforts. They wanted to know what was wrong and what was right in what they were doing while there was still time to change. Gradually, the administrative group became more and more skeptical of the work that the research group was doing.

In addition to the fact that no usable information emanated from the research group, the administrators of the programs had other reasons for uneasiness about this research. The research group seemed more defensive, more inclined toward mystification, less convincing, as they repeatedly argued that the ongoing analysis of base-line data was only a secondary interest, undertaken as a kind of make-work project, until the time came for collection of the post-program data. Increasingly, the administrators of the programs felt that members of the research group were counting on analysis of the base-line data to produce a contribution to their field, and that their continued references to the comparison with postprogram data had the aim of fending off a close scrutiny of their operation. Administrators began wondering whether there would be funds—and, for that matter, staff—for the very difficult pre-postcomparison which was planned.

Still another source of concern developed, though not in any very detailed way. What difference would be made by any findings which might come out of the study? Could any findings really support any conclusions? Suppose that the young people in the Neighborhood Benefit Program area showed changes which were somehow different from those displayed by young people in the neighboring city. It was hard to believe that the difference would be dramatic, but no matter. The cities were already quite different, even before the introduction of the Neighborhood Benefit Program into one of them. (One evidence of their differences was that one, but not the other, had gotten funds from the government for a Neighborhood Benefit Program.) This fact demonstrated that if the attitudes or behavior of youths developed differently in the two cities, it would not necessarily mean that the Neighborhood Benefit Program was the causal agent. An entirely convincing conclusion would not result even from a comparison of those who had participated in the Neighborhood Benefit Program with those who had not participated, assuming that participation could be measured.

Those who chose to participate must have been quite different to begin with from those who chose not to participate. And if there were no differences between youths in the two cities, did this mean that the Neighborhood Benefit Program had no value? In opposition to this possible conclusion could be put the use made of so many of the Neighborhood Benefit Program services. Change or no change, it was clear that what the program made available was being used.

Because of their developing qualms, the administrators of the programs, together with their sponsoring agency, called in a consultant to evaluate the evaluation scheme. The consultant pointed out the Program's commitment to support the research group through the period originally planned for completion of their work. He also pointed out the likely cost of tracking down the original respondents after three years had elapsed, and made estimates of both the length of time and amount of money likely to be necessary for analysis and written presentation of the panel data after the very difficult locating problem had been solved. He made explicit the problems which were involved in generalizing on the basis of data regarding what was, after all, a single instance of a social action, when no information was available which might provide understanding of the form that the instance had taken.

After discussion of the consultant's report, the research group and the administrators of the programs jointly agreed to try to get some sense of what might be gained by comparison of preprogram and postprogram data, by conducting a small-scale study, if possible, before the scheduled time for collection of the postprogram data. It was hoped that a small-scale study might furnish enough information to make it possible to estimate both the difficulties of the larger study and the usefulness of the data which would be gathered.

What happened next seems to be typical of the conclusion of projects for the evaluation of broad-aim action-programs. One of the members of the research group had, some time earlier, accepted another position, and now left the project. The idea of a pilot study proved unworkable without him; it may well have been unworkable even with him. The administrators of the program became increasingly unsympathetic to the research, and increasingly unwilling to sponsor the research group with their funding agency. The director of the research group left the project, with rather bad feelings all around. And so ended the evaluation-study.

Accounts similar to the above can be obtained from many evaluation projects. Here the evaluation team was responsible to individuals who were also administering the action-program, and this produced a number of tensions. Yet, even when evaluation has been conducted by an external agency, the experimental or near-experimental study of an unstandardized, broad-aim, virtually unreplicated action-program has produced the same or very similar problems.

The difficulties that the research group encountered were, for the most part, inherent in a situation where the administrative group needed research information which the research group were committed not to collect; where the primary aim of the research depended on detecting that component of change exerted by a government-sponsored program upon a group of youngsters who were moving through one of the most changeful periods of their lives; and where the research systematically neglected the form being taken by the program which it was studying and the ways in which the institutional system of the area responded and was itself affected by the program. Any such enterprise might be expected to have heavy going. We shall first list the technical difficulties, and next the administrative difficulties, which might be expected in a research enterprise of this sort.

TECHNICAL PROBLEMS

(1) *The problem of developing criteria.* Evaluation asks the extent to which predetermined goals are reached. But how will such goals as increased opportunity, a more responsive institutional system, and a richer cultural atmosphere show themselves? What operations can be chosen, in advance, to decide whether these goals have or have not been realized? It turns out that there are so many different ways in which changes related to such broad aims may take place that a very great number of indicators must be included in the study, and even then there is no assurance that something has not been omitted. The alternative, of course, is simply to study the program in operation and to attempt to infer from qualitative evidence what its accomplishments might have been. But this is not possible in the experimental mode.

(2) *The situation is essentially uncontrolled.* Setting up comparison situations is an attempt to insure that

changes in the experimental condition will not be mistakenly credited to the experimental intervention when, in fact, some other, alien, factor is responsible. The idea is that every other factor except the experimental intervention will also be present in the comparison situation and that, therefore, if there are differences in the experimental situation between the preprogram and the postprogram measurements, and none in the comparison situation, the responsibility can confidently be assigned to the experimental intervention. But this application of scientific methodology—actually, misapplication—does not recognize the extent to which communities are open to all sorts of idiosyncratic experiences, from the personalities of mayors through the location decisions of industries. What the comparison "sample" really accomplishes, from a statistical point of view, is that a single case in which there is no intervention is being compared with a single case in which there is an intervention. The statistical merit of this procedure is very close to zero.

(3) *The treatment is not standardized.* It is general experience that the form taken by a broad-aim program will differ in different communities, in response to different needs and tolerances. Each community experiences a different mixture of program emphases or, considering the program as a whole, a different attempt at social action. The result is that unless careful attention is paid to just what happened within the community, it is not possible to say what it is which is being evaluated. Experimental evaluation neglects this careful study of the intervention process itself, assuming in-

stead that what took place was what was supposed to have taken place.

(4) *The experimental design discourages unanticipated information.* The possible results of an experiment can easily be listed in advance: the intervention does or does not produce change in one or another characteristic. Negative results are not very helpful, because although they signal some flaw in theory or operationalization, they do not make evident the nature of the problem. The need in the study of broad-aim programs is for something more: a conscientious attempt to find the reasons for failure and the forms of unanticipated success, as well as to identify the anticipated changes which happened and the ones which did not. The broad-aim program is a major undertaking, and the issue is not the simple-minded one of "Does it work?" but the much more important one of "When such a program is introduced, what then happens?"

*   *   *

These are the primary technical problems associated with the experimental evaluation of broad-aim programs. Let us now consider some of the administrative problems that such a program is likely to encounter.

ADMINISTRATIVE DIFFICULTIES

(1) *There may be conflict over program-development.* In the experience which we report here, the research group did not attempt to direct the development of the action-program, except for the suggestion that different sections of the community get different components of the action-program. But in other cases, the evaluation group has considered it essential to

monitor the action-program to ensure that it does not take a form too different from that initially proposed. They require that the program hold still while it is being evaluated, instead of constantly modifying itself, metamorphosing from one thing to another. But any effective administrator who is committed to the success of a program will insist on modifying the program as he learns more about his staff, his situation, and the initial reaction engendered by his first attempts. In response to this, the research group may become embattled with the administration of the program, or may withdraw into an unwillingness to recognize the extent to which the program is being modified.

(2) *Operationalizations may become leading goals.* In the discussions with administrators, the research group may come to some understanding that particular operationalizations of program-aims represent what the administrators hope to achieve. If the aim of the program is cultural enrichment, then the administrators might agree with the research group that increased consumption of reading matter would be a fair form of evidence of program success. The problem is that the operationalization may thereupon take on an importance far out of keeping with the program's actual, broader, goals—that, in this example, an emphasis on reading as a way of achieving cultural enrichment, in preference to, say, museum attendance or painting or the development of musical groups, would become a feature of the program. The example may suggest that this is an easily avoidable difficulty, but in real situations the lure of the operationalization is more subtle, and

it is much more difficult to identify the way in which the process of evaluation has itself structured—and to that extent limited—the action-program.

(3) *The research staff may know less, rather than more, about the consequences of the program than the action group knows.* The experimental approach is apt to result in the research staff's being relatively ignorant regarding what is happening in the field in response to the action-program. To an objective observer, this is merely paradoxical; to a member of the program's administrative staff, it may be a source of anger or distress. It means that the program's staff cannot turn to the research group for the information that it requires for intelligent operation. In time, the research group will be defined as irrelevant, or even as a burden. But since the action-group will continue to need information regarding the state of the community, and the effectiveness of its operation, to date, it is likely to go farther than simply deciding that the research enterprise is of no help, and actually to sponsor a second research enterprise which is concerned with the issues important for its operation. This arrangement has rich potential for misunderstanding, rivalry, and conflict.[1]

CONCLUSION

The purpose of this paper is to call into question the easy assumption that experimental design is always the best way to decide whether action-programs are having desirable effects. It is for the most part an essay in destructive criticism. The more constructive parallel essay on the methods of research which would be appropriate for the study of the effects of broad-aim programs would be more difficult to write, because there are fewer models to use. Nevertheless, it is possible to see what would be the outlines of a more effective methodology.

First, a more effective methodology would be much more descriptive and inductive. It would be concerned with describing the unfolding form of the experimental intervention, the reactions of individuals and institutions subjected to its impact, and the consequences, so far as they can be learned by interview and observation, for these individuals and institutions. It would lean toward the use of field methodology, emphasizing interview and observation, though it would not be restricted to this. But it would be much more concerned with learning than with measuring.

Second, it is very likely that the conceptual framework of the approach would involve the idea of system, and of the intervention as an attempt to change the system. The systems perspective alerts the investigator to the need to identify the forces which are mobilized by the introduction of the program, the events in which aspects of the program are met and reacted to by individuals and institutions already on the scene, and the ways in which actors move in and out of the network of interrelationships of which the program is a constituent. It alerts the investigator to the possibility that important forces which have few interrelationships with the existent system—in this sense, alien forces—may appear on the scene. It urges the investigator to think of the action-program as just one more input into the system, and prepares him to deal with such issues as the way in which the program makes a place for itself, the new stresses it introduces, and the way the system accommodates itself to the program, as well as to address himself to the issue of what individual and institutional benefits the program brought into being.

There is much work to be done in the development of a nonexperimental methodology for evaluation research. Our argument is that this work is justified; that there is need for a more qualitative, process-oriented approach. The way to develop the methodology, we believe, is to begin working in it: to undertake evaluation research, when the action-program requires it, which is concerned with what form the action-program actually took, and with the details of its interaction with its surroundings, from which may be formed an inductive assessment of its consequences. There are, indeed, problems of many sorts associated with nonexperimental approaches, including the mechanics of data-production, the methods of organizing and analyzing data, and the logic of generalization. But the need for the approach is the most important consideration. To fail to recognize this is to insist on an inappropriate methodology just because it is better understood.

NOTE

1. We do not speak here of the many reasons that administrators of action-programs or members of their staffs might have for openly or covertly opposing evaluation. It is a rare action-program in which evaluators are wholeheartedly welcomed. This constitutes an important problem for the researchers, but one outside the scope of this paper.

17. The Evolution of an Evaluation: Methodological Problems in Programs for School Age Mothers

Lorraine V. Klerman, James F. Jekel, John B. Currie,
Ira W. Gabrielson, and Philip M. Sarrel

INTRODUCTION

In this time of technological progress and relative prosperity, the American public has come to expect much from the fields of health, education, and social assistance; but these expectations are continually disappointed by persistent ill health, low levels of education, and poverty among sizeable portions of the population. The traditional methods of delivering services in these fields are increasingly being questioned, and evidence of success is being sought to justify continued funding. Although evaluation has always been considered an integral part of administration, a lack of funds and skilled personnel usually has prevented studies of effectiveness and efficiency from being performed in a thorough and scientific manner. In 1967 Elinson[1] could state that for the preceding 10 year period only 10 reports met his criteria for consideration as evaluative studies in the areas of health and social welfare. More recently the problems of evaluative research have been reviewed by Schulberg, et al.[2] Suchman,[3] Hyman and Wright,[4] Kelman and Elinson,[5] and Freeman and Sherwood.[6]

These authors all agree that the task of determining the effectiveness of entire programs is extremely difficult. In the past it was often possible to study limited program components and determine success or failure; for example, a chest X-ray screening program could be judged by the proportion of a target population reached and by new disease found, although even the usefulness of this kind of evaluation has come under question.[7, 8] Problems of ill health today cannot be separated from a nexus of related problems, such as poverty, racial discrimination, poor schools, and social disintegration. Consequently, multi-faceted programs are created in hope of finding solutions. As programs become more complex, so do the problems of evaluative research, as Suchman[3] pointed out:

> It is not so much the principles of research that make evaluation studies difficult, but rather the practical problems of adhering to these principles in the face of administrative considerations.

A case in point is the "Study of Programs for Teenage Mothers" being undertaken by Yale's Department of Epidemiology and Public Health jointly with the Department of Obstetrics and Gynecology in an attempt to evaluate the effectiveness of programs designed to meet the medical, social, and educational needs of pregnant teenage girls in the cities of New Haven and Hartford, Connecticut. This paper describes the major methodological and administrative problems faced in this effort. It has two

Reprinted with permission from *American Journal of Public Health,* Vol. 63, No. 12, December 1973, pp. 1040–1047.

objectives: 1) to review the compromises with ideal design which have been unavoidable in the process of evolving a workable research design for a complex ongoing service program; and 2) to provide the background information necessary for an understanding of subsequent reports on study findings.

THE DEVELOPMENT OF AN EVALUATIVE RESEARCH EFFORT

Although those responsible for a program usually also "evaluate" it, i.e., make some judgment about its worth, evaluative research utilizing scientific methods and techniques can seldom be done by those actually serving the population at risk due to lack of time, often of skills, and of objectivity. Evaluators from outside the program, on the other hand, may want for clinical insights. A serious evaluation attempt, therefore, frequently requires the interaction of persons associated with research development and others from a service team. The two groups must establish a modus operandi early in the process if the evaluative effort is to succeed.

In the case under study, cooperative arrangements were developed readily when research representatives were invited to consult with service personnel early in the program's history. In 1965 a program had been organized for teenage pregnant girls who obtained antepartum care at the Yale-New Haven Hospital. Later named the Young Mothers Program (YMP), it combined personalized care by a single physician, intensive individual and group social services, and close coordination with community agencies. After a year of

operation, the obstetrician in charge of the program decided to explore the research possibilities of the program with faculty members from the Department of Epidemiology and Public Health. After considerable discussion, both groups decided upon the goal of program evaluation, and a pilot study was undertaken of the medical outcomes of patients served by the YMP from its inception through the spring of 1967. The early results of this study[9] were exciting enough to encourage the research and clinical teams to apply jointly for support for a more intensive evaluative study. (A detailed report on the interaction between research and service personnel which resulted in the development of the research project already has been published.)[10]

THE PROGRAM UNDER STUDY

At the time the research design was developed almost all unwed school age pregnant girls who lived in the New Haven area and applied for clinic care at the Yale-New Haven Hospital were assigned to the special clinic of the Young Mothers Program and received all their care from one obstetrical resident. During the antepartum period he saw each patient regularly for medical care and personal counseling. He was on 24-hour call for deliveries, attended each patient daily during her hospitalization, and was responsible for her care periodically through the early postpartum months. If desired by the patient and permitted by the parents, contraceptive procedures were initiated. (This was in keeping with policies current in 1967.)

Social services were provided by two social workers assigned to the program by the hospital. They met each patient at registration, described the program, and urged attendance at the weekly group sessions. Sometimes a home visit was made and family contact established. Each girl then received individual case work as needed and desired. Social work contact was maintained after delivery by bedside visits and after discharge by periodic group meetings for several months.

The obstetrician and the clinic nurse participated in the group sessions led by the social workers. Occasionally they were joined by a pediatrician who answered questions about child care. Discussion focused on the girl's social problems, including her relationship with her family and the putative father, and educational or vocational plans. The purpose of these group sessions was the modification of the girl's attitudes, values, and behavior through group discussion techniques and information.

Education and other services were provided through the Polly T. McCabe Center, which was supported by the New Haven Board of Education, the New Haven antipoverty agency, and other community organizations.[11] All of the YMP clinic patients were urged to attend the special educational program at the Center, and most of them did. The school staff and the hospital social workers coordinated their efforts through individual contacts and joint conferences.

By the time intake into the research sample began, this program had changed extensively due to externally induced staff changes. The obstetrical resident who had begun the program was meeting his military obligations in another state and consequently the responsibility for obstetrical care was divided between a staff obstetrician, who saw the patient at the initial visit and all subsequent visits up to the 28th week of pregnancy, and a 3rd-year obstetrical resident who followed her through the rest of her antepartum period. These two physicians shared the deliveries and postpartum follow-up. Program continuity was further disrupted by the departure of the two original social workers and pregnancy leave for the clinic nurse. The second and third years of the project brought additional staff changes which will be described later as examples of the research problems created when the research unit does not have control over the program being evaluated.

THE RESEARCH DESIGN

The first application to the Children's Bureau in 1967 stated the objectives of the proposed study as follows: to determine the impact of the YMP, a hospital-based, comprehensive medical, social, and educational program for the teenage unwed mother, on the course of her pregnancy and on her subsequent physical and psychological health and social development and on the physical and psychological health and social development of her child. These objectives were to be met through a prospective, controlled study. (See Campbell, "Reforms as Experiments"[12] for alternative methods of evaluation.) Two hypotheses provided further specification:

Teenage unwed mothers who actively participate in the YMP will fare significantly better than similar girls enrolled in other prenatal care programs on a series of indicators including health during pregnancy, ease of labor and delivery, health in postpartum period, educational achievement, and familial and social relationships.

The infants of the mothers actively participating in the YMP will be significantly healthier at birth and in the subsequent years and will score significantly higher on indicators of development than will infants of similar mothers enrolled in other prenatal care programs.

Intake into the sample began with those girls who registered for antepartum care in the special YMP clinic after September 1, 1967 and was to continue for two years. All girls who at registration were 17 or under, unmarried, residents of New Haven, and eligible for clinic care, and whose pregnancy terminated at the Yale-New Haven Hospital after 20 weeks gestation were included in the research sample.

Data were collected starting with registration and continuing through the antepartum period, labor and delivery, and two years postpartum. Collection methods included abstracting of hospital and school records, completion of rating forms by obstetricians, nurse-midwives, and social workers, and home interviews by members of the research staff not identified with the clinic service team. In order to determine the impact of the program, it was planned to contrast the "experimental" group, namely the participants in the YMP, with other groups of pregnant teenagers.

The basic prospective, longitudinal, multi-faceted, evaluative character of the research design has been maintained over the succeeding four years, with some minor modifications resulting from changes in the service program itself and from the research staff's evolving understanding of the problems of evaluation.

DESIGN DIFFICULTIES

Many practical problems were encountered in attempting to meet the criteria for a valid evaluative research design: 1) sampling equivalent experimental and control groups; 2) isolation and control of the stimulus; and 3) definition and measurement of the criteria of effect.[3]

FINDING AN ADEQUATE CONTROL GROUP

Probably the most critical problem the research project faced was the lack of a true control group. To provide the most accurate evaluation of the effectiveness of the program for teenage mothers would have required the random allocation of the eligible members of the population into an experimental group, which would receive the full package of augmented services both at the special clinic and in the special educational program, and a control group which would receive traditional obstetrical services at the hospital clinic and either homebound or no instruction. Even if the clinical staff had considered it ethical to split the sample, the Board of Education would not have excluded students from the special educational program for research purposes. In addition, patients or families of patients placed in the control group might have protested the inequity.

Several alternatives to the randomized split sample were considered. One possibility was to compare participants in the YMP with contemporaneous nonparticipants at the same hospital. This was discarded almost immediately for two reasons: 1) the probability that self-selection would introduce bias, i.e., the more motivated patients would participate in the YMP and the less motivated be left for the control; and 2) the small number of nonparticipants. A second possibility was to reach into the past, before the development of the YMP, for a control sample which had not received the special services described earlier. This approach, however, might introduce extraneous factors such as differences in the population served, and changes in medical practices, educational achievement levels, or community attitudes over time. A third approach was to compare simultaneously the medical, educational, and other achievements of the YMP participants with those of similar patients elsewhere who were not receiving special services. The third alternative was chosen initially. The entire study was to remain prospective in character and a "contrast" group was to be sought whose intake would cover the same period of time as the experimental group.

The contrast group was to meet several criteria: 1) demographic and socioeconomic characteristics similar to the YMP participants; 2) approximately the same size as the YMP; 3) easily accessible from New Haven; 4) not participating in any augmented medical, social, or educational services; but, 5) receiving a level of medical care equivalent to that received in New Haven prior to the inception of the YMP. The use of teenage obstetrical patients at another hospital in New Haven was considered, but rejected because of the small numbers available, differing demographic characteristics, evidence that the hospital might soon establish a program similar to the YMP, the availability of the special school services to patients at both hospitals, and indications that some of the teenagers who might have sought antepartum care there in the past were now coming to the Yale-New Haven Hospital because they had heard of the YMP services. Clinics which served teenage obstetrical patients in neighboring cities were considered, but they were not approached because of the possibility of programs being developed while the study was under way and other theoretical and practical considerations.

Finally the search for a contrast group receiving no special services was abandoned. Instead, a population participating in a special program with a different orientation, the Inter-Agency Services program in Hartford (IAS), was chosen as the control group. While New Haven's YMP was a hospital-based program with medical and social work components and a strong relationship to a special school, Hartford's IAS was social agency-based and included social services and education. Obstetrical care for IAS clients was arranged by referral to private physicians or to the obstetrical clinics of three Hartford hospitals.

This decision created a research design which measured not the differences between the presence of a program and its absence, but between two types of programs whose objectives were basically the same, but whose approaches were different. Although this was not the ideal design, the research staff members believed that they would be able to observe and measure differences in outcomes between the two programs, and that the hospital-based model, YMP, because of its attempt to integrate the medical and educational components, would be more likely to reach its objectives than the social agency-based one, IAS.

By the end of the second research year, doubts were expressed about IAS as a contrast group. A more positive opinion of the Hartford program had developed with increased contact. Also, the early data from IAS aroused suspicions that because intake was through a social agency it was reaching a selected group of pregnant girls in contrast to the mixed group enrolled in the YMP, where intake was through the hospital's obstetrical clinic. With this information, the alternative possibilities for a control group were reconsidered.

Despite the problems involved in a retrospective study, the decision was made to supplement the basic YMP-IAS contrast with a study of a group of girls who had received care at the obstetrical clinic of the Yale-New Haven Hospital prior to the inception of the YMP. This would provide a comparison of the medical, educational, and social outcomes in the YMP sample with the outcomes in another sample presumably demographically and socioeconomically similar. The

control sample would have received approximately the same quality of medical care, but been offered no special services.

The control sample was chosen from patients who attended the Yale-New Haven Hospital's clinics in the 18 months prior to the active involvement of the YMP's original obstetrical resident in the care of teenage obstetrical patients (September 1963 through March 1965). Only those patients who met the same criteria as the YMP and IAS samples were chosen, i.e., 17 or under, unmarried, resident of New Haven at clinic registration, and pregnancy terminated at the Yale-New Haven Hospital after 20 weeks gestation. Table 1 compares the three samples along selected dimensions and indicates that their characteristics are similar but not identical.

All of the problems anticipated in studying this control sample materialized, plus a few unexpected ones. Respondents were difficult to locate—the high rate of mobility in a lower-income group was aggravated further by urban renewal. School records were more difficult to find for the 1963–65 control than for the 1967–69 YMP group. Non-comparability in contraceptive status emerged because giving contraceptive advice or prescriptions was illegal in Connecticut until June 1965, a point after all the control group had delivered and before any of the experimental group had done so. An unanticipated difficulty arose because of a marked lowering of age at first pregnancy in New Haven (Table 2). Consequently the control group is older than the YMP sample, and age can make a difference in obstet-

TABLE 1. SELECTED CHARACTERISTICS OF THE YMP, IAS, AND
OBSTETRICAL CLINIC POPULATIONS

	YMP		IAS		Obstetrical clinic	
	N = 180		N = 160		N = 83	
	No.	%	No.	%	No.	%
Age at registration (years)						
11–12	1	0.6	—	—	1	1.2
13	8	4.4	—	—	1	1.2
14	26	14.4	13	8.1	2	2.4
15	34	18.9	43	26.9	14	16.9
16	62	34.4	59	36.9	31	37.3
17	49	27.2	45	28.1	34	41.0
Race						
Black	169	93.9	152	95.0	74	89.2
White, not Puerto Rican	6	3.3	5	3.1	5	6.0
White, Puerto Rican	5	2.8	3	1.9	3	3.6
Mulatto	—	—	—	—	1	1.2
Birthplace						
New Haven	66	36.7	—	—	29	34.9
Hartford	1	0.6	59	41.8	—	—
Other Connecticut	6	3.3	5	3.5	2	2.4
Other New England states	2	1.1	3	2.1	—	—
Middle Atlantic states	14	7.8	6	4.3	4	4.8
Southern states	86	47.8	57	40.4	45	54.2
Other continental United States	1	0.6	1	0.7	—	—
Puerto Rico	4	2.2	3	2.1	3	3.6
Non-United States	—	—	7	5.0	—	—
Unknown	—	—	(19)	—	—	—
Previous pregnancies						
0	168	93.3	146	91.3	74	89.2
1	10	5.6	14	8.7	6	7.2
2	2	1.1	—	—	3	3.6
Total number in household including client—antepartum period						
1–3	33	18.5	30	18.9		
4–5	40	22.5	54	34.0	Information not	
6–7	43	24.2	35	22.0	complete	
8 or more	62	34.8	40	25.2		
Unknown	(2)	—	(1)	—		
Type of household—antepartum period						
Patient only	2	1.1	2	1.3		
With mother only	94	52.5	75	46.9		
With both parents	57	31.8	58.	36.3	Information not	
With husband (married after registration)	2	1.1	—	—	complete	
With others (related & unrelated)	20	11.2	23	14.4		
Foster	4	2.2	2	1.2		
Unknown	(1)	—	—	—		

rical complications and reaction to motherhood.[13] Also unanticipated was an increased incidence of venereal disease in the YMP group as compared to the control. This was partly due to more rigorous case-finding. Since 1967 all obstetrical patients have been tested for gonorrhea using an efficient culture medium (Thayer-Martin) while in the past only those with obvious signs were cultured. In addition, there has been a marked increase in the incidence of VD in the adolescent population.[14]

The research team is attempting to find ways of dealing with the problems raised by the absence of an ideal control group. Fortunately, the older control group would be expected to have fewer obstetrical and social problems. Any bias would not favor the YMP. If the YMP group has better outcomes than the control despite its lower age distribution, the program's effectiveness will be more striking. The contraceptive and venereal disease differences seem to pose unsolvable problems. Hopefully, the missing records and missing people may be discovered by diligent follow-up.

MAINTAINING THE STIMULUS

Change in the major program being evaluated (YMP) posed another serious methodological problem. The research staff had to face both significant changes in the service personnel and more gradual, subtle drift in the pattern of services over time. Examples of the first are the changes already noted, from a single resident providing care to a staff-resident pattern which occurred just as the research project started; and large-scale personnel changes in the summer of 1969 which necessitated the decision to close intake into the research sample in June 1969, two months earlier than anticipated to avoid the injection of an uncontrolled variable.

As research intake entered its second year it seemed as though key elements of the program, individualized attention and continuity of care, might be lost completely by the assignment of the medical component of the YMP to obstetrical residents on rotation. This personnel shift, dictated by manpower problems, was reconsidered when the research staff suggested that such a change might be sufficient reason to terminate the study. Continuity of care was maintained, on at least the level of the previous year by introducing a new staff physician and by greater use of nurse-midwives in obstetrical care; but this in turn added new variables which are being considered in the analyses.

Occasionally the research staff became aware of program modification by chance only after it had been in existence for several months. Since the clinical staff was always very pleasant and cooperative, and generally kept the research team informed of changes, it seems probable that the communication of change to the research team was dependent on the perception by the clinicians that a given program change had implications for the study design.

An example of such a change was the development of a YMP waiting list. To encourage pregnant teenagers to come to clinic early in their pregnancy, when preventable conditions could be detected and treated, the original policy had been to give clinic appointments as soon as pregnancy was confirmed. The increasing number of patients and the resistance of the staff to large and long clinic sessions resulted in the development of a backlog. Opinions differed as to whether this reduced the quality of care. Some felt the waiting period would produce adverse results, but others felt it was preferable to provide good care to a few rather than poor care to many. Both dilemmas, clinical and research, were real. Since number of weeks of gestation at registration was to be both a dependent variable, to determine the effectiveness of the program in motivating potential participants to early registration, and an independent variable, to test its association with outcome, the waiting list added difficulties to the analyses and interpretation.

Because of its inability to control the program changes, the research team found it necessary instead to study their effect. For example, in the area of personnel, within the limits set by the small size of the total sample, attention is being focused on whether one method of provision of service, e.g., midwives, is more favorably perceived

by the patients than another, e.g., obstetrician; or whether the outcomes are different under one pattern than another. If there are no differences, then the outcomes for the total YMP sample will be compared with the IAS contrast group and the 1963–65 control group. If there are differences each subgroup will have to be compared with the controls separately.

Summarizing, the goal of program evaluation can best be served when the same individuals have control over both the clinical and research components of the evaluation, providing the research team is independent enough to remain objective. Although this research project did not have such control, it did have influence over program direction since the project grant supported three of the staff members during the period they provided services to study subjects. This clinical support, wisely recommended by the Children's Bureau staff, enabled a consistently high level of services to be maintained, and it reimbursed the clinicians for the time spent in data collection.

TABLE 2. AGE AT DELIVERY FOR UNWED MOTHERS UNDER 18 YEARS, NEW HAVEN, CONN., 1963–1969.

Year	N	12–15		16–17	
		No.	%	No.	%
1963	55	11	20.0	44	80.0
1964	66	10	15.2	56	84.8
1965	75	16	21.3	59	78.8
1966	91	20	22.0	71	78.0
1967	112	30	26.8	82	73.2
1968	133	42	31.6	91	68.4
1969	140	42	30.0	98	70.0

SOURCE: Vital Statistics of New Haven, Conn. 1963–1969

DEFINING THE CRITERIA

Another problem not yet resolved, is precisely what criteria should be used to evaluate the program. Technically the task of goal-setting should belong to the program planners rather than to the research staff. The clinical staff felt very deeply what it wanted to accomplish, but often was unable to express these feelings in operational terms. The researchers found that it was their task to translate the clinicians' discussions of goals into objective terms. Sometimes these interpretations were accepted, but often the research staff was told that its thinking was too limited, or even wrong. For example, the clinicians' ambivalent attitude, when a subsequent pregnancy in a YMP participant was mentioned, suggested that the prevention of subsequent pregnancies was a program goal. This interpretation was met with the statement from the clinicians, "These girls have as much right as any other women to become pregnant," despite the fact that some of the girls under discussion were as young as 13 or 14 years.

Eventually the research staff defined the scope of the research by establishing a series of short- and long-range criteria for determining program success. Little disagreement ensued from the short-range goals: a healthy pregnancy, an uncomplicated delivery, and a healthy infant. The long-range criteria, however, brought the researchers into more sensitive areas. The following were suggested: completion of high school or equivalent; employment; economic independence; marriage; and deferment of subsequent pregnancies until after marriage or until at least two years had passed since

the previous birth. The clinicians, and even some members of the research staff, felt that some of these criteria were culture-bound and represented an attempt to impose middle-class values on other populations. Many discussions have been held about whether a high school diploma really signifies educational achievement or merely symbolizes the ability to stay in school until graduation; or the importance of a job versus being a full-time mother; or the stability of teenage marriages. Undoubtedly there are alternative ways of looking at these issues, but these criteria appear to be important in today's world, and the use of them enables the research staff to communicate meaningfully with others interested in programs for pregnant girls.

Equally important was the elimination of those criteria which, although they might be acceptable as goals, were not realistic in terms of the service program. For example, the infant's health and development after the immediate neonatal period were deleted as outcome measures because the services offered were considered insufficient to produce results detectable by survey research techniques within the two-year postpartum period.

MEASUREMENT DIFFICULTIES

As the problems with the research design began to come under control, the research staff turned its attention to the difficulties inherent in the measurement of program results.

SPECIFICATION OF POPULATIONS AND VARIABLES

Agreement tentatively had been reached about the criteria of effect, but now more specific definitions of populations and variables were needed in order to proceed. For example, who was to be considered a program participant? Full participation would have included periodic clinic visits from the fourth month of pregnancy through several months postpartum, two or more interviews with the social worker in the hospital and at home, participation in group sessions, and attendance at the McCabe School. But many of those who registered for the YMP did not cooperate in one or more of these areas. The decision was made not to establish arbitrary criteria for "participation" but rather to try to study degrees of participation, the pre-existing characteristics of high and low participants, and the relationship of degree of participation to outcomes.

Initially an extensive listing of the variables to be used in testing the hypotheses was compiled, but new insights into the program brought new thoughts about these variables. Were Emergency Room visits during the antepartum period to be considered positively or negatively? They might indicate a lack of rapport with the YMP clinic staff, or an unusual amount of physical or psychological ill health among the patients, or sensitivity to early signs of difficulty.

Often measures, selected as "hard" and universally accepted proved to be "soft" and somewhat controversial. What amount of weight gain should be considered excessive in an adolescent? How should toxemia be defined? What complications of labor were preventable? How should the study deal with girls who had pre-existing medical problems which further complicated their pregnancies? These and similar problems plagued the staff as they attempted to convert study hypotheses into testable components.

LONGITUDINAL ANALYSIS

Early data analyses made it apparent that cross-sectional ways of dealing with data from a longitudinal study were inadequate. For example, the first report on subsequent pregnancies was quite misleading because it failed to take into account the period at risk. The introduction of epidemiological concepts was essential to the solution of this problem. The life table method was adapted first to the problem of comparing the rate of subsequent deliveries between the YMP participants and the controls. Although the results in the YMP group were not as favorable as had been hoped, the method did show that the YMP population was delaying subsequent pregnancies longer than the controls and this finding was statistically significant. (These results were reported in a subsequent article.) The life table method also will be utilized to compare school drop-outs among the several populations.

CONDENSING THE DATA

One problem confronting the project was the management of a large number of variables. Any single variable may be an inadequate measure of program effectiveness, but in aggregate such variables define outcomes. In the obstetrical component, for example, several conditions such as toxemia are considered measures of maternal and child health and may reflect the quality of care. Most of these events occur rarely, and therefore the ability of statistical tests to show difference is small unless the samples are large. Another problem with the interpretation of many variables is that one program may show superior outcomes on several indicators while another may rank higher on others. On balance which program is better?

One possible solution to the problems mentioned above may be the combining of several variables into one or more indices or scores which will facilitate comparison between programs and which will also increase the amount of data contained in the index, thereby hopefully increasing statistical power. Interestingly, although scoring systems have been developed in the maternal and child health field to detect which women are a higher risk during pregnancy[15] and to study the association between specific types of maternal conditions and the infant's health,[16] no composite score was found which would enable programs to be compared in terms of maternal health and/or infant health. The research staff developed such scores by assigning a set of weighting constants or factors based on judgment and prior experience.

ASSOCIATION AMONG VARIABLES

As already indicated, the research project involves a wide range of dependent variables including complications of pregnancy, labor and delivery problems, infant health, educational achievement, development of family life, etc. Influencing these variables are two types of independent variables: 1) those which precede participation in the program, such as demographic and socioeconomic characteristics; and 2) those which measure program partici-

pation, such as number of weeks of gestation at first antepartum visit, number of antepartum visits, or percentage of group sessions attended. Obviously there may be associations between these two types of independent variables as well as clustering among the variables in each group. The direct and indirect influence of demographic and socioeconomic variables on outcomes through qualitative and quantitative participation in the programs is of particular interest to the research personnel. The staff is seeking appropriate measures for allocating the successes or failures of the programs to pre-existing characteristics and to program participation. Since much of the data is nominal or ordinal in character, this problem is quite difficult.

GENERALIZATION OF FINDINGS

An additional question which has stimulated much discussion among the members of the research staff is the generalizability of the findings of this project. Several authors have reviewed this type of problem and offered a solution by distinguishing between "program testing," which is evaluation of a total service product, and "variable testing," which is evaluation of the effectiveness of specific components of a program. Suchman[3] comments:

> Program testing has almost no generalizability, being applicable solely to the specific program being evaluated. Generalizations (to other projects, populations, times) have the status of untested hypotheses. This is a major reason why so many evaluation studies appear repetitive—one can never be certain that a program which works in one situation will work in another. To the extent that evaluative research can focus

upon the general variables underlying a specific program and test the effects of these variables rather than the effectiveness of the program as a whole, it may hope to produce findings of greater general significance.

Separating out the different components and evaluating them individually appears to be at variance with the frequently expressed concept that what is important for pregnant school age girls is a total program. Nevertheless, the basic validity of this dilemma has forced the project increasingly to focus on evaluation of components of the total program. An example is the question of the success of the YMP and IAS in the educational sphere. No special services (aside from homebound instruction) were provided to the control group, a special school but with limited classes and hours was available to the Hartford group, and a special school which attempted to duplicate the material being taught in the student's regular classes was provided to the YMP participants. Comparison of outcomes in terms of high school graduation should give some information about the relative success of these three approaches to educational programming.

SUMMARY AND CONCLUSIONS

At the end of the fourth year of a 5½-year-project, the research staff has reviewed its progress. On the debit side, the lack of control over the program being studied has caused more problems than anticipated. A mechanism should have been developed which would have prevented major changes in the program while the study was proceeding. Also detrimental was the impossibility of obtaining a true control group. This difficulty was managed by using two control groups, in one of which the pregnant girls participated in a different type of service program (IAS/Hartford) and in the other the girls had no special program (obstetrical clinic—New Haven).

On the positive side the research project is providing data about programs for pregnant teenagers, a subject which has too often been discussed in terms of opinions based on wish fulfillment and impressions based on small samples followed for short periods of time. Unsubstantiated claims about the value of programs caring for teenage pregnant girls are being heard less often as clinicians are increasingly seeking factual material in which the variables and the samples are more clearly defined. The experience gained in the project may provide useful methods of analyses which will permit valid comparisons among samples in the maternal and child health field. By using a composite index of success of obstetrical programs[17] and the life table analyses of subsequent pregnancies,[18] programs will be able to contrast their results and reach conclusions about the effectiveness of different ways of serving teenage mothers.

The research team has already faced many problems and suspects that the most difficult ones still lie ahead. Yet its members feel the endeavor will be worthwhile, not only by showing that some programs for teenage mothers accomplish their objectives, but also by demonstrating the feasibility of evaluative studies of complex ongoing programs.

REFERENCES

1. Elinson, J. Effectiveness of Social Action Programs in Health and Welfare. Report of 56th Ross Conference on Pediatric Research. Columbus, Ohio: Ross Laboratories, 1967, pp. 77–81.
2. Schulberg, H. C., et al. (eds.). Program Evaluation in the Health Fields. New York: Behavioral Publications, Inc., 1969.
3. Suchman, E. A. Evaluative Research. New York: Russell Sage Foundation, 1967.
4. Hyman, H. H. and Wright, C. R. Evaluating Social Action Programs. Chapter 27 in The Uses of Sociology, Lazarsfeld, P. F., et al. (editors). New York: Basic Books, Inc., 1967.
5. Kelman, H. R. and Elinson, J. Strategy and Tactics of Evaluating a Large Scale Medical Care Program. Medical Care 7, 2: 79–85, 1969.
6. Freeman, H. E. and Sherwood, C. C. Social Research and Social Policy. Englewood Cliffs, N.J.: Prentice-Hall, Inc., 1970. [Reprinted in this volume, No. 13, pp. 205–220]
7. Yerushalmy, J. R., et al. The Role of Dual Reading in Mass Radiography. Am. Rev. Tuberculosis 61, 4: 443–464, 1950.
8. Greenberg, R. A. Mass Survey Detected Lung Cancer in Conn., 1949–1953. Conn. State Med. J. 20, 11: 857–863, 1956.
9. Sarrel, P. M. and Klerman, L. V. The Young Unwed Mother. Am. J. Obstet. & Gynec. 105, 4: 575–578 (Oct. 15), 1969.
10. Klerman, L. V., et al. The Interaction Between Research Consultants and a Clinical Team: A Case Study in Obstetrics. Health Education Monographs 29: 11–27, 1969.
11. Holmes, M. E., et al. A New Approach to Educational Services for the Pregnant Student. J. School Health 40, 4: 168–172, 1970.
12. Campbell, D. T. Reforms as Experiments. American Psychologist 24, 4: 409–429, 1969. [Reprinted in this volume, No. 12, pp. 172–204]
13. Oppel, W. C. and Royston, A. B. Teen-age Births; Some Social, Psychological, and Physical Sequelae. AJPH 61, 4: 751–756, 1971.
14. Hurney, G. J. Gonorrhea in Connecticut. Conn. Health Bulletin 84, 4: 83–90, 1970.
15. Nesbitt, R. E. L. and Aubry, R. H. High Risk Obstetrics II: Value of Semiobjective Grading System in Identifying the Vulnerable Groups. Am. J. Obstet. & Gynec. 103, 7: 972–985, 1969.
16. Shapiro, S., et al. Relationship of Selected Prenatal Factors to Pregnancy Outcome and Congenital Anomalies. AJPH 55, 2: 268–282, 1965.
17. Jekel, J. F., et al. An Analysis of Statistical Methods for Comparing Obstetrical Outcomes: Infant Health in Three Samples of School-Age Pregnancies. Am. J. Obstet. & Gynec. 112, 1: 9–19, 1972.
18. Currie, J. B., et al. Subsequent Pregnancies Among Teenage Mothers Enrolled in a Special Program. AJPH 62, 12: 1611.

18. Experimental Methodology and Innovative Social Programming

Francis G. Caro

Researchers with disciplinary roots in the behavioral sciences characteristically regard the formal experiment as the preferred model for the evaluation of innovative social programming. (See, for example, Campbell, 1969 and Rivlin, 1971.) So that sound inferences can be made regarding the effectiveness of an intervention, it is recommended that those receiving the innovative treatment be compared with an equivalent group that does not receive the innovative treatment. Random assignment of potential recipients to experimental and control conditions is considered an ideal procedure for assuring comparability of groups. The strategy calls for repeated measurement of those conditions in which change is sought.

The evaluation literature is full of complaints of researchers about resistance of administrators and practitioners to formal experimentation (Caro, 1971 and Weiss, 1972). Administrators are often unwilling, for example, to permit random assignment of potential service recipients to experimental and control conditions. Reluctance of program operators to specify objectives makes it difficult for researchers to develop suitable change measures. Administrators are often less than fully cooperative in giving researchers access to clients for measurement purposes. Administrators are also often interested in introducing significant changes in the treatment before researchers have collected data on sufficient numbers of cases for the statistical analysis they consider essential.

With their interest in expanding opportunities to conduct evaluation studies incorporating true experimental designs, researchers have been reluctant to consider the possibility that formal experimentation is not always an appropriate evaluation strategy.

Rossi (1966), who notes the high cost of experimental evaluation, is something of an exception. He recommends initially that correlational studies be conducted to identify relatively promising interventions. Rossi recommends that experimental evaluation be limited to the few innovative programs that pass that screening successfully. Weiss and Rein (1969) through the analysis of an ill-fated attempt at experimental evaluation, argue that other evaluation approaches are likely to be more appropriate in community-wide interventions with multiple objectives. They argue that an experimental orientation may lead researchers to over-emphasize outcomes to individuals. Not only is it technically difficult for researchers to conduct such studies, but a bias toward experimental methodology may distract them from attention to institutional issues that may be of much greater immediate importance than outcomes to individuals.

The current paper uses a case analysis to raise further questions about the conditions under which experimental evaluation is appropriate in innovative social programming. The case is of particular interest because of the strong role which evaluative researchers with an experimental orientation played in the execution of the project. In contrast to the more common social intervention in which research is a secondary concern, research considerations were given the highest priority. The project was specifically structured to accommodate research design and measurement requirements. It will be argued here that research involvement in the operation of the project seriously limited possibilities for valid generalization of findings. Further, the general preoccupation with research and the substantive issues of primary research concern may have contributed to serious weaknesses in the intervention itself. The case will be used to suggest that certain forms of innovative social programming are best served by an evaluation strategy that makes restrained use of experimental methodology. Implications of the passive role of policy makers in the project's implementation also will be considered. It will be argued that policy makers must work closely with researchers in the formulation of evaluation strategies for demonstration projects.

THE CASE EXAMPLE

Substantively, the case concerns problems of basic care of the elderly and other adults who are both old and seriously disabled. Its central premise is that, in the United States presently, excessive emphasis is placed on institu-

tional care, which is costly, unpopular, and often unnecessary. Alternatively, the project proposed to make a variety of in-home services available to persons who because they were indigent were a responsibility of public welfare and who because they were seriously disabled were candidates for institutionalization. The in-home services were to be financed by Medicaid funds that would otherwise have been used to pay for institutional care. It was hypothesized that in-home services could be offered at a cost to the public no greater than that of institutional care. It was also hypothesized that in-home services would make possible a life situation qualitatively superior to that available in institutions. Favorable results were to be used to bolster the argument for permanent and widespread Medicaid financing of medical and non-medical in-home services for the indigent disabled who would otherwise require institutional care.

The project was far more complex organizationally than it was substantively. Principally involved were a state agency concerned with the elderly, a private research group, a state department of public welfare, a local agency concerned with coordination and development of services for the elderly, several other local agencies which provided specific services, a local administrative unit created for purposes of the project, and three administrative units of the Department of Health, Education, and Welfare in Washington.

As the recipient of a federal demonstration grant, the state unit on aging had overall responsibility for the project. The demonstration grant was to cover costs of administration, research, and service development. Services, themselves, were to be financed through the existing Medicaid program which was administered by the state department of public welfare. The private research group contracted with the state unit on aging to conduct the external evaluation required by federal officials.

Permission had to be obtained from the federal regional office and the department of public welfare for Medicaid financing of the project's services. Service payment procedures had to be reviewed by another state agency which established rates for services purchased by the state. Project personnel had to develop procedures for recruiting and screening potential clients. In addition, a procedure for the certification of their eligibility for Medicaid by public welfare personnel had to be worked out. On the basis of a grant from the state unit on aging with matching funds from the city council, a local agency assumed responsibility for service development and coordination. Contracts had to be negotiated with the local agencies which were to provide specific services. A procedure had to be developed for transmitting bills from local service providers through the service coordinator and the project to the department of public welfare. Project personnel with the service coordinator had to work out case planning, case management, and quality control procedures.

EMPHASIS ON OUTCOME
EVALUATION

Evaluation considerations weighed heavily in the implementation of the project. The project was structured to accommodate a methodologically sound test of the effects of services on the lives of individuals. The implications of that decision to structure the project around a strong outcome evaluation are the central concerns of this case analysis.

To guard against internal threats to the validity of inferences that might be made regarding the outcome of services, the project was cast as a formal experiment. Client assignment to experimental and control conditions was not only random but double blind. So that neither clients nor service providers could subvert the design, evaluative researchers assumed control of the intake process for the project. Efforts were made to keep community knowledge of the project to a minimum. Potential participants were not encouraged to apply for a publicly financed service. Rather, they were invited to be nominally paid participants in a study of the service needs of the elderly. They were told initially that their participation in the study might make them eligible for publicly financed services. On the basis of data obtained in the research interview, judgments about appropriateness for home services were made by clinicians employed by the research unit. Some study participants were screened out on the basis of insufficient need for service; others were excluded on the grounds that their conditions were so serious that their needs could not be adequately addressed through in-home services. Those found appropriate for home care were randomly assigned to the experimental and control conditions. Members of the experimental group were offered home care services. No provisions for services were made through the project for any other persons interviewed.

IMPLEMENTATION PROBLEMS

In its implementation, the project was beset by problems. Approvals for Medicaid financing of services and the proposed payment method were not readily forthcoming. Additional local services thought to be important were not developed. Recruitment of research subjects was much more difficult than anticipated. In fact, recruitment of potential subjects became the major preoccupation of a social service staff which had expected to be concerned with service development, case management, and quality control. Social service personnel found it difficult to ask other agencies to refer potential research subjects to them when clients could be referred directly for services without facing the risk of screening and randomization through the research project. In its first year of operation, the project recruited fewer than half the subjects called for by the research design.

The researchers were unable to control the experimental treatment itself as adequately as research subject recruitment. What was to differentiate the experimental group from controls was the availability of Medicaid financed in-home services. As the project was implemented, another new but more limited source of public funds became available for the same services for much of the potential population to be served. A question arose over whether the Medicaid funds should be used as a supplement to or substitute for the more generally available service funds. When arrangements for Medicaid financing of services were not realized, all services had to be funded through the more generally available source. Because the pool of service funds was small, experimental subjects were able to receive a much more modest configuration of services than anticipated. Previously available services were offered on a temporary or intermittent basis. No new services could be developed. Experimental subjects were referred through the project for publicly funded services. Control subjects were not referred for services through the project but could receive the same publicly funded services if they applied themselves. In effect, then, referral for service through the project became the experimental treatment.

Relatively late in the life of the project, permission was granted to use Medicaid funds to finance rather extensive in-home services for experimental subjects. Relaxation of eligibility criteria also made it somewhat easier to recruit subjects to the experiment. Nevertheless, the experimental service component never did operate as expected. Most experimental subjects never received the rich services originally anticipated. Either subjects did not need (or want) extensive services or appropriate services were not available.

DISCUSSION

A case could be made that the emphasis on experimental evaluation and some of the implementation problems were not unrelated. Fully occupied with tasks introduced by the experimental evaluators, project administrators may have had insufficient time and energy to deal with other problems. The administrative efforts used in explaining and defending the randomization procedure and in recruiting research subjects might instead have been directed at arrangements for securing Medicaid financing. The relationship between an emphasis on experimental evaluation and the absence of Medicaid financing, however, may have been more direct. It was important for the research group to control the intake process to assure the experiment's double blind features. In an operating program, eligibility determination would have been a public welfare responsibility. Public welfare's involvement in the project's development was de-emphasized so that it would not interfere with the research group's case finding assessment and randomization procedures. At the same time, public welfare did not make the availability of Medicaid service funds one of its priorities. If public welfare had been invited to participate fully in the project's development, Medicaid financing may have been more readily available.

The low level of use of services on the part of experimental subjects when Medicaid funds did become available could be explained as a gross overestimate on the part of project planners of the scope of the problem. Alternately, the low level of service demand could be attributed to the project's avoidance of community visibility and its unusual procedures for client recruitment. It is conceivable that if the innovative service program had been well publicized through conventional referral channels and if interested persons had been encouraged to apply, many more persons eligible and in need of extensive services would have applied.

The role which the evaluation group played in the client intake process also had inevitable implications for potential generalization of the results of the project to an operating program. Because potential clients were sought as participants in a study, the project could not provide a basis for estimating the number of characteristics of applicants which might be expected if the availability of publicly financed services were freely publicized. Those who would agree to participate in a study could not be assumed to be identical to those who would apply for a public program.

Further, it is not clear how the screening process used in the project could be generalized to an operating program. An informational base for the screening was obtained through a structured instrument. Research subjects were led to believe that the instrument was administered strictly for research purposes. Individuals who knew that the information they provided might affect their eligibility for a desired public program might have responded to the instrument's more interpretive questions very differently. If an individual desired public, in-home services and believed it would help to establish his eligibility, he might exaggerate, for example, his loneliness, anxiety, or depression. In the project, clinicians enjoyed a great deal of freedom in making judgments about the appropriateness of in-home services for specific research subjects. In an operating program, eligibility determiners under pressure from applicants, family spokesmen, and social service personnel might make very different eligibility judgments.

From a social science research perspective, the approach to evaluation used in the project had impressive qualities. Perhaps its strongest feature was its design. The random assignment of eligible persons to experimental and control conditions assured comparability of experimental and control groups. The double blind feature of the design provided further assurance that differences between the groups would not stem from spurious factors such as the Hawthorne effect. It also provided protection against the possibility of subversion of the design by zealous practitioners committed to providing service to all in need. The successful implementation of such a strong research design in a project concerned with human services in a community setting must be considered an extraordinary achievement.

In retrospect, it can be argued that the project's ambiguous and seemingly weak treatment did not deserve to be tested with the highly sophisticated design that was used. It might also be argued that some of the skill and energy used in developing and implementing the experimental design might have been better used in shoring up the treatment.

A major but often implicit contribution of the behavioral science approach to program evaluation is the assumption that programs are finally to be judged on the basis of outcomes to those at whom programs are directed. The behavioral science perspective is in marked contrast to the accreditation approach which judges programs on the basis of structural characteristics

(Glass, 1971). It is also in contrast to what may be called a program accounting perspective which invites judgments on the basis of the quantity and efficiency of services. As Etzioni (1960) has suggested, a focus on outcomes may be more than a technical perspective; it may be an assertion that organizational structures are to be judged exclusively as instruments in the realization of announced objectives. Etzioni argues that reform values are often better served by a perspective which is less exclusively concerned with outcomes of organized efforts and more appreciative of the strengthening of organizational capabilities.

That perspective may be usefully applied to the present case. The impact evaluation's focus on the health and morale of those to be served may have contributed to an underestimation of the difficulties of creating the structural conditions through which the desired outcomes may have been achieved. With the heavy emphasis on outcomes to individuals, the structuring of the project to maximize a soundly designed outcome study seemed justified. An evaluative perspective concerned equally with structural developments and outcomes to individuals may have anticipated administrative problems and dictated that more project resources be directed to organizational problems and that the evaluation itself minimize the administrative challenges it generated for the project.

ALTERNATE EVALUATION STRATEGIES

The question may be raised whether the project may have been better served by an alternate evaluation strategy.

One conspicuous alternative would have been simply to delay the start of the experimental evaluation. The project might have been initiated simply as a service with project resources concentrated on the development of a viable service demonstration. When the service program was established and working smoothly, the experimental evaluation may have been introduced on a prospective basis (i.e., testing of the effects of service would have been limited to individuals entering the project after the start of the experimental study).

Slightly more elaborate would have been what will be referred to here as a "phased" approach to evaluation. Initiated in the earliest stages of the project would have been unobtrusive evaluation activities concerned with the project's success in creating conditions necessary for an effective program. At the outset, the evaluation would have been concerned with the project's achievement in creating necessary organizational components. Evidence of insurmountable obstacles might have led to a recommendation of radical alteration or termination of the project. Subsequently, the evaluation would have dealt with the service operation. It would have been concerned with the project's ability to recruit, serve, and retain clients in numbers and with an efficiency which could be considered reasonable. The information obtained through these early evaluation activities would have been used to judge whether the project was sufficiently promising to warrant an experimental outcome evaluation. Methodologically, the early stages of the evaluation would have been kept simple. Data would have been ob-

tained through observation, examination of documents, informal interviews with administrators, practitioners, and consumers, and through the analysis of the project's financial and service records. The project's performance would have been judged according to its own developmental goals and according to administrative experiences with comparable programs (e.g., public welfare's experiences in contracting for services with nursing homes).

That there may be serious hazards in the use of a phased approach to evaluation should be clearly recognized. If a controlled experimental evaluation is introduced only after a project has passed more proximate tests of its viability, for example, difficulties of introducing an experimental design may be increased. When an intervention is entirely new, the withholding of services from members of a control group can be defended on grounds, such as the highly untested nature of the intervention and the limited availability of the new approach. Control of information about the availability of the intervention and, hence, effective limitation of demand for its services is easiest when it is entirely new. Once a service intervention has been made available to a population, it is far more difficult to impose the controls over its use necessary if there is to be an experimental evaluation. Potential solutions to this problem are available. One is to conduct the experimental study on a population not otherwise eligible but nonetheless similar. In the project described here, for example, the experimental study might have been done on a population with an income level slightly above that required for Medicaid eligibility. Alternately, an experimental study may be launched at another site if the intervention itself can be transported readily. Campbell (1969) has suggested in these situations that research funds be used to finance services for those receiving the experimental treatment.

Still another possible concern is that if the experimental evaluation is not undertaken immediately, it may never be done at all. It is possible that a new program approach with a plausible rationale, efficient administration, acceptable cost, and professional and client acceptance will attract considerable attention. It may gain widespread adoption even in the absence of strong research evidence showing its effectiveness (Rivlin, 1971). A delay in the introduction of experimental evaluation may be seen as a dangerous invitation to the premature diffusion of an inadequately tested intervention.

A question must be raised at this point about the seriousness of the damage that may arise from the diffusion of an imperfectly tested intervention. In the pharmacology literature there are, of course, enough reports of disastrous effects of inadequately tested medications to suggest that thorough experimental testing of new drug therapies is necessary before widespread use is permitted. In the case of social programs, however, the risks are not likely to be of the same nature. In the case of social programs, such factors as substantial time lags in the emergency of long-term effects, difficulties in measurement of long-term effects, and obstacles to the use of experimental designs make it necessary that evaluative judgments be based on proximate rather than ultimate measures of effec-

tiveness. Educational programs, for example, are often judged on the basis of evidence concerning the transmission of knowledge rather than success in adult life. Further, it is rarely considered likely that innovative social programs may have any harmful effect. More often, the pertinent question is whether they can be shown to have any effect at all of any kind.

In the present case, widespread dissatisfaction with present arrangements for care of infirm older persons may justify the adoption of imperfectly tested reform measures. Dissatisfaction with the quality of life in nursing homes is widespread. The cost of such care is also a matter of public concern. In considering an alternative form of care as an added option rather than as a substitute for nursing home care, policy makers may find it reasonable to accept an alternative if it can be mounted, attract and retain clients, and be offered at a modest price. In this case, subtle differences between institutional and in-home services in effects on health, morale, and even mortality of those served may be of more academic than social policy importance. Still another possibility is that gross data on the viability of in-home services may be sufficient to persuade policy makers to accept in-home services as a matter of principle. Experimental evidence of subtle effects on the health or morale of those served may only persuade them to endorse or seek improvements in the specific form of in-home services.

EVALUATION AND POLICY ISSUES

The situation described here is one in which a policy decision was made to invest in a test of publicly financed in-home services for the indigent disabled. Beyond that fundamental commitment, specific choices regarding the development of the project were left to research methodologists. Although most of the discussion has focused on evaluation research, the paper has at least as much to do with social policy formation as it does with evaluation methodology. Project development was guided by evaluation research requirements with important but neglected social policy implications. Even if they command resources and some control over programming, evaluation researchers play a useful role in program development only if their work is addressed to policy issues. The paper suggests that policy makers may find it hazardous to rely on the researcher's explicit or implicit definition of the basic program development strategy. If their investment in evaluation research is to be productive, policy makers will do well to specify the information they hope to derive from innovative interventions and to prepare themselves to participate in negotiations regarding basic evaluation strategy. Funding agents and program administrators should be able to identify the sequence of issues to be addressed through a project. They should know when an innovative program is confronted with major developmental problems and have some insight into the information which is needed to judge the project's ability to overcome those problems. Further, they should be able to recognize the stage in program development where an experimental test of effectiveness is warranted.

REFERENCES

Campbell, Donald T., "Reforms as Experiments," *American Psychologist,* Vol. 24, No. 4 (April, 1969), pp. 409–429. [Reprinted in this volume, No. 12, pp. 172–204]

Caro, Francis G., "Issues in the Evaluation of Social Programs," *Review of Educational Research,* Vol. 41, No. 2 (1971), pp. 87–114.

Etzioni, Amitai, "Two Approaches to Organizational Analysis: A Critique and a Suggestion," *Administrative Science Quarterly,* Vol. 5 (1960), pp. 257–278.

Glass, Gene V. The Growth of Evaluation Methodology. AERA Curriculum Evaluation Monograph Series, No. 7. Chicago: Rand McNally, 1971.

Rivlin, Alice. *Systematic Thinking for Social Action.* Washington, D.C.: Brookings Institution, 1971.

Rossi, Peter H., "Boobytraps and Pitfalls in the Evaluation of Social Action Programs," *Proceedings of the American Statistical Association,* 1966, pp. 127–132. [Reprinted in this volume, No. 15, pp. 239–248]

Weiss, Carol. *Evaluation Research: Methods of Assessing Program Effectiveness.* Englewood Cliffs, N.J.: Prentice-Hall, 1972.

Weiss, Robert and Martin Rein, "The Evaluation of Broad-Aim Programs: A Cautionary Case and a Moral," *Annals of the American Academy of Political and Social Science,* Vol. 385 (September 1969), pp. 133–142. [Reprinted in this volume, No. 16, pp. 253–262]

19. The External Politics of the National Income Transfer Experiment

Peter H. Rossi and Katharine C. Lyall

All large-scale, policy oriented research projects are conducted within a political context, and all research operations create their own internal political systems. The context for a research project includes the organizations within which the project is embedded, the relations with sponsors and sources of funds, audiences that are willing or not willing to learn of results, and sometimes even the subjects of the research or their organized representatives. For large-scale policy oriented research sponsored by a controversial government agency, these elements of context impinge with particular force. The National Income Transfer (NIT) project was no exception: There were several instances when the project moved perilously close to the kitchen fire even though the support of its sponsor, OEO, was strong and unwavering. The nature of these events and how they were successfully handled are integral parts of the lessons to be learned from NIT. . . .

PRESSURES FOR EARLY DISCLOSURE OF FINDINGS[1]

The NIT Experiment was designed to run for three years. Although there were plans for interim reports to OEO, there were no set plans for widespread public release of early findings. Rather the plan was to provide findings for public release in the form of a final report to be issued sometime after the experiment had run its planned course. To be sure, close running tabs would be kept on the NIT families but more as an administrative monitoring than for the purpose of providing interim information on findings. This long-term perspective was consistent with the expectation that it was the policymaking needs of some years beyond the completion of the experiment that were being served: Few expected that some form of NIT would be placed on the political agenda during the course of the experiment itself.

Yet the political atmosphere that led to approval of the experiment itself was also a climate that was inclined to look upon the idea of negative income tax plans as at least conceivable, if not desirable. Hence, within a few months after the NIT Experiment was started, the new Nixon administration began to think of an overhaul of the existing welfare system. The general idea of a negative income tax program as a replacement for all or a part of the existing welfare system had been hovering on the margins of the federal government's policy agenda for some years. As early as 1965 the Council of Economic Advisors undertook a study of negative income tax plans recommending in 1966 that a more extended

Adapted from Peter H. Rossi and Katharine Lyall, *Reforming Public Welfare: A Critique of the Negative Income Tax Experiment* (New York: Russell Sage Foundation, 1976), pp. 157–168. Copyright © 1976 Russell Sage Foundation. Reprinted by permission.

study be made of this promising idea. Early in 1968, President Johnson appointed a commission to study income maintenance, the commission to report within two years of establishment. In the summer of 1968 hearings on income maintenance programs were initiated by the Joint Economic Committee of the Congress.

All of these events had taken place before the first payment was made to the first families enrolled in Trenton, New Jersey. At the same time as the debate over the design of the experiment was going on, the new Nixon administration with Daniel Patrick Moynihan on board began to explore the possibilities of welfare reform with negative income tax plans receiving particular attention. By the middle of April 1969, the president had delivered in a message to Congress a plan for reform that hopefully would correct some of the deficiencies of the then current welfare system.

Within the White House staff, two different approaches were being debated: Daniel Moynihan and George Schultz were leaning toward a plan that would have a high guarantee and strong work incentives, while the president's economic advisor, Arthur Burns, stressed a much lower guarantee and work requirements. By the end of the summer of 1969, a compromise Family Assistance Plan (FAP) was devised and by the beginning of October, legislation embodying FAP was introduced into Congress. In short, the NIT Experiment had been barely under way for a year and had yet to complete enrollment of families in Scranton, Pennsylvania, when legislation embodying some of the ideas of a negative

income tax proposal was introduced into Congress.

It is not at all clear how much the NIT Experiment influenced the FAP legislation at this stage. Certainly the technical staff of OEO and HEW who had participated in the formulation and approval of the NIT Experiment were involved as consultants to the various participants in the process. Moynihan was certainly aware of the experiment, as later events were to prove. Perhaps the clearest point of contact between the experiment and the groups that were arguing over policy formulation was over the administration of an income maintenance plan: In setting up the NIT Experiment much thought had gone into the question of an appropriate accounting period, and information on this score was fed into the early discussions in the executive branch that led to formation of FAP.

As the FAP legislation in 1969 came before the House Ways and Means Committee, Harold Watts (director of the Institute for Research on Poverty at the University of Wisconsin which held the prime contract for the project) offered to ranking Minority member Congressman John W. Byrnes (Wisconsin) to testify on FAP, an offer that the Ways and Means Committee took up in November 1969. Watts's testimony in an open meeting of the committee was in favor of the FAP legislation, pointed out the general similarity between the design of the experiment and the drafting of the FAP legislation, and made some suggestions concerning the accounting period to be employed.

The Ways and Means Committee

requested that the NIT Experiment staff testify again in January 1970 but this time behind closed doors. Watts, David Kershaw, and Lee Bawden[2] testified in this session. The testimony given in this session also emphasized the administrative aspects of the NIT Experiment experience. Kershaw, a principal investigator who managed field operations, testified in fairly vague terms on his impressions of the results of the NIT Experiment thus far, indicating that he could not discern any meaningful trend in work response.

Around the same time as the NIT principals were testifying, a "leak" appeared in the *New York Times* to the effect that the Ways and Means Committee staff had uncovered a "secret study" that projected a very heavy work disincentive response to FAP and possibly an incentive for breaking up families. In response to this rumor, the administration began to press for some harder data from the NIT Experiment. Moynihan is reputed to have expressed his displeasure in no uncertain terms to John Wilson, then director of Research, Plans, Programs, and Evaluation at OEO, that the NIT Experiment had been going for more than a year and that some hard results ought to be available. At the same time, Kershaw had communicated to OEO that he thought it would be possible to put together some data on the first 500 or so families that had been enrolled initially. Wilson gave the go-ahead signal to Kershaw and within the short space of a few weeks, Kershaw and Watts *hand-tallied*[3] some of the data from 509 of the first-year enrolled families.

The hand-tallied results were incor-porated into a report written by Watts and Kershaw entitled "Preliminary Results of the New Jersey Work Incentive Experiment." The results purportedly showed that there was no discernible work disincentive nor were there any severe changes in consumption patterns among experimental families that were receiving payments. Wilson discussed the preliminary results in a cabinet meeting. President Nixon incorporated the generally optimistic findings into a speech he gave at a governors' conference, and the "preliminary report" was released to the public in the middle of February. It should be noted that the preliminary report contained statements to indicate that the findings were partial, tentative, and subject to change when data from other sites would be available and when a longer time experience with the experiment was assessed.

Thus within less than eighteen months of the beginning of the experiment, some of its results were beginning to filter into the policymaking process. However, it should be clear from this account that the infiltration was far from optimum. First, although the first year's experiences of the initial group of families were of some interest, it was not at all clear that these data were of sufficient quality and generality to warrant much attention. The New Jersey cities were the first sites at which families were selected: The early data series on income, work effort, and consumption patterns were early recognized as bearing significant defects; and hand-tallying was a far from reliable mode of data processing although a subsequent check by the General Accounting Office (GAO) found that the data had been coded and tallied correctly. In addition, the initial group of families was drawn disproportionately from among blacks and Puerto Ricans, groups from whom it would be hard to draw generalizations about the total impact of FAP on the working poor.

Second, although FAP had some kinship to the NIT Experiment, there were also some very critical differences. FAP was designed to supplement the existing welfare system by providing payments to the working poor while the NIT plan was intended as a replacement. NIT had no built-in work requirements while FAP contained both manpower retraining features and a work availability requirement that led to its being called "work-fare." The level of guaranteed support in FAP was identical to that of the least generous plan being tested in NIT. It should be noted that these differences did not invalidate an extrapolation of NIT to FAP: First, NIT did turn out to be in competition with the existing welfare systems of New Jersey and Pennsylvania; second, few expected that the work requirements of FAP could be effectively implemented; finally, the FAP plan was one that was at the lower limits of the policy space of the experiment, even though as a treatment, the lowest plan was so far inferior to the local welfare plans that few eligible families assigned to that plan elected for NIT payments.

Third, and most important to the present discussion, the testimony of NIT personnel and the release of preliminary results were interpreted as partisan behavior of the experimenters. Watts's early testimony was certainly volunteered in an effort to be helpful to

the FAP proposal. All of the testimony presented was offered at the request of the administration or administration supporters.

The testimony also brought the NIT Experiment to the attention of the mass media. Television reporters asked for access to experimental families, requests which were consistently turned down.

The most important immediate consequence of entry into the public attention was a decision by the GAO to audit the experiment. GAO officials sensed that the preliminary report might play an important role in the then upcoming Senate Finance Committee Hearings, wondered how preliminary and tentative were the findings, and decided to audit the experiment.[4]

They asked for access to the raw data series in order to evaluate the data series, including names of participating families (possibly to check directly with them whether data on families were correct). Kershaw resisted giving complete access to GAO investigators, the critical point being information that would reveal the identity of participating families. Accepting this compromise, GAO investigators sampled some of the data and issued a report. GAO investigators emphasized the tentative character of the preliminary findings, expressed some satisfaction with data quality and the tabulation of findings, and endorsed the continuation of the experiment as a valuable aid to the policy formation process.

Despite the GAO report's generally favorable findings, the impact of the GAO investigation was, ironically, to undermine the credibility of the *Preliminary Report.* Representatives on the Ways and Means Committee interviewed in 1972 remembered the testimony of the NIT personnel adding a qualifying phrase to the effect that they also remembered something was wrong with their data that the GAO had to look into. The sting of the GAO investigation was not modified by Watts's issuance of a later report entitled "Adjusted and Extended Preliminary Results from the Urban Graduated Work Incentive Experiment."

By the time that the FAP legislation came up for hearings in the Senate Finance Committee, the NIT Experiment and its personnel had taken on a decided partisan look in the minds of those who were opposed to the FAP legislation. When Watts testified before the Senate Finance Committee, Senator John J. Williams (Delaware) dismissed his testimony by asking only one question: whether Watts's salary was being paid by OEO.

Senator Williams also struck hard at the NIT Experiment by demanding of OEO that the agency produce a list of the names and addresses of participating families suggesting that funding for the experiment would be cut off if compliance was not forthcoming. Senator Williams' request created considerable consternation among NIT staff and OEO since congressional subpoena power could have compelled disclosure if the senator had been willing to push the issue that far. Apparently feeling that his objections to FAP had gone far enough, Senator Williams did not push his request for access to "raw data," when OEO refused to honor his request on the grounds that the data were collected under promises of confidentiality.

The 1969–1970 version of FAP legislation did not pass through Congress, achieving approval of the House but falling short of necessary support in the Senate.

A second version of FAP was introduced into the next session of Congress in the fall of 1970. NIT personnel volunteered to introduce some new data into congressional hearings on this second go-around, but OEO officials were more cautious. Besides, the new tabulations made by Harold Watts showed a slight work disincentive. OEO officials argued that the release of such preliminary data might do some harm to the FAP legislation.

OEO eventually gave permission to Watts and Kershaw to send additional findings to the House and Senate. Not much attention was paid to their findings partially because the issues that engaged the attention of congressmen were no longer ones of work disincentives but of the effects of overlapping welfare programs to which the NIT Experiment could make little contribution. But, some of the lack of attention to the NIT results was a matter of discounting what had come to be regarded as a partisan and somewhat shaky source of information. In the recollections of congressmen interviewed later, the impact of the GAO report on the previous (1970) preliminary report was considerable.[5]

A hindsightful analysis of the NIT experiences in trying to be relevant to the decision making process reveals the dangers that are involved. First, it is apparently easy to become identified as a partisan if one pursues the apparently contradictory roles of advocate of a plan and the bearer of scientific findings. Reasonable questions raised about the findings tend to accentuate the perception of one's role as advocate. Second, it is difficult to resist the pressures of the sponsor. OEO was very much part of the executive branch: The public release of the preliminary report by OEO was correctly seen by Congress as a partisan move. It should also be noted that the NIT staff willingly volunteered to assemble the preliminary report, a move that they were later to regret, at least partially.[6]

Finally, the incident with Senator Williams firmly brought to mind on how fragile a base are erected researcher promises to respondents of confidentiality. Until there is some statutory foundation on which the promise of confidentiality can be based, confidentiality cannot be guaranteed. Had Senator Williams wished to pursue the matter and had he the support of his colleagues, the raw data of the NIT Experiment could have been subpoenaed. Possibly NIT personnel and OEO would have chosen to fight such a subpoena through the courts; even so the outcome would have been in doubt.

THE MERCER COUNTY PROSECUTOR AND THE NIT EXPERIMENT

Threats to the promises of confidentiality extended to participating families from local sources as well. As the experiment began to achieve some publicity in the latter part of 1969, the county prosecutor of Mercer County (in which Trenton is located) began to inquire into the possibility that some of the participating families may have been accepting payments from both the experiment and public welfare. NIT payments not reported to welfare authorities constituted evidence of neglect, if not intentional fraud, on the part of participating families.[7]

Almost any system of confidentiality can be broken if enough attention is given to the problem. The county prosecutor managed to determine the names of a few families in Trenton who were on the welfare rolls and also participating in the experiment and in late 1969 issued a subpoena to Mathematica to produce the records of payments to about a dozen participating families.

It should be noted that when the experiment first started it would have been legally impossible for participating families that remained intact to have been eligible for AFDC in New Jersey since payments could only be made to households in which there were no work-eligible males. When the New Jersey welfare law was changed early in 1969 extending coverage to families with an unemployed male parent present (AFDC-UP), some of the families participating in the experiment became eligible for welfare payments. Families initially enrolled in Trenton were told that they could receive payments from both although they were advised that they had to report welfare payments as income on their monthly report forms and that they were legally obligated to report experimental payments to welfare authorities.[8] Families enrolled in other sites that were solicited after AFDC-UP had been enacted in New Jersey were told that they had to choose between welfare and NIT payments and could not receive both.

Mathematica's response to the county prosecutor's subpoena was to give the prosecutor a summary of the payments made to the families about whom information was requested but to resist opening the records of all families to the prosecutor's office. In a move to quash the subpoena, Mathematica argued that to open the records was to violate the pledge of confidentiality made to participating families, that the experiment served a useful purpose, and that whatever apparent fraud had been committed may have arisen out of the understandable confusion in participating families' minds between the two systems of payments. Mathematica's arguments were backed by statements from OEO officials about the importance of the experiment and careful applications of pressure on the county prosecutor from a variety of sources.

For a period of nearly a year the county prosecutor's office persisted in its attempts to subpoena Mathematica's records on participating Trenton families. Mathematica countered by handing over summaries of NIT payments made to families about whom specific requests were made but continued to resist turning over more complete records. At several points, David Kershaw indicated his willingness to go to jail rather than break Mathematica's pledges of confidentiality.

A compromise was eventually reached in which the NIT Experiment assumed the liability for whatever overpayments were made by the Mercer County welfare department, a sum that totaled approximately

$20,000 for the eighteen-month period that the fourteen families were receiving dual payments. In addition, quarterly checks were instituted with the welfare departments at all the sites in which participating families' names were checked against the welfare rolls. The rules were then changed for Trenton families to prohibit dual participation.

As in the case of Senator Williams' request for raw data, the subpoena power of the Mercer County prosecutor was never put to the ultimate test.[9] The subpoena was never quashed, it was withdrawn when the compromise involving repayment was reached. Hence, the issue whether pledges of confidentiality would be upheld by the courts as sufficient reason for withholding detailed information on participating families was never tested.

This incident was to prompt HEW to ask the National Academy of Sciences/National Research Council Committee on Federal Evaluation Research to conduct a study of the problem of confidentiality to research evaluating social programs. The committee with the aid of legal scholars has drawn up a suggested federal statute extending to evaluation research the same protections extended to members of the press concerning the materials obtained in confidence from informants. Whether this legislation is ever to be presented to Congress is largely a matter of conjecture.[10]

CONCERNING SOME EXTERNAL POLITICAL PROBLEMS OF CRITICAL SOCIAL POLICY RESEARCH

The vast bulk of social research has proceeded over the past fifty years without serious challenges to the informal pledges of confidentiality extended routinely by social researchers to their respondents. Much of the research, however, has only been remotely related to social policy, and little has had as close a connection with ongoing policy formation as in the case of NIT and the consideration of FAP in Congress. An additional vulnerability of the NIT field experiment is that it involved the possibility that participating families by virtue of their participation could be involved in seeming fraud.

Two lessons may be drawn from the NIT Experiment: First, it is important to build up and retain an image of impartiality as opposed to an image of partisanship. The attempt on the part of NIT researchers to act in the dual (and somewhat contradictory) role both of advocates of FAP and as the bearers of empirical data relevant to critical policy questions did little to build confidence in the outcome of the experiment. The experiment was perceived as flawed, and the experimenters as just another set of administration partisans.

Second, the legal foundations on which social researchers promise confidentiality are very insecure. Up to this point, the researchers have met the issue by finding a compromise that avoids bringing the issue to a clear resolution in the courts, a solution that only postpones the inevitable possibly in the hope that customary procedures will achieve some recognition in the courts.[11] It does appear as if some policymakers intuitively understand this vulnerability and use threats to subpoena raw data as means of placing pressures upon social researchers. It

should be borne in mind that it is not at all clear how Senator Williams could have used access to raw data as means to his goal of discrediting the FAP proposal. Giving publicity to specific participating families might undermine the conduct of the experiment but would not be useful directly to Williams' cause. Similarly the indictment of a few families in Trenton for welfare fraud would certainly have made participating families in Trenton and in other New Jersey sites uneasy enough to drop out of the experiment, but it is hard to envisage that the welfare department in Mercer County would be materially improved by the county prosecutor's move although it is easy to see that the prosecutor could make some personal mileage out of his move.[12]

Finally, a comment must be made on the curious conjunction between the start of the experiment and the arrival of some sort of NIT proposal at the top of the political agenda. It is apparent that the political conditions that make it possible to conduct field experiments are the *same* political conditions that make it likely that a related proposal will appear on the agenda. Hence, the NIT Experiment, which was seen by the OEO administrators and NIT personnel as providing results relevant for a distant future, turned out to be badly timed for consideration as relevant to the FAP proposal. That this is not a circumstance that is unique to NIT can be seen from similar examples in other areas. For instance, at the same time that the current (Ford) administration is considering submitting a bill that would set up a national health insurance plan, HEW has just launched a long-term field experiment testing the impact of such insurance on the consumption of medical care. It is now quite clear that the results of the experiment, designed to provide information relevant to the design of a national health insurance plan, will not be anywhere near ready when a plan will be presented to Congress. Another set of examples are the current housing voucher experiments. There has been enough discussion of housing vouchers in the Nixon and Ford administrations to make one suspect that this too will appear in the form of proposed legisla-tion long before results from the experiments are in.

This mistiming of field experiments on prospective social policies suggests that long-term field experiments conducted under the sponsorship of policymakers may turn out to be prematurely obsolescent. Instead, it may be necessary to consider other ways of sponsoring field experiments, which would be further removed from policymakers and the immediacy of their concerns.

NOTES

1. For a more detailed exposition of these events and an analysis of the impact of the NIT Experiment on the formulation of FAP and the decision-making process within Congress and the executive branch, see Margaret Boeckmann, "The Contribution of Social Research to Social Policy: A Study of the New Jersey Income Maintenance Experiment and the Family Assistance Plan" (Ph.D. diss., The Johns Hopkins University, 1973). Dr. Boeckmann's dissertation research was supported by a Russell Sage Foundation project. This section is based largely on the extensive discussion of the relationships between the NIT Experiment and Congress during congressional consideration of FAP contained in Chapter 4.

2. Lee Bawden was the principal investigator of the Rural Income Maintenance Experiment being conducted by the Institute for Research on Poverty in two rural sites, one in Wisconsin and the other in North Carolina.

3. Hand-tallies were necessary because the data, although available on tape, had been formatted in so awkward a form that it was not possible to be retrieved in a useful fashion. Indeed one of the major problems that had to be overcome before final reports were produced was to reformat the computer software system.

4. Under a 1967 amendment to the poverty act, the GAO was assigned the responsibility to audit the performance of all OEO programs.

5. The discounting of the NIT Experiment's results is aptly illustrated in the following excerpt from a personal interview (reported in Boeckmann, "The Contribution of Social Research," p. 196) with Geoffrey Patterson, legislative aide to Senator Abraham Ribicoff:

I guess that in 1970 there had been some discrediting of the experiment. That the size of the sample was small. That they had reported findings too early. I remember that when I had suggested to the senator that we use it in a statement to support our idea that by providing a FAP type approach that you would actually be encouraging people to work, he said, "No let's not emphasize that experiment because of its controversial nature." And I know that the Finance Committee had been attacking it. And whenever you are using data to support your position, you always try to come up with the strongest data possible you can, and if that information has already been attacked fairly strongly, you decide well, we will drop that and go on to something that we have a great deal of confidence in.

6. Watts has expressed the view that he did not feel it would have been socially responsible to withhold interim information useful in the policy debate, stating "The one principle I did regard as important was to assure equal accessibility to the partial and preliminary findings to all participants in the policy process—not just the immediate sponsors of the project." (Personal communication, July 1975.)

7. Families receiving welfare payments were supposed to report immediately all change in income that might affect such payments. This is a rule that is not very rigorously enforced, as most studies of the administration of public welfare show. The discretion that is allowed caseworkers in most welfare systems is often exercised in overlooking earnings from casual and intermittent employment, employment of secondary wage earners (teenagers), and so on. A thorough investigation of almost any welfare roll will bring to light instances in which some families are receiving at any one time more than they are due under current rules and regulations. Thus a "cheap shot" for any state's attorney would be to institute an investigation into "welfare fraud."

8. This decision was made in order to maintain faith in the original agreements made with enrolling families in Trenton. Since there was initially no problem of overlap with AFDC, no mention was made in the enrollment process of the possibility of conflicts with welfare. Hence, NIT administrators felt that it would be more in line with the original understandings undertaken with Trenton families to allow participation jointly in welfare and the experiment.

9. A very similar case involving the county prosecutor of Bergen County who wished to examine records for participating families in Jersey City was also solved by a similar compromise. The amount of overpayment in Jersey City was considerably smaller since rules prohibiting dual payment had been in effect from enrollment on and families apparently understood the rules.

10. National Research Council, *Protecting Individual Privacy in Evaluation Research* (Washington, D.C.: National Academy of Sciences, 1975).

11. There has also been some concern with insuring that data files are confidential by stripping identifying information from such files. This move assumes that if the data are subpoenaed and such moves are upheld by the courts, the data do not contain enough detail to constitute an unwilling breaking of confidentiality pledges.

12. Something may be gained by the state's attorney in the way of favorable publicity as a prosecutor who is hard on "welfare cheaters."

20. Responding to Skid Row Alcoholism: Self-Defeating Arrangements in an Innovative Treatment Program

Lincoln J. Fry and Jon Miller

Based upon twenty-seven months of participant observation in a skid row mission, this study explores some of the factors that contributed to the ineffectiveness and ultimate failure of what began. as a highly promising alcoholism rehabilitation program. The program was very generously funded from state and local resources; it was technically and philosophically innovative; it was highly professionalized and staffed by young, bright, eager practitioners. Further, it was located in the treatment quarters of an established, highly regarded religious organization that could add stability and experience to this impressive array of financial and professional resources. Despite these advantages the experiment could be credited with almost no positive impact on the alcoholism problem surrounding it, and its professional staff could be seen to change from confidence, to desperation, and finally to disengagement as the failure of the program became apparent.

The study describes how the initial optimism generated by this program was eventually overwhelmed by internal and external considerations. The program began with ambiguous and conflicting goals which led to organizational conflicts involving the competing vested interests of participants. A

related factor was the absence of workable technologies for achieving stated objectives.

Before we describe the evolution of the program in more detail, a brief comment on the difficulty of defining and measuring organizational goals and effectiveness seems useful. Assessing the effectiveness of organizations has always been an elusive task. Perhaps in reaction, Warren (1973) has taken social scientists to task for continuing to support ineffective large-scale comprehensive and coordinating strategies designed to alleviate urban social problems. These strategies increasingly consist of interorganizational and interdisciplinary networks designed to present a "unified" attack on a specific problem. They often have vigorous advocates, yet clear guidelines have not been established to measure or promote effectiveness, at either the organizational or interorganizational level. Organizational effectiveness is usually conceptualized in terms of the degree of goal-achievement (Etzioni, 1961, 1964; Thompson, 1968); however, goals have proven hard to identify. As a result, Etzioni (1964) finds it necessary to distinguish between "real" and "stated" goals while Perrow (1961) identifies "stated" as distinct from

From *Social Problems*, Vol. 22, No. 5, June 1975, pp. 675–688. Reprinted by permission of the authors and the Society for the Study of Social Problems.

"operational" goals. When goals are stated imprecisely they may provide little insight for the observer to record the operation of the organization and measure its effectiveness. However, it is equally important to remember that when goals are imprecisely defined this fact may itself be a factor preventing the organization's participants from moving in any consistent direction. More than any other single factor, the inability clearly to specify and implement its objectives condemned the project we are about to describe to failure.

AN INNOVATIVE TREATMENT PROGRAM

A major piece of state legislation made funds available for counties in California to create "comprehensive" alcoholism treatment systems. This legislation was designed to promote cooperation between different levels of government and agencies involved in alcoholism treatment; its major impact was to create interorganizational treatment ventures, especially between the state department of vocational rehabilitation and county health departments. Prior to this legislation, alcoholism treatment was offered by a number of separate local, county and state government agencies, and by private organizations. In the system we studied, one county-wide treatment system was developed with the new funding which centered on services previously offered by the health department. Four clinics made up the system; three of the four clinics were joint ventures between the county health department and the state department of vocational rehabilitation.

The fourth clinic was located in a skid row mission operated for a number of years by a large philanthropic religious organization. Data for the present study were collected primarily within this unusual mixed clinic and mission setting. The study involved twenty-seven months of participant observation, supplemented by questionnaires and strategic interviews.[1]

The Mission

The mission, which could accommodate two hundred and thirty-five residents, occupied the first five floors of a building originally built as a hotel. The first floor contained office space, kitchen and dining areas, and a chapel. The second floor housed a medical clinic, a detoxification unit, and further office space. Residents lived in single, double, and dormitory style rooms on the upper floors.[2]

The mission's management structure consisted of a titular head, charged with responsibility for the spiritual well-being of residents, and a business manager responsible for financial affairs. Resident responsibility rested with the house manager and his assistant. These two, both recovered alcoholics, supervised the house staff recruited from the resident alcoholic population. The house manager was an employee of the religious organization and could be moved from one facility to another. The manager had been in this mission six years when the study began. House staff, on the other hand, were attached only to a particular facility and their employment was transitory.[3]

Located on the main thoroughfare of a major metropolitan skid row, the building which housed the mission appeared more modern than the typical structures lining the street; these were primarily other missions, old hotels, pawn shops and cheap bars. Men in various stages of intoxication populated the street, some sleeping in doorways. The major visible activity conducted on the street appeared to be drinking, primarily wine from bottles in brown paper bags. Periodically, paddy wagons appeared and took some of the men to jail, usually those who appeared unable to care for themselves.

The other missions on the street offered the traditional "three hots and a cot" as their major service to alcoholics. In contrast, this facility had always stressed long term residency and treatment. Whether recruiting from the streets, "walk-ins," or through its court program, the mission had traditionally admitted residents based upon an assessment of the individual's determination to stop drinking and to show a commitment to the work ethic. Treatment involved religious meetings and employment services; Alcoholics Anonymous meetings were held in the facility once a week. Employment consisted of "day work," with some hope of eventually finding steady work allowing a resident to leave the mission altogether. Most treatment activities were scheduled in the evening and focused on the religious activities and the residents' commonly shared drinking problem.

The Clinic

The clinic added to this mission was not a completely new venture. Previously, several professional and clerical personnel had been housed in the mission, including a social worker, a part-time physician for physical examinations, a social service aide, and a clerk. As a result of new funding, increased resources were provided by the agencies involved in the program and, most important, an interdisciplinary treatment team was added. The purpose of this team approach was to concentrate the technical expertise of several fields on the single problem of alcoholism and to coordinate this effort with that of the mission.

The health department provided a number of members for the interdisciplinary team, including several social workers and nurses, a public health investigator, a recreation therapist, and several part-time counselors. The state department of vocational rehabilitation provided the team with a rehabilitation counselor, several part-time physicians for physical examinations, a part-time job developer and several social service aides. Both the county and the state provided clerical staff. In addition, the state provided the rehabilitation counselor with a budget which included money to be used for room and board for selected patients as well as for training and educational expenses. This vital financial resource in the hands of the treatment team was to become an important factor in the evolution of the program.

The clinic expansion began when a rehabilitation counselor was assigned to the mission. At this time, those professional personnel employed in the mission prior to the increased funding were replaced by other professional personnel recruited specifically to staff the interdisciplinary team. This made clear from the outset that the clinic was to be committed to a counseling technology dispensed through the team method, a group practice in which a number of professionals (four or five, in this setting) meet with a single patient (Horwitz, 1970). Through their mutual interaction consensus theoretically develops between patient and team as to the course of treatment.

Alcoholics who entered the mission had a choice. They could become clinic patients or they could be designated just as residents of the mission facility. Non-clinic residents were to be under the sole jurisdiction of the religious organization. Both types of patients were live-ins, and were not segregated within the mission. The clinic facility provided minimal out-patient services. The planning which provided for the expanded services offered in the mission was intended to broaden the mission's sources of patients. In addition to the surrounding skid row, the sources of recruitment became the probation department, the court system, hospitals, other clinics within the county system, and walk-ins. The mission had received residents from the criminal justice system before the team-oriented clinic was added, but the public health investigator attached to the team had a formal responsibility to work with the court system and to expand the number of alcoholics sent to the mission by the courts.

EMERGING DIFFICULTIES

Early Organizational Problems: Ambiguous Goals and Competing Interests

The clinic became operational with the usual optimism expressed by the county treatment system and by the religious organization. Initially everyone agreed that the clinic represented a change from the old method of alcholism treatment on skid row and that the clinic was a harbinger of the future. This consensus was largely illusory and short-lived because the immediate changes created by the clinic expansion were more far-reaching than the simple addition of another treatment modality would warrant. The team approach affected all aspects of the mission environment in fundamental ways and the unanticipated sources of contention were many.

The clinic team immediately began to recruit its own patients, to establish training, educational, and job development programs for these patients, and to acquire some degree of influence over how the mission operated. As a result, the first problem that emerged was establishing working relationships and mutual objectives for the mission and the clinic. These relationships had not received much attention until after the clinic began to function and the consequence was the alienation of the mission's resident staff at the very outset of the program when it was least prepared to tolerate strain. In the beginning, a series of meetings was initiated between the mission's management and clinic personnel in order to establish mutually acceptable policies. These meetings took place primarily between the titular head of the mission and the rehabilitation counselor attached to the interdisciplinary team, with the house manager and his staff excluded for several months. The house staff's anger over this exclusion was further accentuated because all the professionals replaced in the transition to the clinic's team treatment had been considered friends by the house staff because they had rarely interfered in the internal operation of the mission. Both the clinic and mission's management became aware, belatedly, that the exclusion of the house staff from policy-making was a major source of resentment but not until there was serious damage to the working environment. In fact, after this point the clinic personnel never enjoyed the full confidence of the house staff. The house staff found a major source of support gone and in its place a new group of professionals who threatened all their time-tested procedures.

Within weeks, a second problem arose over the proper role of medical treatment in the mission and clinic. Both the clinic and the mission indicated that alcoholism treatment was their primary goal but there was no agreement over the proper approach to take. This was another problem not fully aired before the venture began. The mission's management stressed the medical aspects of alcoholism and requested that a medical director be appointed to head the clinic. The clinic personnel refused to endorse the medical approach to alcoholism treatment or the call for a medical director because they defined the interdisciplinary team model as an alternative to medical treatment. They thought counseling was a more promising approach and the medical services provided by the clinic were, ideally, relegated to a supplementary role.

This debate over approaches to alcoholism treatment led to a basic disagreement over the use of drugs in the mission. Consistent with their stress on the medical model, the mission's management was adamant that all of the residents, clinic and non-clinic, be required to take antabuse (a substance which makes alcoholics violently ill if they drink alcohol). The clinic was at best ambivalent about the use of antabuse and related medications, including tranquilizers, which they considered inconsistent with the counseling treatment approach. They thought patients heavily medicated were not as likely to "get in touch with themselves." The clinic compromised by requiring antabuse for all mission residents, while it was understood that the medical director issue would be reconsidered at a later date. In fact, a medical director was never appointed during the course of the study, an outcome representing a considerable victory for the bureaucratic autonomy of the treatment team. However, the agreement to prescribe antabuse was a high professional and philosophical price to pay for this concession.

A third source of early disagreement between mission and clinic involved general personnel procedures. Since the clinic primarily hired recent graduates for regular positions and filled part-time positions with graduate students, the professional staff was unusually young. The house staff and the residents complained bitterly that these new professionals were simply not old enough, despite their training, to understand resident problems. (A common complaint from the residents was that they had been on skid row before some of the staff were born.) At the same time, the mission's management had complaints about the clinic's young staff, with a miniskirted graduate student a major source of consternation.

Persistent Strains: Employment, Social Control and Recruitment

The problems we have described so far would seem sufficient to drain off much of the initial enthusiasm for the program. Yet, in the face of these early sources of strain, the interdisciplinary team members continued to show enthusiasm for their work. Before long, however, an instance of open conflict developed in the area of employment that went to the heart of the program. Employment was the core element of the treatment effort. The state department of vocational rehabilitation to which the clinic was accountable defined success strictly in terms of employment. This agency provided all of the case service monies in the clinic and this money was used legitimately only if related to employment potential. As a result, successful rehabilitation was initially defined by the clinic as ninety days working and not drinking. The mission also relied on employment as the major indicator of success, but without a specified time period. The mission relied on the resident's ability to leave and become self-supporting as the major indicator of success. Neither the clinic nor the mission were actually concerned with alcoholism treatment *per se,* as the primary operational criterion determining success.

The clinic and the mission had separate employment programs that began to compete for residents appearing to be likely candidates for rehabilitation. Each side was critical of the other's approach to the role of employment in

the rehabilitation process. The clinic stressed steady work. Day work was not steady work and therefore could not contribute to the rehabilitation of clinic patients. The mission, on the other hand, felt that the clinic's approach to employment was a clear indicator that no realistic conception existed of the type of people who populated the mission. The mission staff thought taking a job in a strange location with a steady work routine spelled disaster for skid row alcoholics. The clinic stressed employment away from skid row and had an employment arrangement with an outside industrial firm. The mission staff thought this would leave the resident isolated, alone in a room in a strange location, and the alcoholic's immediate reaction would be to begin drinking again. A return to skid row would quickly follow and the mission would be defeated once again.

The clinic personnel were antagonistic toward the day labor program of the mission for several reasons. First, day labor is characteristic of the skid row scene. Referred to as "slave markets," day labor offices usually provide skid row residents with just enough money for wine and a "flop" for the night. The clinic felt residents should change their life style and that day labor merely kept them on skid row. Furthermore, the religious organization collected room and board from each resident's day labor effort while the residents were not charged anything if they did not work. Clinic personnel considered this "negative reinforcement" for working. The dispute over the proper role of employment in rehabilitation was never really resolved and it remained an inescapable source of strain between the clinic personnel and the mission staff.

Several of the persistent sources of strain appeared by the close of the first holiday season after the clinic team was introduced. The holidays were a significant rite of passage for most of the clinic personnel. There was a huge turn-over and loss of patients in the facility over Christmas and New Year's because of the drinking associated with this period. This devastation of the clients had an effect upon the staff and their attitudes toward the clients as well as their work role within the mission because it demonstrated just how ephemeral the effects of their efforts could be. After these heavy patient losses, the clinic became much more defensive, and less confident, about its approach to treatment and its role in the mission.

Many team members began to complain that their patients were forced to leave the mission because of arbitrary decisions made by the house staff. A more general controversy arose over whether both the clinic and the mission staff tried to "protect their own." Team members accused the house staff of allowing certain individuals to drink in the mission with immunity from the rule that this was an automatic reason for dismissal. The clinic staff believed this questionable privilege was reserved for special, i.e., non-clinic patients. At the same time, the house staff raised a similar complaint about the clinic staff: the professionals were accused of not recognizing minor drinking as an infringement upon the rule against drinking. They were also charged with giving their patients second and third chances to remain in the

facility once caught drinking. In short, both the clinic and the mission staff accused the other of subverting the established primary goal of the mission, alcoholism treatment based upon total abstinence in an alcohol-free environment.

The house manager had almost sole power to dismiss residents from the facility. In principle, he could be overruled by the titular head of the mission, but this rarely happened. As a result of the controversy over dismissal of residents, the mission's management was pressured to agree to a policy put forward by the clinic that dismissal of clinic patients should only be by mutual agreement. The clinic gained this concession primarily because of the money paid for the room and board of clinic patients. This was an important financial resource for the mission, and it gave the clinic leverage not otherwise available. Management's agreement to share social control with the clinic was interpreted by the mission's staff as a sell-out, an indication that money was more important to management than their own responsibility to maintain order in the mission.

The conflict between mission staff and the clinic over these issues became so severe that residents began to have to take sides and distinct camps emerged within the patient population based upon these allegiances. Employment again became the crucial factor in this polarization. The residents were caught in a bind. Since day labor was the only reliable source of ready cash, they were reluctant to offend the head of the day labor office by fraternizing with the clinic personnel, for this might mean being turned away from the day labor office. Clinic personnel also put pressure on the residents: continuing on day labor jobs indicated a patient was not sincere about changing his life style and this activity could bring him into disfavor with the clinic personnel. It was not unusual for team members to request residents to quit the day labor office and formulate a workable training or job development plan in order to receive the special benefits the clinic could offer.

As distinct camps among the residents became visible, a distinct recruitment pattern emerged. The clinic began to recruit surprisingly highly qualified patients through its linkages with various referring agencies. When the clinic began its operation, recruits had been more or less "pot luck." As time passed, clinic patients became differentiated from the typical house non-clinic resident as well as from the alcoholics who populated the surrounding streets. The educational levels of some of these patients were impressive. The list included engineers, accountants, data processing specialists, white collar workers, and numerous skilled craftsmen. Some unique skills were represented, including a former college math professor and a herpetologist. Individuals with high levels of education and skill are not unknown though uncommon among the skid row alcoholic population. The clinic actively recruited this type of client.

The clinic's recruitment pattern can be explained by the need to demonstrate the superiority of their approach to alcoholism treatment. The clinic not only tried to prove its superiority to the mission, it also felt pressure to meet the expectations imposed by the larger county clinic system. They recruited atypical clinic patients because such patients seemed "easy rehabs," if the major problem for the practitioner was to find work for the client, not to train and then place him. This impression was mistaken because all major employment efforts met with failure. Yet the clinic continued to recruit this type of patient. A common request at patient assignment sessions was, "Please give me someone with at least a high school education or preferably some college; they do much better in my group." Given the very low incidence of success with these patients, it is not clear what "doing better" meant. Nevertheless, the preference for skilled and previously successful clients persisted.

A number of clinic patients had little or no previous skid row experience. One reason was the increasing number of recruitment efforts within the criminal justice system (the probation department and the courts) rather than within the surrounding skid row area. Other clinics in the county-wide treatment system but outside the skid row area also referred clients to the mission clinic because it was the only live-in facility available in the county system. Because of this pattern of recruitment and referral, many men were brought to skid row who otherwise might not have come there.

The mission's recruitment pattern also began to change at about the same time, for much the same reason. Admittance from the street came to resemble a referral system. House staff began to screen and admit "walk-ins" only on the basis of personal acquaintance or prior residence in the facility. Those obviously drunk and likely to be troublesome were turned away even though the facility had its own detoxification unit. Skid row residents, and especially those most obviously in need of detoxification and treatment, found it more difficult to gain access to the facility.

While the mission and the clinic came to resemble each other more in terms of the selectivity of their recruitment systems, their relationship with each other grew worse. The mission staff felt the clinic was a waste of time and money, and no longer took pains to hide this opinion. They justified their hostility by claiming the clinic was actually hurting rather than helping residents, that the hand-outs of training, education, transportation, or clothing money the clinic could provide only gave alcoholics wine money. The mission thought the professionals were allowing the patients to con them, thus retarding rehabilitation. Mission staff felt if alcoholics really wanted help, they would come to the mission staff and not play the "clinic game." The mission approach was defined as both morally and technically superior, and the clients who opted for the mission approach were seen as better, more deserving individuals.

As the study drew to a close, both the clinic and the mission staff withdrew from their positions of open conflict and their relationship may be characterized as one of avoidance and indifference. The only continuing positive overlap between the clinic's program and the rest of the mission's treatment efforts was in the area of recreation. The residents reacted posi-tively to bingo, ping-pong, and other forms of recreation provided by the clinic, but little else. The original goal of interorganizational cooperation between the public clinic and the private mission never really became operational.

Internally, the clinic began to concentrate more on perfecting the functioning of the interdisciplinary team, even though the patients in the mission rarely reacted in a positive manner to meeting with the team. Success, always elusive in the mission environment, became harder to achieve and the tenor of the team sessions began to change as more clients were rejected and as the team became steadily more dictatorial with those clients it retained.[4] The team began to withdraw from the treatment arena and the team began to meet more and more often without patients. On several occasions the team shut down the clinic completely to go on day-long retreats. The stated purpose of each of these trips was to "get the team together."

Technological Deficiencies

In time there came a period of evaluation of the role of the clinic in the mission. The religious organization was of little help in this respect because it had never kept records designed to measure program effectiveness. The clinic staff felt at a professional disadvantage because they were saddled with the same success criteria as the rest of the county treatment system, and at the same time had to work with the worst (least employable) clients in the system. Most of the other clinics served more middle-class clients. Much discussion arose in the administration of the county clinic system about eliminating the "unproductive" mission clinic from the treatment system. It is in this context that the technological deficiencies of alcoholism rehabilitation became apparent.

Support for the notion of technological failure came from the role medication played late in the study. Fairly early in the program, as the initial optimism began to wane, the clinic personnel had joined the administrators and staff of this mission in approving the use of antabuse. This reliance on drugs eventually expanded to other kinds of medication, including tranquilizers, and by the time the study ended, thirty-six different kinds of medication were dispensed to house residents. The clinic personnel, so confident of the interdisciplinary team technique earlier, began to abandon this approach to treatment and to rely on medication as a means to control (if not permanently alter) patient behavior, especially drinking behavior. Ironically, a new problem appeared when the abuse and misuse of medication became a major problem in the facility.

The residents reacted negatively to all of the treatment technologies used in the mission environment including the clinic's team approach, the mission's religious program and the Alcoholics Anonymous meetings. The majority of residents saw treatment as something they had to bear in order to stay in the mission.[5] They were acutely aware of the distribution of power, and especially their own lack of power. From their perspective, the major pay-off from treatment was determined

not by its therapeutic (technological) effectiveness, but by the way it affected the individual's position in the mission in terms of privileges and advantages. For instance, when queried about the role Alcoholics Anonymous played in his own rehabilitation, the secretary of the house meeting replied, "I hate A.A." When asked why he was the secretary (house leader) of the A.A. meeting in the mission, he replied, "It was the only good job open, the only one of importance I could get."

INTERPRETATIONS

Many of the problems besetting this relatively small organization are probably also endemic to large scale treatment and social change efforts. For this reason our observations have implications that could lead to a better understanding of massive program failure. Most such programs begin with an ill-defined problem to solve, and have difficulty in agreeing on a consistent technological approach. There is little agreement on how to conceptualize or treat alcoholism, a problem that also characterizes other problem areas such as mental illness, criminality and poverty.

Planning and coordination efforts typically proceed with little understanding of the internal organizational problems likely to be encountered. In the situation analyzed here, for example, the clinic was opened even though the professional staff lacked several vital pieces of information. The clinic personnel did not know how their services would affect the local treatment population, originally intended to be the alcoholics found on this particular skid row. The mission had provided services to some of these alcoholics for a number of years and they were not an unknown group. Yet for reasons that were more financial, organizational and political than therapeutic, the clinic initiated practices that excluded the local treatment population from the mission. Referrals came more and more from the criminal justice system and other agencies even though the local skid row population was a target population in the planning strategy. A system of funding used by the clinic which provided more money for referrals helps to explain this divergence from a major stated goal. Increased availability of money to the organization inadvertently served to exclude many members of the target population from treatment.

Clinic staff were also ignorant of what the mission residents wanted in the way of services and therefore did not anticipate their lack of response to the program. They reacted with bewilderment when the residents rejected their treatment efforts and extensive vocational rehabilitation program. Staff idealism and compassion were steadily eroded by disappointment and cynicism. When surveyed, the residents indicated they wanted medical services, not counseling services, and demonstrated throughout the course of the program that they did not want to return to the world of steady work. Yet the clinic did not abandon its initial strategy in order to reflect these patient preferences. When the team members did change their approach, they turned to medication as a mechanism of control (an indirect confession of failure) more than as a mechanism of treatment. The inference is that the pa-

tients' definition of the problem is a key variable in the success of a treatment program.

The clinic entered the mission environment without an understanding of the mission staff and its existing power structure. The failure to comprehend the power and legitimacy enjoyed by the house manager was a major oversight. There never really was a honeymoon period, and the failure to negotiate a working relationship with the house staff contributed to the conflict which lasted for the duration of the study. The elimination of those professional individuals who had established an unobtrusive relationship with the mission's staff before the clinic started exacerbated this situation.

Looking at the situation from the other side, the house staff became increasingly hostile toward the clinic. This hostility arose partly from the failure of the professional staff to negotiate with them and the feeling that the clinic personnel did not legitimate their skill in dealing with alcoholics. The professional staff never asked them for advice, and the clinic disrupted their position in the power structure of the organization. House staff had to share power over residents with the clinic staff and at the same time did not control the new sources of reward, especially the financial rewards, available to the clinic staff. House staff felt that a ticket to a baseball game, which they could provide, could not compete with offers of long term training, and education, transportation, and clothing allowances.

The clinic team members were unprepared for this hostility and as a result their performance changed dramatically over the course of the study. Resentment toward the religious organization grew as the team came to believe that the religious organization, especially its management, placed little value on them as a treatment resource. The constant plea by the mission for a medical director to oversee the team's activities was crucial here.

The result was that the clinic and the mission staff worked frequently at cross purposes, each attempting to make the other look bad in the eyes of the patients. Each expressed the belief that the other was callous and not using the proper approach to the residents' problems. The factionalism between the two staffs in turn was a source of tension for the residents. They all lived together and exchanged their grievances because no distinction was made between clinic and non-clinic residents in room assignments. The mission did have a high retention rate for this type of facility. Patients averaged slightly over five months in terms of total residence while most likely to be in their second stay within the facility. Despite its problems, the mission still compared favorably with other facilities on skid row even though residents did not see either the mission or the clinic as an avenue to reintegration into the outside world.

Added to these internal problems, the clinic was required to accept unrealistic performance criteria imposed by the larger clinic system. Certainly the initial criterion (ninety days working without drinking) was clear, but the clinic was able to achieve this standard only in rare cases. Actually, to keep patients from drinking was even

more difficult than finding them work. This fact explains why alcoholism treatment, *per se,* was progressively de-emphasized while control occupied more and more attention. The change of the clinic staff's attitude toward antabuse was a reflection of their lack of viable treatment technology.

The clinic team also became much more selective in accepting patients in an attempt to provide better performance indicators. At the same time a harshness and dictatorial tone entered into their contact with patients. Patients who did not accept the teams' definition of the seriousness of their drinking problem, or the teams' plan for treating the problem, were dismissed as "not ready" for treatment. This view was certainly a turn-around from the altruistic and optimistic attitude of the professional staff when the study began. The house staff also became perceptibly harsher in their interactions with patients; and in this respect the clinic and mission staffs became more alike in their relationships with residents.

Eventually, the clinic did manage to have the performance criterion lowered. Ninety days working and not drinking became sixty days of the same. However, the clinic found this criterion no easier to live with, and they ultimately began to disregard the drinking criterion and to concentrate on work only. They actually had no real way of determining whether the client had complied with the official standard unless the client lost his job *because* of drinking or re-entered the mission for being drunk.[6] There were never any clear statistical indicators of success regardless of the criterion utilized. Records were poor, with little cooperation between agencies. Decriminalization of alcoholism made police records unreliable indicators and the changing success criterion meant that individuals could be readmitted and processed as new cases after being previously closed as rehabilitated.

CONCLUSION

This study described factors contributing to the ineffectiveness of a skid row alcoholism treatment organization. Problems involving ill-defined goals, conflicts over resources and vested interests and inadequate technology were discussed, and the section just concluded has indicated how these problems were intensified by a lack of background planning, coordination, and cooperation between subgroups in the organization. The findings support the conclusions reached by others who have reported on the overwhelming ineffectiveness of efforts to intervene in the skid row alcoholism problem (Spradley, 1970; Wiseman, 1970; Rubington, 1973). We can now say with some confidence that part of the reason for failure of ambitious planning and coordinating strategies is the failure to credit these research findings. Certainly, the kinds of problems the clinic encountered in the mission environment were well documented in the literature before the program began and some of these problems could have been minimized or avoided by learning from the mistakes of previous ambitious but ineffective programs.

If any single finding in this study stands out, it is that where the problems discussed here exist and where they are not anticipated and taken into account by planners, no amount of funding will produce an effective program, nor will the recruitment of a young, expert and committed staff, nor the adoption of a model of interorganizational (public and private) cooperation guarantee success. In fact, these ambitious strategies may have directly counterproductive effects. In the present case, the program established an avenue to skid row for clients who might not otherwise have found their way there and at the same time, it deflected the mission from the treatment of many of the alcoholics in the area surrounding the mission, a consequence which seriously questions the wisdom of locating new and largely untested treatment services in an established facility. The consequences may be to erode an established (and, at least partially effective) treatment strategy without creating the conditions of success for a new strategy. In fact, the final conclusion to be drawn from this case history is that the planning and coordinating strategy responsible for creating the clinic actually contributed to the skid row alcoholism problem.

NOTES

1. For a description of the instrument and the sampling procedure utilized, see Fry and Miller, 1975.

2. The physical location of the clinic and some of the residents changed toward the end of the study when a new wing was opened in the building.

3. Another type of mission personnel was found in the mission environment. Known

as salvationists, these individuals engaged in street missionary work and in the spiritual program within the facility. They did not have direct control over the residents.

4. For further discussion of team-patient interaction, see Fry and Miller (1974). We do indicate that patients in the entire county system reacted unfavorably to the team approach and that the entire system experienced problems in delivering service. However, the mission patients appeared to have the most negative reaction among the system client population.

5. An exception to the negative reaction to treatment is the residents' feelings toward medical services. When surveyed, physicians and nurses were overwhelmingly chosen as the occupational groups most qualified to treat alcoholism.

6. The success criterion was an irritation in another way. Clinic personnel were faced with the problem of maintaining contact with patients who began working. Once they received a paycheck, residents tended to want to move out of the facility. Since out-patient services were minimal, the resident who moved out lost support from and contact with the clinic. The staff were faced with the necessity to verify employment status in order to record a success, which was sometimes difficult. As a result, conflict developed between client and clinic because of the staff's insistence that they not move out until they had been working for whatever time period met the success criterion at that time. Yet the clinic never advocated extended out-patient services.

REFERENCES

Etzioni, Amitai.   1961   A Comparative Analysis of Complex Organizations. Glencoe: The Free Press.

Fry, Lincoln J. and Jon Miller.   1974   "The impact of interdisciplinary teams on organizational relationships." The Sociological Quarterly 15 (Summer): 417–431.
   1975   "Observations on an emerging profession." Unpublished manuscript.

Horowitz, J. J.   1970   Team Practice and the Specialist. Springfield, Illinois: Charles C. Thomas.

Perrow, C.   1961   "The analysis of goals in complex organizations." American Sociological Review 26: 854–866.
   1965   "Hospitals: technology, structure and goals." Pp. 910–971 in J. C. March (ed.), Handbook of Organizations. Chicago: Rand McNally.
   1970   Organizational Analysis: A Sociological View. Belmont, California: Wadsworth Publishing Co.

Rubington, E.   1973   Alcohol Problems and Social Control. Columbus, Ohio: Charles E. Merrill.

Spradley, J. P.   1970   You Owe Yourself a Drunk: An Ethnography of Urban Nomads. Boston: Little, Brown & Co.

Thompson, James D.   1968   "Models of organization and administrative systems." Pp. 95–405 in The Social Sciences: Problems and Orientations. The Hague: Mowton/UNESCO.

Warren, R. L.   1973   "Comprehensive planning and coordination: some functional aspects." Social Problems 20: 55–64.

Wiseman, J. P.   1970   Stations of the Lost: The Treatment of Skid Row Alcoholics. Englewood Cliffs, New Jersey: Prentice Hall.

21. An Experiment on the Social Effects of Good Housing

F. Stuart Chapin

Is the condition of a slum family improved by rehousing in a model public housing project? An affirmative answer to this question is assumed as the justification for the expenditure of millions of dollars. Is there any proof of this assumption aside from common sense expectation?

This study is an effort to measure the effects of good housing upon former slum families rehoused in Sumner Field Homes of Minneapolis, originally a project of the Housing Division of the PWA, and since 1937, under the management of the USHA.

The most interesting findings of this study are: (1) no significant change in moral or in general adjustment in 1940 as compared to 1939, either for the 44 "experimental families" resident in the project, or for the "control group" of 38 families residing in the slum; (2) both the resident and control groups gained in social participation from 1939 to 1940, but the resident families gained twice as much in absolute score as the control group; (3) both resident and control groups gained in social status from 1939 to 1940, but the residents showed a gain of greater magnitude; (4) a score made on the "condition of the furnishings of the living room" showed for the residents a striking gain, but for the control group, a

real loss for the 12-month period; and (5) both residents and control groups had improved in the percentage of families "use-crowded" in 1940 over 1939, but the gain of the residents was about three times that of the control group.

Thus the improvements in condition accrue in much larger degree to the residents of the project, and seem to justify the housing program in so far as the facts of this single study are concerned.

Three important questions intrude at this point: (1) were the measures of change or gain reliable and dependable; (2) were the magnitudes of the changes or gains sufficiently large to be significant; and (3) to what extent was rehousing *per se* the cause of these changes or gains? The answer to these pertinent questions requires a description of the methods used in this study.

The study was planned in 1938 to test the hypothesis: the rehousing of slum families in a public housing project results in improvement of the living conditions and the social life of these families. Sumner Field Homes was selected as the test case. In an earlier study of 1935–1936, we reported on the immediate effects of slum clearance and temporary rehousing of 171 slum families.[1] The present

This study was made possible by a grant from the fluid funds of the Graduate School of the University of Minnesota, and was conducted with the cooperation of the USHA and a subcommittee of the Committee on Hygiene of Housing of the APHA. The fieldwork and analyses were under the supervision of Julius A. Jahn, research assistant in sociology.

Reprinted with permission from *American Sociological Review,* Vol. 5, 1940, pp. 868–879.

study is, therefore, a followup conducted upon a more systematic and experimental procedure. To test the hypothesis of improvement, we selected 108 project families (1939) as the "experimental group" and 131 families in slum neighborhoods as the "control group."

The experimental group of resident families were those admitted to the project after December 16, 1938. The families in the control group were living in the slum and were chosen from the "waiting list," i.e., from the group of applicants fully investigated by the USHA agents but not immediately accepted as residents because they lived in poor housing not definitely substandard, or their income was uncertain, or there was some question of economic or social stability. They remained as eligible rejects or deferred cases for later reconsideration provided subsequent applicants did not meet the requirements in sufficient numbers to fill up the project. There were about 603 families in the "waiting list." For the reasons given, they were a group comparable to residents. The control group of slum families was 21.3 percent larger than the experimental group of residents to allow for shrinkage from moving away, refusals or other reasons.

How to measure the effects of good housing? Are residents of the project better adjusted than slum residents? The attempt to measure the effects of good housing utilized four sociometric scales that have been applied successfully in other recent studies: a slum family study in Minneapolis in 1935–1936,[2] and a WPA relief study in St. Paul in 1939.[3]

The scales measure: (1) *Morale,* or the degree that the individual *feels* competent to cope with the future and to achieve his desired goals; (2) *General Adjustment,* or the *feelings* about his relationship to other persons, toward present or future social conditions and toward present social institutions; (3) *Social Participation,* or the degree to which an individual *actually* engages in the organized activities of his community in terms of membership, attendance, contributions, committees, and offices; and (4) *Social Status,* or the position the family occupies with reference to the average prevailing household possessions of other families in the community.

Interviewing of residents and non-residents began in February 1939 and continued intermittently through July 1939, when a total of 239 had been interviewed, 108 residents and 131 non-residents. A group of 12 interviewers, graduate students in sociology and social work at the University of Minnesota, were used. Only two were paid; the remainder were volunteers. The visitors were instructed in a group meeting and each was provided with sheets of typed directions before going into the field. *Entré* to the families was obtained by the visitor stating that he was collecting information about people's opinions as part of a wider study being made under the direction of a university scientist. No mention was made of any connection of this study with the USHA. In this way, it was felt that a more spontaneous response would be obtained. The interview furnished the following data.

Minnesota Survey of Opinions, two sheets with 31 questions about the individual's attitudes, to be filled in by the subject. After the interview, the *Moral score* and the *General Adjustment score* may be extracted from the subject's marked response by a simple system of weighing and scoring. It takes the subject from 20 to 30 minutes to fill this in.[4]

Social Participation Scale, one sheet for entries on each group affiliation of subject recorded in five entries under five columns by the visitor in reply to questions answered by the subject. It takes 10 or 15 minutes to fill in the subject's answers.[5]

Social Status Scale, one sheet containing 21 entries filled in as observations made by the visitor, with perhaps one or two non-inquisitorial questions. Can be completed in 5 minutes' observation.[5]

The flow chart illustrates the actual shrinkage from the initial group of 108 resident families to the final group of 44 resident families, and from the initial group of 131 slum families not resident in the project (called the control group) to the final group of 38 families. At each point in the study, the elimination of families is shown with the reason for it.

The 103 resident families and the 88 nonresident families that were interviewed in 1939 were matched on the following factors:

1. Race or cultural class of husband (Negro, Jew, mixed white);
2. Employment of husband (private, unemployed, OAA, WPA);
3. Occupational class of husband (I-professional, II-managerial, III-clerical, etc., using the Minnesota Rating Scale of occupations);
4. Number of persons in the family (2, 2–3, 3–5, etc.);
5. Income of the family ($690–814, 815–939, etc.).

When so matched, the results of interviewing to obtain scores on *Morale* and on *General Adjustment,* as well as scores on *Social Participation* and *Social Status,* showed the two groups to be very much alike. In fact, none of the critical ratios of the absolute differences in scores were statistically significant and in all cases were −1.01 or less. This result establishes the fact that the initial experimental group and the initial control group matched on five factors began the experiment in 1939 (visiting was from Feb. 1 to July 31) with a common base or zero point from which to measure change or gains.

Five additional matching factors were then added because it was found that the responses on the *Morale* and *General Adjustment* scales were made chiefly by housewives. These five factors were:

6. Race or cultural class of wife;
7. Employment of wife;
8. Occupational class of wife;
9. Age of wife (16–20, 21–30, etc.);
10. Years education of wife (1–4, 5–8, etc.).

This process eliminated 47 cases from the experimental group of residents, and 12 cases from the control group of nonresidents for the reasons shown on the flow chart. This brought us to the end of the 1939 study with measurements on 56 cases of residents and 76 cases of nonresidents or controls.

The next step was taken a year later (Feb. 1 to May 31, 1940), when the followup eliminated 12 more cases from the resident group and 38 more cases from the nonresident group for the reasons listed on the flow chart.

FLOW CHART OF EFFECTS OF GOOD HOUSING IN MINNEAPOLIS, 1939–1940

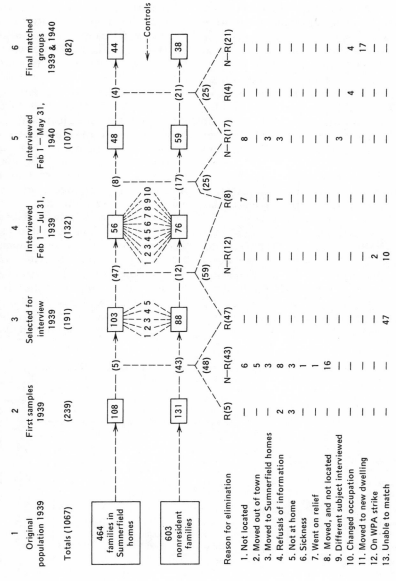

This left final groups of 44 resident families and 38 nonresident families matched on ten factors and which were occupants of the same dwelling unit in 1939 and in 1940. This also added one more constant matching factor.

The mean scores were then calculated for these two matched groups and the 1939 values were compared with the 1940 values. The differences or gains are shown in Table 1, together with the critical ratios of these changes.

It will be observed that the changes in morale and in general adjustment were very small, absolutely and relatively, and that the critical ratios of these changes show them to be not statistically significant (that is, less than 2). On the other hand, the measured changes in social participation and in social status were large in absolute magnitude and were statistically significant. This observation applies with special emphasis to the residents,

who gained more in magnitude and with statistically significant gains.

There are two explanations of the insignificant changes in morale and in general adjustment. First, when the raw scores on Morale and General Adjustment of Table 1 are converted into standard scores by the Rundquist-Sletto tables,[6] it appears that the morale and general adjustment of these housewives of slum families were about at the level of the normal population. Since they were evidently not depressed or variant, it was to be expected that a change in residence for one year would have only slight effect. Second, the Morale and General Adjustment scores of the experimental group in 1939 were obtained after occupancy of a dwelling unit in the housing project, so that if any gain had been experienced in relation to improved housing, it would have taken place earlier. The Survey of Opinions form which yielded the scores on morale and on general

TABLE 1. MEASURED CHANGES ASSOCIATED WITH HOUSING

	Means of Measures of Effect			
Groups Compared	Morale* Scores	General* Adjustment Scores	Social Participation Scores	Social Status Scores
Residents (N=44)				
1939	60.1	45.0	1.73	60.5
1940	60.2	44.0	6.34	86.7
Mean change	0.1	−1.0	4.61	26.2
Critical ratio of mean change	0.12	−0.97	3.69	4.27
Nonresidents (N=38)				
1939	58.0	42.4	2.76	61.1
1940	56.6	41.2	4.87	82.2
Mean change	−1.4	−1.2	2.11	21.1
Critical ratio of mean change	−1.28	−1.34	2.88	3.82

* Reverse scales, hence minus change interpreted as a gain.

adjustment was not part of the interviews conducted by agents of the USHA when making an initial investigation of applicants, since to have included this additional form would have increased the time of interview beyond the limit thought to be appropriate by the USHA; consequently, we were obliged to use this *Survey of Opinions* form in later interviews made by graduate student and social work visitors as described above. However, all of the *Social Participation* and *Social Status* scores, as well as the information as to percentage of families use-crowded, were obtained as part of the initial interviews made by the USHA visitors, and include all of the 1067 families in 1939. The 1940 information on all scales was obtained by graduate students and social workers.[7] Since the changes measured on morale and general adjustment were so indeterminate, our remaining argument will be based upon the substantial changes in (a) social participation, (b) condition of furnishings in the living room, and (c) percentage of families in each group use-crowded.

In order to orient our procedures and findings to the requirements of technical research, we may now re-state our thesis in terms of two null hypotheses: (1) there are no changes in social participation, condition of the living room and in percentage use-crowded, if differences in composition of the experimental group and the control group are held constant in respect to the ten matching factors, race of husband, employment of husband, occupation of husband, number of persons in the family, income of family, race of wife, employment of wife, occupation

of wife, age of wife, and years education of wife; (2) the observed changes in social participation, condition of the living room, and percentage use-crowded, are not greater than those that could occur between two groups selected by random sampling from the same population. If these two null hypotheses are disproved by the results of this study, it will then be permissible to conclude that the assumption of the USHA program of slum clearance and rehousing *has not been disproved by the findings of this experiment.*

It will be observed that one of the conditions of the first null hypothesis is the constancy of the ten matching factors. These factors were held constant throughout the period of the experiment. A further word is relevant, however, as to the procedure in matching. The matching process when carried out in strict manner involves identical individual matching, that is, each individual in the experimental group is matched against another individual in the control group exactly similar in respect to the ten matching factors. Since this rigorous process of matching[8] inevitably leads to heavy eliminations of cases that can not be paired on all factors, we resorted to the expedient of pairing two or more from the experimental group against one case of the control group within a stated range. To put the matter in different phraseology, the families in the nonresident group were paired against the families in the resident group when one or more nonresident families had the same classification according to the list of matching factors as one or more of the resident families. As indicated, this procedure was less rigorous than identical individual matching but gave us greater freedom in the pairing process, prevented excessive elimination of cases, yielded terminal groups of larger size, and was followed by determinate results.

The absolute differences shown in rows (3) and (6) of Table 2 are the evidence for disproof of the first null hypothesis. In short, despite matching on ten factors there were differences between the experimental group and the control group in respect to social participation, condition of the living room and percentage use-crowded. We find in this table, therefore, evidence to disprove the first null hypothesis and consequently to conclude that the assumption of favorable effect of the housing program on slum families is not disproven by the results of this study.

The reliability of the changes appearing in rows (3) and (6) of the table is related, first, to the standardization of the scales used in obtaining the differences, and second, to the size of the standard errors of these differences. As to the first point, namely the stan-dardization of the scales, it may be stated briefly that we have previously published the reliability coefficients and the validity coefficients of these scales, thus displaying the evidence for the claim that both scales are dependable instruments of observation. The second point, namely, the significance of the absolute differences in terms of the standard errors of the differences of the means, may be most satisfactorily considered by comparison of the critical ratios. When a critical ratio of a difference or of a change has a numerical value of 3, the odds of such a difference being due to chance factors in random sampling is about 1 in 370. When the critical ratio is 2, the odds are about 1 to 20. With this in mind, we now consider the last two columns of Table 3.

It will be seen from the last column of this table that the gains made by the resident group are far more significant in terms of probability than the gains of the nonresident group in every comparison. In fact, the only category in which nonresidents made a gain of any appreciable importance was in social

TABLE 2. CHANGES IN MEASURES OF EFFECTS OF HOUSING, 1939–1940

Groups Compared		Rows	Mean Social Participation Scores	Mean Scores, Condition of Living Room	Percentage Use-Crowded
Residents	1939	(1)	1.73	−0.2	50.0
N=44	1940	(2)	6.34	+3.0	6.0
	Mean change	(3)	+4.61	+3.2	−44.0
Nonresidents	1939	(4)	2.76	+3.5	44.7
N=38	1940	(5)	4.87	+2.2	28.9
	Mean change	(6)	+2.11	−1.3	−15.8

TABLE 3. CRITICAL RATIOS OF THE GAINS OR LOSSES OF TABLE 2

Measures of Effects of Housing	Mean Gain of Residents and Nonresidents in Year Period 1939–1940		Critical Ratio of this Gain	Odds of Such a Gain Being Due to Chance Alone in Random Sampling	
1. Social participation	Resident	+ 4.6	+3.69	1 in	4,638 chances
	Nonresident	+ 2.1	+2.88	1 in	267 chances
2. Condition of living	Resident	+ 3.2	+2.28	1 in	46 chances
room	Nonresident	− 1.3	−1.14	1 in	3 chances
3. Decline in percent-	Resident	−44%*	−4.44	1 in	92,593 chances
age use-crowded	Nonresident	− 15.8%*	−1.43	1 in	6 chances

* A decline in percent use-crowded (negative sign) in interpreted as a gain.

participation, but even here the contrast to the gain made by the residents is striking. Since the odds of finding chance differences of this size between 1939 and 1940 are extremely slight for the resident group, and since at the outset and throughout the comparison the resident and nonresident groups were matched on ten factors, we may conclude that there is a high probability that the gains were due to the housing factor; namely, the program of rehousing slum families.

Since the gains in (1) social participation and (2) condition of the living room occur together, that is, appear in the same families for the same period studied, is it not possible to obtain a measure of the probability of occurrence of these factors together or in a pattern? The answer to this question is "yes." There is a probability formula for the so-called "multiple critical ratio" that enables us to combine the two measured differences. When this is used we find that the multiple critical ratio of the residents is 4.23, and of the nonresidents is only 1.23. This means that the odds of finding a combined

difference on these two measurements, or a pattern of differences on these housing factors in the magnitude shown, is one in 37,593 chances for the residents, and only one in 4.5 chances for the nonresidents. This combined analysis shows, therefore, that the probability in favor of the resident's gain not being due to chance is overwhelming.

Final proof that the gains of the residents are *due solely to their improved housing* would require that we had listed all the community and personal influences that operated in the period studied and then controlled by matching, all of these differences *excepting only* the fact that the resident group were in the project and the nonresident group were in the slum. Obviously such a task would have been impossible to perform. We did, however, control by matching ten factors of a personal and social nature, which, if not controlled, might have explained the differences eventually found. With these ten factors controlled or held constant throughout the experiment, we found by application of probability formulas

TABLE 4. SOCIAL PARTICIPATION OF RESIDENT AND NONRESIDENT GROUPS

Social Participation Levels	Residents Frequency of Types of Participation		Nonresidents Frequency of Types of Participation	
	1939	1940	1939	1940
None	29	16	26	13
1. Member	14	44	15	30
2. Attend	12	42	16	30
3. Contribute	13	37	13	24
4. Committee	0	5	1	2
5. Office	0	4	3	3
Total families	44	44	38	38

that the differences measured could not have been due to chance in any reasonable expectation that reasonable persons would insist upon. Consequently, we may conclude that the results of the experiment have disproved the second null hypothesis, and this means that the assumption of the USHA program that rehousing improves slum families has not been disproved.

Sociological research continually reveals the existence of configurations and patterns of several factors. One such pattern of factors discovered in this study was the occurrence together of higher social participation score with improved condition of the living room and less use-crowding. Since we have hitherto been dealing with these conditions in terms of scores (numerical symbols), it may be helpful to show the gross facts of observation from which these scores were derived. Tables 4, 5, 6 and 7 do this.

Table 4 shows that the residents gained at every level of participation at least twice as much as the nonresidents gained. The question now may be asked, what kind of organizations were included in these gains? Table 5 supplies the answer to this question. It will be seen that the greatest gains of the residents were in (1) the Sumner Field Tenants' Association and its subsidiaries, (2) Sunday school, and (3) other organizations. What was the nature of these "other organizations"? Table 6 supplies the facts. It will be seen that in "other organizations," the residents gained by diversification and variety in their social contacts, probably a beneficial gain.

An explanation of the scores on condition of the living room and the subsequent differences or gains in these scores that were summarized in Table 2, can be obtained by examining Part II of the *Social Status Scale.*[9] In spite of the apparent subjectivity of these categories of observation, they are in fact very reliable, as has been shown by coefficients of reliability of $+.72$ to $+.97$ obtained from repeated observations of the same homes.

Table 2, which measures differences and gains in terms of the percentage of

TABLE 5. ORGANIZATIONS PARTICIPATED IN BY RESIDENT
AND NONRESIDENT GROUPS

Types of Social Organizations	Residents Number of Persons Participating			Nonresidents Number of Persons Participating		
	1939 (1)	1940 (2)	Diff. (2–1)	1939 (1)	1940 (2)	Diff. (2–1)
1. Sumner Field Association	0	13	13	0	0	0
mothers' club	0	4	4	0	0	0
2. Neighborhood House clubs	1	1	0	0	1	1
3. Church or Sunday School	7	11	4	16	17	1
clubs	1	2	1	1	2	1
4. Unions	0	1	1	0	1	1
5. Other	6	14	8	7	12	5
Total	15	46	31	24	33	9

TABLE 6. TYPES OF SOCIAL ORGANIZATIONS INCLUDED IN THE
"OTHER" OR MISCELLANEOUS CLASSIFICATION IN TABLE 5

Residents		Nonresidents	
1939	1940	1939	1940
2 Social		2 Social	
2 Insurance		2 Veterans	2 Veterans
1 Bowling		1 Lodge	1 Lodge
1 Bridge	2 Bridge	1 Kindergarten	1 Mother's
	1 Mahjong	mother's club	1 Women's
	1 Home Ec.	1 Scout	1 Scout
	1 Delta Theta Pi		3 Card
	1 W.F.B.A.		(or bridge)
	1 Sokol		
	3 P.T.A.		3 P.T.A.
	1 Charity		
	1 Relief Corps		
	1 Scout		
	1 Citizen's		
6	14	7	12

TABLE 7. CHANGES IN USE-CROWDING OF RESIDENT AND
NONRESIDENT GROUPS

Type of Use-Crowding	Residents N=44		Nonresidents N=38	
	1939	1940	1939	1940
1. Dining room	1	0	3	1
2. Kitchen	0	0	0	0
3. Bedroom, or D. R. & K.	21	3	14	9
4. B. R. & D. R. & K.	0	0	0	1
Total	22	3	17	11

families use-crowded, may be explained by the information contained
in Table 7 above. Here it will be seen
that the 22 families (or 50 percent of
the 44 resident families) classified as
use-crowded, used their living room as
a dining room also in one case in 1939
and had no such double use in 1940.
They used their living room as a bed-
room also, or as a dining room and
kitchen also, in 21 cases in 1939; but
in 1940, there were only three such
cases. This was a real gain in the functional purpose of the living room and
represented less confusion of function
in 1940 than in 1939. Similar analysis
for the nonresident group shows much
less gain in these respects.

Inasmuch as the results of this study
were presented at the beginning, it
may be useful to conclude our discussion with an attempt to place the
methodology of this "experiment" in
relation to similar procedures hitherto
used by the author. Since 1916, we
have been interested in the possibilities
of using "the experimental method" in
sociological research and in 1917, published an early attempt to delineate the
field.[10] This paper was followed by
several others[11] so that we have re-

cently come to the tentative conclusion
that the essential point in the application of a method somewhat like that of
"the experiment" in natural science research is the procedure that we have
called "analysis by selective control."
The present paper is the most complete
application of this method we have yet
attempted. Consideration of the variations in techniques used suggests that
there are three forms of analysis by
selective control. These are stated below.

1. Cross-sectional analysis by selective control, in which an "experimental group" is matched on selected factors against a "control group" for a
given date or time. This form is illustrated in our WPA-Relief study of
1939.[12]

2. Retroactive-retrospective analysis by
selective control, in which an "experimental group" is matched on selected
factors against a "control group" for a
common date or time earlier than the
present, and then followed through to
a present date. This form is illustrated
in the St. Paul high school student
study,[13] made by Mrs. Christiansen.

3. Projected analysis by selective
control (the "normal" experimental de-

sign), in which an initial "experimental group" is matched on selected factors against an initial "control group" for a common date or time, and then followed up for a second series of measurements at a future date or time. The present study of the effects of good housing is an illustration of this third form of analysis by selective control.

NOTES

1. F. Stuart Chapin, "The Effects of Slum Clearance and Re-housing on Families and Community Relationships in Minneapolis," *Amer. J. Sociol.,* March 1938, 744–763.

2. *Ibid.*

3. F. Stuart Chapin, and Julius A. Jahn, "The Advantages of Work Relief over Direct Relief in Maintaining Morale in St. Paul in 1939," *Amer. J. Sociol.,* July 1940, 13–22.

4. These scales and their norms will be found in E. A. Rundquist and R. F. Sletto, *Personality in the Depression,* U. of Minn. Press, 1936.

5. These scales and their norms will be found in F. S. Chapin, *Contemporary American Institutions,* 373–397, New York, 1935; and F. S. Chapin, "Social Participation and Social Intelligence," *Amer. Sociol. Rev.,* April 1939, 157–166.

6. *Ibid.,* 389–391.

7. A year is perhaps only a short time for changes in morale and in general adjustment to register. The very slight gain on these measures shown by the nonresidents reflects perhaps the improvement in economic conditions and in general prosperity. Data on total unduplicated public welfare case count for Minneapolis show a substantial improvement in 1940 over 1939. The index of store sales of the IX Federal Reserve Bank shows a change from 94 for the first six months of 1939 to 97 for the corresponding period of 1940.

8. A systematic analysis of the effects of precision of control by matching appears in our recent article, "A Study of Social Adjustment Using the Technique of Analysis by Selective Control," *Social Forces,* May 1940, 476–487.

9. The portion of the *Social Status Scale* referred to is as follows:

PART II: CONDITION OF ARTICLES IN LIVING ROOM

To provide some objective rating of qualitative attributes of the living room, such as "aesthetic atmosphere" or "general impression," the following additional items may be noted. The visitor should check the words that seem to describe the situation. Some of the weights are of minus sign, and so operate as penalties to reduce the total score of the home.

18. Cleanliness of room and furnishings:
   a. Spotted or Stained (−4) _____
   b. Dusty (−2) _____
   c. Spotless and dustless (+2) _____

19. Orderliness of room and furnishings
   a. Articles strewn about in disorder (−2) _____
   b. Articles in place or in useable order (+2) _____

20. Condition of repair of articles and furnishings
   a. Broken, scratched, frayed, ripped, or torn (−4) _____
   b. Articles or furnishings patched up (−2) _____
   c. Articles or furnishings in good repair and well kept (+2) _____

21. Record your general impression of good taste
   a. Bizarre, clashing, inharmonious, or offensive (-4) ————————————
   b. Drab, monotonous, neutral, inoffensive (-2) ————————————
   c. Attractive in a positive way, harmonious, quiet and restful ($+2$) ————————

10. F. Stuart Chapin, "The Experimental Method and Sociology," *The Scientific Monthly,* Feb. 1917, 133–144; March 1917, 238–247.

11. F. Stuart Chapin, "The Problem of Controls in Experimental Sociology," *J. Educ. Sociol.,* May 1931, 541–551; "The Advantages of Experimental Sociology in the Study of Family Group Patterns," *Social Forces,* Dec. 1932, 200–207; and "Design for Social Experiments," *Amer. Sociol. Rev.,* Dec. 1938, 786–800.

12. F. Stuart Chapin and Julius A. Jahn, "The Advantages of Work Relief over Direct Relief in Maintaining Morale in St. Paul in 1939," *Amer. J. Sociol.,* July 1940, 13–22.

13. F. Stuart Chapin, "A Study of Social Adjustment Using the Technique of Analysis by Selective Control," *Social Forces,* May 1940, 476–487.

22. The Kansas City Preventive Patrol Experiment: A Summary

George L. Kelling, Tony Pate, Duane Dieckman, and Charles E. Brown

INTRODUCTION AND MAJOR FINDINGS

Ever since the creation of a patrolling force in 13th century Hangchow, preventive patrol by uniformed personnel has been a primary function of policing. In 20th century America, about $2 billion is spent each year for the maintenance and operation of uniformed and often superbly equipped patrol forces. Police themselves, the general public, and elected officials have always believed that the presence or potential presence of police officers on patrol severely inhibits criminal activity.

One of the principal police spokesmen for this view was the late O. W. Wilson, former chief of the Chicago Police Department and a prominent academic theorist on police issues. As Wilson once put it, "Patrol is an indispensable service that plays a leading role in the accomplishment of the police purpose. It is the only form of police service that directly attempts to eliminate opportunity for misconduct. . . ." Wilson believed that by creating the impression of police omnipresence, patrol convinced most potential offenders that opportunities for successful misconduct did not exist.

To the present day, Wilson's has been the prevailing view. While modern technology, through the creation of new methods of transportation, surveillance and communications, has added vastly to the tools of patrol, and while there have been refinements in patrol strategies based upon advanced probability formulas and other computerized methods, the general principle has remained the same. Today's police recruits, like virtually all those before them, learn from both teacher and textbook that patrol is the "backbone" of police work.

No less than the police themselves, the general public has been convinced that routine preventive patrol is an essential element of effective policing. As the International City Management Association has pointed out, "for the greatest number of persons, deterrence through ever-present police patrol, coupled with the prospect of speedy police action once a report is received, appears important to crime control." Thus, in the face of spiraling crime rates, the most common answer urged by public officials and citizens alike has been to increase patrol forces and get more police officers "on the street." The assumption is that increased displays of police presence are vitally necessary in the face of increased criminal activity. Recently, citizens in troubled neighborhoods have themselves resorted to civilian versions of patrol.

Adapted from *The Kansas City Preventive Patrol Experiment: A Summary Report* by Kelling *et al.* (Washington: Police Foundation, 1909 K Street, NW, Washington, D.C. 20006, 1974). Reprinted by permission of the Police Foundation.

Challenges to preconceptions about the value of preventive police patrol were exceedingly rare until recent years. When researcher Bruce Smith, writing about patrol in 1930, noted that its effectiveness "lacks scientific demonstration," few paid serious attention.

Beginning in 1962, however, challenges to commonly held ideas about patrol began to proliferate. As reported crime began to increase dramatically, as awareness of unreported crime became more common, and as spending for police activities grew substantially, criminologists and others began questioning the relationship between patrol and crime. From this questioning a body of literature has emerged.

Much of this literature is necessarily exploratory. Earlier researchers were faced with the problem of obtaining sufficient and correct data, and then devising methodologies to interpret the data. The problems were considerable, and remain so.

Another problem facing earlier investigators was the natural reluctance of most police departments to create the necessary experimental conditions through which definitive answers concerning the worth of patrol could be obtained. Assigned the jobs of protecting society from crime, of apprehending criminals, and of carrying out numerous other services such as traffic control, emergency help in accidents and disasters, and supervision of public gatherings, police departments have been apprehensive about interrupting their customary duties to experiment with strategies or to assist in the task of evaluation.

It was in this context that the Kansas City, Missouri, Police Department,

under a grant from the Police Foundation, undertook in 1972 the most comprehensive experiment ever conducted to analyze the effectiveness of routine preventive patrol.

From the outset the department and the Police Foundation evaluation team agreed that the project design would be as rigorously experimental as possible, and that while Kansas City Police Department data would be used, as wide a data base as possible, including data from external measurements, would be generated. It was further agreed that the experiment would be monitored by both department and foundation representatives to insure maintenance of experimental conditions. Under the agreement between the department and the foundation, the department committed itself to an eight-month experiment provided that reported crime did not reach "unacceptable" limits within the experimental area. If no major problems developed, the experiment would continue an additional four months.

For the purposes of measurement, a number of hypotheses were developed, of which the following were ultimately addressed:

(1) crime, as reflected by victimization surveys and reported crime data, would not vary by type of patrol;

(2) citizen perception of police service would not vary by type of patrol;

(3) citizen fear and behavior as a result of fear would not vary by type of patrol;

(4) police response time and citizen satisfaction with response time would vary by experimental area; and

(5) traffic accidents would increase in the reactive beats.

DESCRIPTION OF THE PREVENTIVE PATROL EXPERIMENT

The impetus for an experiment in preventive patrol came from within the Kansas City Police Department in 1971. While this may be surprising to some, the fact is that by that year the Kansas City department had already experienced more than a decade of innovation and improvement in its operations and working climate and had gained a reputation as one of the nation's more progressive police departments.

Under Chief Clarence M. Kelley, the department had achieved a high degree of technological sophistication, was receptive to experimentation and change, and was peppered with young, progressive and professional officers. Short- and long-range planning had become institutionalized, and constructive debates over methods, procedures and approaches to police work were commonplace. By 1972, this department of approximately 1,300 police officers in a city of just over half a million—part of a metropolitan complex of 1.3 million—was open to new ideas and recommendations, and enjoyed the confidence of the people it served.

As part of its continuing internal discussions of policing, the department in October of 1971 established a task force of patrol officers and supervisors in each of its three patrol divisions (South, Central and Northeast), as well as in its special operations division (helicopter, traffic, tactical, etc.). The decision to establish these task forces was based on the beliefs that the ability to make competent planning decisions existed at all levels within the department and that if institutional change was to gain acceptance, those affected by it should have a voice in planning and implementation.

The job of each task force was to isolate the critical problems facing its division and propose methods to attack those problems. All four task forces did so. The South Patrol Division Task Force identified five problem areas where greater police attention was deemed vital: burglaries, juvenile offenders, citizen fear, public education about the police role, and police-community relations.

Like the other task forces, the South task force was confronted next with developing workable remedial strategies. And here the task force met with what at first seemed an insurmountable barrier. It was evident that concentration by the South Patrol Division on the five problem areas would cut deeply into the time spent by its officers on preventive patrol.[1] At this point a significant thing happened. Some of the members of the South task force questioned whether routine preventive patrol was effective, what police officers did while on preventive patrol duty, and what effect police visibility had on the community's feelings of security.

Out of these discussions came the proposal to conduct an experiment which would test the true impact of routine preventive patrol. The Police Foundation agreed to fund the experiment's evaluation.

As would be expected, considerable controversy surrounded the experiment, with the central question being whether long-range benefits outweighed short-term risks. The principal short-term risk was seen as the possibility that crime would increase drastically in the reactive beats; some officers felt the experiment would be tampering with citizens' lives and property.

The police officers expressing such reservations were no different from their counterparts in other departments. They tended to view patrol as one of the most important functions of policing, and in terms of time allocated, they felt that preventive patrol ranked on a par with investigating crimes and rendering assistance in emergencies. While some admitted that preventive patrol was probably less effective in preventing crime and more productive in enhancing citizen feelings of security, others insisted that the activities involved in preventive patrol (car, pedestrian and building checks) were instrumental in the capture of criminals and, through the police visibility associated with such activities, in the deterrence of crime. While there were ambiguities in these attitudes toward patrol and its effectiveness, all agreed it was a primary police function.

Within the South Patrol Division's 24-beat area, nine beats were eliminated from consideration as unrepresentative of the city's socio-economic composition. The remaining 15-beat, 32-square mile experimental area encompassed a commercial-residential mixture, with a 1970 resident population of 148,395 persons and a density of 4,542 persons per square mile (significantly greater than that for Kansas City as a whole, which in 1970

with only 1,604 persons per square mile, was 45th in the nation). Racially, the beats within this area ranged from 78 percent black to 99 percent white. Median family income of residents ranged from a low of \$7,320 for one beat to a high of \$15,964 for another. On the average, residents of the experimental area tended to have been in their homes from 6.6 to 10.9 years.

Police officers assigned to the experimental area were those who had been patrolling it prior to the experiment, and tended to be white, relatively young, and somewhat new to the police department. In a sample of 101 officers in the experimental area taken across all three shifts, 9.9 percent of the officers were black, the average age of the officers was 27 years, and average time on the force was 3.2 years.

The 15 beats in the experimental area were computer matched on the basis of crime data, number of calls for service, ethnic composition, median income and transiency of population into five groups of three each. Within each group, one beat was designated reactive, one control, and one proactive. In the five reactive beats, there was no preventive patrol as such. Police vehicles assigned these beats entered them only in response to calls for service. Their noncommitted time (when not answering calls) was spent patrolling the boundaries of the reactive beats or patrolling in adjacent proactive beats. While police availability was closely maintained, police visibility was, in effect, withdrawn (except when police vehicles were seen while answering calls for service).

In the five control beats, the usual

level of patrol was maintained at one car per beat. In the five proactive beats, the department increased police patrol visibility by two to three times its usual level both by the assignment of marked police vehicles to these beats and the presence of units from adjacent reactive beats.

Other than the restrictions placed upon officers in reactive beats (respond only to calls for service and patrol only the perimeter of the beat or in an adjacent proactive beat), no special instructions were given to police officers in the experimental area. Officers in control and proactive beats were to conduct preventive patrol as they normally would.

It should be noted, however, that the geographical distribution of beats (see Figure 1) avoided clustering reactive beats together or at an unacceptable distance from proactive beats. Such clustering could have resulted in lowered response time in the reactive beats.

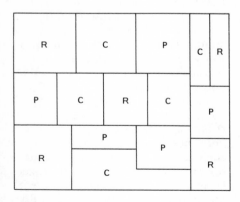

P = Proactive   C = Control   R = Reactive

FIG. 1. Schematic representation of the 15-beat experimental area

It should also be noted that patrol modification in the reactive and proactive beats involved only routine preventive patrol. Specialized units, such as tactical, helicopter and K-9, operated as usual in these beats but at a level consistent with the activity level established the preceding year. This level was chosen to prevent infringement of these specialized units upon experimental results.

Finally, it should be noted that to minimize any possible risk through the elimination of routine preventive patrol in the reactive beats, crime rate data were monitored on a weekly basis. It was agreed that if a noticeable increase in crime occurred within a reactive beat, the experiment would be suspended. The situation, however, never materialized.

While the Kansas City experiment began on July 19, 1972, both department and Police Foundation monitors recognized by mid-August that experimental conditions were not being maintained, and that several problems had arisen. Chief Kelley then saw to it that these problems were rectified during a suspension of the experiment.

One problem was manpower, which in the South Patrol Division had fallen to a dangerously low level for experimental purposes. To correct this problem additional police officers were assigned to the division and an adequate manpower level restored. A second problem involved violations of the project guidelines. Additional training sessions were held, and administrative emphasis brought to bear to ensure adherence to the guidelines. A third problem was boredom among officers assigned to reactive beats. To counter this, the guidelines were modified to allow an increased level of activity by reactive-assigned officers in proactive beats. These revisions emphasized that an officer could take whatever action was deemed necessary, regardless of location, should a criminal incident be observed. The revised guidelines also stressed adherence to the spirit of the project rather than to unalterable rules.

On October 1, 1972, the experiment resumed. It continued successfully for 12 months, ending on September 30, 1973. Findings were produced in terms of the effect of experimental conditions on five categories of crimes traditionally considered to be deterrable through preventive patrol (burglary, auto theft, larceny—theft of auto accessories, robbery and vandalism) and on five other crime categories (including rape, assault, and other larcenies). Additional findings concerned the effect of experimental conditions on citizen feelings of security and satisfaction with police service, on the amount and types of anti-crime protective measures taken by citizens and businessmen, on police response time and citizen satisfaction with response time, and on injury/fatality and non-injury traffic accidents. The experiment also produced data concerning police activities during tours of duty, and police officer attitudes toward preventive patrol.

DATA SOURCES

In measuring the effects of routine preventive patrol, it was decided to collect as wide a variety of data from as many diverse sources as possible. By so doing, it was felt that overwhelming evidence could be presented to prove or disprove the experimental hypotheses.

To measure the effects of the experimental conditions on crime, a victimization survey, departmental reported crime, departmental arrest data, and a survey of businesses were used. While reported crime has traditionally been considered the most important indicator of police effectiveness, the accuracy of both reported crime and arrest data as indicators of crime and police effectiveness has come under scrutiny in recent years. Both types of data are subject to wide degrees of conscious and unconscious manipulation, and to distortion and misrepresentation. Because of these, a criminal victimization survey was used as an additional source of data.

Victimization surveys were first used by the President's Commission on Law Enforcement and Administration of Justice. These surveys revealed that as much as 50 percent of crime was unreported by victims, either from neglect, embarrassment, or a feeling that the crimes were not worth reporting. Although victimization surveys also have their limitations, they can be an important way of measuring crime. Thus a victimization survey was used by the experiment to measure this key outcome variable.

To measure the impact of experimental conditions on community attitudes and fear, attitudinal surveys of both households and businesses (in conjunction with the victimization surveys) and a survey of those citizens experiencing direct encounters with the police were administered. Estimates of citizen satisfaction with police services were also recorded by participant observers.

Overall, in collecting data for the experiment, the following sources were used:

Surveys and Questionnaires

1. Community Survey
   victimization
   attitudes
   rates of reporting
2. Commercial Survey
   victimization
   attitudes
   rates of reporting
3. Encounter Survey—Citizens
   attitudes
   perceptions
4. Encounter Survey—Officers
   attitudes
   perceptions

5. Encounter Survey—Observers
   attitudes
   perceptions
6. Noncommitted Time Survey
7. Response Time Survey
   observers
8. Response Time Survey
   citizens
9. HRD Survey
10. Officer Questionnaire

Interviews and Recorded Observations

1. "Player" Observations
2. Officer Interviews

3. Participant Observer Interviews
4. Participant Observer Transaction Recordings

Departmental Data

1. Reported Crime
2. Traffic Data
3. Arrest Data

4. Computer Dispatch Data
5. Officer Activity Analysis Data
6. Personnel Records

Because many of these sources were used to monitor the degree to which experimental conditions were maintained or to identify unanticipated consequences of the experiment, only findings derived from the following data sources are presented in this report:

Community Survey

The community survey, which measured community victimization, attitudes and fear, was taken on a before and after basis. A sample of 1,200 households in the experimental area (approximately 80 per beat) was randomly selected and interviewed in September of 1972. In September of 1973, 1,200 households were again surveyed, approximately 600 chosen from the same population as the 1972 survey (for a repeated sample) and 600 chosen randomly from the experimental area (for a non-repeated sample). Since 11 cases had to be excluded because of missing data, the 1973 sample totalled 1,189.

Commercial Survey

The commercial survey involved interviews conducted both in 1972 and 1973 with a random sample of 110 businesses in the experimental area to measure victimization rates and businessmen's perceptions of and satisfaction with police services.

Encounter Survey (Both Citizen and Participant Observers)

Because household surveys tend to interview relatively few citizens who have experienced actual contact with the police, citizens in the three experimental areas who experienced direct encounters with police officers were interviewed. Although three survey instruments were developed (one to elicit the response of the citizens, a second for the police officers, and a third for the observers riding with the officers) only the observer and citizen responses were analyzed. Identical questions were used as often as possible. The survey was conducted over a four-month period (July through October, 1973). Interviewed were 331 citizens who were involved in either an officer-initiated incident (car check, pedestrian check or a traffic violation) or citizen-initiated incident (one in which the citizen called for police service: burglary, robbery, larceny, assault, etc.).

Participant Observer Transaction Recordings

While the community encounter survey focused on the location of the police-citizen contact, the observer transaction recordings focused on police-citizen interactions in terms of the assignment of the officer involved

(reactive, control or proactive beats). These data were obtained by observers while riding with officers assigned to the experimental area, and involved observer estimates of citizen satisfaction as a result of direct contact with the police. Observations covered all three watches in all 15 beats. As a result, 997 incidents of police-citizen transactions were systematically recorded.

Reported Crime

Monthly totals for reported crime by beat over the October 1968 through September 1972 (pre-experimental) period and over the October 1972 through September 1973 (experimental) period were retrieved from departmental records. Time-series analyses were then performed on these data to produce the findings.

Traffic Data

Two categories of traffic accidents were monitored: non-injury and injury/fatality. Monitoring was maintained over two time periods, October 1970 through September 1972 for the pre-experimental period, and October 1972 through September 1973 for the experimental period.

Arrest Data

Arrest data by month and beat for the experimental year and the three preceding years were obtained from departmental records.

Response Time Survey

Police response time in the experimental area was recorded between May and September 1973 through the use of a response time survey completed by the participant observers and those citizens who had called the police for service. In measuring the time taken by the police in responding to calls, emphasis was placed on field response time (i.e., the amount of time occurring between the time a police unit on the street received a call from the dispatcher and the time when that unit contacted the citizen involved). In measuring citizen satisfaction with response time, the entire range of time required for the police to answer a call was considered (i.e., including time spent talking with the police department operator, police dispatcher, plus field response time).

Methodology and Maintenance of Experimental Conditions

Because multiple dimensions of the possible effects of the experiment were examined, differing methods of analysis were applied to the data generated. Detailed discussions of these and other factors concerning the experiment's methodology, including a discussion of the sampling error, can be found in the technical report and its appendices. A discussion of the methods used to determine the extent to which desired levels of patrol coverage were achieved, the degree to which experimental conditions were maintained, and whether the criminal world realized that routine patrol strategies had been modified and to what extent patterns of behavior changed as a result can be found in Chapter III of the technical report. In summary, the data sources used to analyze these factors point to the overall maintenance of experimental conditions.

Spillover Effect

One major concern in an experiment of this type is the so-called spillover or displacement theory, i.e., that as crime decreases in one area due to increased police presence, it will increase in other, usually contiguous, areas. This would mean that the effect of the experiment within the experimental area would be offset by counter-effects in other areas. To test this, various correlations between contiguous beats were calculated and analyzed. Except for auto theft, there were no noticeable alterations in the correlations of crime levels. These results, combined with an examination of the actual monthly crime figures, tend to indicate that, in general, there was no spillover effect. Results of the calculations can be found in the appendices to the technical report.

EXPERIMENTAL FINDINGS

The essential finding of the preventive patrol experiment is that decreasing or increasing routine preventive patrol within the range tested in this experiment had no effect on crime, citizen fear of crime, community attitudes toward the police on the delivery of police service, police response time, or traffic accidents. Given the large amount of data collected and the extremely diverse sources used, the evidence is overwhelming. Of the 648 comparisons made to produce the 13 major findings that follow, statistical significance occurred only 40 times between pairs, or in approximately 6 percent of the total. Of these 40, the change was greater 15 times in reactive beats, 19 times in control beats, and 6 times in proactive beats.

Effects on Crime, Reporting and Arrests

Finding 1: Victimization

The Victimization Survey found no statistically significant differences in crime in any of the 69 comparisons made between reactive, control and proactive beats.

This finding would be expected for such categories as rape, homicide and common or aggravated assault. For one thing, these are typically impulsive crimes, usually taking place between persons known to each other. Furthermore, they most often take place inside a building, out of sight of an officer on routine preventive patrol. The spontaneity and lack of high visibility of these crimes therefore, make it unlikely that they would be much affected by variations in the level of preventive patrol.

Given traditional beliefs about patrol, however, it is surprising that statistically significant differences did not occur in such crimes as commercial burglaries, auto theft and robberies.

Nonetheless, as measured by the victimization survey, these crimes were not significantly affected by changes in the level of routine preventive patrol.

Finding 2: Departmental Reported Crime

Departmental Reported Crimes showed only one statistically significant difference among 51 comparisons drawn between reactive, control and proactive beats.

Statistical significance occurred only in the category of "Other Sex Crimes." This category, separate from "Rape," includes such offenses as molestation and exhibitionism. Since this category

is not traditionally considered to be responsive to routine preventive patrol, however, it appears likely that this instance of significance was a statistically random occurrence.

Finding 3: Rates of Reporting Crime

Crimes citizens and businessmen said they reported to the police showed statistically significant differences between reactive, control and proactive beats in only five of 48 comparisons, and these differences showed no consistent pattern.

Of the five instances of statistical significance, three involved vandalism and two residence burglary. But where statistical significance was found, no consistent pattern emerged. On two occasions the change was greater in the control beats, on two occasions greater in the proactive beats, and once it was greater in the reactive beats. Given the low number of statistically significant findings combined with a lack of consistent direction, the conclusion is that rates of reporting crimes by businessmen and citizens were unaffected by the experimental changes in levels of patrol.

Finding 4: Arrest Patterns

Police arrests showed no statistically significant differences in the 27 comparisons made between reactive, control and proactive beats.

While arrest totals for 16 categories of crime were determined, it will be noted that in seven categories—common assault, larceny-purse snatch, homicide, non-residence burglary, auto theft, larceny-auto accessory, and larceny-bicycle—either the number of arrests was too small to allow for statistical analysis, or the pre-experimental pattern of arrests was so distorted that statistical significance could not be determined. On the basis of the comparisons that could be made, however, the conclusion is that arrest rates were not significantly affected by changes in the level of patrol.

Effects on Community Attitudes

Citizen Fear of Crime

The experiment measured community attitudes toward many aspects of crime and police performance to determine whether varying levels of routine preventive patrol—reactive, control, proactive—had any significant effect upon these attitudes. Previous investigators, including Roger Parks and Michael Maltz, have shown that citizens can recognize, or at least sense, changes in levels of service or innovations in policing.

Thus, through the Community and Commercial Surveys which provided the victimization information used in the previous section of this summary, citizen attitudes toward crime and police were also measured before and after the experiment.

The first attitude measured was citizen fear of crime, determined by (1) a series of questions in the Community Survey designed to probe levels of fear; (2) a series of questions in the Community Survey regarding protective and security measures taken by citizens; and (3) questions in the Commercial Survey about protective and security measures used by businessmen at their place of business.

Finding 5: Citizen Fear of Crime

Citizen fear of crime was not significantly

affected by changes in the level of routine preventive patrol.

In the Community Survey, citizen estimates of neighborhood safety and perceptions of violent crimes were obtained. Citizens were then asked what they thought the probability was that they might be involved in various types of crime, including robbery, assault, rape, burglary and auto theft.

Of the 60 comparisons made between experimental areas, statistical significance was found in only five cases. Three involved the probability of being raped, one the probability of being robbed, and one the probability of being assaulted. The change in the level of fear was greater in reactive beats four times and greater in proactive beats once.

Yet when statistical significance is found, the patterns are inconsistent. For example, all cases in which the change in the reactive beats are significantly higher than in other beats are found in the repeated sample. These findings are not confirmed by the non-repeated sample, however. The one area in which control registered the higher change occurs in the non-repeated sample, but this is not confirmed by the repeated sample.

The findings thus lead to the conclusion that citizen fear is not affected by differences in the level of routine preventive patrol.

Finding 6: Protective Measures (Citizens)

Protective and security measures taken by citizens against the possibility of being involved in crime were not significantly affected by variations in the level of routine preventive patrol.

The questions asked of citizens in

the Community Survey on this subject dealt with the installation of such devices as bars, alarms, locks and lighting, the keeping of various types of weapons or dogs for protection, and the taking of certain actions, such as staying inside, as preventive measures.

Here, 84 comparisons were made between experimental areas, with statistical significance occurring 11 times. The significance occurred most often (6 times) in those beats where preventive patrol had not changed, that is, in control beats. The change in the reactive beats showed significance three times, and in the proactive beats twice. There is no apparent explanation for the fact that the use of protective measures supposedly increased in the control beats relative to the other two conditions. For the most part, the findings are inconsistent and occur either in the non-repeated sample or the repeated sample but never uniformly in both.

Thus, as measured by the use of protective and security measures, experimental preventive patrol conditions did not significantly affect citizen fear of crime.

Finding 7: Protective Measures (Businesses)

Protective and security measures taken by businesses in the experimental area to protect offices or other places of business did not show significant differences due to changes in the level of routine preventive patrol.

In the Commercial Survey, businessmen were asked such questions as whether they had installed alarm systems or reinforcing devices such as bars over windows, whether they had hired guards, or whether they kept watch-dogs or firearms in their places of business.

All told, 21 comparisons were made and statistical significance was found once, where the change in the control beats was the greater as compared with the reactive beats.

Because this was a telephone survey, however, some problems with the findings were evident. Briefly, some businessmen were reluctant to talk about protective measures over the phone to persons unknown to them. This is discussed more fully in the technical report.

The conclusion remains, however, that preventive patrol variations seem to have little effect on fear of crime as indicated by protective measures taken by commercial establishments.

Citizen Attitudes Toward Police

In addition to investigating citizen fear of crime and criminals, the preventive patrol experiment delved into citizen attitudes toward the police. Residents in the experimental area were asked, for instance, about the need for more police officers, about variations in patrol, police officer reputations and effectiveness, police treatment of citizens, and about their satisfaction with police service.

The attitudes of businessmen toward police were studied in the course of the preventive patrol experiment for a variety of reasons. One was simply that businessmen's attitudes have seldom been studied in the past, although these people are often affected by crime in ways more crucial to their survival than are citizens in general. It is not only the businessman's personal comfort and safety that may be involved, but also the ability to remain in business that may be affected by crime. At the same time, businessmen are often influential in their communities. For these reasons, assessing their attitudes is often crucial to the development of new policing programs. Therefore, businessmen were asked similar questions about police effectiveness, treatment of citizens and so forth.

While the study of such attitudes is valuable in obtaining the impressions of a significant cross-section of the community, most of the citizens and businessmen interviewed were unlikely to have experienced recent actual contact with the police. Thus, another part of the preventive patrol experiment focused on determining citizens' responses to actual encounters with police officers. To determine such responses, citizens themselves, the police with whom they came in contact, and trained observers were all asked to complete reports on the encounter. Citizens were interviewed as soon as possible after the incident. Separate questionnaires were used, depending on whether the encounter was initiated by an officer or by a citizen.

Finally, a fourth measure was used to determine citizen attitudes. Here, in what has been given the title "Police-Citizen Transactions," the trained observers focused on the outcome of police-citizen interactions in terms of the patrol assignment of the officer involved, that is, reactive, control or proactive.

The next findings deal with citizen attitudes toward police, businessmen's attitudes toward police, police-citizen encounters initiated either by citizens (calls for service) or police (traffic arrests, suspect apprehension, etc.) and finally police-citizen transactions.

Finding 8: Citizen Attitudes Toward Police

Citizen attitudes toward police were not significantly affected by alterations in the level of preventive patrol.

A large number of questions in the Community Survey were designed to measure citizen attitudes toward the police. As a result, more comparisons were made here than in other cases and more instances of statistical significance were found. Altogether, 111 comparisons were made and statistical significance occurred 16 times. Items with significant differences included the need for more police officers in the city, the reputation of police officers, citizens' respect for police, police effectiveness, harassment, and change in neighborhood police officers.

Of the 16 instances of significance, the change in reactive beats was greater five times, in control beats ten times, and in proactive beats once, demonstrating no consistent pattern of statistical significance. The indication is that there was little correlation between level of patrol and citizen attitudes.

Finding 9: Businessmen's Attitudes Toward Police

Businessmen's attitudes toward police were not significantly affected by changes in the level of routine preventive patrol.

Like citizens in the Community Survey, businessmen in the Commercial Survey were asked about their attitudes toward police. Some of the questions in the Commercial Survey were similar to those in the Community Survey and some specially selected with regard to businessmen's interests.

In all, 48 comparisons were made to measure differences in businessmen's attitudes, but no statistically significant differences were found or even approached. The clear indication here is that variations in the level of preventive patrol have no effect on businessmen's attitudes.

Finding 10: Police-Citizen Encounters

Citizen attitudes toward police officers encountered through the initiative of either the citizen or the officer were not significantly affected by changes in patrol level.

Citizen attitudes were measured by both questions asked of citizens themselves and observations of trained observers. Citizens and observers alike were asked about such items as response time, characteristics of the encounter, the attitude and demeanor of officers in the encounter, and citizen satisfaction. Observers in officer-initiated encounters also recorded things not likely to be noted by citizens, including the number of officers and police vehicles present.

Including both citizen-initiated and officer-initiated encounters, a total of 63 comparisons were made and no statistically significant differences were found.

Finding 11: Police-Citizen Transactions

The behavior of police officers toward citizens was not significantly affected by the officers' assignment to a reactive, control or proactive beat.

The finding is distinct from the previous finding in that the focus here is upon the police-citizen interaction in terms of the beat assignment of the officer rather than on the location of the contact. (Many police contacts with citizens take place outside of the officer's beat.) Data were recorded by participant observers riding with the officers.

In all, 18 comparisons were made between experimental areas, and no statistically significant differences were found.

Other Effects

Experimental Findings in Regard to Police Response Time

The time it takes police officers to respond to a citizen call for assistance is usually considered an important measure of patrol effectiveness. The general principle is that the lower the response time, the more efficiently the police are doing their job.

But there are difficulties in determining how to measure response time given the numerous possible segments involved. For instance, is the response time cycle complete when the first officer arrives at the scene? Or when the last of several officers dispatched reaches the scene? Or when the first officer contacts the person making the call? For the purposes of the preventive patrol experiment, response time was defined as the time between receipt of a call from a dispatcher to the point when that unit contacted the citizen involved. In measuring citizen satisfaction with response time, the entire range of time required was considered, beginning with the citizen's contact with the police switchboard operator.

Response time was studied to see if experimental conditions would have any effect on the amount of time taken by police in answering citizen calls for service. Before the experiment began, the hypothesis was that experimental conditions would affect response time, particularly in the proactive beats. It was believed that since more officers were assigned to proactive beats, response time would be significantly reduced in those beats.

Finding 12: Response Time

The amount of time taken by police in answering calls for service was not significantly affected by variations in the level of routine preventive patrol.

To obtain this finding, data were gathered on such matters as distance from police car to scene of incident, mean time from receipt of calls to start of call, mean time from receipt of call to arrival at scene, and observer's estimate of patrol car speed. Citizen estimates of time and satisfaction were also measured.

In the area of response time, a total of 42 comparisons were made between patrol conditions. Statistical significance occurred only once: in the number of officers present at the scene of incidents in the reactive beats. The reason for this is unclear, but it can be theorized that police officers were exhibiting their concern for the safety of fellow officers and citizens in reactive beats.

While variations in the level of patrol did not significantly affect police response time, the Kansas City findings suggest that more research is necessary. It appears that response time is not only the result of rate of speed and distance, but also reflects the attitude of the officers involved and possibly other variables not investigated in this study.

Experimental Findings in Regard to Traffic Accidents

Does police visibility through routine preventive patrol have an effect upon traffic accidents? A common hypothesis is that it does, that reduction in patrol, for instance, will be followed by an increase in traffic accidents. Therefore the preventive patrol experiment involved some study of the presumed relationship.

The finding in this area is presented with considerable caution, however, since traffic patterns played no role in the selection of the experimental beats. It is possible (and in fact likely, given the area involved) that traffic patterns in the experimental area are not representative, and thus would not allow for reliable findings. In addition, the findings involved only accidents reported to the department by citizens and do not take into account accidents which occurred but were not reported.

Finding 13: Traffic Accidents

Variations in the level of routine preventive patrol had no significant effect upon traffic accidents.

A total of six comparisons were made in this area, with statistical significance not occurring in any.

Summary and Conclusion: Experimental Findings

Of the 648 comparisons used to produce the major findings of the preventive patrol experiment, statistical significance between pairs occurred 40 times representing approximately 6 percent of the total. Of these 40 findings, the change in the reactive beats was greater 15 times, in the control beats 19 times, and in the proactive beats 6 times. Given the large amount of data collected and the extremely diverse sources used, the overwhelming evidence is that decreasing or increasing routine preventive patrol within the range tested in this experiment had no effect on crime, citizen fear of crime, community attitudes toward the police on the delivery of police service, police response time or traffic accidents.

POLICE USE OF NONCOMMITTED TIME

Since routine preventive patrol is conducted during noncommitted time (time available for answering calls for service), it was deemed important to determine how officers typically spend their noncommitted time. An observer survey was developed to measure use of noncommitted time and to assess the effects of experimental conditions upon officer allocation of noncommitted time. The survey classified activity during noncommitted time into "stationary," "mobile," and "contacting personnel in the field." Each category was further divided between "police related" and "non-police related."

Over a ten-week period (1,230 hours of observation), some 60 percent of the observed time was found to be noncommitted. This figure varied little from one experimental area to another.

Police patrol officers assigned to the reactive beats tended to spend more of their noncommitted time (22.1 percent) on non-police related mobile and stationary activities (e.g., eating, resting, girl watching, personal phone calls, driving to relieve boredom, pleasure riding) than did their proactive and control counterparts (16.6 percent and 16.4 percent respectively).

Examined in terms of individual police officers, the observations again revealed that regardless of experimental conditions, police officers spent approximately the same amount of their noncommitted time on non-police activities (25.5 percent) as they spent on mobile police-related activities (23.5 percent). Police officers did not typically spend all their time aggressively battling crime.

Six general kinds of noncommitted time activity were noted and classified by the participant observers:

stationary police related (report writing, waiting for tows, surveillance, traffic ordinance enforcement, etc.);

stationary non-police related (eating, resting, reading, rest calls, girl watching, phone calls, visits, sleeping, watching movies or sporting events, etc.);

mobile police related (looking for suspicious cars, people, stolen autos, traffic violations, training new patrol officers, watching buildings and residences, etc.);

mobile non-police related (driving to relieve boredom, girl watching, personal errands, etc.);

contacting personnel in the field, police related (exchanging information about crime suspects, discussing cases, policies, etc.);

contacting personnel in the field, non-police related (general talk about hunting, cars, sex, vacations, jokes, etc.); and *residual* (traveling to and from station, court, garage, headquarters, repair, etc.).

POLICE OFFICER ATTITUDES TOWARD PATROL

Because the primary goal of the preventive patrol experiment was to measure the effectiveness of routine patrol as a crime deterrent strategy, the experiment opened to question a traditionally held theory of policing. Like other departments across the country, the Kansas City Police Department strives to attain its objectives (reduction and prevention of crime, provision of services requested by the public, maintenance of citizen feelings of security, etc.) in large part through patrol activities, including heavy reliance on routine preventive patrol.

Many of the officers involved in the initial stages of the preventive patrol experiment reacted predictably to reduction in routine patrol, warning that the reduction would be quickly followed by increases in crime and citizen fear. Reaction from other officers outside the experimental area was similar.

It was felt, therefore, that an assessment of officer attitudes toward patrol and toward the experiment itself would provide valuable information and be highly relevant to the issues at hand. To gather information, a questionnaire was designed and distributed to all police officers assigned to the 15-beat experimental area.[2] In addition, officer interviews, participant observer interviews, a human resources development questionnaire (administered department-wide by the Police Foundation and the department for general use) and discussions with Police Academy training personnel were also used.

Discussions with academy officials and Kansas City police officers lead to the conclusion that the tradition of preventive patrol is passed on to new officers in a very informal manner. A Kansas City police officer's initial exposure to the patrol concept occurs at the academy, where guest speakers from various units of the department incorporate the concept of routine patrol into their talks whenever relevant. This in itself tends to imply that routine preventive patrol is considered a primary method for apprehending criminals and reducing and preventing crime. No formal attempt, however, is made to provide police recruits with a systematic assessment of the value, methods or effectiveness of preventive patrol.

Kansas City police officers receive their first field experiences under the supervision of training officers, whose influence upon the recruits is clearly significant. For while recruits are receiving a practical field experience, the training officers are further reinforcing the perceived efficacy of routine preventive patrol through a myriad of informal techniques. This process fails, however, to provide recruits with a method of assessing the utility of individual patrol activities. It places the recruits in a position of having to determine for themselves the value of routine preventive patrol only after having been influenced by the duties and responsibilities already encountered in the field and as interpreted by their training officers.

The informal training given to recruits appears to stress the development of a "systematically unsystematic" approach to patrol. No alternative methods are suggested. As a result, the officer's only option lies in the choice of location of patrol (within an assigned boundary) rather than in method. The ambiguity in this approach results in varied orientations toward patrol among supervising sergeants as well as patrol officers.

One source of data used to determine the importance attached to the patrol function by police officers was the Human Resources Development questionnaire, which asked, among other things, how respondents rated the patrol function in terms of its importance within the department, and how much time they felt the department should allocate to that function. Three-fourths of those surveyed in the South Patrol Division more than moderately agreed that routine patrol was the most important function of the department, while most officers then indicated that patrol, along with investigating crimes and assisting in emergencies, was the most important activity to which department time should be allocated.

But in-depth interviews with 18 police officers and the six observers revealed two distinct orientations toward patrol and an ambivalence toward patrol's value. On the one hand, many of the officers interviewed felt that patrol was less effective in preventing crime than it was in enhancing citizen feelings of security. (One possible reason for this could be the fact that few crimes-in-progress are come upon by patrolling officers, and thus "good" arrests—resulting in the clearance of a crime—rarely result from routine patrol activity.) On the other hand, many officers tended to feel that such basic

preventive patrol activities as car, pedestrian and building checks were instrumental in the apprehension of criminals and the deterrence of crime, despite the infrequency of criminal arrests resulting from such checks. (Albert Reiss cites a New Orleans police study which found that only 15.5 percent of some 40,375 pedestrian checks resulted in arrests, while a 1972–1973 survey undertaken by the South Patrol Task Force in Kansas City found that only 6.1 percent of 1,002 patrol stops resulted in arrests.)

A majority of the interviewed officers said the only way to increase patrol's deterrent effectiveness would be through the greater use of unmarked police vehicles, i.e., a move toward less visibility. Another change frequently favored was fewer uniformed and more plainclothes officers. Those surveyed seemed to feel that the police uniform was most useful as a symbolic tool for eliciting immediate response to authority in situations where deference to authority was the quickest path to order. But they cited the uniform's obvious disadvantage of affording criminals instant recognition of police presence. A similar viewpoint argued for the greater use of unmarked police vehicles. The officers felt that clearly marked police vehicles helped in the prevention of automobile accidents and tended to enhance citizen feelings of security. But on the other hand, many of the officers felt that marked cars militated against the apprehension of criminals by again affording instant recognition. The general consensus among those interviewed was that officers should be allowed to drive not only departmental unmarked cars (with spotlights and two-way radio antennas) but also their own personal vehicles or cars similar to those driven by civilians.

AUTHORS' OBSERVATIONS AND CONCLUSIONS

The initial impetus behind the Kansas City preventive patrol experiment was the issue of time and staff resources. When the South Patrol Task Force began its deliberations, the concern was that any serious attempt to deal with priority problems would be confounded by the need to maintain established levels of routine patrol. Thus, in addition to testing the effect of various patrol strategies on such factors as crime, citizen fear and satisfaction, and response time, the experiment equally addressed the question of whether adequate time can be channeled to the development, testing and evaluation of new approaches to patrol.

From the beginning phases of this experiment, the evaluators formed hypotheses based upon certain assumptions. One primary assumption was that the police, as an institutionalized mechanism of social control, are seriously limited in their ability to both prevent crime and apprehend offenders once crimes have been committed. The reasons for these limitations are many and complex. But they include the very nature of the crime problem itself, the limits a democratic society places upon its police, the limited amount of resources available for crime prevention, and complexities within the entire criminal justice system.

As a result of these limitations, many have rightly suggested that we must now begin revising our expectations as to the police role in society.

Because there are programmatic implications in the findings of this experiment, several cautionary comments are offered.

During the course of the experiment a number of preliminary findings were reported initially and subsequently reprinted in and editorialized upon in many major newspapers. A weekly news magazine carried a brief and cryptic report on the experiment, suggesting that it had produced evidence that patrol officers were unnecessary. This was subsequently picked up by a television network and given further exposure. Public response to these stories was unfortunate, but predictable. Unfamiliar with the issues of the experiment, and yet highly sensitive to these issues, some saw the study as justification for limiting or reducing the level of policing. Many saw it as a justification for two-officer cars. Others, fearing some of the conclusions drawn above, simply rejected the study out of hand.

Such implications are unfortunate. Given the distinct possibility that the police may more effectively deal with the problems of crime if they work more closely and systematically with their communities, it may be that an increase rather than a decrease in the number of police is warranted. It may be that, given a different orientation and strategy, an increase in the number of police would increase chances for preventing crime. Those who drew manpower reduction conclusions from the preliminary findings assumed that if the crime prevention strategies currently being used did not work, no crime prevention strategies would work. This is not believed to be the case and such an implication is not supported by this study. Police serve a vital function in society, and their presence is of real and symbolic importance to citizens.

Nor does this study automatically lead to any conclusions about such programs as team policing, generalist-specialist models, minority recruitment, professionalization of the police or community relations programs. These are all package phrases embracing a wide variety of programs. While some recent works attempt to define the exact nature of these programs, most such terms remain ambiguous and for some, offensive.

These programs are attempting to deal with particular problems in the field of policing, including police and citizen alienation, the fragmented nature of police work, the inability to provide adequate supervision for police officers, the inability to coordinate the activities of officers in a variety of areas, the inability to adequately transmit information from officer to officer, from beat to beat, and from watch to watch, and the antiquated, quasi-military organizational structure in predominant use. These problems exist, but they were not the concern of this study.

The relevance of this study is not that it solves or even attempts to address many of these issues which admittedly are interdependent and central to the ability of the police to deal with crime. Rather, the experiment has demonstrated that the time and staff resources do exist within police departments to test solutions to these problems. The next step, therefore, will be to use that time and these findings in the development of new approaches to both patrol and policing.

NOTES

1. In this report, routine preventive patrol is defined as those patrol activities employed by the Kansas City Police Department during the approximately 35 percent of patrol duty time in which officers are not responding to calls for service, attending court or otherwise unavailable for self-initiated activities. (The 35 percent figure was a pre-experimental estimate developed by the Kansas City Police Department for use in determining officer allocation.) Information made available daily to patrol officers includes items such as who in their beats is wanted on a warrant, who is wanted for questioning by detectives, what criminals are active in their beats and type and location of crimes which have occurred during the previous 24 hours. The officers are expected to be familiar with this information and use it during their non-committed time. Accordingly, routine preventive patrol includes being guided by this information while observing from police cars, checking on premises and suspicious citizens, serving warrants, checking abandoned vehicles, and executing other self-initiated police activities. Thus routine preventive patrol in Kansas City is informed activity based upon information gathered from a wide variety of sources. Whether Kansas City's method of preventive patrol is typical is hard to say with exactness. Clearly, some departments place more emphasis on pedestrian checks, car checks, and field interrogating than does Kansas City (experiments on some of these activities are now taking place elsewhere). Preventive patrol as practiced in Kansas City has some unique characteristics but for the most part is typical of preventive patrol in urban areas.

2. A 90+ percent response rate was generated.

23. The Impact of Head Start: Executive Summary

Victor Cicarelli

This report presents the results of a study on the impact of Head Start carried out for the Office of Economic Opportunity from June 1968 through May 1969 by Westinghouse Learning Corporation and Ohio University.

The study attempted in a relatively short period of time to provide an answer to a limited question concerning Head Start's impact; namely: Taking the program as a whole as it has operated to date, to what degree has it had psychological and intellectual impact on children that has persisted into the primary grades?

The very real limitation of our study should be established at once. The study did not address the question of Head Start's medical or nutritional impact. It did not measure the effect of Head Start on the stability of family life. It did not assess the impact of Head Start on the total community, on the schools, or on the morale and attitudes of the children while they were in the program. The study is therefore a limited and partial evaluation, but one based on solid, useful, and responsible research.

We were not asked to answer all the questions that might have been asked. Those that we did ask (and answer), however, were the right questions to ask first. This is an ex post facto study; we therefore did not have the opportunity to observe the Head Start classrooms whose output we measured, nor could we attempt to ascertain various kinds of secondary social or mental health benefits.

The basic question posed by the study was:

To what extent are the children now in the first, second, and third grades who attended Head Start programs different in their intellectual and social-personal development from comparable children who did not attend?

To answer this question, a sample of one hundred and four Head Start centers across the country was chosen. A sample of children from these centers who had gone on to the first, second, and third grades in local area schools and a matched sample of control children from the same grades and schools who had not attended Head Start were administered a series of tests covering various aspects of cognitive and affective development (listed below). The parents of both the former Head Start enrollees and the control children were interviewed and a broad range of attitudinal, social, and economic data was collected. Directors or other officials of all the centers were interviewed and information was collected on various characteristics of the current local Head Start programs. The primary grade teachers rated both groups of children on achievement motivation and supplied a description of the in-

Reprinted with permission from *The Impact of Head Start: An Evaluation of the Effects of Head Start on Children's Cognitive and Affective Development,* Vol. 1 (Bladensburg, Md.: Westinghouse Learning Corp., June 1969), pp. 1–11. This volume is out-of-print. It is available only through the Educational Resources Information Center (ERIC).

tellectual and emotional environment of their elementary schools.

Analyses of comparative performances on the assessment measures of all children in the study were conducted for each selected center area. Findings were combined, then, into the total national sample (called the overall analysis) and into three major subgroupings of centers formerly attended by the Head Start children, the latter being classified by geographic region, city size, and racial/ethnic composition. All the findings were also related to the type of program attended, i.e., summer or full-year program.

The major findings of the study are:

1. In the overall analysis for the *Metropolitan Readiness Tests (MRT)*, a generalized measure of *learning readiness* containing subtests on word meaning, listening, matching, alphabet, numbers, and copying, the Head Start children who had attended full-year programs and who were beginning grade one were superior to the controls by a small but statistically significant margin on both "Total Readiness" and the "Listening" subscore. However, the Head Start children who had attended summer programs did not score significantly higher than the controls. (This particular cognitive measure was used in grade one because it does not require the ability to read.)

2. In the overall analysis for the *Stanford Achievement Test (SAT)*, a general measure of children's *academic achievement*, containing subtests on word reading, paragraph meaning, spelling, arithmetic, and so on, used to measure achievement at grades two and three, the Head Start children from both the summer and the full-year pro-

grams did not score significantly higher than the controls at the grade two level. While the children from the summer programs failed to score higher than the controls at grade three, an adequate evaluation of the effect of the full-year program at this grade level was limited by the small number of programs.

3. In the overall analysis for the *Illinois Test of Psycholinguistic Abilities (ITPA)*, a measure of *language development* containing separate tests on auditory and vocal reception, auditory and visual memory, auditory-vocal association, visual-motor association, etc., the Head Start children did not score significantly higher than the controls at any of the three grade levels for the summer programs. In the case of the full-year programs, two isolated differences in favor of Head Start were found at grade two for two subtests of the *ITPA*, namely, "Visual Sequential Memory" and "Manual Expression."

4. In the overall analysis for the *Children's Self-Concept Index (CSCI)*, a projective measure of the degree to which the child has a *positive self-concept*, the Head Start children from both the summer and the full-year programs did not score significantly higher than the controls at any of the three grade levels.

5. In the overall analysis for the *Classroom Behavior Inventory (CBI)*, a teacher rating assessment of the children's *desire for achievement* in school, the Head Start children from both the summer and the full-year programs did not score significantly higher than the controls at any of the three grade levels.

6. In the overall analysis for the *Children's Attitudinal Range Indicator*

(*CARI*), a picture-story projective measure of the child's *attitudes toward school, home, peers, and society,* the Head Start children from the full-year programs did not score significantly higher than the controls at any of the three grade levels. One isolated positive difference for summer programs was found on the "Home" attitude subtest at grade one.

7. The above findings pertain to the total national sample. As mentioned previously, additional analyses were made for three subgroups of the national sample: geographic regions, city-size groups, and racial/ethnic composition categories. Analysis of the summer programs by subgroups revealed few differences where Head Start children scored higher than their controls. *Analysis of the full-year programs by the same subgroupings revealed a number of statistically significant differences in which, on some measures (mostly subtests of cognitive measures) and at one or another grade level, the Head Start children scored higher than their controls.* There were consistent favorable patterns for certain subgroups: where centers were in the Southeastern geographic region, in core cities, or of mainly Negro composition. Even though the magnitudes of most of these differences were small, they *were* statistically significant and indicated that the program evidently had had some limited effect with children who had attended one or another of these types of full-year centers.

8. Apart from any comparison with control groups, the scores of Head Start children on cognitive measures fall consistently below the national norms of standardized tests. While the former

Head Start enrollees approach the national level on school readiness (measured by the *MRT* at first grade), their relative standing is considerably less favorable for the tests of language development and scholastic achievement. On the *SAT* they trail about six-tenths of a year at second grade and close to a full year at grade three. They lag from seven to nine months and eight to eleven months respectively on the *ITPA* at first and second grades.

9. Parents of Head Start children expressed strong approval of the program and its effect on their children. They reported substantial participation in the activities of the centers. Parents of full-year enrollees tended to be slightly better educated but with a slightly lower income than parents of summer enrollees; summer programs enrolled a larger proportion of white children.

Viewed in broad perspective, the major conclusions of the study are:

1. Summer programs appear to be ineffective in producing any gains in cognitive and affective development that persist into the early elementary grades.

2. Full-year programs appear to be ineffective as measured by the tests of affective development used in the study, but are marginally effective in producing gains in cognitive development that could be detected in grades one, two, and three. Programs appeared to be of greater effectiveness for certain subgroups of centers, notably in mainly Negro centers, in scattered programs in the central cities, and in Southeastern centers.

3. Head Start children, whether from summer or from full-year pro-

grams, still appear to be considerably below national norms for the standardized tests of language development and scholastic achievement, while performance on school readiness at grade one approaches the national norm.

4. Parents of Head Start enrollees voiced strong approval of the program and its influence on their children. They reported substantial participation in the activities of the centers.

An analysis of covariance random replications model was used for the main analysis of the data obtained in this study. This statistical procedure was cross-checked by both a non-parametric analysis (with appropriate matchings) and an analysis of covariance with individuals rather than centers as the basic unit. Overall results with all procedures were similar.

In sum, the Head Start children can not be said to be *appreciably* different from their peers in the elementary grades who did not attend Head Start in most aspects of cognitive and affective development measured in this study, with the exception of the slight but nonetheless significant superiority of full-year Head Start children on certain measures of cognitive development.

A variety of interpretations of the data are possible. Our measures were taken after children had been out of Head Start from one to three years, in order to detect persisting effects. It is conceivable that the program does have a significant impact on the children but that the effect is matched by other experiences, that it is contravened by the generally impoverished environment to which the disadvantaged child returns after he leaves the Head Start

program, or that it is an intellectual spurt that the first grade itself produces in the non-Head Start child. Or it is possible that the Head Start program has a significant impact on the children who attended, but that the presence of these improved children in the classroom has raised the level of the whole class to the point where there are no longer statistically reliable differences between the Head Start and non-Head Start children. A further possibility exists that Head Start has been of considerable impact where adequately implemented, but lack of more positive findings reflects poor implementation of the program. Or it is possible that Head Start has been effective only with certain types of pupils, and so on.

In any case, the study indicates that Head Start as it is presently constituted has not provided widespread significant cognitive and affective gains which are supported, reinforced, or maintained in conventional education programs in the primary grades. However, in view of the mixed results from the full-year findings, the impact on the parents, the obvious values of the medical and nutritional aspects of the program, and the critical need for remediating the effects of poverty on disadvantaged children, we make the following recommendations:

1. Summer programs should be phased out as early as feasible and converted into full-year or extended-year programs.

2. Full-year programs should be continued, but every effort should be made to make them more effective. Some specific suggestions are:

a. Making them a part of an intervention strategy of longer duration, perhaps extending downward toward infancy and upward into the primary grades.

b. Varying teaching strategies with the characteristics of the children.

c. Concentrating on the remediation of specific deficiencies as suggested by the study, e.g., language deficiencies, deficiencies in spelling or arithmetic.

d. Training of parents to become more effective teachers of their children.

3. In view of the limited state of knowledge about what would constitute a more effective program, some of the full-year programs should be set up as experimental programs (strategically placed on a regional basis), to permit the implementation of new procedures and techniques and provide for an adequate assessment of results. Innovations which prove to be successful could then be instituted on a large scale within the structure of present full-year programs. Within the experimental context, such innovations as longer period of intervention or total family intervention might be tried.

4. Regardless of where and how it is articulated into the structure of the federal government, the agency attempting the dual research and teaching missions presently assigned Head Start should be granted the focal identity and organizational unity necessary to such complex and critical experimental programs. Their basis of funding should take cognizance of both the social significance of these missions and the present state-of-the-art of programs attempting to carry them out.

In conclusion, although this study indicates that full-year Head Start appears to be a more effective compensatory educational program than summer Head Start, its benefits cannot be described as satisfactory. Therefore we strongly recommend that large-scale efforts and substantial resources continue to be devoted to the search for more effective programs, procedures, and techniques for remediating the effects of poverty on disadvantaged children.

24. Head Start: Comments on the Criticisms

John W. Evans

Since its release, the Westinghouse study has occasioned considerable, even bitter, debate. If we are to understand the heat that has spiced this controversy, in my opinion we must look less to the purely methodological issues in the exchange and more to the fact that the findings of the study have been difficult to accept. Head Start has been the showcase program of the war on poverty. As a bold new effort to prevent the numbing effects of poverty on small children, it elicited immediate national sympathy as well as the support and involvement of the education profession. It is not surprising that so many have rushed to the defense of such a popular and humane effort. I am persuaded, however, that if the study had found positive Head Start effects there would have been very few questions raised about adequacy of sample size, the appropriateness of covariance analysis, the matching of control and experimental groups, etc. In the eyes of many, the Westinghouse study attacks Head Start and this is being mean to kids.

Motivation and social conscience aside, however, we are still left with the question, "Is the study any good?" My answer is yes, and I'll try to set forth the reasons why I think so and why I think many of the criticisms that have been made of the study have very limited validity in the context of evaluating ongoing social action programs. In doing this I should make clear that I am a protagonist in the debate. The study was designed in my office and we contracted for it to be carried out.

With the study now completed and the criticisms of it before us, it remains my judgment that it is by far the best evaluation that has been carried out on Head Start and provides the best evidence we have on the program's overall effectiveness in the all-important areas of cognitive and social personal development.

Below I cite the major criticisms that have been made of the study and comment on each of them.

1. The study is too narrow. It focuses only on cognitive and affective outcomes. Head Start is a much broader program that includes health, nutrition, and community objectives, and any proper evaluation must evaluate it on all these objectives.

It is true the Westinghouse study did not evaluate all aspects of Head Start. It was explicitly limited to the cognitive and affective objectives and this limitation is clearly stated in several places in the report. The limitation was made for several reasons. First, our experience has been that one of the reasons why so many evaluations have failed to produce much of anything is because they have aspired to do too

Reprinted with permission from *Britannica Review of American Education*, Vol. 1, 1969, edited by David G. Hays. (Chicago: Encyclopaedia Britannica, Inc., 1969), pp. 253–260.

much. We did not think it was feasible to cover all the Head Start objectives in the same study, so we purposely limited the study's focus to those we felt were most important. Second, despite its many other objectives, in the final analysis Head Start must be evaluated on the extent to which it has affected the life chances of the children. In order to achieve such effects, cognitive and motivational changes are essential. Third, while Head Start has objectives other than cognitive and affective change, these other objectives are in large part *instrumental* to the cognitive and affective objectives. That is, the program is attempting to improve children medically and nutritionally *in order to* make it possible to change them cognitively and motivationally. This means that one need not necessarily look directly at success on the instrumental objectives in order to determine whether or not success is being achieved on the ultimate cognitive and affective objectives. Finally, even if these arguments are discounted, it seems clear that among all of its objectives, the cognitive and affective ones are so important that failure to achieve success on them should cause us to be seriously concerned about the program even if we agree it is successful in achieving its nutritional, medical, and other objectives.

2. The study fails to give adequate attention to variation within the Head Start program. It lumps Head Start programs together into an overall average and does not explore what variation there may be in effectiveness as a function of differing program styles

and characteristics. The study, therefore, fails to give any guidance as to what changes in the program should be made.

This criticism is essentially correct. The limited and explicit purpose of this evaluation was to provide an indication of the overall effectiveness of the Head Start program, an indication long sought by Congress and the Bureau of the Budget but one that could not be gleaned from any of the previous evaluations done of Head Start. Most of the previous studies were done without control groups and were not based on national samples. As a result, it was not possible to get from them the answer to the question, "How effective on the whole has the Head Start program been in improving children's motivation and cognitive abilities?" This was the limited question this study addressed. It purposely did not get into detailed measurement of program variation because it wished to provide an answer to the basic question in a reasonably short period of time and because a division of labor had been established within the Office of Economic Opportunity (OEO) whereby the Office of Research, Plans, Programs, and Evaluation (RPP&E), a staff office overseeing all OEO programs, would take responsibility for the evaluation of the overall effectiveness of all OEO programs, and the respective program offices (e.g., Head Start) would be responsible for evaluations of the effect of different program variables, strategies, and techniques.

3. The sample of full-year centers in the study is too small to provide confidence in the study's

findings. Because of such a small sample, the lack of statistically significant differences between the Head Start and control groups is to be expected and gives a misleading indication of no program effect. With such a small sample it would take quite large differences to reach a satisfactory level of statistical significance. Thus, many differences that are of an appreciable *practical* magnitude fail to achieve statistical significance because of the small sample.

The randomly selected 104 Head Start centers were chosen in order to provide an adequate *total* sample which was then broken down in an approximate 70–30 division to reflect the proportion of summer and full-year programs. On retrospect this was an erroneous and unnecessary decision since we decided relatively early we would at no time combine the summer and full-year samples. If we were doing the study over, we would select a larger number of full-year centers. The main advantage of a larger number of full-year centers, however, would be to allow more analysis of subgroups within the full-year sample. It is unlikely the study's principal conclusions would be altered by a larger sample. A detailed "power of the test" analysis showed that with the present sample size and variance, the statistical tests are capable of detecting differences between the experimental and control groups below the level of what would be practically meaningful (Madow's comments to the contrary notwithstanding).

4. The sample is not representative. Many of the original randomly chosen centers had to be eliminated.

It is likely the sample is not perfectly representative of the entire universe of Head Start centers. It is, however, as representative as it is practically possible for any sample to be. There were two main reasons for not being able to include all of the centers from the original random selection. First, in some small rural locations nearly all eligible children had been included in the Head Start program and it was therefore not possible in these communities to locate any control children (i.e., those who were eligible for Head Start but had not attended). Second, in some communities a local rule prohibited testing of children in the school system. These factors will affect the sample of any study and are simply restricting conditions we will have to live with. When these conditions occurred and centers had to be rejected, substitute centers were randomly chosen to replace them. Comparison of the final sample with the total universe of Head Start centers showed the two to be very similar on rural-urban location, racial composition, size of the center, teacher-pupil ratio, kind of staff services, median age of the children at enrollment, parent participation, and program objectives.

5. The measures used in this study and indeed all existing instruments for measuring cognitive and affective states in children are primitive. They were not developed for disadvantaged populations and they are too gross and insensitive to pick up the real and

important changes Head Start has produced in children. This is especially true of the unvalidated affective measures used in the study.

It is entirely possible that this is true. However, most of the cognitive measures are the same ones being used by other child development and Head Start researchers doing work on disadvantaged children. In those relatively few cases where previous studies have shown positive changes on these very same measures, they have seldom been questioned or disregarded because of the inadequacy of the instruments. The Westinghouse study attempted to use the best instruments available. Many of them have been used on disadvantaged populations. The results of the study merely say that, using the best instrumentation available, few appreciable differences are found between children who had Head Start and those who did not. If someone wishes to argue that the instruments are worthless, this is certainly a point of view that can be taken. Such a view, however, seems more of an effort to find some way to reject the study's unpleasant findings than an impartial effort to assess the evidence in hand. There are only two choices: we can use the instruments we have or we can substitute our personal judgments about Head Start's impact. I think it is important to temper the latter with the former. No great claims are made for the affective instruments. The Westinghouse staff found after exploration that no instruments were available so they developed some. The limited experiences in this study do not provide enough

evidence to determine whether their efforts were successful or not.

6. The study is based on an ex post facto design which is inherently faulty because it attempts to generate a control group by matching, post facto, the Head Start children with other non-Head Start children. Since we can never be sure that the two groups have been matched on all relevant factors (e.g., parental motivation in getting their children into the program, etc.), the study may be comparing two unlike groups. If so, this would obscure the effect of Head Start.

It is always possible in any ex post facto study that failure to achieve adequate matching can occur. Ex post facto studies, however, are a respected and widely used scientific procedure if not one that provides the greater certainty of the classic before-after experimental design carried out in controlled laboratory conditions. This study was intentionally designed as an ex post facto study because of time considerations. It took nearly a year to complete; a longitudinal study would have required four or five years. Longitudinal studies are better and they should be done. But in the interim we need some basis for judging program effectiveness that is more rigorous and objective than our personal judgment. In the Westinghouse study the two groups were matched on age, sex, race, and kindergarten attendance. Any residual differences in socioeconomic status were equated by two different statistical procedures, a random replication covariance analysis and in a nonparametric matching procedure. Both statistical techniques, which equated the two groups on parents' occupation, education, and per capita income, yielded the same results.

7. The study tested the children in the first, second, and third grades of elementary school—after they had left Head Start. Thus, rather than demonstrating that Head Start does not have appreciable effects, it merely shows that these effects tend to fade out when the Head Start children return to poverty homes and ghetto schools.

There are several answers to this point. First, the study explicitly focused on the "effects of Head Start that persisted into the elementary grades." If the program's effects are so weak or ephemeral they do not persist even into the elementary grades, then they are without much practical value. To make this point clear, we need only realize the untenability of asking Congress each year for $300 million to carry out a program whose effects we know last for only a few weeks. The Follow Through program was set up to deal with the possibility that Head Start's effects might fade out and subsequent reinforcement would be needed. The Follow Through program, however, is and will continue to be for the next several years, a limited experimental program. Until Head Start is having positive effects that are not fading out or until Follow Through or some other program is operating in such a manner as to provide the needed subsequent reinforcement, we cannot merely continue unchanged a $300-

million-a-year national program that is not making children appreciably different from what they would have been without the program.

While the Westinghouse study makes clear it is measuring only the residual effects of Head Start (i.e., those that persist into the elementary grades), and the study therefore cannot speak with authority on whether there is little original Head Start effect or whether there was a major effect that subsequently faded out, the assumption that there is a major effect that fades out is without much support at this time. Some of the analyses carried out by Westinghouse suggest it is primarily the absence of any appreciable original effect rather than the fade out of an achieved effect that accounts for the absence of appreciable differences between the Head Start and control children in the elementary grades. One half of the first-grade full-year sample consisted of centers and children who attended Head Start prior to entering kindergarten. By the time this group reached the first grade it had been over a year since they left their Head Start experience. The other half of the first-grade, full-year sample, however, went directly from Head Start to the first grade (with only the summer period intervening). These two groups were compared on all of the cognitive and affective measures and there were few significant differences between them.

8. The study's comparison of Head Start with non-Head Start children in the same classrooms fails to take into account secondary or spillover effects from the Head

Start children. The children who have had Head Start are likely to infect their non-Head Start peers with their own greater motivation and interest in learning. Their presence in the classroom is also likely to cause the elementary school teacher to upgrade her general level of teaching or to give more attention to, and therefore produce greater gains, in the less advanced non-Head Start group. Thus, the study minimizes Head Start's effect by comparing the Head Start children with another group of children that has been directly improved by the Head Start children themselves.

This is certainly a possibility. However, most of the previous before-after studies of Head Start's cognitive effect have shown at most small gains—so small it is hard to imagine their having such major secondary effect on teachers and peers. Moreover, the first grade children in the Westinghouse study were tested during the early part of their first grade year, prior to the time when such secondary influence on teachers or peer children would have much of a chance to occur. On the direct child measures (Metropolitan Readiness Test, Illinois Test of Psycholinguistic Abilities, etc.) there were only marginal differences between the Head Start and control children at that time. Also, on the Children's Behavior Inventory, a teacher rating instrument, there were few significant differences between the two groups, indicating that the teachers were not able to perceive any difference

between the motivation of the Head Start and non-Head Start children. In light of these findings, it is hard to see how spillover could contaminate the control group.

9. Unless researchers are virtually certain of their procedures and findings, studies like this can do great harm to the hard-won national effort to eliminate poverty. The new Republican administration, which came to office on promises to cut back the poverty program, could use this study to eliminate Head Start and to deemphasize other child remediation efforts.

It seems sophomoric to have to observe that knowledge can always be misused but that this fact can never be used as a justification for not finding things out. While evaluations can be misused, and probably will be, it is important to note that in the present case this did not occur. The results in fact were quite the contrary. In his February 19th message to Congress, President Nixon said:

Head Start is still experimental. Its effects are simply not known—save of course where medical care and similar services are involved. The results of a major national evaluation of the program will be available this Spring. It must be said, however, that preliminary reports on this study confirm what many have feared: the long term effect of Head Start appears to be extremely weak. This must not discourage us. To the contrary it only demonstrates the immense contribution the Head Start program has made simply by having raised to prominence on the national agenda the fact—known for some time, but never widely recognized—that the children of the poor mostly arrive at school age seriously deficient in the ability to profit from formal education, and already significantly behind their contemporaries. It also has been made abundantly clear that our schools as they now exist are unable to overcome this deficiency. In this context, the Head Start Follow Through Program, already delegated to HEW by OEO, assumes an even greater importance.

In sum, while most of the criticisms made of the Westinghouse study have some degree of validity, they are the kind of criticisms that could be made about virtually any piece of social science research conducted outside the laboratory, in a real world setting, on disadvantaged children, with all of the logistical and measurement problems such studies entail.

This study set out to accomplish, in a reasonable period of time, an assessment of the extent to which Head Start has achieved some of its major objectives. In my judgment it did what it set out to do and did it well. It should, therefore, be one of the principal sources of information we use in forming our judgment about Head Start and what its future course should be.

The purpose of the study was not to test the idea of Head Start but to assess its implementation—an implementation that is not in the form of a limited demonstration program (like Follow Through, for example) but one that is a large nationwide program, well into its fourth year, and operating at the level of $300 million per year. What the study has shown is that this implementation leaves a great deal to be desired. By the time they reach the first grade, children who have gone through Head Start are not appreciably better off in the cognitive and affective areas than those who have not. For those of us who want so much for this program to be successful in changing the lives of disadvantaged children, this is a hard pill to swallow. But attempting to reject the unpleasant findings by pointing to the methodological defects in this study is a counterproductive thing to do. If we persuade ourselves that Head Start is a successful program because we want to believe it, when in fact it is not, we only postpone the achievement of the objectives that we all so earnestly seek. Our posture at this point should not be to search for ways of discrediting the Westinghouse study because it has produced unpleasant findings but rather to take its findings, which are consistent with most other studies, and get on with the task of making the changes in the Head Start program that are required if it is to achieve the remediation of disadvantaged children we all desire.

25. An Evaluation of the Effectiveness of the OEO Legal Services Program

Anthony Champagne

In view of the current controversy over the legal services program (Pious, 1972), it is important to answer the question: What has been the impact of the OEO projects? The question will be answered by determining the degree of effectiveness of the program in meeting its goals of individual case handling, law reform, and community development.[1] In addition, evaluations of the effectiveness of legal services as determined by administrators of agencies and institutions relevant to poor people, poverty community group leaders, and the legal community will be discussed.

Before the discussion, it should be pointed out that the term "effectiveness" as used in this research is somewhat impressionistic and refers to the degree of success in achieving program goals. Such a subjective measure of effectiveness is common in evaluations of broad social programs where it is difficult, if not impossible, to measure social outcomes (Shipman, 1971).

Two sets of data will be used in this examination of program effectiveness.

THE DATA

The data from which this analysis is taken involve two previously confidential program evaluations—an independent evaluation done by the Auerbach Corporation for the Office of Legal Services and one conducted by the John D. Kettelle Corporation for the Office of Economic Opportunity.

The Kettelle evaluation, which was begun in 1970 and completed in 1971, involved 37 local legal services projects, visited by eight teams of four trained evaluators, three of whom were attorneys and one of whom was a community analyst. Those evaluators described the quality and types of activities of the legal services projects and included their impressions of the effectiveness of the projects in achieving legal services goals. The evaluators also interviewed and recorded the impressions of members of the community regarding legal services program effectiveness.

This evaluation performed a number of functions. One function was to esti-

AUTHOR'S NOTE: This research was partly funded by a grant from the University of Illinois Research Board. The author is indebted to J. Roger Detweiler, acting Director of the Office of Planning and Technical Assistance, Office of Legal Services, and to Mr. Fred Baldwin, formerly of the Office of Evaluation, Office of Economic Opportunity. The author is also grateful to Professors Stuart Nagel, P. G. Bock, Karl Johnson, and Jan Gorecki for their valuable comments and suggestions.

Reprinted from *Urban Affairs Quarterly*, Vol. 9, No. 4, June 1974, pp. 466–488, by permission of the Publisher, Sage Publications, Inc.

mate the degree of access that the legal services program provided indigents. The evaluation also compared the costs of the legal services program to costs of equivalent services provided by the private bar. It compared the costs of judicare with the costs of legal services and also determined the cost-effectiveness of various forms of legal services delivery systems. For example, it determined whether a rural legal services project was more expensive to operate than an urban one. Finally, the Kettelle evaluation determined the degree of legal services activity devoted to goals other than individual case-handling. Although it was not the goal of the Kettelle research to determine the effectiveness of legal services, the data allow for such an analysis (John D. Kettelle Corporation, 1971: iv-3–iv-16).[2]

The 37 OEO legal services projects examined by Kettelle are viewed as a sample representative of all legal services agencies. The Kettelle Corporation selected the sample in such a manner that they believed it was representative of the full scope of the legal services program along such dimensions as degree of effort of the legal services projects in serving the poverty community, the goal orientation of the program, the age of the individual projects, region in which the projects are located, degree of urbanism, density of the target population, proportion of the target population that is in poverty, size of the project staff, and ethnic composition of the target community (John D. Kettelle Corporation, 1971).

The Auerbach evaluation was also begun in 1970 and was designed to examine those OEO legal services agencies which were not evaluated by the Kettelle Corporation. Two hundred one OEO-funded legal services projects were involved in this evaluation.[3] The analysts of the Auerbach Corporation believe that conclusions drawn from this sample of legal services projects are applicable to the entire program.[4]

The data for the Auerbach evaluation were gathered by trained evaluators who visited the legal services projects for several days. These evaluation teams consisted of an attorney, a professional social worker, and a professional management analyst from the Auerbach Corporation (1971: 1-1, 3-1–3-4).

The primary purpose of the Auerbach evaluation was to provide individual reports on the legal services projects which provided a history of the project, a study of the types of issues with which the agency was involved, an evaluation of the environment within which the projects operate, and an evaluation of the director of the project and the staff attorneys. A secondary goal of this evaluation was to develop a system for comparing legal services agencies. Such a system was designed to aid administrators in the Office of Legal Services in evaluating legal services project performance in systematic fashion, to provide assistance to administrators in discovering factors which are critical to the success of legal services projects, and to examine the interrelationships among the factors which were deemed crucial to project success (Auerbach Corporation, 1971).

The evaluators for both these consultant firms spent several days at each legal services project. During this time, they conducted extensive interviews with the project director. Staff attorneys were also interviewed, as were other staff members of the project. Representatives of the project's board of directors, members of the legal community, representatives of poverty community groups, and administrators of agencies and institutions of relevance to poor people were also interviewed.

The interviewees were not chosen randomly, but were chosen to give a representative sample of opinion on the legal services project from a wide variety of people affected by and involved in the project.

Because of advance planning and, perhaps, the professional status of the interviewers, there was no problem in getting individuals to respond to the evaluators' questions. One problem, however, is that there is a considerable amount of missing data. Particularly in the Kettelle data, many questions were so detailed that respondents were not able to answer them. More general attitudinal and evaluative questions tended not to have the missing data problem.

Because the goal was to obtain a representative sampling of community opinion rather than establishing quotas on respondents or types of respondents, questioning proceeded until the evaluators judged that they were able to correctly gauge community sentiment on the project.

The evaluators then filled out questionnaires about the interviews and wrote a report on the project. Three significant differences exist in the two evaluations:

(1) As already mentioned, in more de-

tailed questions, considerable missing data exist in the Kettelle study.
(2) The Auerbach data are much more extensive but less intensive than the Kettelle. Fewer persons were interviewed in a shorter amount of time in the Auerbach evaluation.
(3) The Auerbach data are less subject to quantitative analysis than the Kettelle data.

The coding sheets filled out by the Auerbach evaluators were limited and do not lend themselves to a determination of agency and institution, legal community, or poverty community group leadership evaluation of legal services. The Auerbach evaluation of legal services contains only quantitative data on the evaluators' determination of the effectiveness of the program. Evaluations of the program from other groups are only available in the written reports on the projects (Auerbach Corporation, 1971).

The small number of projects examined by each evaluation team makes it unlikely that the biases of any one team would affect the ratings for the program as a whole. A number of other means were used to reduce the possibility of rater bias.

(1) The teams were required to give reasons for their scores. Thus, whatever the ratings, they had to be justified by verbal reports on why the project was given a specific numerical rating.
(2) The evaluation teams received training prior to conducting their evaluation and technical guidance from the management analyst who made up part of the evaluation team.
(3) The evaluators were not employees of the legal services program or any related OEO program, so they did

not have a vested interest in scoring legal services well or poorly.

(4) In addition to their own evaluation, they gathered information on legal services from other members of the community. This additional evaluation material from nonteam members would likely provide a check on team member evaluations.

Individual team member biases in the Kettelle evaluation were controlled by having the entire team agree on the evaluation score. In the Auerbach evaluation, each team member consulted with one another after a project evaluation. Each member then suggested an evaluation score and gave reasons for that score. The evaluation scores were then averaged.

In spite of the obvious shortcomings of these data such as the nonrandom procedure for selecting legal services projects and respondents plus the missing data problems, these two evaluations are clearly the best data available on a wide variety of legal services projects. It should be added that the evaluations were much more sophisticated than traditional evaluations of government programs.[5]

AGENCY EFFECTIVENESS

The Kettelle Evaluation

The legal services projects in the Kettelle sample were rated on an overall scale ranging from 1 to 12 in order to classify projects as to whether they were operating in a fashion appropriate to the general goals of the legal services program. Effectiveness scores are not available in the Kettelle sample on the specific goals of the program. Figure 1 shows the number and percentage of

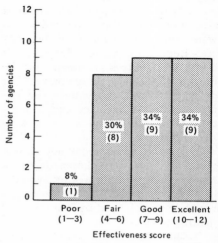

FIG. 1: Overall effectiveness of Kettelle sample of legal services agencies

agencies which received numerical scores equivalent to poor, fair, good, and excellent ratings. Most of the projects received a rating of good or excellent in the overall rating. Only 1 of the 27 projects given an overall rating by the Kettelle evaluators received a poor rating.

The Auerbach Evaluation

The Auerbach evaluators also used an overall rating scale which ranged from 1 to 12. Figure 2 gives that overall rating. According to the Auerbach evaluators, roughly the lowest one-fourth of the scale should be considered a low rating which indicates that the projects have such critical deficiencies that they should probably be closed down or cut back. The second lowest one-fourth of the scale should be considered a moderately or fairly low rating which indicates that the projects have problems in providing representation to poor people in accordance with OEO standards. The second highest one-fourth of the scale indicates the projects are performing efficiently, and the top one-fourth of the scale indicates that the projects are considered very efficient and strong forces in the War on Poverty (Auerbach Corporation, 1971: 171).

In keeping with what one might expect given the difficulty in defining effectiveness, the rating given by the Auerbach evaluators differs somewhat from the overall rating given by the Kettelle evaluators. Most legal services projects are rated fairly low by the Auerbach evaluators in overall effectiveness, though 38% of the agencies recieved a fairly high or high rating, which indicated that the projects were performing efficiently.

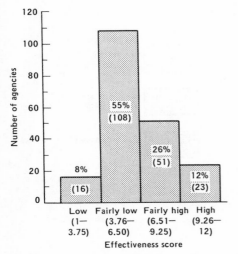

FIG. 2: Overall effectiveness of Auerbach sample of legal services agencies

The Auerbach data also contain effectiveness measures for the specific goals of legal services (see Figure 3). The effectiveness measure in case handling is quite good. Most of the agencies scored as generally effective and 21% scored as exceptionally effective. The rating for law reform was much worse than the rating for case handling. Forty-one percent of the projects were rated as ineffective. Most of the projects were rated as generally effective and only 10% were rated as exceptionally effective. The ratings for community development were similar to the ratings for law reform. Thirty-six percent of the projects were rated as ineffective, most were rated as generally effective, and 13% were rated as exceptionally effective.

It may be thought the fewer law reform activities, the greater the effectiveness due to the possibility for greater concentration of attorney time and energy on specific cases. This is not the case. Agencies which were rated as effective in law reform were also rated as having high law reform activity. The correlation between law reform effectiveness and high activity is positive and quite high (r = +.83).[6]

THE COMPATIBILITY OF LEGAL SERVICES GOALS

Figure 3 indicates that legal services projects are strongest in pursuing individual case-handling and weakest in the law reform goal. It is also important to determine whether one of the reasons for this emphasis on individual case-handling at the expense of other program goals is that the goals necessarily conflict with one another.

Edgar and Jean Cahn have suggested

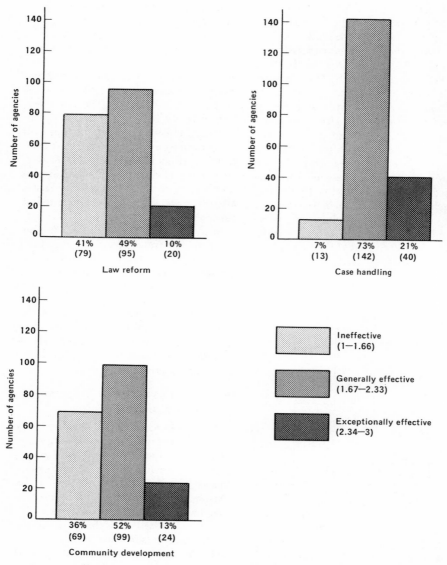

FIG. 3: Effectiveness in achieving legal services goals (Auerbach Sample)

that the goals conflict, since an agency has to ignore the quality of its individual case-handling in order to devote time to its law reform activities. They tend to see the effectiveness of agencies in a given goal area as the result of devotion of most agency time, energy, and money to one goal to the exclusion of other goals (Cahn and Cahn, 1966: 928). In order to test whether the goals conflict, effectiveness scores were correlated with each other. If the goals conflict, a low or even a negative correlation among the effectiveness scores would be expected. A negative correlation would indicate that agencies which were seen as effective in pursuing one goal were not viewed as effective in pursuing other goals.

In the Auerbach data, there is a high positive correlation between effectiveness in individual case-handling and law reform effectiveness ($r = +.61$). Similarly, a strong correlation exists between effectiveness in individual case-handling and effectiveness in community development ($r = +.56$). The correlation between law reform effectiveness and community development effectiveness is also strong and positive ($r = +.67$). These correlations suggest that agencies which are viewed as performing strongly in pursuit of one goal are also viewed as performing strongly in pursuit of other goals. Agencies may exist which emphasize one goal at the expense of others, however. This comment in the evaluation report of one agency illustrates this point:

[It] is an innocuous agency which provides good quality routine legal services for indigent clients. The project handles predominately individual services cases and has no plans to initiate action in other OLS [Office of Legal Services] goal areas. The project has failed to establish itself in the poverty community as an aggressive advocate of the poor, either through community education or cooperation with other agencies.[7]

It may also be that an agency can perform well in two goal areas and not perform well in a third. Clients of an agency which was effective in case-handling, for example, may educate other segments of the poverty community about the agency and the rights of poor people. An agency whose goal was individual case-handling may even pursue a community education goal in order to generate individual cases. Possibly an agency which was effective in law reform would also be effective in community education because of the necessity of reaching the poverty community in order to obtain an appropriate law reform case. Thus, some of the goals of the program may conflict, such as the law reform and the case-handling goals. The high positive correlation between effectiveness variables may only be spurious, the result of agencies high in case-handling also being high on community development effectiveness and agencies high on law reform scoring high on community development. This hypothesis was tested by using partial correlations which statistically control for the presence of a third variable which may be causing a spurious correlation between two variables.

When the effect of community development effectiveness upon individual case-handling and law reform effectiveness is controlled in the Auerbach data, the correlation between case-handling and law reform remains positive and moderately high (r = +.38). After controlling for the effect of the law reform effectiveness variable, there is still a positive correlation between case-handling effectiveness and community development effectiveness (r = +.26). Similarly, when the effect of case-handling effectiveness is controlled, the correlation between community development and law reform effectiveness remains relatively high (r = +.48). It appears, therefore, that the goals of the legal services program do not inherently conflict, at least in a statistical sense. The positive correlation between the effectiveness variables is not the result of agencies being successful in only two of the three goal areas.

Time Devoted to Legal Services Goals

Of course, lack of a conflict among legal services program goals may still mean that a goal can be overemphasized and act to the detriment of other goals. The more time attorneys spend on individual case-handling, the less they can spend on law reform. Even though an agency is acting effectively in pursuing a goal, more time and effort may need to be given to that goal. It is possible that some attorneys may even spend so much time on case-handling that they could not spend time on any other activity.

As it is, most attorney time is already spent on individual case-handling. Table 1 presents an adjusted estimate[8] of the mean allocation of attorney time among legal services agencies evaluated by the Kettelle Corporation. Though law reform does receive

eighteen percent of attorney time, the effort in time seems small, compared, for example, to the emphasis placed upon such activity by former national Office of Legal Services Director Earl Johnson. Johnson believed that law reform should be the main goal of the program (Pious, 1971: 378). Another national director of the Office of Legal Services, Burt Griffin, argued that economic development should be a major goal of legal services, yet only a small percentage of attorney time seems to be devoted to economic development (Pious, 1971: 386).

Comment by Legal Services Directors about Program Accomplishments

Legal services project directors do recognize the importance of goals other than individual case-handling. The Kettelle evaluators asked the project directors to mention what they thought were the most significant accomplishments of their project in the past calendar year. Many of the responses indicated quite significant gains for poor people. Among the significant cases described by the directors were actions related to reforming the law in the courts. These cases included such activities as a class action suit against a state welfare provision which held that people had to live in the state for ninety days before receiving welfare benefits. The suit became moot shortly after it was filed, since the state welfare department responded to the threat by eliminating the regulation.[9]

The accomplishments of the agencies also included numerous attempts at legislative law reform—lobbying

TABLE 1. ADJUSTED ESTIMATE OF MEAN ALLOCATION OF
ATTORNEY TIME AMONG LEGAL SERVICES GOALS (KETTELLE SAMPLE)

Legal Services Goals	Mean Percentage of Attorney Time
1. Individual representation	53
2. Law reform	18
3. Economic development	7
4. Community education	7
5. Group representation	7
6. Other	8
Total	100

and otherwise promoting the interests of poor people through legislation. One such attempt at legislative law reform involved the establishment of a local consumer protection agency (Pious, 1971).

Instances of accomplishment in the community development area were also common. Many agencies have apparently been very active in establishing tenant organizations for poor people who live in public housing. Legal services projects have also promoted such economic development activities as organizing and incorporating a black radio station and a poor people's credit union (Pious, 1971).

Though many directors did emphasize case-handling as their most significant accomplishment, the overwhelming number of accomplishments which were mentioned were not case-handling, but involved law reform activities as well as all forms of community development. When case-handling was mentioned as an accomplishment, such matters as the following were mentioned: legal services obtained a writ of *habeas corpus* for a man who had been unlawfully detained by the police, and legal services engaged in "solving problems for 600 poor people" (Pious, 1971).

Administrators Rate the Effectiveness of OEO Legal Services

Still another way to determine the effectiveness of legal services in the local community is to ask representatives of various segments of the community which may be affected by legal services. Administrators of agencies and institutions of relevance to poor people[10] are one such group which should be affected by legal services.

What has been the effect of the interaction between legal services and agencies and institutions dealing with poor people? In the judgment of the Kettelle evaluators, of 221 agencies and institutions which had some contact with legal services, 37% were affected very little or not at all by the activity of the legal services program. Twenty-four percent of these agencies and institutions had had their regulations, practices, or service affected somewhat. Thirty-eight percent were affected considerably or extensively. Of course, some agencies which remained unaffected by legal services may not have needed to change their procedures for relating to poor people. Even if all 221 agencies had needed to change their procedures, there was at least some change in 62% of the contacts between legal services projects and the agencies. This record of success is quite respectable, and it strongly indicates that legal services projects meet with considerable success when they do direct their efforts toward changing policies of agencies which may discriminate against poor people.

POVERTY GROUP LEADERS RATE THE EFFECTIVENESS OF OEO LEGAL SERVICES

Poverty group leaders were also asked to rate the effectiveness of legal services.[11] According to the information obtained by the Kettelle evaluators, when legal services came in contact with government agencies, the poverty group leaders were sure in 49% of the cases that there had been a change in agency policy which favored the poverty community. In another 28% of the cases, the community leaders were either unable to determine whether there had been a change in policy or the contact with the agency was such that a change was not needed. In only 23% of the contacts were community leaders sure there was no change in agency policy. In about two-thirds of the cases where the community leaders detected a change in agency policy, that change involved an agency adopting a more responsive attitude to the poverty community. The other one-third of policy changes actually involved a change in agency regulations.

In order to determine how effective

poverty community leaders felt legal services were in a number of issue areas, they were asked by the Kettelle evaluators to rank the effectiveness of the legal services program on a scale of 1 to 5. A score of 1 indicated that the legal services agency had no effect in the issue area, a score of 5 indicated legal services had substantial effectiveness. Table 2 gives the mean effectiveness scores for each of the issue areas.

Even though 4 areas had scores a bit below 3, most of the scores are slightly above 3. A score of 3 means that the poverty community leaders believed that legal services agencies were somewhat effective in that issue area. In only three cases was the score of community group leaders 3.5 or above. Such a score approaches the "considerably effective" category. In one of these cases, domestic relations, the score was above 4. In general, it appears that poverty groups do not tend to regard the work of legal services as ineffective, though they recognize a need for considerable improvement. Interestingly, two issue areas are included in the table which strongly suggest law reform activity. One is a category for suits against government agencies and the other is a category for implementing federal, state, or local civil rights legislation. These issue areas are ranked 3 and 6 in the rank ordering of 12 issue areas. The high ranking for the suits against government agencies category suggests that, at least from the perspective of poverty community groups, the fears expressed by Edward Sparer are groundless. Sparer (1965) was concerned that legal services agencies would not vigorously pursue litigation against government agencies for fear

TABLE 2. COMMUNITY GROUP RANKING OF THE EFFECTIVENESS OF
LEGAL SERVICES IN VARIOUS ISSUE AREAS (KETTELLE SAMPLE)

Issue Area	Mean Score [a]
1. Domestic relations	4.02
2. Landlord/tenant	3.71
3. Suits against government agencies	3.50
4. Wage garnishment or debtor/creditor cases	3.38
5. Juvenile delinquency	3.31
6. Housing codes	3.30
7. Consumer protection	3.20
8. Implementing federal, state, or local civil rights legislation	3.14
9. Fair employment practices	2.94
10. Bankruptcy	2.83
11. Employee/employer disputes	2.83
12. Criminal cases	2.82

a. Rounded to the nearest hundredth.

that these agencies would retaliate against the legal services agency. In addition, the rankings of 3 and 6 for the two law reform categories suggest that Jean and Edgar Cahn (1966: 928) were inaccurate when they expressed the belief that rising caseloads would cause legal services projects to emphasize only individual case-handling. They argued that, since high caseloads would make it impossible to pursue law reform, agency effectiveness would only be measured in terms of effectiveness in case-handling.

Economic development has been another issue area that has been emphasized as an important goal for legal services to pursue (Pious, 1971: 386). In responding to the Kettelle evaluators, poverty group leaders tended not to believe the program had contributed much to the development of their area. Only fourteen percent of the leaders felt that legal services had contributed to development by aiding

in creating new businesses which were run by the people in the area. Four percent believed legal services had persuaded business to employ more poor people. Only two percent believed the program had aided in improving wages or working conditions of the poor people who worked. Eight percent believed legal services had been helpful in the development of cooperative or credit unions in the poverty community and only seven percent believed legal services had contributed to the development and operation of day care centers. Many unions have long been hostile to admitting poor people into their ranks,[12] but only three percent of the poverty community leaders felt that legal services had been active in inducing unions to admit more people from the poverty community to union membership. Only seven percent of the community leaders felt legal services had been active in obtaining loans or other financial assistance for poor people. Seventeen percent felt legal services had been active in other areas of economic development. If legal services could be considered truly effective in the economic development of poverty communities, a much higher percentage of poverty community leaders should believe that there had been legal services activity in all the component areas of economic development.

Though these effectiveness scores show a definite need for improvement in legal services activities, 95% of community group leaders in the Kettelle sample agreed that legal services projects are providing services which would otherwise be unobtainable. Indeed, 59% of the respondents believed that OEO legal services was the only way that poor people could get legal help. Sixty-four percent of the leaders believed legal services projects sensitive to the needs of poor people, 14% that it was moderately sensitive, and 23% that it was insensitive.

THE LEGAL COMMUNITY RATES
THE EFFECTIVENESS OF OEO
LEGAL SERVICES

Private Practicing Attorneys

The third major group in communities serviced by legal services which was asked by the Kettelle evaluators to rate the effectiveness of the legal services program is the legal community.[13] The Kettelle data indicate that, if the legal services project in their community were eliminated, sixty percent of the attorneys believed that poor people would not receive any legal assistance. In spite of the emphasis on the professional responsibility of lawyers to represent indigents,

only eighteen percent of the attorneys believed that pro bono work could substitute for legal services agency activities. The remainder of the attorneys believed that some other legal aid program could take legal services' place (the public defender was one most often mentioned).

Attorneys tend to believe that the services provided by OEO legal services are of good quality. Over three-fourths of the attorneys had had a case where a legal services attorney was involved. They were asked to rate how effectively the legal services attorney serviced his client by comparing the services to those that the private bar might offer. Eleven percent of the attorneys felt the services were inferior to those of the private bar. Fifty-two percent believed the services were equal to and 37% believed the services were better than the services offered by the private bar. Thus, it appears that, contrary to Billie Bethel and Robert Walker (1965), poor people do not suffer by having a legal services attorney. Even if poor people could get a private attorney to handle their case, lawyers tend to believe that poor people would receive equal or better services from a legal services attorney.

Bethel and Walker (1965) make other criticisms of legal services. They imply that legal services programs will increase the size of courts' dockets. Though hardly a good reason for depriving poor people of legal help, an increased court docket can damage the quality of the judicial system for everyone and thus becomes an important question. Only two percent of the attorneys interviewed by the Kettelle evaluators felt legal services for poor people brought about a decrease in court dockets. Forty-six percent felt that there had been no change. Fifty-two percent of the attorneys did feel there had been an increase. The perceived increase in court dockets may suggest the need for expansion of the court system along with the expansion of opportunities for individuals to obtain lawyers.

Another criticism of legal services is that the program affects the volume of business of private attorneys (Bethel and Walker, 1965). This point is critical, since it has been suggested that support for legal services in the legal community will vary in inverse proportion to the degree of business legal services takes from the private bar (Caplan and Johnson, 1965). Most of the attorneys (57%) felt that there had been no effect on the volume of business of private attorneys. Some attorneys (22%), perhaps because the ex-

pansion of legal services to poor people expands the amount of litigation throughout society, believed that the program had brought about an increase in the volume of business for private attorneys. Only 21% of the attorneys interviewed by the Kettelle Corporation felt there had been a decrease in business that could be attributed to the legal services program.

Judges' Ratings

Since judges are a particularly important segment of the legal community, the Kettelle Corporation asked them to rank the effectiveness of legal services. The 79 judges who were interviewed readily admitted that legal services had been effective in a number of issue areas. Table 3 presents the mean ratings of judges in response to a question asking them to rate the effectiveness of legal services in various issues on a scale of 1 to 5. A score of 1

TABLE 3. JUDGES' RANKING OF THE EFFECTIVENESS OF LEGAL SERVICES IN VARIOUS ISSUE AREAS (KETTELLE SAMPLE)

Issue Area	Mean Score[a]
1. Domestic relations	4.12
2. Criminal cases	4.06
3. Suits against government agencies	3.93
4. Juvenile delinquency	3.82
5. Housing codes	3.79
6. Landlord/tenant	3.77
7. Wage garnishment or debtor/creditor cases	3.69
8. Implementing federal, state, or local civil rights legislation	3.67
9. Fair employment practices	3.50
10. Consumer protection	3.46
11. Employee/employer disputes	3.35
12. Bankruptcy	3.00

a. Rounded to the nearest hundredth.

represents a rating of no effectiveness and a score of 5 indicates a rating of substantial effectiveness.

Judges scored every issue area as one where legal services had at least some effectiveness (a score of 3). In two issue areas, the score was above 4, which indicated considerable effectiveness; in six other issue areas, the scores approached considerable effectiveness. No score approached the substantial effectiveness score of 5, but the judges gave quite high scores on the effectiveness of the program in twelve issue areas.

In the discussion of Table 2, it was noted that poverty leaders also gave scores on the effectiveness of legal services in a number of issue areas. In general, judges scored a number of issues differently from community groups. Judges tended to give higher scores and, on some issues such as criminal cases, there was a substantial difference in scoring. Both judges and community group leaders, however, saw legal services as most effective in the area which has traditionally involved legal aid, domestic relations. Both also gave relatively high scores to the law reform issues. Such scores of two vastly different groups in the community suggest that legal services has been widely recognized as being an effective organization for promoting the rights of poor people in a wide variety of issue areas.[14]

Interestingly, the two issue areas which suggested considerable law reform activities received fairly good scores. The category for suits against government agencies ranked third among the twelve issues. The category for implementing federal, state, or local civil rights legislation received a lower ranking of 8.

In addition to being asked to rank the effectiveness of legal services, the Kettelle Corporation asked the judges how they thought poor people would receive legal assistance if there were no legal services project in their community. Over half the judges (57%) said that poor people would not receive legal assistance. The other judges felt that poor people might be able to receive assistance through private attorneys, use of lawyer referral services, or through such governmentally supported legal assistance programs as public defender offices.

Judges were more likely than attorneys to believe that, if there were no legal services program, the poor would still receive legal assistance ($r = +.12$). The correlation is small and perhaps indicates a slightly greater awareness among judges of alternatives to legal services or slightly more faith in the pro bono activities of the legal profession.

Of the 79 judges, 74 had had the opportunity of seeing the operation of the OEO legal services program firsthand. That is, a legal services attorney had appeared before them in court. These judges were asked how effectively the legal services attorney performed in comparison to how the judge felt a private attorney would perform if he were handling the case. Eight percent of the judges felt that the legal services attorney did not handle the case as well as would a private attorney. Fifty-nine percent of the judges felt the case was handled as well as if it had been a private attorney's case. Of special interest were the statements of

33% of the judges. They felt that the quality of legal services was superior to the representation that would have been provided by the private bar. From the standpoint of providing quality legal representation to poor people, it would appear that the OEO legal services program provides representation which is as good as or better than the representation provided by private attorneys.

Interestingly, there is no difference between judges and attorneys as to whether legal services attorney representation is better than private attorney representation. The correlation is minute and statistically nonsignificant ($r = +.02$). If one believes legal services attorneys are more effective than private attorneys, there is a greater likelihood that one would believe poor people would not be served without a legal services program ($r = +.18$). This correlation indicates that those with a high regard for legal services attorneys cannot foresee another system of representation which could do the job that the legal services program is doing.

SUMMARY AND CONCLUSIONS

Expert evaluator opinion indicates that legal services has been somewhat successful from the standpoint of overall effectiveness, as well as in pursuing its goals of individual case-handling, law reform, and community development. Legal services appears to have performed exceptionally well in case-handling, though its record in law reform and community development is also impressive.

The three legal services goals do appear to be compatible. Agencies which successfully pursue the case-handling goal are also likely to be successful in law reform and community development. It is true, however, that an overwhelming amount of legal services attorney time is spent on the case-handling goal. The primary orientation of legal services is case-handling in spite of the project directors' general belief that the most significant accomplishments of legal services involve law reform or perhaps community development activity.

Three key groups in the local communities—administrators of government agencies, poverty group leaders, and the legal community—also rated the effectiveness of legal services. Legal services proved quite successful in changing the regulations of agencies and institutions if those regulations tended to discriminate against poor people. Poverty group leaders rated the effectiveness of legal services quite highly. They felt that legal services had been successful in working on behalf of poor people in changing policies of agencies and institutions to favor poor people. Poverty group leaders also tended to feel that legal services had performed well in a number of issue areas, though they felt legal services had performed poorly in economic development activities. The legal community also felt that legal services has been a successful program. Attorneys felt that quality of legal services had been quite good and that the program had not tended to interfere with private attorney business. Judges ranked the quality of legal services highly in twelve issue areas. They felt legal services gave better aid to indigents than private, practicing attorneys.

Such an evaluation clearly shows that the legal services program has been quite successful in meeting its goals and, therefore, in providing for the legal needs of poor people. Unfortunately, the success of the program has caused a number of political leaders to concern themselves with the program—a concern aimed, oddly enough, not at improving what this research shows as being an already successful program, but in reducing the program's effectiveness (Sullivan, 1971).

NOTES

1. For a discussion of legal services goals, see U.S. General Accounting Office (1969).

2. The name of the John D. Kettelle Corporation is now Kappa Systems, which is located in Willow Grove, Pennsylvania.

3. Every legal services project other than those evaluated by Kettelle was not evaluated by Auerbach. Projects which were not evaluated by Kettelle or Auerbach were either (1) backup centers (OEO-funded organizations that do not actually engage in case-handling); (2) new projects that were just getting started; or (3) legal aid organizations that were not receiving OEO funding when evaluations began.

4. Personal correspondence, August 1, 1972.

5. The nature of the data can only be briefly described here. For detailed information, see John D. Kettelle Corporation (1971) and Auerbach Corporation (1971). For an analysis of government program evaluations, see Shipman (1971: 198–200).

6. The correlation measure used is Pearson's r.

7. Confidential evaluation report on file in the Office of Legal Services, Washington, D.C.

8. The estimates in the original data added to more than 100%, so the estimate was adjusted proportionally to add to 100%. This table presents only a very rough estimate. Many project directors did not respond to all questions concerning time spent pursuing legal services goals. Many answers were inconsistent—that is, they were verbal responses instead of numerical.

9. The verbal response was recorded within the Kettelle data base.

10. The following administrators of agencies and institutions were interviewed: community action program and other community organizations, 52; welfare, 47; economic development, 42; public administration and general services, 36; other, 35; police and courts, 31; schools, 23; employment, 20; housing authority, 16; health, 6; consumer protection agency, 1.

11. The following types of poverty group leaders were interviewed: neighborhood groups, 49; other, 21; economic development, 20; Spanish-speaking, 16; housing, 14; migrants/Indians/natives, 14; welfare, 13; black groups, 13; civil rights, 11; senior citizens, 6.

12. As an example of problems in getting unions to open their ranks, see In re State Commission for Human Rights (1967).

13. The types of attorneys who were interviewed are as follows: private attorneys, 83; judges, 79; government attorneys, 38; bar association officers, 27; law school professors, 24; justices of the peace, 4; other, 2.

14. Correlations were also calculated to determine if there was agreement between judges and community group leaders within the same community. This was done to see whether judges in the community scored the effectiveness of legal services differently

from community group leaders. Due to missing data, the sample size was small, often falling far below the original agency sampling of 37 projects. As a result of this small sample size, it was impossible to use statistics in a meaningful manner. In order to statistically determine whether judges and community leaders rank legal services differently, a much larger sample is needed, perhaps a sample as large as the Auerbach sample. It is unfortunate that the Auerbach sample does not contain these ratings.

CASE

In re *State Commission for Human Rights* (1967) 277 N.Y.S. 2d 287.

REFERENCES

Auerbach Corporation (1971) Office of Legal Services Individual Project Evaluations: Final Report. Philadelphia.
Bethel, B. and R. K. Walker (1965) "Et tu, Brute!" Tennessee Bar J. 1 (August): 321–324.
Cahn, E. S. and J. S. Cahn (1966) "What price justice: the civilian perspective revisited." Notre Dame Lawyer 41 (Fall).
Caplan, G. M. and E. Johnson, Jr. (1965) "Neighborhood lawyer programs: an experiment in social change." University of Miami Law Rev. 20 (Fall): 184–191.
John D. Kettelle Corporation (1971) Evaluation of Office of Economic Opportunity Legal Services Program: Final Report. Paoli, Pennsylvania.
Pious, R. (1972) "Congress, the organized bar, and the legal services program." Wisconsin Law Rev. 1972 (Spring): 438–446.
——— (1971) "Policy and public administration: the legal services program in the War on Poverty." Politics and Society 1 (May).
Shipman, G. A. (1971) "The evaluation of social innovations." Public Admin. Rev. 31 (March/April).
Sparer, E. V. (1965) "The role of the welfare clients' lawyer." UCLA Law Rev. (January).
Sullivan, L. A. (1971) "Law reform and the legal services crisis." California Law Rev. 54 (January): 1–28.
U.S. General Accounting Office (1969) Effectiveness and Administration of the Legal Services Program Under Title II of the Economic Opportunity Act of 1964. Washington, D.C.: Government Printing Office.

26. Champagne's Assessment of Legal Services Programs: An Evaluation of an Evaluation

Richard A. Berk

For the vast majority of public programs, no scientific evaluation is ever undertaken. With poorly defined goals, empirical measures of dubious quality, and *ad hominum* criteria for judging effectiveness, a program's life expectancy typically depends on considerations marginally related to reasonably objective assessments of performance. It is now widely accepted that the community action program of Lyndon Johnson's War on Poverty, for example, was in trouble from its inception because of vague legislation, sloppy monitoring, and political exigencies (Moynihan, 1969; Marris and Rein, 1967; Clark and Hopkins, 1968). And while there is no such thing as a totally objective evaluation (it is not even clear what that could mean), one could certainly argue that the process should be explicit, accessible to the public, and subject to some universalistic rules of evidence.

Given the inadequate procedures by which the fates of programs are usually determined, Champagne's evaluation of OEO's legal services program deserves careful consideration. Between the samples gathered by the John D. Kettelle Corporation and those by the Auerbach Corporation, virtually all legal services programs functioning during 1970 and 1971 were canvassed. Teams of four "trained evaluators" vis-

ited each site for a period of about five days to examine project records and interview program personnel, community leaders, and representatives of local agencies and institutions. From these sources, evaluators constructed broad ordinal judgments of each program (e.g., excellent, good, fair, poor) and these "effectiveness" ratings were used as measures of program performance. Champagne's paper is exclusively an examination of these ratings and similar general assessments by people interviewed at each site. From his analysis, the following findings can be abstracted.

First, it seems that there was indeed a program. While this may seem a trivial point, there have been numerous instances where programs (and not just poverty programs) were funded and money spent, but where no activity actually occurred. There is still considerable controversy in Chicago, for example, surrounding massive funding to the Black P. Stone Nation for "community development."

Second, the data suggest the programs were reasonably consistent with commonsense notions of legal assistance. Again, this is not a trivial point. In community action programs, funds were used in such diverse ways that they approximated unspecified "'block grants." In other words, community

Reprinted from *Urban Affairs Quarterly*, Vol. 9, No. 4, June 1974, pp. 490–509, by permission of the Publisher, Sage Publications, Inc.

action programs provided money for many different neighborhood activities which evolved locally with little relation to any common ends and means. This may have been a useful way to assist poor people (Vanecko, 1969), but should not be perceived as a coherent national program. Questions have also been raised about "programs" funded by the Law Enforcement Assistance Administration. While the enabling legislation was justified in terms of crime prevention and the upgrading of police personnel, as well as more efficient criminal apprehension, the purchase of police hardware has consumed a disproportionate share of the money. While blame is difficult to affix, legislative intent may have been considerably subverted. In contrast, Champagne's analysis suggests that OEO's legal services program was more specifically conceived than community action and more fairly implemented than many LEAA programs.

Third, Champagne argues that at least three types of activities were often initiated: "case-handling, law reform, and community development." While it is unclear how these three were distributed across all legal assistance programs (in part because of the incomplete nature of the data), some program diversity is suggested. There is evidence that the "treatment" (i.e., the legal service program) sometimes involved as many as three major sub-treatments.

Fourth, the evaluation teams were apparently able to arrive at some form of consensus about the sites they visited. While the process through which raters ("evaluators") interacted is unclear (apparently their assessments

were *not* independently produced), the construction of mean ratings suggests that the initial individual evaluations were perhaps not too divergent. Even though reliability was not formally measured, one would hope that the means do not mask large interrater variance.[1] Such variability would have meant that a "central tendency" was an artificial, forced consensus and, hence, a very misleading statistic. In short, if one assumes that the mean ratings reflect more than an artificially constructed statistical consensus, the rater reliability may be substantial.

Fifth, very few of the programs were judged "low" or "poor" in "effectiveness" by the raters. While the references for these words are not specified and the term "effectiveness" is never defined, one can infer that the rating teams felt that most of the programs were meaningfully implementing the intent of the legal services program. In other words, "trained" and reasonably objective observers felt that the majority of programs were at least somewhat effective.

Sixth, in the Auerbach data rater judgments about effectiveness across "case-handling," "law reform," and "community development" were correlated positively. When raters thought a program was effective in one activity they were likely to think it was effective in others.

Seventh, rater judgments from the Kettelle data about time allocations of legal services attorneys indicate that time was not distributed equally to all activities. Further, individual representation may have gotten the lion's share of time.

Eighth, "in the judgment of Kettelle evaluators" about two-thirds of the local agencies contacted (e.g., welfare departments) had been affected by the legal services program. While there is no way to judge the representativeness of the sample,[2] one can probably conclude a nontrivial number of city and state "administrators" claimed their organization had been affected by legal services.

Ninth, in the Kettelle data, some sample of "poverty group leaders" claimed that legal services were generally somewhat effective. However, some tasks were believed to be more effectively implemented than others.

Tenth, in the Kettelle data, some sample of legal professionals claimed legal services were generally somewhat effective. For example, they often stated that the services provided were equal to or better than legal assistance available without the program.

Eleventh, in the Kettelle data, some sample of judges who had seen legal services attorneys in action generally assessed them to be at least as effective as other types of counsel. However, some kinds of tasks were allegedly handled better than others.

In summary, a set of neighborhood activities may well have existed roughly consistent with the intent of OEO's legal services program, which "trained" outside evaluators judged to be at least moderately "effective." In addition, interviewed "representatives" of local institutions, community groups, and the legal profession claimed that, in general, many of the programs were "effective," depending on the type of activity specified.

While there is some nontrivial value in these findings, there are many weaknesses in the analysis which cannot be ignored. By way of introduction, it is critical to recognize that the data is essentially an *opinion poll,* in which assessments by trained raters and some selected representatives from local institutions are presented. *The actual practices of legal services programs are not reported.* Thus, we have no idea if specific programs judged more "effective" processed more cases or won more suits for clients. We do not know if positive assessments from "community representatives" were based on actual performance, the publicity surrounding alleged performance, or some other factor(s). For instance, there is considerable evidence from other research that citizen evaluations of *specific* public services are heavily dependent on the global popularity of city officials like the mayor (Rossi et al., 1974). Hence, without some explicit grounding in actual practices, many of the study's findings may reflect more the psychological processes of attitude formation than reasonably accurate judgments about programs. For example, the correlations reported between rater assessments of the effectiveness of case-handling, law reform, and community development may simply be a "halo" effect, and the positive partial correlations do not in any way refute this interpretation.

The data are not only an opinion poll, but a poll from a very special set of respondents. We are told of judgments by evaluators, representatives of local agencies, and "community leaders." Nowhere are *clients* of the program formally interviewed. Indeed, there is no evidence of *any* systematic contact with the people who are supposed to benefit from legal services! Hence, the reported assessments involve judgments by elites and outsiders about undocumented activities for invisible clients.

In addition, we have little notion of what the critical words used by evaluators and respondents actually denote. The word "effective" is obviously central to the entire analysis, and we know virtually nothing of its meaning. "Effectiveness" implies at a minimum that benefits exceed costs, but neither is defined, let alone examined with data. Also, we do not know for whom the program is supposed to be "effective," and this is troublesome, since a variety of parties could gain or lose. From a cynical perspective, the surest winners were the companies paid to gather the data. Further, we are plagued by the question: effectiveness compared to what—conditions prior to the existence of legal services program or other forms of legal assistance? To rationalize these definitional problems, as Champagne does on page 1, by saying that such subjectivity is common in evaluations of broad social programs seems a half-hearted effort to transform vice into virtue.

There is much that can be learned from the many other weaknesses in the evaluation, and they will be discussed in a more general framework for evaluation research. This may assist other evaluators in avoiding similar difficulties.

CRITERIA FOR EVALUATION METHODOLOGIES

In essence, I have begun arguing that severe methodological problems undermine much of the credibility in the Champagne-Auerbach-Kettelle data. However, credibility in evaluation research rests on several different criteria which in practice must be considered carefully. Though there are many ways to organize a discussion of these specifics, the scheme devised by Campbell and Stanley (1966) and later extended by Cook and Campbell (1974) is especially compelling and will be employed here.

Cook and Campbell suggest that sound evaluation techniques must maximize four kinds of validity. Though this list is not exhaustive, it is an excellent place to begin.

Conclusion Validity

Conclusion validity involves two criteria: (1) the treatment (e.g., a legal aid program) must precede the effect (e.g., more civil suits won) in time, and (2) the treatment and effect must covary. For longitudinal effects, this reduces to showing that a "real" change occurred after a treatment was introduced. There is an implicit "nontreatment" before the pretest and a treatment between the pretest and posttest. One first assesses the "effect" by comparing the pretest with the posttest, while arguing that the difference (or some other disparity) is not a function of the particular samples of observations available.[3] If a "real" effect appears, it is necessarily associated with the treatment. For cross-sectional effects, there is no pretest. Rather, two (or more) posttests are compared. Each posttest has been preceded by a different treatment (one of which may be "no treatment"), and any nonsampling differences are then necessarily *associated* with alternative treatments. ("Association" does not necessarily imply causality.) More powerful evaluation designs combine longitudinal and cross-sectional observations (see Campbell and Stanley, 1966). One of the convenient aspects of evaluation work is that usually the researcher knows the time ordering of treatments and observations. For some kinds of cross-sectional data like attitude surveys, the ordering of variables in time is far more problematic.

In longitudinal qualitative studies, plausible conclusion validity rests on a detailed discussion of a sequence of events. For example, one might carefully describe how police protection improved after a lawsuit seeking more equitable or appropriate deployment of patrolmen. Cross-sectional qualitative studies might compare descriptions of cities where such suits had been won with those where suits had been lost. In both cases, sampling issues would be addressed by arguing from a wealth of detail that "real" effects are more plausible than sampling "accidents."

Quantitative methodologies typically rely on statistical procedures, and here conclusion validity formally addresses the application of appropriate statistics and degree of sampling error. If improved police protection is the specified outcome, plausible conclusion validity would be phrased in terms of statistics sensitive to a change in protection and a probability assessment of the alternative explanation of "chance." Thus, one might report that, after the lawsuit, the mean time for police to respond to calls dropped a "statistically significant" amount. Or one might report that cities in which

suits had been won enjoyed "statistically significant" shorter response times than those in which suits had been lost.

In the Champagne-Auerbach-Kettelle material, conclusion validity derives from much weaker methodologies. First, many respondents were in essence asked what kinds of changes they noted after the introduction of the legal services program. In other words, respondents were asked to make a longitudinal judgment: are things different from before the legal services program existed? Such conclusions require an accurate assessment of prior conditions, an equally astute perception of conditions after the program's introduction, and an unbiased method of comparison. Since there was no pretest, respondent data rests entirely on *retrospective accounts*. Besides well-known problems with clouded memories and systematic distortions, such judgments demand that informants are able to comprehend very complex events over time. In short, respondents were de facto program evaluators, using their memories as a data base while exercising unspecified methods of longitudinal comparison.

Second, raters visited each program for about a week and apparently judged (among other things) whether conditions had changed after the program's inception. However, they did not have the benefit (or hindrance) of over-time experience with each site and therefore relied on the accounts of others, inferences from current program practices, and comparisons with other kinds of legal services. Therefore, their longitudinal assessments were at least as difficult as any respondent's, while their data base and rules of inference were equally vulnerable. Indeed, they may have compounded the misperceptions of various informants.

Third, the study's conclusion validity involves an assumption that the important differences would be apparent to respondents and raters within a year or two after the program's inception (and sometimes within even a shorter time). Long-range effects or outcomes requiring an incubation period were not tapped because of the timing of site visits. However, should time-lagged effects have been of interest, it is important to emphasize that the retrospective methodology would have been even weaker. Additional longitudinal complexity would have been introduced.

Fourth, we are told that a number of cross-sectional comparisons were also undertaken, especially with alternative forms of legal services. These may have reflected greater conclusion validity, especially for those comparisons where dollar costs were involved. However, Champagne states on page 467 that, for the Kettelle data at least, an evaluation of "effectiveness" per se was not built into the original design, and we are not told how raters arrived at those judgments from the cross-sectional data.

Internal Validity

In essence, internal validity addresses the question of spuriousness: can the outcome be reasonably attributed to the treatment, not some other factor that covaries with the treatment? Typically, there are four ways to improve internal validity. First, one may hold constant factors which are not part of the treatment, but which could affect the outcome. In legal aid programs, one might only provide the service to people within a narrow range of income, so that income could not vary substantially and, hence, be an explanatory variable for treatment effects. Second, one might match the experimental groups to control groups on variables that could affect the program's outcome. For example, experimental and control groups might be of the same race, income, age, and sex. Third, one can often adjust for factors leading to spurious conclusions. There are a variety of statistical techniques (such as analysis of covariance) which can assist in the elimination of rival hypotheses which threaten internal validity. Fourth, one can control for all threats to internal validity through random assignment to treatment and control groups. Randomization defines true experiments and is the best way to ensure internal validity.

While the strengths and weaknesses of these various approaches cannot be discussed here, it is important to note that *none* of these techniques was applied in the Champagne-Auerbach-Kettelle data. Again, we are forced to rely on the judgments of raters and respondents. However, for longitudinal internal validity we not only require that they accurately judge changes after the program was introduced, but that they can specifically *attribute these changes to the program.* This is an extremely complicated kind of assessment and demands that other plausible explanations for the change be considered and eliminated. Internal validity seems especially problematic for the sample of agency representatives who were asked to gauge the impact of legal services programs. How do they decide whether changes in their agencies are a result of legal services or some other factor(s)?

While for conclusion validity cross-sectional comparisons may have been sounder than longitudinal comparisons, for internal validity both types are very weak. For conclusion validity with cross-sectional data, one "only" needs to show that two forms of legal services differ on some set of dimensions like cases processed, cost per case, or cases won. For internal validity, one must demonstrate that the differences in outcomes (e.g., program A won more cases than program B) are a result of the programs themselves, not some other factor. Perhaps some programs processed more cases because their clients brought them simpler problems. Perhaps they won more cases because their local courts were historically more responsive to claims for underprivileged plaintiffs. In short, without more powerful designs which "hold constant" alternative explanations for program effects, internal validity cannot be high. Without high internal validity, the notion of "effectiveness" is extremely misleading.

Construct Validity

Construct validity involves the degree to which operationalized measures fit their theoretical conceptualizations. Suppose one wanted to see if the provision of legal information to the poor through legal counseling would increase court use as a remedy for conflict. One might theorize that, once the poor knew how to use civil suits, they might then take many of their problems to the court. In other words,

better information is the key. Let us also assume an evaluation showed that legal counseling increased the use of the courts and that conclusion and internal validity were high. Despite these compelling results, questions about construct validity could be raised. Perhaps detailed information is not nearly as important as emotional support provided by counselors. In other words, the poor might not need detailed information so much as an authoritative figure encouraging them to use the courts and helping them overcome their fears about dealing with the "system." At first, whether the increased use of the courts resulted from more information or emotional support may seem a trivial distinction. However, suppose one wanted to make the program more efficient. Then it would matter how the treatment was conceptualized. If information were the crucial factor, one might facilitate the process by gathering all potential litigants in a room, providing the necessary information, and answering questions in an impersonal mass production fashion. In contrast, if the crucial factor were emotional support, one might continue to emphasize individualized counseling, where the client's fears could be addressed in detail. Further, one might alter the selection and training of legal counselors depending on which factor was really salient in the treatment.

Perhaps the most obvious problem in the Champagne-Auerbach-Kettelle data is weak construct validity. Normally, this problem is approached in the fit between measure and concepts. However, that comparison assumes the measures are reliable and the concepts clearly defined. Here, neither prerequisite is achieved. First, I have already argued briefly that few of the key concepts are specified with clarity. Champagne acknowledges this weakness. Further, to the degree that definitions exist, they are likely to reflect the conceptions of evaluators and elites, not those for whom the program was designed. The underprivileged might have very different notions of "effectiveness," and according to the data, they did not participate in the evaluation.[4] Second, the reliability of the data is dubious. While one may get a rough sense of some reliability between raters (though no formal assessment), the reliability of respondents seems especially problematic. To begin, there are apparently few respondents per site with coverage of respondent types varying from program to program. For example, in the Kettelle data, 37 sites are assessed by an average of eight "administrators of (local) agencies and institutions" and five "poverty group leaders" (see Champagne's notes 10 and 11). In addition, it appears that there was rarely more than one person interviewed for each agency or local organization. Further, interviewing techniques and instruments are not discussed, so their comparability across respondents cannot be judged. In any case, nowhere is reliability of respondent data formally considered (see Champagne's note 1). Thus, construct validity seems very low because the prerequisites for this judgment are not effectively demonstrated.

External Validity

External validity refers to the degree of agreement that results when one evaluation can be generalized to other kinds of recipients, circumstances, and settings. Assuming that conclusion, internal, and construct validity are high, one still would like to know whether the treatment effects are unique to the situation in which they were tested. For example, legal counseling might produce increased court use by people just above the poverty line, but not below it. The very poor may feel so impotent that a far stronger "stimulus" is needed. If, for instance, a particular program reached only families with incomes of between $6,000 and $8,000 per year, one might question whether the program would work for welfare recipients. Or, if a program emphasized family problems, generalizing its "effectiveness" to programs emphasizing city services would likely be unsound. The careful reader may have already guessed that external validity is typically the most problematic. While there are many useful techniques for minimizing threats to the other kinds of validity, it is difficult to routinely improve external validity. Cook and Campbell provide several suggestions, but compelling external validity must rest on compelling theory about the mechanisms linking the treatment to the outcome, and, unfortunately, social science typically provides meager theoretical assistance.

Given the problems discussed earlier, external validity for the Champagne-Auerbach-Kettelle data may be moot. It is not clear what one would want to generalize. Nevertheless, there are some comments about external validity which should be made. An important strength lies in the near universal coverage of the range of legal services programs. Apparently, the combined Auerbach-Kettelle sample includes almost the entire universe of the programs. Hence, generalization from a sample of the programs to the rest is not problematic.

In contrast, there are major generalization difficulties generated by the sampling techniques used at particular sites. We are told that "the interviewees were not chosen randomly, but were chosen to give a representative sample of opinion on the legal services project from a wide variety of people affected by and involved in the project." Later we are told, "Because the goal was to obtain a representative sampling of community opinion rather than establishing quotas on respondents or types of respondents, questioning proceeded until the evaluators judged that they were able to correctly gauge community sentiment on the project."

From such information, it is impossible to assess the representativeness of the samples (unless we simply take the word of the Kettelle people). If the opinions were tied to some measures of actual program performance, one might feel more confident. But we are only provided with summary statistics of attitudes. In other words, like a Gallup poll, this study claims to *estimate* from a sample the attitudes of some population of people. However, unlike the better public opinion polls, the population is poorly defined, and sampling procedures are at best ambiguous. The implications should be clear. Another evaluation team might go to the same legal services projects and use rigorous (or even the same) sampling techniques and get very different distributions of responses. While it may

be unlikely that the findings from similar elite groups would be completely reversed (i.e., that the majority of programs would be judged ineffective), the proportions reported in this paper could be tremendously altered. One might find, for example, the bar graph on Figure 1 showing thirty percent rather than four percent, of the programs falling within the "poor" category. In other words, since the representatives of the sample are unclear, generalization (external validity) is likely to be unsound.

My discussion of criteria for evaluation research should not be interpreted as an argument for methodological rigor to the exclusion of other factors. Useful applied research should reflect a variety of other considerations since the purpose is to provide information that is not only plausible, but useful and available when needed.

Flexibility of Design

The lives of most social action programs are unpredictable. Regardless of the time spent in planning, a variety of events occur for which there was little preparation. Given this situation, one of the weaknesses of some more rigorous research designs is their inflexibility. Once the design has been specified and implemented, it becomes very difficult to alter the methodology in light of unexpected developments.[5] Qualitative case study research seems especially able to handle unanticipated occurrences, though one typically sacrifices some rigor. Retrospective accounts, as we find in Champagne-Auerbach-Kettelle data, are also useful, but with less credibility than standard longitudinal field work techniques.

Provision of Findings During the Life of the Program

Conscientious administrators are always interested in improving their programs. Hence, if they respect the evaluators, they will try to solicit information which might be useful in bettering the project's performance. Though there is nothing wrong in principle with providing such assistance, many research designs are invalidated through such procedures. In essence, the treatment is being altered during the life of the project with no provision for such changes in the evaluation design. If evaluators anticipate the necessity of providing information to project administrators during the life of the program, they can often build appropriate contingencies into their designs. Field work techniques can quite easily adjust to such demands, but other approaches can also be altered if such changes are anticipated. Unfortunately, the relevance of this issue cannot be easily considered from the Champagne-Auerbach-Kettelle data. We are not told much about the provision of data to local program administrators.

The Nature of Evaluation Data

If the continuation of a social program is to be weighted in light of a variety of costs and benefits, it is crucial to provide findings in a form amenable to such considerations. This has several implications.

(a) Where possible, measurement procedures should reflect units useful for policy. Almost inevitably, this means quantification through such standardized metrics as dollars, events per unit time, events per unit of geographical area, events per population unit, and so on. Unfortunately, at times, these measurement requirements can seriously distort the phenomena of interest, and, though such metrics are desirable, they should not be applied automatically without careful examination of the fit between the phenomena to be measured and the measurement techniques.

(b) Where possible, statistical techniques should be applied which indicate the effects of various inputs on the outputs of interest. In other words, the data should indicate what is the likely outcome from various types and levels of treatments.

(c) The evaluation should be written in a form accessible to people who must use the information. This is frequently a difficult task and requires careful consideration of the audiences involved. In addition, evaluators must learn which parts of their reports are most important for policy makers and highlight these sections.

The Champagne-Auerbach-Kettelle data have interesting strengths and weaknesses in this regard. By using an opinion poll approach, emphasizing a sample of elites, they provide policy makers with the information that many knowledgeable and influential people appear to favor the legal services program. To the degree that policy makers fear or respect such opinions, important data have been collected. On the other hand, if policy makers are interested in the reality of the program's performance divorced from elite assessments of the views of program recipients, the Champagne-Auerbach-Kettelle data have little to offer. The program itself is not evaluated; rather, elite opinions about the program are evaluated.

Moral Considerations

All social intervention programs and their evaluations intrude on people's lives. One important consequence involves the moral questions raised when harm can result from a program. We cannot take the time here to discuss the morality of social programs nor to consider in detail the ethical issues in evaluation. However, it is probably useful to list a few rules of thumb for evaluation methodologies.

(a) The evaluation methodology should be as nonintrusive as possible. The less one meddles in people's lives, the less likely damage will be done. One should even be prepared to sacrifice considerable methodological rigor to avoid the possibility of doing harm.

(b) All individuals who participate as subjects of an evaluation should be guaranteed anonymity. This may mean an evaluator risks contempt of court for failure to divulge information. Where possible, coding systems should be employed which make it impossible to link the *names* of individuals to their data.

(c) No individuals should be permitted to participate as subjects of an evaluation without a reasonable level of informed consent. This means not only providing appropriate information, but taking pains to see that the information is understood.

(d) If the evaluation process may cause some harm, resources should be allocated to compensate subjects or bring about a reversal of the ill effects. For example, if interviews associated with an evaluation methodology cause people to lose time from work, they should be paid for their time and, if desirable, their absence explained to their employer.

(e) Given the possible dangers of social programs, one must always address the question of evaluation for whom. To the degree that a program is supposed to affect people's lives, it seems only just that they be included in the evaluation process; especially in the determination of program goals, the criteria for success or failure, and the final assessment of evaluation results. Social programs should be designed to work *for* people, not *on* people, and this implies that program recipients be active in all evaluations. Professional evaluators and program administrators can provide the necessary technical expertise, but should not be permitted to run roughshod over clients.

In light of these moral issues, the nonintrusiveness of the Champagne-Auerbach-Kettelle evaluation should be commended, because it effectively minimized a variety of potential problems. Evaluators were at each site for a very short period of time and did little more than ask people questions. Clearly, their approach was very nonintrusive and, hence, was unlikely to create problems for respondents. This is one of the real strengths of the evaluation. However, the absence of input from clients must not be ignored. By this criterion, the Champagne-Auerbach-Kettelle study is sorely lacking.

To conclude, good evaluations juggle a variety of desirable goals. It is probably impossible to maximize all four types of validity simultaneously. The tradeoffs are further complicated when other aims are introduced. For example, while randomization strengthens internal validity, randomization may alert program recipients to the artificial nature of the treatment setting and produce reactions which undermine generalization to other situations. Realizing that they are part of an experiment, recipients may resent participation or may become artificially overinvolved (e.g., a "Hawthorne effect"). In either case, should the program move beyond a trial stage when random selection is eliminated, the treatment might then produce very different outcomes. The waters would be further muddied if moral or political considerations make it difficult to apply the treatment to randomly selected experimental and control groups. In short, there are rarely any easy answers or cookbook solutions to these kinds of tradeoffs. Researchers must be familiar with the details of various methodologies and their implications while developing sophistication about the particular settings in which an evaluation is to be implemented.

CONCLUSIONS

Champagne's analysis of the Auerbach-Kettelle data must ultimately rest on the credibility of the reported assessments. There are so many ambiguities and apparent problems that it seems unwise to concur with Champagne that the legal services program was a success. On the other hand, there is no evidence that it was a failure. We know that the preponderance of opinions was favorable, not critical. Further, the positive assessments by judges and private attorneys who would seem to have no vested interest in the program's success cannot be casually dismissed. I would conclude that, while a program did exist roughly consistent with commonsense notions of legal assistance, its value cannot be judged with any acceptable degree of confidence from these data.

I do not want to leave the impression that my criticisms reflect some unrealistic expectations of an imaginary never-never land. There is a large and growing literature on methodologies for the evaluations of social programs which perhaps could have been applied in the evaluation of OEO's legal services program (e.g., Rossi and Williams, 1972; Caporaso and Roos, 1973; Cook and Campbell, 1974). Though no approach is without its problems, many would have provided a more credible assessment.

The range of useful research designs is extensive, including "process research," true experiments, quasi-experiments, and an assortment of post hoc statistical techniques. Sophistication in measurement is also considerable, involving survey approaches of various types, official statistics, unobtrusive measures, qualitative field notes, and census data. Further, such techniques have been frequently discussed in the context of constraints existing in field settings, with political, moral, and practical issues addressed. Most important, there are many sound evaluations currently in the literature (Boruch, 1973) indicating that resourceful evaluation researchers from various disciplines have been able to implement powerful methodologies.

If there is blame to be distributed for the failure to apply more powerful methodologies, it may be placed foremost at the door of OEO. They have sponsored many competent evaluations of other programs and possess the expertise to have critically examined the Kettelle and Auerbach proposals. In short, they know better.

As long as evaluations provide the opportunity for companies to make money, there will always be firms who will claim they can do it better for less. Competition is clearly one method of keeping evaluators from padding research budgets, but it places a heavy responsibility on funding agencies. For the Auerbach-Kettelle data, OEO apparently did not properly fulfill its responsibilities.

NOTES

1. There is a variety of reliability tests that could have been performed. For example, one could have done a one-way analysis of variance using site as the treatment and interrater variability as error. A statistically significant F-ratio would have indicated (under certain assumptions) that there was more variance between sites than between raters, a pretty good commonsense notion of acceptable reliability.

2. Representativeness rests initially on an explicit definition of a population and then on techniques which ensure within the laws of chance a selection of units whose characteristics mirror that of the population. Here no population or selection procedure is clearly delineated. Consequently, some important institutions like the mayor's office may well have been excluded (unless "public administration" includes the mayor's office), while others may well be overrepresented. For example, there were approximately the same number of interviews with "administrators" from welfare agencies as from economic development agencies and both were among the most heavily represented respondents in the Kettelle sample (see Champagne's note 10). In addition, it is important to keep in mind that, separately analyzed, both the Kettelle and Auerbach data are from samples of sites whose representativeness is unspecified.

3. Basically, the sampling issue boils down to whether the effect (pretest versus posttest) could have easily occurred by the luck of the draw. In other words, if the scores in both tests were randomly shuffled, would differences as large as found between pre- and posttest be likely to occur simply through the chance assignment to pre- or posttest.

4. One must not confuse "poverty group leaders" with program recipients. If we have learned one thing from the turmoil of the sixties, "community leaders," like any leaders, do not necessarily represent their constituents accurately. Neither Stokely Carmichael on one side nor Roy Wilkins on the other seemed able to accurately assess black sentiment about civil disorders or determine in any way the behavior of people in the black community. The same can be said for most local leaders.

5. Some more rigorous designs, especially those using multiple and frequent measures, can actually handle a surprising amount of program alteration. As our knowledge of these designs expands, they may begin to approximate the flexibility of some qualitative case study technique.

REFERENCES

Boruch, R. F. (1973) "Problems in research utilization: use of social experiments, experimental results and auxiliary data in experiments." Annals 218 (June).

Campbell, D. T. and J. C. Stanley (1966) Experimental and Quasi-Experimental Designs for Research on Teaching, Chicago: Rand McNally.

Caporaso, J. A. and L. L. Roos, Jr. (1973) Quasi-Experimental Approaches. Evanston: Northwestern Univ. Press.

Clark, K. B. (1968) A Relevant War Against Poverty. New York: Harper & Row.

Cook, T. D. and D. T. Campbell (1974) "The design and conduct of quasi-experiments and true experiments in field settings," in M. O. Dunnettee (ed.) The Handbook of Industrial and Organizational Research. Chicago: Rand McNally.

Marris, P. and M. Rein (1967) Dilemmas of Social Reform. New York: Atherton.

Moynihan, D. P. (1969) Maximum Feasible Misunderstanding: Community Action in the War on Poverty. New York: Free Press.

Rossi, P. H. and W. Williams (1972) Evaluating Social Programs. New York: Seminar.

Rossi, P. H., R. A. Berk, and B. K. Kidson (1974) The Roots of Urban Discontent. New York: John Wiley.

Vanecko, J. J. (1967) "Community mobilization and institutional change." Social Sci. Q. 50, 3.

27. A Reply to Berk

Anthony Champagne

Berk provides a useful criticism of evaluation research, though a number of his comments regarding the Auerbach-Kettelle data deserve further mention. Rather than make a lengthy response to the comments offered by Professor Berk, this reply will briefly mention what I believe are Berk's key points.

The Problem of Client Interviews

Few would doubt the importance of obtaining a "consumer perspective" of the legal services program.[1] If one is to examine the effectiveness of a program such as legal services, it would be ideal to know what the clients of the legal services program feel. Unfortunately, Professor Berk chose not to scan the several volumes of materials on the evaluations prior to criticizing the evaluations (see esp. John D. Kettelle Corporation, 1971). If he would have done so, he would have noted that client interviews were contemplated, a pilot study was made, and the research was later abandoned because of ethical considerations. Many individuals associated with the evaluation believed there was a serious breach of legal ethics in requesting that clients be interviewed. It was felt that the attorney-client privilege would be violated, that the clients would feel compelled to participate in the evaluation, and that clients would feel used by social scientists. The result was an "absence of input from clients," though a victory for ethical research standards.

The Opinion Poll Nature of the Research

As with most data used in the social sciences, "the data are only an opinion poll." Given the unique history of legal services, however, an opinion poll is not a weakness of the evaluation, but a major strength. The OEO legal services program has been one of the most controversial programs of the War on Poverty (Sullivan, 1971). The opinion poll data suggest considerable support for the legal services program at the local level—a finding which should be particularly significant to policy makers.

The Impressionistic Nature of the Data

Berk is correct that longitudinal studies would show much greater conclusion validity. He completely ignores political reality in the case of the legal services program by criticizing the nonexperimental nature of the evaluation. Money has always been a very scarce commodity in the legal services program—a scarcity which can readily place great limitations on the sophistication of one's evaluation methodology.[2]

It should also be emphasized that

Reprinted from *Urban Affairs Quarterly*, Vol. 9, No. 4, June 1974, pp. 510–513, by permission of the Publisher, Sage Publications, Inc.

there is tremendous difficulty in obtaining nonimpressionistic indicators of effectiveness. To Berk, this statement is an attempt "to transform vice into virtue"—a peculiar comment on what is nothing more than fact. In order to illustrate, the number of cases handled might seem to be a good indicator of the degree of services provided to poor people. The problem is that legal services projects define "case" in numerous ways. For some, every person who enters the office is a case; for others, every client in need of litigation is a case; and for still others, every consultation including telephone conversations and community education activities is a case.

Similarly, a nonimpressionistic indicator of law reform effectiveness might be the number of poor people helped as a result of the law reform activity. But on a limited budget, how does one make an estimation of the effectiveness of cases like Shapiro v. Thompson (1969) or Edwards v. Habib (1968).[3]

Though Berk denies it, until funds are available which allow for nonimpressionistic evaluations, his suggestions are in an "imaginary never-never land."

The Overall Usefulness of the Data

Finally, Berk would seemingly solve the methodological limitations of the data by virtually ignoring any conclusions drawn from it. Such a solution is a questionable one, which, if consistently followed, might find one ignoring most data in the social sciences.[4] Particularly in comparison to previous research on legal services,[5] all of which have been impressionistic case studies which were often done without interviewing any segment of the local community, the importance of the Auerbach-Kettelle data in increasing our understanding of the legal services program becomes obvious.

NOTES

1. The original concept of the "consumer perspective" is Edmond Cahn's.

2. Money for the evaluation research on legal services is so scarce that although the Auerbach data were to be updated, improved, and expanded upon in later years, no funds are yet available for such a project.

3. The former voided the use of durational residency requirements for receipt of welfare benefits. The latter voided use of retaliatory evictions.

4. See the excellent discussion of research methodology in Walter (1971).

5. This research includes Masotti and Corsi (1967), Pious (1971), Hannon (1970), and Stumpf et al. (1971).

CASES

Edwards v. *Habib* (1968) 397 F. Supp. 2d 687.
Shapiro v. *Thompson* (1969) 394 U.S. 618.

REFERENCES

Hannon, P. J. (1970) "Legal services in Southern California: a study of the legal services program in action." Ph.D. dissertation. Claremont Graduate School.

John D. Kettelle Corporation (1971) Evaluation of Office of Economic Opportunity Legal Services Program: Final Report. Paoli, Pennsylvania.

Masotti, L. H. and J. R. Corsi (1967) "Legal assistance for the poor: an analysis and evaluation of two programs." J. of Urban Law 44 (Spring): 483-502.

Pious, R. (1971) "Policy and public administration: the legal service program in the War on Poverty." Politics and Society 1 (May): 365–391.

Stumpf, H. P., H. P. Schroerluke, and F. D. Dill (1971) "The legal profession and legal services: explorations in local bar politics." Law and Society Rev. 6 (August): 47–68.

Sullivan, L. A. (1971) "Law reform and the legal services crisis." California Law Rev. 59 (January): 1–28.

Walter, O. [ed.] (1971) Political Scientists at Work. Belmont, Calif.: Duxbury.

28. A National Evaluation of Community Services and the Quality of Life in American New Towns

Raymond J. Burby, III, Shirley F. Weiss, and Robert B. Zehner

Population growth, city problems, and expanding expectations for a better life and a better environment have focused national attention on new communities as a potentially better form of urban development. Depending on definitions and standards, estimates of the number of new communities in America range between 50 and 250 communities which might ultimately house from five to 25 million persons. Regardless of the exact number, this clearly represents an unprecedented level of private commitment to new community development. The private sector's expanding involvement in community building has provided public agencies with an opportunity and a challenge to match excellence in land development with a corresponding level of excellence in community facilities and services.

The primary objective of this article is to evaluate the extent to which this challenge has been met in new community development in the United States. Despite a growing volume of writings on new communities,[1] very little empirical research which

evaluates the actual accomplishments of new communities in meeting human needs has been conducted. Throughout the 1960s the major focus of policy-oriented new community research was on the role of new communities in a national urban growth policy designed to cope with burgeoning population growth and the mounting housing crisis.[2] A second major thrust of new community research dealt with the mechanics of the community development process—including studies on innovation, economic evaluation, education, and governance.[3] These studies have been valuable, but they have not evaluated new community development from the points of view of the actual users of new community environments, the residents. Studies which have focused on residents' responses to new community development have all been limited in scope, both in terms of the number of communities studied and the number of aspects of the community environment evaluated.[4] The research reported here has been designed to overcome these limitations by examining a number of new com-

This article draws on research supported by the National Science Foundation, Research Applied to National Needs, Division of Advanced Productivity Research and Technology, Research Grant GI-34285. Findings, opinions, conclusions, or recommendations arising out of this research grant are those of the authors and it should not be implied that they represent the views of the National Science Foundation. The authors acknowledge with gratitude the contributions of their colleagues and co-principal investigators, Dr. Thomas G. Donnelly and Dr. Edward J. Kaiser.

Reprinted with permission from *Public Administration Review*, May/June 1975, pp. 229–239.

munity service systems in a national sample of new communities.

RESEARCH DESIGN

The approach used to evaluate new community development is based on quasi-experimental design. To provide a sound basis for generalization, comparisons using similar measurements must be made between new communities and alternative forms of urban development. Therefore, the basic research design involves a two-way comparison of new communities with less planned suburban development.

Sample Communities

A national sample of 13 privately developed new communities was selected on the basis of a multi-stage random sampling procedure from a list of "Large Developments and New

Communities Completed or Under Construction in the United States Since 1947," prepared by the Department of Housing and Urban Development.[5] The sample new communities, together with their estimated population, target population, and target acreage, are listed in Table 1. With the exception of Lake Havasu City, which is freestanding, each of these is a suburban community, generally located on the fringe of a metropolitan area. Their populations are predominantly upper middleclass (median income is $17,500), well educated (72 per cent had attended college), and white (96 per cent).

A sample of 13 conventional communities was selected by pairing each new community with a nearby suburban area. Conventional communities were selected so as to match the new communities in terms of location,

TABLE 1. POPULATION AND ACREAGE OF SAMPLE NEW COMMUNITIES

New Community	Estimated Population (1972)	Per Cent of Target Population	Target Population	Target Acres
Park Forest, Ill.	30,600	87	35,000	3,182
Columbia, Md.	24,000	22	110,000	18,000
Sharpstown, Tex.	24,000	69	35,000	4,100
Elk Grove Village, Ill.	22,900	39	58,500	5,760
Reston, Va.	20,000	27	75,000	7,400
Irvine, Cal.	20,000	6	338,000	18,300
Forest Park, Ohio	17,000	49	35,000	3,725
Foster City, Cal.	15,000	42	36,000	2,600
Westlake Village, Cal.	13,000	26	50,000	11,709
North Palm Beach, Fla.	12,500	42	30,000	2,362
Laguna Niguel, Cal.	8,500	21	40,000	7,936
Lake Havasu City, Ariz.	8,500	14	60,000	16,630
Valencia, Cal.	7,000	28	25,000	4,000
Total	223,000	24	927,500	105,704

stage of development and age of housing, type of housing, and price range of housing. Conventional communities differ from the new communities in terms of the degree of planning. They are significantly less planned. The locations of the sample of 13 new communities and 13 conventional communities are shown in Figure 1.

Data

Three types of comparisons are used in evaluating new community service systems. These are: (1) objective characteristics of facilities and services provided in the community, (2) indicators of the performance of service systems, and (3) residents' satisfaction with the quality of facilities and services.

Objective measures of community characteristics were secured through community inventories and professional personnel interviews conducted in the 26 sample communities. On-site community inventories were used to gather data on the number, accessibility, and quality of facilities and services available. Additional objective data and performance indicators were obtained from interviews with a sample of 468 professional personnel who were responsible for administering community associations; elementary, middle, and high schools; health care facilities and services; recreation facilities and services; and school systems. Finally, selected performance data and residents' evaluations were collected through a 90-minute household interview with 2,596 new community residents and 1,298 residents of the conventional communities.

EVALUATION OF COMMUNITY SERVICES

New community service systems considered in this article include primary education, health care, recreation, shopping, and transportation. Major responsibility for some of these service systems, such as primary education, traditionally has been assumed by the public sector. Some services, such as shopping, usually have been provided by the private sector. Many other services, including health care, recreation, and transportation, however, have been provided by both public and private agencies. The mix of who provides what service at what stage of the development process varies considerably among our sample new communities, but in each case it was expected that new community development would result in better services than are typical of new suburban growth. The extent to which this goal has been realized is the subject of the analysis which follows.

Objective Characteristics

The objective characteristics of new community service systems are similar to those of the conventional communities. Table 2 compares the availability and accessibility of services and facilities and selected service program characteristics.

In the case of primary education, the size of the elementary school sites and the mean number of students per classroom are nearly identical in the new and conventional communities, though new community schools are somewhat more conveniently located.

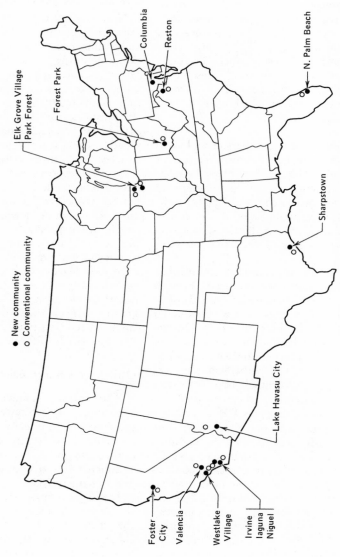

FIG. 1. New and conventional communities

TABLE 2. OBJECTIVE CHARACTERISTICS OF
COMMUNITY SERVICE SYSTEMS, SPRING 1973

Service and Facility Characteristics	*Type of Community*	
	New Communities	*Conventional Communities*
Elementary Schools		
School Plant and Enrollment		
Size of site (mean acres)	11	12
Average classroom size (mean students)	29	28
Accessibility of Schools		
Median road distance from micro-neighborhood[a] to nearest school (feet)	3,600	5,200
Educational Program		
Operating expenditures per pupil (median community)[b]	$1,026	$ 999
Per cent of schools using:		
automated learning	44	40
open space school plan	44	46
team teaching	78	84
ungraded classes	48	46
Health Care		
Health Practitioners and Facilities		
Primary care physicians per 100,000 population (median community)	60	40
Dentists per 100,000 population in community (median community)	42	24
Number of communities with:		
community-based ambulance service	7	8
community hospital	3	3
Accessibility of Health Care Facilities		
Median road distance from micro-neighborhood[a] to nearest (feet):		
general practitioner	6,800	8,800
hospital	14,800	22,200
public health facility	37,000	47,600

(table continued)

TABLE 2 *(cont.)*

	Type of Community	
Service and Facility Characteristics	*New Communities*	*Conventional Communities*
Recreation		
Acreage		
Recreation and open space land per 10,000 population in community (acres in median community)	341	192
Availability of Facilities		
Number of selected facilities per 10,000 population in community (mean):		
totlots	8	2
playgrounds	5	5
parks	3	2
golf courses	1	1
swimming pools and beaches	5	2
tennis courts	8	8
walking paths	7	1
Accessibility of Facilities		
Median road distance from micro-neighborhood[a] to nearest (feet):		
totlot/park/playground	2,100	2,700
golf course	10,500	11,900
swimming pool or beach	3,900	5,000
tennis court	4,600	4,900
walking path	4,800	7,900
Programs		
Recreational operating expenditures per capita	$ 26	$ 10
Number of selected recreational program activities for (mean):		
children	11	10
teenagers	11	9
adults	8	7
Shopping		
Availability of Facilities		
Number of stores per 10,000 population in community (median community):		
supermarkets	1.5	2.0
total number of stores and service establishments	32	55
Number of neighborhood community shopping centers per 10,000 population in community (median community)	1.3	1.4

TABLE 2 *(cont.)*

	Type of Community	
Service and Facility Characteristics	New Communities	Conventional Communities
Number of communities with regional shopping centers	3	2
Accessibility to Shopping Facilities		
Median road distance from micro-neighborhood to nearest (feet):		
convenience store	4,400	4,000
supermarket	4,700	5,600
neighborhood or community shopping center	4,900	7,200
regional shopping center	26,800	30,500
Transportation		
Availability of Services		
Number of communities with:		
intracommunity bus service	8	5
intercity bus service	9	7
commuter bus service	2	2
commuter rail service	1	1
internal walking paths	9	4

a. Micro-neighborhoods are clusters of from five to seven dwelling units.

b. Operating expenditures per pupil are for school districts, rather than individual schools.

Per pupil operating expenditures are also similar. While new communities have been viewed as potential laboratories for educational innovation, these data indicate that new community elementary schools are no more likely to use new educational techniques than schools serving the conventional communities.

New communities had somewhat greater success than the conventional communities in securing health care facilities and services. However, compared to the national average of 82 primary care physicians per 100,000 population,[6] the median new community had only 60 physicians per 100,000 population. Access to the nearest physician was similar in the new and conventional communities, but conventional community residents often had to travel farther to the nearest hospital and public health facility.

Public enthusiasm for new communities has been based, in part, on the assumption that through large-scale planned development more adequate provision can be made for the preservation of open space and the provision of outdoor recreational opportunities. The data indicate that this assumption has been well founded. Per capita recreational and open space acreage and per capita community recreational expenditures in new communities are both considerably larger than those of the conventional communities. In addition, new communities tend to provide recreational facilities which are more accessible to households and to provide a somewhat broader range of recreational program activities.

The provision of adequate shopping facilities is one of the most difficult challenges for new community developers, particularly in the early stages of development. The crux of the problem is that a minimum population base, generally about 12,000 people within a two-mile radius, is needed before even a small shopping center is economically justified. A new community starting from scratch has few such customers, but is expected to provide basic shopping facilities. Data for our sample communities indicate that developers have just begun to solve this "chicken and egg" problem. The number of shopping facilities, standardized by population size, tends to be consistently lower for new communities than for the conventional communities. However, with the exception of convenience stores, new community residents tend to live somewhat closer to selected types of shopping facilities than residents of the conventional communities.

Finally, the data show that new communities generally offer somewhat better transportation facilities than the conventional communities. Differences are greatest for community bus service and the provision of internal walking paths. In addition, new communities are somewhat more likely to have available intercity bus service.

Performance Characteristics

A second perspective on new community service systems is provided by data presented in Table 3 on residents' use of facilities and services. Again, there are few differences between the educational systems of the new and conventional communities. The per cent of elementary school children reading at grade level and parents' evaluation of their children's performance in school are virtually identical in both settings. Although the availability of health resources is somewhat better in new communities, utilization rates are very similar. This is also true of outdoor recreation. The greater number and variety of facilities provided in new communities is not matched by participation rates, which are only marginally higher in new communities than in the conventional communities.

Data on the frequency of use of various shopping facilities show little difference in visits to convenience stores. However, new community residents tend to utilize supermarkets and shopping centers more frequently than conventional community residents.

The greater number of community transportation services and conscious efforts to locate facilities in close proximity to households is reflected in data on automobile mileage and travel distances to facilities used by the sample respondents. Although new community residents tend to own as many automobiles as residents of the conventional communities, their average annual automobile mileage was significantly lower. New community residents also traveled shorter distances to the facilities and services they used

TABLE 3. PERFORMANCE OF COMMUNITY SERVICE SYSTEMS

	Type of Community	
Performance Indicator	*New Communities*	*Conventional Communities*
Elementary Schools		
Per cent of students reading at grade level (median community)	75	75
Per cent of parents who rate child's performance as above average	58	58
Health Care		
Per cent of respondents who wanted to see doctor but did not during past year (median community)	16	17
Per cent of respondents who had a physical check-up in past year (median community)	71	72
Per cent of respondents who have a regular doctor or clinic (median community)	84	84
Median number of visits to doctor or clinic in past year (median community)	2.1	2.2
Recreation		
Per cent of respondents who participated during past year in (median community):		
bicycling	41	31
golf	22	16
swimming	61	56
tennis	22	18
walking and hiking	57	53
Shopping		
Per cent of respondents who use shopping facilities more often than once a week (median community):		
convenience stores	52	49
supermarkets	47	35
shopping centers	16	8
Transportation		
Per cent of respondents with two or more automobiles in household	67	69
Average annual mileage by automobiles of household	23,900	25,700
Median road distance to facilities actually used by respondents (feet):		
elementary school	3,400	6,400
doctor or clinic	28,400	38,000
park or playground	2,000	2,100

(table continued)

TABLE 3 *(cont.)*

Performance Indicator	Type of Community	
	New Communities	*Conventional Communities*
golf course	20,300	31,700
swimming facility	4,600	6,200
tennis court	7,300	7,600
convenience store	4,300	4,600
supermarket	7,200	11,200
shopping center	20,300	27,200
Per cent of respondents who usually walked to:		
school	35	32
convenience store	6	4
supermarket	3	1
shopping center	2	0
work	1	1
Journey to work:		
Median time of trip (minutes)	25	25
Per cent of household heads who are employed in same community as place of residence	14	16

most often, although few chose to walk rather than drive.

While new communities may reduce travel to facilities in and near the community, the data indicate that new community development has had little effect on the journey to work. Median trip times to work by household heads are identical in the new and conventional communities. Furthermore, the ideal of living and working in the same community is no more likely to be achieved in new communities than in conventional suburbs.

Residents' Evaluations

A third means of evaluating new community services is from the points of view of community residents. For each of the service systems discussed in this article, residents were asked to rate the service's overall quality in their community. Results from these questions are summarized in Table 4.

Overall, ratings by residents tend to be highest for recreation, schools, and transportation and lowest for health care and shopping facilities and services. In comparison with residents of the conventional communities, new community residents gave much higher overall ratings to recreation, health care, and ease of getting around their communities. Shopping facilities are rated somewhat better by new community residents, but ratings of schools and convenience to work are about the same.

In summary, the review of the objective characteristics, performance indicators, and residents' evaluations shows that new communities have not succeeded in providing consistently better community service systems than

TABLE 4. RESIDENTS' EVALUATIONS OF COMMUNITY SERVICE SYSTEMS

	Type of Community	
Service System	*New Communities*	*Conventional Communities*
Elementary Schools		
Per cent of parents who rate child's school as excellent or good	79	80
Per cent of respondents who rate schools as better than those in previous community	46	45
Health Care		
Per cent of respondents who rate health care facilities and services as excellent or good	65	54
Per cent of respondents who rate health care facilities as better than those in previous community	25	20
Recreation		
Per cent of respondents who rate overall recreational facilities and services as excellent or good	77	62
Per cent of respondents who rate recreational facilities as better than those in previous community	63	49
Shopping		
Per cent of respondents who rate overall shopping facilities and services as excellent or good	67	63
Per cent of respondents who rate shopping facilities as better than those in previous community	41	36
Transportation		
Per cent of respondents who rate ease of getting around community as better than that of previous community	48	36
Per cent of respondents who rate convenience to work as better than that of previous community	40	40

are typical of less-planned suburban development serving the same segment of the housing market. New communities are achieving their greatest success in providing better recreational facilities and easier access to most community services. Health care is somewhat better in new communities, while in education and shopping new community performance is a little better than that of conventional suburban development.

Environmental Satisfaction and the Quality of Life

Much of what has been written about new communities suggests that the new community is, or should be, a more rewarding environment in which to live than less comprehensively planned suburban communities. Even though new communities do not provide consistently better service systems, it can be argued that many of these services are beyond the direct control or influence of new community developers. In this line of reasoning, the distinguishing feature of new communities is central planning and control of land development which leads to the creation of a better overall living environment and a better quality of life.

To investigate this further, residents were asked to rate: (1) the planning of their communities in comparison with the communities they moved from; (2) the level of their satisfaction with their neighborhood; (3) the overall quality of their community as a place to live; and (4) whether the community would be a better place to live in five years. Also, several questions were directed at residents' quality of life, including satisfaction with their life as a whole and the effect of moving to the community on their quality of life. Responses to these questions are summarized in Table 5.

The data indicate that residents' satisfaction with their living environments is indeed somewhat higher in new communities than in the conventional communities. New community residents are much more pleased with community planning. They are also somewhat more likely to rate their neighborhood and community highly and to believe that their community will improve over time. On the other hand, the data show that new communities do not necessarily lead to a better quality of life than that found in alternative suburban environments. An equal proportion of the respondents living in both settings report that moving has improved the quality of their lives. The proportions of new and conventional community respondents who were completely satisfied with their lives as a whole, 31 and 32 per cent, are also almost identical.

Implications of the Findings

The data presented in this article clearly show that new community development may not offer a panacea for the severe service crises within many urban areas. If new communities are to match excellence in land development with excellence in community services, public agencies must become much more intimately involved in the community development process. There are several indications that such a public-private partnership is beginning to evolve at all levels of government, though the current crisis in the housing and development industries may prematurely stifle many promising beginnings.

The context of federal involvement in new community development was considerably broadened by the passage of Titles IV and VII of the 1968 and 1970 Housing and Urban Development Acts. With the enactment of Title VII in December 1970, Congress found that "the national welfare requires the encouragement of well-planned, diversified, and economically

TABLE 5. ENVIRONMENTAL SATISFACTION AND THE QUALITY OF LIFE

	Type of Community	
Indicator	New Communities	Conventional Communities
Environmental Satisfaction		
Per cent of respondents who rate overall planning of community as better than that of their previous community	75	53
Per cent of respondents who rate their neighborhood highest as a very good place to live	59	56
Per cent of respondents who rate their community as an excellent or good place to live	90	86
Per cent of respondents who feel community will be a better place to live in five years	37	33
Quality of Life		
Per cent of respondents who reported that moving to community improved the quality of their lives	67	67
Per cent of respondents completely satisfied with their life as a whole	31	32

sound new communities, including major additions to existing communities, as one of several essential elements of a consistent national program for bettering patterns of development and renewal." To encourage new community development the New Communities Administration in the Department of Housing and Urban Development was organized and was authorized to provide assistance in the form of loan guarantees, planning grants, loans and grants for land assembly and development, and public service grants during the first three-year period of development. In addition, the Act authorized supplemental grants of up to 20 per cent of project cost for a large number of public facilities. Both public and private new community developers are eligible for assistance. However, few of these provisions were implemented. After approving 17 new community applications through 1973, and none in 1974, the Department of Housing and Urban Development suspended further processing of applications on January 14, 1975.

The federal government has also been directly involved in the development of two new communities. Fort Lincoln, being built on 335 acres of federal land in the District of Columbia, was expected to house 16,000 people by 1976. However, development has fallen far behind schedule and the primary private developer recently abandoned the project. The Tennessee Valley Authority is proceeding with the development of Timberlake, outside Knoxville, as a joint venture between TVA and the Boeing Company. Each partner has devoted substantial funds to undertake initial feasibility and planning studies for this new community. Like Fort Lincoln, however, further development of the project has been stalled by budgetary limitations and the current state of the economy.

Approximately two dozen states have evidenced interest in new communities. These range from New York State, which has three new communities under development, to a number of other states which have established study commissions or held conferences to explore their possible participation in new community development. Local government participation in new community development is expanding from its traditional emphasis on regulation of land use. A local agency, the Lucas County, Ohio, Renewal Agency, is planning the development of a suburban new community known as Oak Openings. Several local agencies are participating with private developers in new community development. These include the Newfields New Community Authority, authorized by the Ohio legislature, which is jointly developing Newfields, Ohio, with a private developer, New Town Urban Research Development Corporation; and, Redwood City, California, which is participating in

the development of the new community of Redwood Shores, with Mobil Oil Estates, Ltd.

Public-private partnerships such as these may lead to the development of new communities which combine the proven land development capability of the private sector with the public sector's capacity to plan and develop community service systems. With public participation in development, the community interest is represented in planning and development decisions from the initial stages of the development process. With adequate local borrowing authority, this offers a means to recognize not only the need for excellence in community services, but also a means to accomplish this end. Greater public participation in community development may also overcome one of the severest criticisms of new community development in the United States, that of monopolistic control of the community by private developers.[7] Collaboration between the public and private interests in community building, if realized, may open up the development process so that both residents' and developers' interests are represented and acted upon. The outcome of such a development process should be better living environments for the next generation of new community residents.

NOTES

1. For an extensive list of citations to the new community literature, see Gideon Golany, *New Towns Planning and Development; A World-Wide Bibliography,* ULI Research Report 20 (Washington, D.C.: ULI-the Urban Land Institute, 1973).

2. A number of substantive reports emerged from these efforts. In particular, see Advisory Commission on Intergovernmental Relations, *Urban and Rural America: Policies for Future Growth.* A Commission Report (Washington, D.C.: U.S. Government Printing Office, 1968), and Donald Canty (ed.), *The New City,* National Committee on Urban Growth Policy (New York: Frederick A. Praeger, Inc., 1969).

3. See, for example, Miller Brown, Neil J. Pinney, and William S. Saslow, *Innovation in New Communities* (Cambridge, Mass.: The MIT Press, 1972); Real Estate Research Corporation, *Economic and Financial Feasibility Models for New Community Development* (Springfield, Va.: National Technical Information Service, U.S. Department of Commerce, 1971); Evans Clinchy, *New Towns, New Schools? A Memorandum on the State of the Art of Educational Planning for New Communities in the United States,* Working Paper No. 1 (New York: Educational Facilities Laboratories, Inc., 1972); and Twentieth Century Fund Task Force on Governance of New Towns, *New Towns: Laboratories for Democracy,* background paper by Royce Hanson (New York: The Fund, 1971).

4. Empirical studies of new community residents include: John B. Lansing, Robert W. Marans, and Robert B. Zehner, *Planned Residential Environments* (Ann Arbor: Survey Research Center, Institute for Social Research, The University of Michigan, 1970); Herbert J. Gans, *The Levittowners* (New York: Pantheon Books, A Division of Random House, Inc., 1967); James A. Prestridge, *Case Studies of Six Planned New Towns in the United States* (Lexington, Ky.: Institute for Environmental Studies, University of Kentucky Research Foundation, 1973); and Carl Werthman, Jerry S. Mandel, and Ted Dienstfrey, *Planning and the Purchase Decision: Why People Buy in Planned Communities* (Berkeley: Institute of Urban and Regional Development, Center for Planning and Development Research, University of California, Berkeley, 1965).

5. New Communities Division, Community Resources Development Administration, U.S. Department of Housing and Urban Development, "Survey and Analysis of Large Developments and New Communities Completed or Under Construction in the United States Since 1947" (Washington, D.C.: The Department, February 1969).

6. Based on 1970 figures for active general practitioners, internists, pediatricians, obstetricians, and gynecologists, and estimated number of osteopaths, National Center for Health Statistics, U.S. Department of Health, Education, and Welfare, *Health Resource Statistics,* DHEW Publication No. (HSM) 72-1509 (Washington, D.C.: U.S. Government Printing Office, 1971).

7. For examples of this critique, see William Alonso and Chester McGuire, "Pluralistic New Towns," in *Frontiers of Planned Unit Development: A Synthesis of Expert Opinion,* Robert W. Burchell (ed.) (New Brunswick, N.J.: Center for Urban Policy Research, Rutgers University, 1973), pp. 251–262; and David R. Godschalk, "New Communities or Company Towns? An Analysis of Resident Participation in New Towns," in *New Towns: Why—And For Whom?,* Harvey S. Perloff and Neil C. Sandbert (eds.) (New York: Praeger Publishers, Inc., 1973), pp. 198–220.

29. Acute Myocardial Infarction: Home and Hospital Treatment

H. G. Mather, N. G. Pearson, K. L. Q. Read, D. B. Shaw, G. R. Steed, M. G. Thorne, S. Jones, C. J. Guerrier, C. D. Eraut, P. M. McHugh, N. R. Chowdhury, M. H. Jafary, and T. J. Wallace

SUMMARY

This is a preliminary report of a co-operative study of 1,203 episodes of acute myocardial infarction in men under 70 years in four centres in the south west of England. The mortality at 28 days was 15%. A comparison is made between home care by the family doctor and hospital treatment initially in an intensive care unit: 343 cases were allocated at random. The randomized groups do not differ significantly in composition with respect to age; past history of angina, infarction, or hypertension; or hypotension when first examined. The mortality rates of the random groups are similar for home and hospital treatment. The group sent electively to hospital contained a higher proportion of initially hypotensive patients whose prognosis was bad wherever treated; those who were not hypotensive fared rather worse in hospital.

For some patients with acute myocardial infarction seen by their general practitioner home care is ethically justified, and the need for general admission to hospital should be reconsidered.

INTRODUCTION

In the past 20 years there has been a rise in the number of deaths ascribed to coronary heart disease. There has been a corresponding increase of interest in its natural history and treatment, particularly in those nations where expectation of life is greater than 65 years and where a high proportion of deaths below this age is due to this disease. The value of various drugs, the role of the intensive care unit, and the use of special ambulances have been studied, but little information is available on the fate of patients treated at home except for the reports by Wright (1964), Sleet (1968), Nichols (1968), and Fry (1968).

From a retrospective survey of general practices in the south west of England in 1964, Wright found that patients developing acute myocardial infarction were treated in hospital and at home in about equal numbers and that the mortality rates in the two groups were similar. Accordingly, as one of a number of trials related to coronary care considered by a Ministry of Health working party under the chairmanship of Lord Platt, a randomized controlled trial was planned in order to compare the fate of patients treated in hospital, initially in an intensive care unit, with that of patients treated at home. If, indeed, intensive hospital care offered important advantages then there would be a need (1) to

Reprinted with permission of the authors and editor of the *British Medical Journal*, August 7, 1971, pp. 334–338.

revise the present practice of the family doctor, (2) to plan for increased coronary care facilities and beds in hospital and, (3) perhaps to develop special ambulances in order to shorten the interval between the patient developing pain and receiving intensive care.

PLAN OF TRIAL

The trial was confined to men under 70 years of age who had suffered a myocardial infarction within the previous 48 hours. Women were excluded because it was felt that home care would be difficult for social reasons. The trial was started in Bristol in October 1966, in Exeter in July 1967, in Torbay in January 1968, and in Plymouth in April 1968. Local general practitioners were contacted and over half agreed to participate—altogether 458.

It was planned that where possible the treatment at home or in hospital would be allocated at random in order to avoid bias in selection. The family doctor carried a sealed envelope stipulating home or hospital care, and the decision on whether a patient could be so selected rested entirely with him. The envelopes were numbered and checked to ensure that the allocation had been adhered to. It was accepted that random selection would not be possible in all patients for the following reasons: *(a)* social conditions might preclude care being given at home, and patients not resident in the area would not be eligible for randomization; *(b)* patients suffering an attack at work, in the street, or in hospital would most likely be treated in hospital without reference to the general practitioners; *(c)* patients or relatives might express a strong desire for home or hospital care; and *(d)* general practitioners might decide that there were medical conditions, which might or might not be associated with the infarction, that precluded random allocation. Therefore, the patients studied fell into four groups.

Elective Hospital

Patients in this group were those who suffered an attack at work, in the street, on holiday, or in hospital and were admitted without the knowledge of their general practitioners, and those whose general practitioner opted for medical or social reasons, including the patient's wishes, for hospital admission.

Elective Home

Those whom the general practitioner considered should be cared for at home, again for medical or social reasons or because of the patient's own wishes.

Random Hospital

Those considered suitable by the general practitioner for random treatment and whose allocation was to hospital intensive care.

Random Home

Those considered suitable by the general practitioner for random treatment and whose allocation was to home.

Criteria for Acceptance

In this study only patients who fulfilled the following criteria were accepted: clinical evidence suggestive of acute myocardial infarction within the previous 48 hours together with either *(a)* evolution of World Health Organization (1959) criteria 1A (e) (the direct injury current) or 1A (a-d) developing after a normal E.C.G., both obtained during the disease event, *or (b)* typical Q and T wave changes (W.H.O. Criteria 1 A a to 1 B. o) in association with a significant rise in the appropriate serum enzyme test (in absence of an irrelevant cause), usually serum lactic dehydrogenase or serum aspartate aminotransferase, *or (c)* subsequent evidence at necropsy of recent myocardial infarct or recent coronary thrombosis.

The same criteria for entry were required for all centres and for all groups of patients. The diagnosis in the hospital groups was confirmed by investigations in hospital, and in the home groups by visits of a research Fellow to the house where at least three E.C.G.s and two blood tests for serum enzymes were taken. Duplicate reading of E.C.G.s was undertaken between the centres to ensure uniform standards of interpretation and to discuss difficulties. Patients treated at home could later be admitted to hospital if for any reason the doctor felt that this was advisable, though for the purposes of analysis they were retained in their original groups.

Data Studied

Details of occupation, past medical history, smoking habits, place of onset of the attack, and other clinical details were recorded on standard forms. Time intervals between the presumed onset of the infarct and admission to hospital were recorded at all centres from the inception of the trial; intervals between

presumed onset and the first medical examination, however, were recorded at only one centre from the outset (see Appendix) but latterly from all centres. Observations on blood pressure, the signs of heart failure, and abnormal rhythm were recorded. As a minimal requirement examinations were standardized at intervals of one, two, four, and seven days after admission to the trial.

In this preliminary report, which is a study of all patients seen in the four centres up to October 1969, deaths before the arrival of medical aid are excluded, and the data on the patients are confined to the study of age, past history of cardiovascular disease, initial systolic blood pressure, and the mortality at 28 days from the onset of the attack.

Treatment

For those kept at home treatment and the amount of activity allowed were decided by the general practitioner. The random hospital patients were admitted to the intensive care unit usually for a minimum of 48 hours and were otherwise cared for in the adjacent medical ward. Most of the elective hospital group were treated similarly, but a few were admitted to other hospitals and did not necessarily have a period of intensive care.

Intensive care involved continuous observation by trained nursing staff in units adapted or built for the purpose. Oxygen and suction were at the bedside, the E.C.G. was monitored continuously, a D.C. defibrillator was in the unit, and pacing facilities were available. Emphasis was placed on quietness, and every attempt was made

TABLE I. TREATMENT GROUP AND AGE

Age (years)	Elective Home	Elective Hospital	Random Hospital	Random Home	Total
<50	14 (13·2%)	161 (21·4%)	32 (18·9%)	24 (13·8%)	231 (19·2%)
50–9	45 (42·5%)	283 (37·5%)	63 (37·3%)	78 (44·8%)	469 (39·1%)
60–9	47 (44·3%)	310 (41·1%)	74 (43·8%)	72 (41·4%)	503 (41·7%)
Total	106	754	169	174	1,203

x^2 Calculated between the four treatment groups and the three age groups = 9·26; not significant.

to prevent the development of dangerous arrhythmias. There was no standardization of drug treatment for either relief of pain or correction of arrhythmias or treatment of heart failure. Anticoagulants were given at the discretion of the physician in charge. As a general policy if the patient's condition was satisfactory after 48 hours in the unit he was transferred to the adjacent medical ward under the care of the same physician. Most patients were mobile in three weeks and discharged by the end of the fourth week.

RESULTS

Altogether 1,203 episodes of infarction were studied. A total of 343 (28%) cases were randomly allocated to home or hospital care, 754 (63%) were electively treated in hospital, and 106 (9%) were electively treated at home. The high proportion of patients sent to hospital is partly due to the inclusion of those whose attack occurred away from home and those where domestic reasons made home care unsuitable. The age distribution and allocation to treatment groups are shown in Table I. There is no significant* difference in age distribution between groups but there is a slight preponderance of younger subjects treated electively in hospital.

The distribution of patients according to the presence or absence of a known history of cardiovascular disease—that is, angina, myocardial infarction, or hypertension—is given in Table II. There is a slight but not significant tendency for cases with such a past history to concentrate in the elective home group.

The systolic blood pressure first recorded for the episode is related to the past history and treatment groups in Table III. It is seen that patients with initial hypotension were more numerous in the elective hospital category, particularly among cases with a past

* "Significant" denotes a significant result of the usual x^2 test at the conventional 5% level. "Highly significant" denotes significance at the 1% level. "Extremely significant" denotes a value well beyond the range of standard statistical tables—that is, significance at a level more stringent than 0·1%.

TABLE II. TREATMENT GROUP AND PAST HISTORY OF CARDIOVASCULAR DISEASE
(C.V.D.) (ANGINA, INFARCTION, OR HYPERTENSION)

	Elective Home	*Elective Hospital*	*Random Hospital*	*Random Home*	*Total*
History of C.V.D.	73 (68·9%)	444 (58·9%)	102 (60·4%)	95 (54·6%)	714 (59·4%)
No such history	33 (31·1%)	310 (41·1%)	67 (39·6%)	79 (45·4%)	489 (40·6%)
Total	106	754	169	174	1,203

x^2 Calculated between the four treatment groups and the presence or absence of a history of C.V.D. = 5·75; not significant.

history of cardiovascular disease. The total figures are statistically significant.

There were 180 deaths within 28 days in the 1,203 cases studied, giving a death rate of 15%. Mortality by age groups and past history of cardiovascular disease is shown in Table IV. It is seen that mortality increases both with age and with such a history and that the latter is present more often in patients of higher age groups.

The mortality is related to initial systolic blood pressure and time of death in Table V. The mortality was four to five times higher in those patients whose initial systolic blood pressure was less than 100 mm and death occurred earlier in the illness.

Comparison of the mortality at 1, 7, and 28 days in the separate treatment groups (Table VI) shows that it was highest in the elective hospital patients. The difference between the total deaths in this group and those in the other groups is statistically significant and is partly due to the large number of deaths occurring on the first day. This difference may be a reflection of the increased frequency of initial hypotension in this group (Table III).

Comparisons between Random Groups

There are no significant differences in the random groups with regard to either age or past history or frequency of initial hypotension. The randomized groups therefore afford a valid basis for comparison of home and hospital care. There was a 4·4% lower mortality for those treated at home, the difference arising in the first week. With 95% confidence we can state that the true difference between the percentage mortalities in the two random groups, and in the circumstances of this trial, lay between 11·3% in favour of home and 2·4% in favour of hospital treatment.

Results for All Treatment Groups

The mortality in the four treatment groups segregated according to the presence or absence of hypotension is given in Table VII, which shows that the initially hypotensive patients had almost five times the mortality of the

TABLE III. INITIAL SYSTOLIC BLOOD PRESSURE BY TREATMENT GROUP
AND PAST HISTORY OF CARDIOVASCULAR DISEASE

B.P.		Elective Home	Elective Hospital	Random Hospital	Random Home	Total
History of C.V.D.	{ <100	7	60	7	8	82
	≥100	66	384	95	87	632
No such history	{ <100	4	34	8	1	47
	≥100	29	276	59	78	442
Total	<100	11 (10·4%)	94 (12·5%)	15 (8·9%)	9 (5·2%)	129 (10·7%)
	≥100	95 (89·6%)	660 (87·5%)	154 (91·1%)	165 (94·8%)	1,074 (89·3%)

χ^2 Calculated between the four treatment groups and presence or absence of initial hypotension (regardless of C.V.D.) = 8·61; significant.

TABLE IV. MORTALITY AT 28 DAYS BY PRESENCE OR ABSENCE OF PAST HISTORY OF
CARDIOVASCULAR DISEASE IN SEPARATE AGE GROUPS

	<50 Years		50–59 Years		60–69 Years		Total	
	No.	Dead	No.	Dead	No.	Dead	No.	Dead
History of C.V.D.	111	16 (14·4%)	285	51 (17·9%)	318	69 (21·7%)	714	136 (19%)
No such history	120	2 (1·7%)	184	17 (9·2%)	185	25 (13·5%)	489	44 (9%)
Total	231	18 (7·8%)	469	68 (14·5%)	503	94 (18·7%)	1,203	180 (15%)
χ^2	11·32 (H.S.)		6·76 (H.S.)		5·16 (S.)		23·2 (H.S.)	

In each age group χ^2 is calculated between the numbers dead or alive at 28 days and presence or absence of a history of C.V.D.

H.S. = Highly significant. S. = Significant.

H. G. Mather, et al.

TABLE V. MORTALITY AND INITIAL SYSTOLIC BLOOD PRESSURE

B.P.	Time of Death (Days)			Total Deaths	Total Patients
	<1	2–7	8–28		
<100	21 (16·3%)	27 (20·9%)	15 (11·6%)	63 (48·8%)	129
≥100	20 (2%)	38 (3·5%)	59 (5·5%)	117 (10·9%)	1,074
Total	41 (3·4%)	65 (5·4%)	74 (6·2%)	180 (15%)	1,203

x^2 Calculated between the numbers dead or alive at 28 days and the presence or absence of initial hypotension = 130; extremely significant.

TABLE VI. COMPARISON OF TREATMENT GROUPS BY MORTALITY

	Elective Home	Elective Hospital	Random Hospital	Random Home	Total
Total Patients	106	754	169	174	1,203
Death					
<1 day	1	34	4	2	41
2–7 days	5	49	8	3	65
8–28 days	6	44	12	12	74
Total deaths	12	127	24	17	180
	(11·3%)	(16·8%)	(14·2%)	(9·8%)	(15%)

x^2 Calculated between elective hospital and the other three groups (taken together) and the numbers dead or alive at 28 days = 5·6; significant. If deaths within 1 day are ignored x^2 = 1·64; not significant.

non-hypotensives. The mortality of the hypotensive patients is consistent in the four groups, but in the non-hypotensive patients it is significantly higher in the hospital groups compared with the two home groups combined. The random groups share in this contrast but not to a statistically significant degree.

Of the 280 patients treated at home 57 were later transferred to hospital. These patients have been kept in their original group for the purpose of the analysis. The mortality in these 57 transferred patients was higher than in those retained at home and resembled the main group of elective hospital cases.

Of the 180 patients who died within 28 days necropsy evidence was available for 97, of whom 85 had been treated in hospital. In all but five of the total number evidence of coronary thrombosis/infarction was positively identified; in the remainder severe coronary atheroma was found.

DISCUSSION

There were no significant differences between the two random groups with regard to any of the characteristics recorded. The group treated at home included somewhat fewer young patients and patients with hypotension, but the differences were within chance limits. Thus the randomization seems to have been effective. The differences in mortality between these groups when studied as a whole or according to initial blood pressure were not significant. The question of whether the random groups were representative of all the cases must be considered. Inevitably those patients whose attack occurred away from their home would be sent to hospital, as would those whose domestic arrangements were unsuitable and some with important medical complications. The random groups comprised subjects whose attack occurred at home and who were first seen by their family doctor. They do, however, typify the clinical problem confronting the general practitioner.

The elective hospital group is the largest and is heterogeneous, comprising patients whose attack occurred in the street, at work, or in hospital; those whose medical or social conditions demanded admission; those who expressed a strong preference for care in hospital; and some who were first seen by a doctor other than their own. The group contains more cases with initial hypotension (Table III); these contribute to the higher death rate in this group as their fate was no better when treated in hospital compared with at home. When the initially non-hypotensive patients are considered separately (Table VII) the hospital groups still fare worse than those treated at home.

It would be inappropriate to deduce from the above figures that domiciliary treatment is preferable in all cases to hospital treatment. Firstly, we have already seen that there was a tendency for patients with hypotension to be sent electively to hospital, and there appears to be no difference between the groups regarding the mortality of this complication. It is noteworthy that this feature, carrying as it so often does the implication of extensive myocardial damage, is one which has proved particularly unresponsive to therapy—even intensive care. It is possible that patients with hypotension also respond especially badly to the stress of a move into hospital. Secondly, it is appreciated that when judging from the figures for hypotension the randomized groups (for whatever reason) contained a larger proportion of the less seriously ill patients. Thirdly, there has been no attempt in this interim analysis to assess in the different groups the incidence of factors such as ectopic beats, arrhythmias, and defects of conduction, which are likely to be amenable to intensive care.

Finally, analysis of the length of time that elapsed between the symptomatic onset of the infarction and the calling of medical help has so far been undertaken only in Bristol (see Appendix). This omission deprives our preliminary report of a further factor for comparison of the random hospital with the elective hospital groups, and between the home and hospital groups in general; for it is known that the fatality rate after myocardial infarction is highest immediately after the incident and falls steeply over the first few hours. It does not, however, detract from the validity of the comparison between the two randomized groups.

TABLE VII. COMPARISON OF TREATMENT GROUP MORTALITIES ACCORDING TO INITIAL BLOOD PRESSURE

	Elective Home	Elective Hospital	Random Hospital	Random Home	Total
B.P. <100					
Total	11	94	15	9	129
Dead	6 (54·5%)	46 (48·9%)	7 (46·7%)	4 (44·4%)	63 (48·8%)
B.P. ≥100					
Total	95	660	154	165	1,074
Dead	6 (6·3%)	81 (12·3%)	17 (11%)	13 (7·9%)	117 (10·9%)

x^2 Calculated between home and hospital care and the numbers of initially non-hypotensive cases dead or alive at 28 days = 4·5; significant.

x^2 Calculated between the four treatment groups and the numbers of initially hypotensive cases dead or alive at 28 days = 0·2; not significant.

It must be emphasized that this research was done in an operational setting without publicity to the public or doctors which might influence their normal habits. Moreover the mortality rate compares favourably with that reported from other centres (Lawrie et al., 1967; Lown et al., 1967; Pentecost and Mayne, 1968; Thomas et al., 1968; Norris et al., 1969).

This interim analysis suggests that a randomized comparative trial of the efficiency of domiciliary treatment versus hospital intensive care is a proper and ethical study. It also implies that we should reconsider the grounds on which general practitioners have in the past sought admission of their patients to hospital for medical as distinct from social reasons. The high death rate in the initially hypotensive subjects wherever they are treated might indicate the need for a partial return to the concept of a patient being "too ill to move" if he is hypotensive. Since the initially normotensive patients fare rather better at home (Table VII) it would seem reasonable to keep them

there unless complications occur. It may be that multiple ectopic beats, conduction defects, and other dysrhythmias should prompt early admission to intensive care units which are specifically equipped to deal with such complications. In patients with these complications some form of mobile intensive care may be useful. Yet our observations on mortality raise the question of whether these arrhythmias do not occur more frequently in hospital than at home; even our final report will not answer this direct, as patients are not monitored at home.

Many patients who have suffered a cardiac infarct express a preference for home care because of fear of hospitals or because of a desire to stay with their relatives and to be cared for by their own family doctor. Our findings provide no evidence to suggest that their choice is necessarily mistaken.

We gratefully acknowledge the co-operation of large numbers of general practitioners, without whom this work could not have been done. Professor A. L. Cochrane assisted in the planning of the trial and Dr. G. Ford and Dr. J. M. G. Wilson, of the Department of Health, were of great help in its organization. The expenses were covered by a grant from the Department of Health and Social Security.

APPENDIX

The time intervals between the presumed onset of myocardial infarction and first contact with a doctor for the Bristol patients only are given in Table VIII. Altogether 51% of all cases were seen within four hours of onset, and the proportions seen early did not differ significantly in the four treatment groups. The table indicates the higher mortality within 28 days which prevails among cases with shorter delay times. Of the 455 patients admitted to hospital only one died between first contact with a doctor and arrival in the intensive care unit. It is therefore evident that at least a modest coverage of the earlier stages in the natural history of the disease has been obtained.

TABLE VIII. TIME FROM ONSET OF SYMPTOMS TO FIRST CONTACT WITH DOCTOR IN 615 CASES IN BRISTOL

Delay time (Hours)	No.	% of Total	Treatment Group				Died Within 28 Days
			Random Home	Random Hospital	Elective Home	Elective Hospital	
0–1	117	19	12	16	17	72	30
1–2	111	18	10	16	9	76	21
2–4	84	14	12	15	12	45	12
4–12	125	20	23	19	19	64	16
12–48	68	11	12	11	13	32	5
Unknown but ≤48	110	18	1	4	20	85	17
Total	615	100	70	81	90	374	101

REFERENCES

Fry, J. (1968). *Schweizerische medizinische Wochenschrift,* 98, 1210.
Lawrie, D. M., *et al.* (1967). *Lancet,* 2, 109.
Lown, B., Fakhro, A. M., Hood, W. B., jun., and Thorn, W. (1967). *Journal of the American Medical Association,* 199, 188.
Nichols, J. B. (1968). *Practitioner,* 200, 700.
Norris, R. M., Brandt, P. W. T., and Lee, A. J. (1969). *Lancet,* 1, 278.
Pentecost, B. L., and Mayne, N. M. C. (1968). *British Medical Journal,* 1, 830.
Sleet, R. A. (1968). *British Medical Journal,* 4, 675.
Thomas, M., Jewitt, D. E., and Shillingford, J. P. (1968). *British Medical Journal,* 1, 787.
World Health Organization (1959). *Technical Report Series,* No. 168.
Wright, H. J. (1964). Unpublished data.

30. Determining the Social Effects of a Legal Reform: The British "Breathalyser" Crackdown of 1967

H. Laurence Ross, Donald T. Campbell, and Gene V. Glass

The social effects of a legal reform are examined in this paper utilizing the Interrupted Time-Series research design, a method of analysis that has broad potential use in studies of legal change more generally. A previous demonstration of the applicability of this design to the sociology of law concerned the Connecticut crackdown on speeders (see Campbell and Ross, 1968; Glass, 1968). In that study, the substantive findings were that the crackdown had little effect on the highway death rate, and that it introduced certain unexpected and undesirable changes into the legal process in Connecticut. The present study concerns a similar attempt to lower the highway death rate through changes in the law, specifically the British Road Safety Act of 1967. Critical scrutiny of the data indicates that in this instance the legal change quite impressively achieved its goal.

The British crackdown attempted to get drunken drivers off the road, and thus took aim at a scientifically demonstrated correlate of automobile accidents. The Connecticut crackdown, in contrast, was based on commonsense considerations unsupported even by correlational studies. Its sponsors claimed success prematurely, before

such possibilities as random variation and statistical regression could be ruled out as explanations of an apparently striking decline in accident rate. In the present study, similar claims turned out to be justified.

In presenting this report, we hope for two consequences. Substantively, we hope that officials concerned with traffic safety will consider adopting a legal reform which has proved in one notable instance to be effective in reducing traffic deaths; methodologically, we hope to increase awareness of the need for hard-headed evaluation of legal and administrative reforms, and of the value of experimental and quasi-experimental designs for this purpose.

INTERRUPTED TIME-SERIES ANALYSIS

The Interrupted Time-Series is a quasi-experimental design (Campbell and Stanley, 1966; Campbell, 1969) for studying the effect of a given "treatment" on a variable that is repeatedly measured over a period of time before and after the application of the treatment. Like all quasi-experimental techniques, the time-series design is a substitute for an unfeasible true experiment. The true

AUTHORS' NOTE: This study was supported in part by National Science Foundation Grant G51309X.

Reprinted from *American Behavioral Scientist*, Vol. 3, No. 4, March/April 1970, pp. 494–509, by permission of the Publisher, Sage Publications, Inc.

experiment requires randomized assignments of subjects to experimental and control groups, but the time-series design can be used, albeit with greater equivocality, in situations lacking randomization.

The essence of an Interrupted Time-Series design is the extension of a typical before-and-after study to a series of observations at various times removed from the experimental treatment, both before and after. To illustrate, the typical before-and-after study concerns only points immediately prior and subsequent to the treatment, as in Figure 1, which compares accidental deaths in Connecticut before and after the crackdown on speeding. It is very difficult to interpret any change from before to after the treatment for various reasons, discussed in more detail in our full presentations. Briefly, these reasons are:

(1) History. The change observed may be due to simultaneous events other than the experimental treatment.
(2) Maturation. The change may be part of some long-term trend.
(3) Instrumentation. The measured change may be based on a change in the means of measuring, rather than in the thing being measured.
(4) Testing. The change may be caused by the initial measurement rather than by the treatment.
(5) Instability. The apparent change may be no more than chance or random variation.
(6) Regression. If the group was selected because it was extreme on some measure, statistical rea-

soning indicates that it will appear less extreme on subsequent tests, even though the intervening treatment may be completely ineffectual.

A study of Figures 1 and 2 of Campbell and Ross (1968: 38, 42) will illustrate the relevance of time-series data to four of these six threats to validity. In this Connecticut case, maturation and testing are pretty well ruled out by the extended data series inasmuch as *both* posit processes that would have existed in prior years and inasmuch as the 1955–1956 drop is not interpretable as a continuation of trends manifest in 1951–1955. History and instrumentation are not controlled by this design, but an examination of plausible alternative causes such as winter weather and possible changes in record-keeping make this implausible as rival explanations of the 1955–1956 drop. It is on the threats of instability and regression that the time-series presentation exposes weaknesses invalidating the public pronouncements of the Connecticut experiment.

Instability was a possibility totally neglected. *All* of the 1955–1956 change was attributed to the crackdown; the Governor of Connecticut stating, "With a saving of forty lives in 1956, a reduction of 12.3% from the 1955 motor vehicle death toll, we can say the program is definitely worthwhile." When the prior years are examined it becomes obvious that the 1955–1956 shift is typical of the usual annual shifts, rather than being exceptionally large. The problem of regression was likewise overlooked. When a treatment is applied because of extremity on some score (e.g., remedial reading courses applied to persons because of their low reading comprehension scores) it is likely that subsequent scores will on the average be less extreme due to statistical regression alone, even if the treatment has had no effect. The problem of regression is not easy to communicate briefly. It will be helpful to think of a time-series that fluctuates completely at random. If one moves along the series, selecting points that are extraordinarily high, on the average subsequent points will be lower, less extreme and closer to the general trend. In the Connecticut case it appears certain that the great 1954–1955 increase instigated the crackdown. Thus the point where the treatment was instigated was selected for its height. Therefore, a good part of the 1955–1956 decrease must be attributed to statistical regression.

Legal change is a subject for which the Interrupted Time-Series design seems eminently suited. True experiments can seldom be performed in the law because all persons receive the treatment at the same time or because, even if only some receive it, legal or practical considerations prevent the necessary randomization. If a policy strikes a legislature or an administrative body as being a good idea, it is adopted wholesale; if it seems unpromising at first glance, it may not be tried at all. Moreover, even when a change is adopted "experimentally," it is seldom applied at random to one group of people and not to another similarly situated group. The experimental change is typically put into full-scale effect for either an arbitrarily limited time or for a single jurisdiction chosen

nonrandomly from among many others. The time-series design is appropriate in these circumstances.

The opportunity to work with time-series design in studies of legal change is enhanced by the fact that there are numerous series of data that are routinely gathered by governmental bureaus and agencies. Examples are general and specific crime rates, institutional commitments, case loads, economic indexes, and accident rates. Because these data are routinely gathered, their measurement is not taken by participants as a cue that a study is being done (Webb et al., 1966). Generalization to other groups involves fewer theoretical problems than for laboratory experiments because of the much greater similarity between field of experimentation and field of application.

The special relevance of time-series data for questions of legal impact has no doubt frequently been recognized, even though simple before-and-after figures, or percentage change from the previous year remain the commonest means of reporting. Time-series data have been employed by Stieber (1949) and Rose (1952) in studies of the effects of compulsory arbitration; by Wolfe, Lüke and Hax (1959), Rheinstein (1959) and Glass (forthcoming) in studies of divorce law; and by Walker (1965) and Schuessler (1969) in studies of the effects of capital punishment. But the formal development of the method, the analysis of its strengths and pitfalls, the development of appropriate tests of significance, are all too recent for the method to have received the widespread application it deserves. We have previously reported a

negative application, primarily rejecting the Connecticut claims. In the present paper we report an optimistic one,
in which effects claimed in press releases
stand up under scientific scrutiny.

ALCOHOL AND TRAFFIC ACCIDENTS

The Legislation and Background

The sponsors of the British Road
Safety Act of 1967 based their action
on a voluminous scientific literature
which showed association between accidents, particularly serious ones, and
blood alcohol, particularly in high
concentrations. In a recent review of
the literature, three studies of fatal accidents were cited in which the proportion of drivers with alcohol in their
bloodstreams ranged from 55 to 64%.
In single-vehicle accidents, three other
studies revealed alcohol in from 71 to
83% of the victims (Automobile Manufacturers Association, 1966). One of
the latter studies matched the deceased
drivers with a sample obtained later of
drivers in the same location at the same
hour. Only 23% of the controls had a
concentration of .02% or more of alcohol in their blood, compared with
71% of the deceased drivers.

There were similar findings in reports of several correlational studies of
nonfatal accidents. The U.S. Department of Transportation recently issued
a report containing the following
summary:

Scientific investigation of actual crashes
and the circumstances in which they
occur and laboratory and field experiments show very clearly that the higher
a driver's blood alcohol concentration:
—the disproportionately greater is
the likelihood that he will crash;

—the greater is the likelihood that he
himself will have initiated any
crash in which he is involved; and
—the greater is the likelihood that
the crash will have been severe.
[House Committee on Public Works,
1968: 15]

The British government, then, had
a good theoretical basis on which to
form their program of control. The attempt was further justified by claims of
success in similar programs in the
Scandinavian countries (Andanaes,
1966). The state of knowledge about
alcohol and accidents is quite different
from the existing knowledge about the
effect of speed, which indicates no
simple relationship with accidents.

Since 1925, it had been an offense in
Britain to drive while under the
influence of alcohol. However, as one
British lawyer explained:

I knew only too well how easy it was
to secure acquittal from a charge of
drunken driving in the United King-
dom. The form one adopted for the defense was always to insist on a jury trial;
the evidence as to drunkenness was always given by the Police Surgeon who
had made the drunken man carry out
some rather extraordinary tests, many of
which perfectly sober people could not
carry out. You would inevitably find
that your jury consisted of people like
myself, honest, law-abiding citizens
who both drove motor cars and also
drank alcohol. The inevitable reaction
of juries faced with a case of this nature
was "there but [for] the grace of God go
I . . . Not Guilty" [Insurance Institute
for Highway Safety, 1968: 40].

Legislation in 1962 permitted blood
and urine tests, with certain presump-
tions to be raised in the event of the

driver's refusal to cooperate. The stimulus for additional legislation was a continued rise in automobile-related deaths and serious injuries. Deaths had peaked in 1966 at 7,985, a culmination of a steady rise throughout the 1950s and 1960s. Injuries peaked a year earlier, but remained quite high (384,000) in 1966.

The new legislation, put into effect on October 9, 1967, was not particularly radical as compared, for instance, with Scandinavian procedures, or even with the laws in several American states. However, the Act was well publicized in Britain and included the following features:

(1) The criterion of impairment was set at a blood alcohol level of .08%. This is a more stringent standard than that prevailing in most American states, but less so than that prevailing in Norway and Sweden (.05%) or in Czechoslavakia, Bulgaria, and East Germany (.03%). A blood alcohol level of .08% might be barely reached if a 160-pound man drank three drinks in quick succession on an empty stomach (Campbell, 1964).

(2) Police were authorized to give an on-the-scene breath test. This test, called the Breathalyser, gave its name to the crackdown in the British press. The test may be administered to a driver if "the constable has reasonable cause— (a) to suspect him of having alcohol in his body; or (b) to suspect him of having committed a traffic offense while the vehicle was in motion." The test may also be given to any driver involved in an accident. A driver who fails the breath test is brought to the police station for a (more accurate) blood or urine test, on the basis of which a charge is made.

(3) A mandatory punishment was instituted, consisting of "disqualification" (license suspension) for one year and a fine of £100 or imprisonment for up to four months, or both. Severe penalties were also instituted for failure to submit to the breath test or to either the blood or urine tests.

(4) The specific starting date for the new regulations was given advance publicity. This provides an essential aspect making the study interpretable. A very gradual change of enforcement would have produced results indistinguishable from a gradual change in long-term trends.

Although official publicity campaigns greatly increased public awareness of the new procedures and penalties, particularly of the on-the-scene breathalyser test, enforcement was probably not much increased. During the first six months after the act was initiated, only 20,000 drivers had to take the test, and fewer than half of them failed it. A report commissioned by the Insurance Institute for Highway Safety states "that in reality [the British driver's] chances of being apprehended for driving after drinking are no greater than they were before" (Bennett and Westwick, 1968: 10).

Claimed Results

As in the case of the Connecticut crackdown, the fact of fewer casualties in the period immediately following the institution of the reform was interpreted as evidence of an effect. The Ministry of Transport in its official press releases was considerably more restrained than the governor of Connecticut had been, but its claims were based on much the same kind of reasoning. For instance, a press release of March 21, 1968, was headlined: "Road Casualties in 1967 Lowest Figure for Nine Years." This release documented the fact that in the last three months of 1967 casualties had declined by sixteen percent and deaths had declined by twenty-three percent; readers were reminded that the Road Safety Act came into force on the 9th of October. On December 11, 1968, the Ministry of Transport issued a press release headline: "First Twelve Months of 'Breath Test.' 1,152 Fewer Dead on Roads." Although the term "cause" was never used, the report contains statements about "casualty savings" and "gaining safety from the new legislation." The magnitude of the shift, particularly in the night hours when the casualty rate declined by a third, makes the British interpretation less offensive than the official line in Connecticut. Our statistical analyses, in fact, support the press releases. But the claims failed to indicate that thought had been given to such obvious alternative causes of the decline as instability of the casualty rate, regression from peak statistics, and other safety-related events taking place at the same time.

INTERRUPTED TIME-SERIES ANALYSIS OF THE BREATHALYSER CRACKDOWN

The Statistics

A graphic presentation of some of our time-series analysis of the Breathalyser crackdown is shown in Figure 1. Our analyses are based upon statistics made available to us by the British Ministry of Transport, including breakdowns going beyond the data reported in their press releases, some of which were made especially at our request.[1] We report here only a portion of our analyses, selected so as to display the major results and to illustrate the method. For the full presentation, including alternative analyses, see Glass et al. (forthcoming).

All Hours and Days

Data on total monthly casualty rates by seriousness of casualty are available back to 1961. For the present analysis, we have focused upon the combination "fatalities plus serious casualties," since specific hour and day analyses, to be discussed later, were only available in that form. These data have been smoothed in two stages: first, the rates for months of 28, 29, and 30 days in length have been extrapolated to 31-day equivalents (by multiplying the obtained rates by 31/28, and so forth). Second, a yearly cycle of seasonal variation has been removed. (In this cycle, January is lowest, August through December high.) The average monthly rate prior to the crackdown has been used to compute a monthly correction such that the mean annual correction is zero. These corrections have been added to, or subtracted from, the 31-day rates. The crackdown began on October 9, 1967. In order to plot October as a purely posttreatment value, an additional prorating has been employed.[2] Without the prorating, October 1967 would have had a plotted value of 7681, instead of 7226 shown.

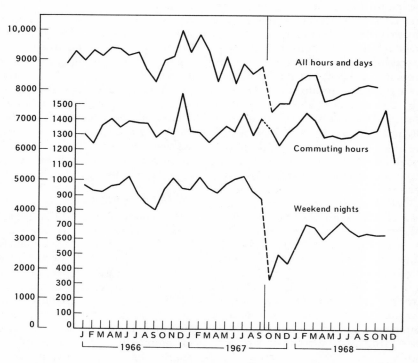

FIG. 1. [Authors' Note (added in press): We have just been informed by the Ministry of Transport that, through error, the data we were supplied for weekend nights are actually for the periods Thursday midnight to 4:00 A.M. Friday; Friday 10:00 P.M. to 12:00 P.M.; Friday midnight to 4:00 A.M. Saturday morning; and Saturday 10:00 P.M. to 12:00 P.M. By the inclusion of the late Thursday night (Friday morning) data and by the omission of the late Saturday night (Saturday morning) data, we have underestimated the weekend night effects. We have also been informed that the data labeled "commuting hours" should have been labeled "closed hours," as it includes closed hours for Saturday and Sunday as well as for the weekdays.]

Visual inspection of the all-hours-and-days graph supports the hypothesis that the crackdown had an effect. A simple nonparametric consideration offers further confirmation: the September-October drop of 1967 is the largest one-month shift not only for the three years plotted in Figure 1, but also for the total series going back to January 1961. The odds against this are 93 to 1. This holds true even if the uncorrected value for October 1967 is used. The most sophisticated test of significance in this situation is that developed by Box and Tiao (1965).[3]

Taking out the annual seasonal cycle

is a problematic matter (and even more so in the shorter series that follows). Our procedure is only one of many, all of which are unsatisfactory in one way or another. Can the effect be noted in these all-hours-and-days data without the annual cycle being removed? Only if one compensates for it by eye, or by seasonally controlled comparisons. The largest shifts in the uncorrected data tend to be the annual December-January drops, four out of seven larger than our focal September-October 1967. On the other hand, the 1967 September-October drop of 1,654 (or of 1,199 if October be left with the eight precrackdown days uncorrected for) greatly exceeds the seven other September-October shifts, being three times as large as the largest of them.

Weekend Nights

Going back continuously until January 1966, the Ministry of Transport has monthly statistics by hours of the week. From their analyses and press releases, it was apparent that Friday and Saturday nights, from 10:00 P.M. to 4:00 A.M. the following morning, were the hours in which the effect of the Breathalyser was strongest. The bottom time-series in Figure 1 depicts these data. Here, the figures have been prorated to four Fridays and four Saturdays each month. Rather than attempt to estimate seasonal cycles on the basis of these few data, it seemed appropriate to use the monthly corrections based on all hours and days, proportionately reduced in magnitude.

These data provide striking evidence of efficacy. The casualty rate seems to initially drop some forty to forty-five percent, and to level off with a net reduction of perhaps thirty percent.

The September-October 1967 drop is four times as large as any other month-to-month change. The Box and Tiao statistic produces t in excess of 6.50 for likely magnitudes of effect, for which the chance probability is less than .0000001.

For these weekend nights, the data are convincing visually even when seasonal corrections are not made. Even then, the 1967 September-October drop far exceeds any other month-to-month change, including the December-January ones.

We have chided the typical administrator for being too quick to announce success without taking into account instability, and without adequate sampling time periods before and after the legal change. But when does the administrator have enough evidence? This is in part a function of the prior instability of the series, and in part a function of the magnitude of the change. In the present instance, using the Box and Tiao test and the common acceptance level of a chance probability of less than .01, the administrator could have announced a significant drop after only one posttreatment month. As a matter of fact, after only one month the t value was 8.63 where $p < .01 = 2.86, p < .001 = 3.88$. Even for the all-hours-and-days data, he would have had to wait only one month, at which time the t value was 3.27.

Commuting Hours as a Control

While both series of data considered so far indicate that the crackdown had an immediate effect, it becomes important to know to what extent that effect has been sustained. Such considerations involve inferences as to what the long-term trends would have been without the crackdown. On the basis of increased traffic volume, one would expect a steady rise. On the basis of increased availability of divided and limited access highways, one would expect a decline. The trend was actually downward 1961–1963, markedly upward 1963–1965, and slightly downward from January, 1966 until the crackdown. Thus there are no grounds here for extrapolation.

What one needs in such cases is a "control group" or some other control comparison. In the Connecticut case, we were able to use data from adjacent and similar states for this purpose, assuming similar weather, vehicles, and safety changes in the absence of a crackdown. Such comparisons never achieve the effectiveness of the randomly assigned control groups of true experiments, but are nonetheless useful. Because of differences in drinking and closed hours, as well as rate of automobilization and highway construction, Irish or Belgian data would be of less use as a control than were other states for Connecticut, but they would still be of value.

But control data series need not come solely from different persons, groups or populations. In the present situation, a valuable comparison would come from those high accident hours least likely to be affected by drinking. Commuting hours during which British pubs and bars are closed seemed ideal. Casualties on the five working days between the hours of 7:00 to 10:00 A.M. and 4:00 to 5:00 P.M. were chosen (pubs close after lunch at 2:30

P.M.). These monthly rates were prorated to 23 working days per month. These data showed a distinctly different annual cycle than did the all-hours-and-days data; rather than January being the lowest month, August was, whereas August was the highest in the all-hours-and-days cycle. November and December were high in both cycles. These differences made it inappropriate to use the 1961–1967 annual cycle used for the other two curves. Since the commuting-hour data showed much the same cycle each of the three years (except that the high was November rather than December in 1968) and since there was only trivial indication of effect, the three years of these data were averaged to get the annual cycle, which was then removed from the series.

In Figure 1, the middle line represents the resulting commuting-hours series. There is visibly no effect of the crackdown, nor does the Box and Tiao test show one, when applied to the series as graphed, or to an alternate way of removing the annual cycle. (The graphed approach would have some bias in the direction of minimizing the September-October 1967 shift.)

Ideally, this commuting-hour series would provide a control comparison against which we could decide whether or not the Breathalyser enforcement was being maintained or had abated. Insofar as it is relevant for this purpose, the crackdown had a maximum impact for the first three or four months and has leveled off since. But at the end of 1968 there was still a definite saving of some thirty percent in the weekend-night rates.

The appropriateness of the comparison is weakened by the dissimilarity shown in its annual cycle. Yet it is the nearest thing we have. If it is to be of value we need to do better than has been done here with the annual trend. Data subsequent to the crackdown continue to be collected, and four or five years from now we will have available a better estimate of the commuting-hour annual cycle.

The Threats to Validity

In the presentation of the Interrupted Time-Series design at the beginning of this paper, we listed six threats to validity. In the presentation so far of the British crackdown, we have paid attention primarily to the threat of instability—the only one, it should be remembered, to which tests of significance are relevant.

Reviewing the other threats, *maturation* seems out: the October 1967 drop is not plausibly interpretable as part of a general trend manifested prior to the crackdown. *Testing* and *instrumentation* seem unlikely: the procedures for recording and publicizing traffic casualties were well established prior to the crackdown and did not change on account of the crackdown. But this is not a trivial matter. The official categories of "seriously injured" and "slightly injured" obviously call for a judgment the threshold for which could change if the record-keepers were strongly motivated to make a good show. Crime rates, for example, have shown such fluctuations (Etzioni, 1968; Campbell, 1969: 415). In this regard it is comforting to note that for the all-days-and-hours figures, for which fatalities are separately available, they show as marked effects as do serious injuries. (In the crime studies cited, homicides and murders were markedly less susceptible to recording bias than were lesser crimes. See Campbell, 1969.) *Regression* seems implausible here, for, in marked contrast to the Connecticut case, the crackdown was not a reaction to a peak crisis, but rather to a chronic condition, as inspection of the series indicates.

There remains the catchall category labeled *history*—discrete events other than the experimental treatment that occurs simultaneously with them. In quasi-experimental thinking, when a set of hypotheses cannot be ruled out mechanically through design, the researcher bears the burden of seeking out the reasonable hypotheses included therein and ruling them out or allowing for them individually. The following explanations have been suggested as possible alternative or additional explanations of the change in the British casualty rate in October of 1967 (Bennett and Westwick, 1968).

(1) *The publicizing of crackdown.* The government conducted a two-phase publicity campaign concerning the crackdown, from September 25 through December 21, 1967. This large-scale effort involved several hundred thousand pounds spent for paid advertising, in addition to donations of large amounts of free time by public radio and television. The campaign publicized and explained the crackdown.

Although the publicity campaign may have helped the crackdown produce its effect—indeed, it may be considered as a part of the crackdown—the continued lower casualty rate is inconsistent with the idea that the publicity campaign acted independently. It seems reasonable to posit that the publicity campaign made the crackdown more effective, and to expect that the effect of the crackdown might be increased with additional publicity campaigns. An additional reason for doubting the independent effect of the publicity campaign is the known ineffectiveness of most safety publicity; a similar safety campaign conducted in Britain in 1964, on the same scale and with the same media as the 1967 campaign, had no notable effect on the casualty rate.

(2) *Improvements in traffic controls.* Within the past two or three years, there have been some important improvements in traffic control in Britain. For instance, the priority of vehicles at traffic circles has been resolved, and signs posted accordingly; "halt" and "yield" signs had been posted to control entry to major arteries; and intersections known to be dangerous had been reworked.

Perhaps part of the observed change in the casualty rate is due to these efforts, but the introduction of reforms in traffic control can best be conceived as a gradual program rather than as a sudden one, whereas the change in the data is abrupt. In addition, traffic signs would not be expected to have a greater effect at night than during the day.

(3) *Tire inspection.* New tires must now meet the standards of the British Standards Association.

However, since the proportion of vehicles with new tires increases very gradually, the comments concerning the traffic control program apply here and rule out explaining much of the observed change in these terms.

(4) *Reduction in two-wheeled vehicles.* Motorcycles and motor scooters have a high accident rate; the number of these vehicles in use is alleged to have decreased very sharply in 1967, one estimate being as much as thirty percent (Bennett and Westwick, 1968). The reduction is said to be due to a temporary increase in the purchase tax on these vehicles, which was rescinded in 1968.

The factual basis of this explanation is challenged by statistics maintained by the Ministry of Transport showing that the use of motorcycles and motor scooters declined only about fourteen percent in 1967. This decline was part of a general, long-term decline in the use of these vehicles, and was about average in amount. A decline of this form is unlikely to produce an abrupt effect in a causally related variable. Just to be sure, we have examined all-hours-and-days figures separately for cars and for two-wheeled motor vehicles. The sharp October 1967 drop exists in both series, but is much more marked for four-wheeled cars.

(5) *Improvement in traffic law enforcement in London* has been suggested as a cause of the decline. Since there is no demonstrated sharp and direct relationship between law enforcement and accident rates, this explanation can be discounted.

(6) *Highway traffic* has grown less rapidly in Britain since 1965 than before that date. However, since growth has continued, albeit at a slower pace, an absolute decrease in the number of accidents does not seem reasonably explained by this fact. The actual volume of traffic in Britain increased by six percent in 1967.

(7) *British insurance companies* offer an enormous discount for claim-free driving. However, this is no innovation, and any effect that it might have on casualties would not be expected to follow the form of our data.

CONCLUSION

The Interrupted Time-Series design used in this study of the British crackdown on drinking and driving has ruled out a wide variety of potential alternative explanations of the observed decline in casualties. The only serious contenders to the hypothesis that the crackdown saved lives and injuries are a group of hypotheses each of which refers to a simultaneous event that might be expected to have a similar effect. However, close attention to each of these rules them out as plausible explanations of much of the change observed at the time of the crackdown. Our conclusion is that the crackdown, with its attendant publicity, did save lives and prevent injuries, and that it continues to have an important beneficial effect on British highways.

Substantively, we have shown that a relatively simple and inexpensive legal reform has produced the results for which it was intended. We believe that the British Act, with appropriate modifications, would meet the requirements of constitutionality in the United States; and although direct generalization is not possible, we can see no reasons why such action would not have a similarly beneficial effect in this country. Officials charged with responsibility for highway safety might well be urged to consider this adoption.

Methodologically, we have demonstrated a technique for evaluating the effect of social changes generally and legal changes in particular. This technique ought to be used more frequently than it is at present by both pure and applied social research. The student of society does not need experimental control to assess the effect of a change, providing he knows the limits of the techniques he uses and proceeds sensibly rather than mechanically. If the resulting knowledge is imperfect, the same problem applies in a slightly lesser degree to the best controlled laboratory experiments when one tries to generalize beyond the laboratory. In contrast, the ability to generalize to a large population outside the laboratory is inherent in this and other quasi-experimental techniques where the basic experiment itself is conducted in a similar field situation. Uniquenesses in such settings make it of course desirable to have replications and cross-validations.

The administrator who wants to adopt an innovation such as this should introduce it in such a way that its effectiveness can be reconfirmed in his own setting. For this purpose, where the Interrupted Time-Series is all that is feasible, rules should be kept in mind.

First, an abrupt, strong, dateable point of impact should be sought, since gradual innovation cannot be distinguished from secular trends. Second, the available time-series records should be continued so as to preserve comparability. Third, the innovation should be introduced when the problem is at a chronic level, rather than in response to crisis. Fourth, the administrator should seek out control series, from adjacent political units or from subset data within his own polity.

NOTES

1. For these data, we are indebted to N. F. Digance and J. M. Munden, Directorate of Statistics, Ministry of Transport, London. Their help is gratefully acknowledged.

2. This prorating procedure assumed that the rate for the first nine days of October 1967 was characteristic of October 1961–1966 and of the year 1967. The average October value was 9042. January-September of 1967 ran 1.058 times the average January-September 1.058 × 9042 = anticipated October 1967 of 9566, 8/31 of which is 2468. The actual total for October 1967 was 8269, of which we assume that 8269 − 2468 = 5801 occurred during October 9 to 31. Expanding 5801 for 23 days to a 31-day month produces 7814. (This is then corrected for seasonal trend by subtracting 588, to achieve the plotted point of 7226.) It is obvious here, in the monthly prorating to 31 days, and in the prorating of weekends below, that for a scientific or legislatively authoritative analysis, we should have been given access to records by days rather than by months. However, this was not feasible.

3. Their model assumes that the time-series is subjected to an influence at each time which tends to move the series up or down, and that in the long run these influences—if they could be examined individually—would follow a normal distribution. Though a new influence enters maximally at each point, the effect of the influence is felt on the series at points beyond its initial appearance. Thus the statistical model specifically takes into account the nonindependence of adjacent observations in a time-series. It is with respect to this typical nonindependence of real data that attempts to solve the problems of time-series analysis with simple regression models fail. Data which conform to the statistical model will not show regular periodic cycles. Since most systems which are partially affected by weather and other annual phenomena show yearly cycles, it is necessary to remove such cycles in the data before analysis. Subsidiary autocorrelation analyses verify the absence of cycles. Glass, Tiao, and Maguire (1970) have modified the model to allow for the data to show constant rates of "drift," increase or decrease, over time. It is this modified model which has been used here, applied to the total series, beginning January 1961. For all the likely values of the effect, the t values are 4.0 or larger, which indicates that the shift is of a magnitude that would occur by chance less than once in 10,000 similar series.

REFERENCES

Andanaes, J. (1966) "The general preventive effects of punishment." Univ. of Pennsylvania Law Rev. 114 (March): 949-983.

Automobile Manufacturers Association, Inc. (1966) The State of the Art of Traffic Safety: A Critical Review and Analysis of the Technical Information on Factors Affecting Traffic Safety. Cambridge: Arthur D. Little.

Bennett, R. O. and E. H. Westwick (1968) "A report on Britain's road safety act of

1967." Prepared for the Insurance Institute of Highway Safety.

Box, G. E. P. and G. C. Tiao (1965) "A change in level of non-stationary time series." Biometrika 52: 181–192.

Campbell, D. T. (1969) "Reforms as experiments." Amer. Psychologist 24 (April): 409–429.

———— and L. Ross (1968) "The Connecticut crackdown on speeding: time-series data in quasi-experimental analysis." Law & Society Rev. 3 (August): 33–53.

Campbell, D. T. and J. C. Stanley (1966) Experimental and Quasi-Experimental Designs for Research. Chicago: Rand-McNally.

Campbell, H. E. (1964) "The role of alcohol in fatal traffic 'accidents' and measures needed to solve the problem." Michigan Medicine 63 (October): 699–703.

Etzioni, A. (1968) "Shortcuts to social change?" The Public Interest 12: 40–51.

Glass, G. V. (1968) "Analysis of the Connecticut speeding crackdown as a time-series quasi-experiment." Law & Society Rev. 3 (August): 55–76.

————, H. L. Ross, and D. T. Campbell (forthcoming) "Statistical analyses of the impact of the British road safety act of 1967."

Glass, G. V., G. C. Tiao, and T. O. Maguire (forthcoming) "Analysis of data on the 1900 revision of the German divorce laws as a quasi-experiment." Law & Society Rev.

Insurance Institute for Highway Safety (1968) Highway Safety, Driver Behavior: Cause and Effect. Washington.

Rheinstein, M. (1959) "Divorce and the law in Germany: a review." Amer. J. of Sociology 65: 489–498.

Rose, A. M. (1952) "Needed research on the mediation of labor disputes." Personnel Psychology 5: 187–200.

Schuessler, K. F. (1969) "The deterrent influence of the death penalty," pp. 378–388 in W. J. Chambliss (ed.) Crime and the Legal Process. New York: McGraw-Hill.

Stieber, J. W. (1949) Ten Years of the Minnesota Labor Relations Act. Minneapolis: Industrial Relations Center, University of Minnesota.

U.S. House Committee on Public Works (1968) 1968 Alcohol and Highway Safety Report. Washington: U.S. Government Printing Office.

Walker, N. (1965) Crime and Punishment in Britain. Edinburgh: Edinburgh Univ. Press.

Webb, E. J. et al. (1966) Unobtrusive Measures: Nonreactive Research in the Social Sciences. Chicago: Rand-McNally.

Wolfe, E., G. Lüke, and H. Hax (1959) Scheidung und Scheidungsrecht: Grudfrägen der Ehescheidung in Deutschland. Tübingen: J. C. B. Mohr.

NAME INDEX

SUBJECT INDEX